ROMANTIC ANDROGYNY

ROMANTIC ANDROGYNY

The Women Within

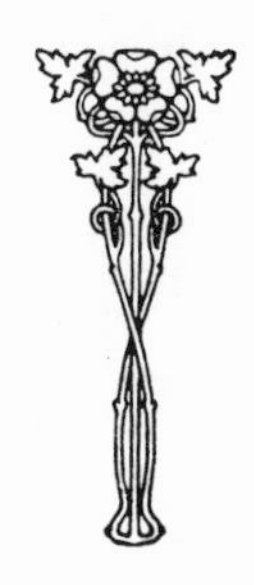

Diane Long Hoeveler

The Pennsylvania State University Press
University Park and London

"Blake's Erotic Apocalypse: The Androgynous Ideal in *Jerusalem*" reprinted by permission from *Essays in Literature* 65 © 1979.

Library of Congress Cataloging-in-Publication Data

Hoeveler, Diane Long.
Romantic androgyny : the women within / Diane Long Hoeveler.
p. cm.
ISBN 0-271-00704-4 (alk. paper)
1. English poetry—19th century—History and criticism. 2. English poetry—Men authors—History and criticism. 3. Androgyny (Psychology) in literature. 4. Femininity (Psychology) in literature. 5. Men authors, English—Psychology. 6. Women in literature. 7. Romanticism—England. I. Title.
PR585.A49H6 1990
821'.709352042—dc20 89-71135

Printed in the United States of America

It is the policy of The Pennsylvania State University Press to use acid-free paper for the first printing of all clothbound books. Publications on uncoated stock satisfy the minimum requirements of American National Standard for Information Sciences—Permanence of Paper for Printed Library Materials, ANSI Z39.48-1984.

This book is dedicated to the "Women Within" my own life:

to the memory of my grandmother
Lina Hansen Long

to the memory of my mother
Constance Pugliese Long

to my daughter
Emily Ann Hoeveler

"A bird of the air shall carry the voice, and that which has wings shall tell the matter"
Bettelheim, *Uses of Enchantment*, 259

Sister and mother and diviner love,
And of the sisterhood of the living dead
Most near, most clear, and of the clearest bloom,
And of the fragrant mothers the most dear
And queen, and of diviner love the day
And flame and summer and sweet fire, no thread
Of cloudy silver sprinkles in your gown
Its venom of renown, and on your head
No crown is simpler than the simple hair.

Wallace Stevens,
"To the One of Fictive Music"

Contents

Abbreviations

AS:	*American Scholar*
B:IQ:	*Blake: An Illustrated Quarterly*
BMMLA:	*Bulletin of the Midwest MLA*
BS:	*Blake Studies*
BSQ:	*Boehme Society Quarterly*
CI:	*Critical Inquiry*
CJ:	*Classical Journal*
CLS:	*Comparative Literature Studies*
CR:	*Centennial Review*
EC:	*Eighteenth Century*
EIC:	*Essays in Criticism*
ELH:	*English Literary History*
ES:	*English Studies*
ESC:	*English Studies in Canada*
FR:	*Feminist Review*
HAB:	*Humanities Association Bulletin*
HR:	*History of Religion*
HT:	*History Today*
IJP:	*International Journal of Psychoanalysis*
JAAC:	*Journal of Aesthetic and Art Criticism*
JEGP:	*Journal of English and Germanic Philology*
JES:	*Journal of European Studies*
KSJ:	*Keats-Shelley Journal*
KSR:	*Keats-Shelley Review*
MLQ:	*Modern Language Quarterly*
MLR:	*Modern Language Review*

NLH:	*New Literary History*
NR:	*Nassau Review*
PLL:	*Papers in Language and Literature*
PMLA:	*Publications of the Modern Language Association*
PQ:	*Philological Quarterly*
PR:	*Psychoanalytic Review*
PS:	*Prose Studies*
REL:	*Review of English Literature*
RP&P:	*Romanticism Past and Present*
RS:	*Research Studies*
SCR:	*South Carolina Review*
SECC:	*Studies in Eighteenth-Century Culture*
SEL:	*Studies in English Literature*
SIR:	*Studies in Romanticism*
SP:	*Studies in Philology*
SR:	*Sewanee Review*
SVEC:	*Studies in Voltaire and the Eighteenth Century*
TSLL:	*Texas Studies in Language and Literature*
UTQ:	*University of Toronto Quarterly*
WC:	*Wordsworth Circle*
WHR:	*Western Humanities Review*
WS:	*Women's Studies*
XUS:	*Xavier University Studies*
YFS:	*Yale French Studies*

Preface

Writing a study in the late 1980s of "images of women" in English Romantic poetry could be seen as an act of extreme naïveté or worse. Anglo-American feminist criticism has moved much beyond an examination of "images of women" in poetry written by males, and yet, ironically, no such study exists for the major poetry of English Romanticism.[1] It would seem, then, that those working in the field have moved on before completing the necessary preliminary examina-

1. See Toril Moi's analysis of the differences between Anglo-American and French feminist theory in *Sexual/Textual Politics: Feminist Literary Theory* (London: Methuen, 1985), as well as Anne K. Mellor's succinct discussion of the major distinctions between the two methodologies in the context of the English Romantic period in *Romanticism and Feminism*, ed. Mellor (Bloomington: Indiana University Press, 1988), 3–6. Helen E. Haworth, "'A Milk-White Lamb that Bleats'? Some Stereotypes of Women in Romantic Literature," *HAB* 24 (1973), 277–93, argues that all the women who appear in Romantic poetry are portrayed in domestic roles. Irene Tayler and Gina Luria's "Gender and Genre: Women in British Romantic Literature," in *What Manner of Woman*, ed. Marlene Springer (New York: New York University Press, 1977), 98–123, stands as the fullest attempt to discuss both "real" women and the images of women during the Romantic period. More recently, Deborah A. Gutschera, "'A Shape of Brightness': The Role of Women in Romantic Epic," *PQ* 66 (1987), 87–108, argues that female characters in Romantic epic should be read as "human rather than divine, immediate rather than remote," or, in other words, real rather than symbolic.

tion that this work attempts. There have been studies on isolated female figures within the poetry, such as Barbara Schapiro's *Romantic Mother*, and a voluminous bibliography exists within the periodical literature on the feminine in one or more poems. But Schapiro's study focuses exclusively on the maternal in the poetry of Shelley, Keats, Coleridge, and Wordsworth as she can be understood through the object-relations theorists on narcissism: Heinz Kohut, Otto Kernberg, Melanie Klein, W. D. Fairbairn, and D. W. Winnicott.[2]

This book, however, examines the symbolic feminine—the full configuration of the Romantic version of the Eternal Feminine—as she recurs in poetry whose persistent subtext presents the androgynous unification of masculine and feminine qualities within the Romantic male poetic psyche. I have not attempted, therefore, to discuss every female character within all the poetry written by the six canonical male Romantic poets. Such a task would be indeed beyond the scope of one volume. Instead I have chosen to focus on the various symbolic configurations of the feminine in those poems that either implicitly or explicitly reinforce an androgynous ideology, that is, that attempt to valorize the appropriation of feminine qualities by male heroes. This study will claim that male poets self-consciously employed the feminine as "Other" and as an alternative source of value in order to engage in a fictional completion of their own psyches, and that a large proportion of the "women" in the poetry of the major Romantics cannot be understood apart from this radical metaphoric tradition of literary absorption/cannibalization. What this study demonstrates, to paraphrase Mary Jacobus, is that no "woman" exists in texts that reveal the contours and contortions of masculine desire. That is, a careful analysis of the texts instead demonstrates either the feminine's presence as a triangular mediator between aspects of the masculine mind or various traces of her metaphoric absence, her *différance* (Derrida's term), or her *disruptive excess* (Irigaray's term).[3]

2. See Barbara Schapiro, *The Romantic Mother: Narcissistic Patterns in Romantic Poetry* (Baltimore: Johns Hopkins University Press, 1983), ix. Schapiro claims that the "finest Romantic poetry . . . reveals the efforts of [the narcissistic] self to overcome its angry, self-destructive attachment to the mother, to give the woman back her wholeness, her separate reality, and thereby to make itself whole" (130). But I would assert that the mother is only one guise taken by the Romantic woman, and that she never possesses any ontological "wholeness" apart from her absorption in the masculine/androgynous psyche.

3. Most recently this phenomenon has been fruitfully explored by Alan Richardson, "Romanticism and the Colonization of the Feminine," in *Romanticism and Feminism*, ed. Mellor, 13–25, and Marlon B. Ross, *The Contours of*

A preliminary word is necessary here at the outset about my use of the terms "female," "feminine," "male," and "masculine." In her seminal study *Toward a Recognition of Androgyny* (1973), Carolyn Heilbrun observes that "it is impossible to write about androgyny without using these terms in their accepted, received sense," which she then defines: "Masculine" represents traits of force, competence, competition, aggressiveness, and violence; "feminine" embodies qualities of tenderness, intuitiveness, passivity, and submission (xv). There can be no denying the fact that the English Romantic poets adhered to such an ideology of sexual and sexist polarization, and that their use of androgyny as a psychic goal was a poetic technique designed to merge the fictional masculine and feminine in one new and redeemed being—the androgynous male poet. I will, then, use the terms "masculine" and "feminine" when discussing culturally determined gender characteristics and qualities that are not necessarily possessed by men or women exclusively. For instance, Shelley feminizes Keats in *Adonais* by attributing to him such culturally determined qualities as tenderness and sensitivity, while Blake masculinizes Vala as a phallic woman throughout *The Four Zoas*. But I use the terms "male" and "female" to refer to the reality of actual biological sexes. At times these distinctions become a bit confusing, but I intend to demonstrate that the Romantic poets subscribed to an ideology of the feminine that determined their literary presentations of virtually all the "women" in their poetry. Further, this ideology caused their poetic efforts to focus on the male hero and the male reader, although at a few points we glimpse their attempts to escape the massive masculine bias—the phallogocentrism—that characterizes most of their texts. Most of the symbolic women analyzed in this study, however, exist almost purely as symbols of the Eternal Feminine within the male poetic psyche. Realizing this fact can tell us a great deal about these poets' attitudes towards women, as well as the culture's conscious and unconscious misogynistic construction of gender ideologies.

The women who appear in this study stand, then, as emblems of the feminine as she emerges from and returns to her origin within the male

---

Masculine Desire: Romanticism and the Rise of Women's Poetry (New York: Oxford University Press, 1989). See Mary Jacobus, "Is There a Woman In This Text?" *NLH* 14 (1982), 117–41; rpt. *Reading Woman: Essays in Feminist Criticism* (New York: Columbia University Press, 1986), 83–109; Jacques Derrida, *Of Grammatology*, trans. Gayatri Spivak (Baltimore: Johns Hopkins University Press, 1976), 188; Luce Irigaray, *This Sex Which Is Not One*, trans. Catherine Porter (Ithaca: Cornell University Press, 1985), 78.

psyche. That is, she is totally defined by her role in relation to the male; she is either his mother, his sister, his beloved, his temptress, his muse, or some combination of those roles. Ultimately, she is as ephemeral as his current needs, his fantasies, his longings for escape from mortality and sexual polarization. She tropes the limitations of the body as well as the fantasy of escape from the body. She images his best and worst fantasies about life, love, death, creativity. She is radically "Other" to him, and, as such, she is crucial to his quest for identity and selfhood. She is his scapegoat, the cause of his failures, and at other times, the reason for his fictional salvation. She cannot be understood finally apart from his radical attempts to incorporate her and in doing so to transform both her—Nature—and himself—Culture—into a new ideal, the androgynous Culture Hero.

A word is necessary here about the critical methodologies that I have employed. My use of several different psychoanalytic structures is predicated on my respect for Freud, Lacan, and the French Feminists as poets, that is, as creators of imaginative and poetic fantasies, ideologies of the (usually male) mind. The fact that I do not adhere exclusively to any one psychoanalytic school is based on my belief that all of these writers have attempted to couch their "theories" in the formulae of bourgeois respectability—whether biological science, structuralism, or psycholinguistics. I employ, for instance, Freudian and Lacanian myth without subscribing to any belief in their systems, hence my eclecticism, otherwise known as "pluralism." As for feminist criticism, it has developed over the past twenty years along two distinctly different lines, the French and the Anglo-American, and these two approaches have been conventionally seen as opposed to each other in both theory and practice. But it seems that the two approaches—psychoanalytical/theoretical or historical/experiential—are not mutually exclusive and can in fact both be fruitfully employed to elucidate literature by and about women. To discuss women as symbols/signs/images of the "Other" is also to discuss the social and cultural ideologies that have created and reinforced those representations. I have, therefore, attempted to bring together the insights gained from what Elaine Showalter has called "gynocriticism"—"the images and stereotypes of women in literature . . . woman-as-sign in semiotic systems"—with the theories of the French feminists on troping the female as "Other." Alice Jardine's call for "gynesis"—seeing women not as objects of "Otherness" but as a process of liberating the unconscious from the tyranny of binary oppositions—is very pertinent to my focus on the androgynous impulse.[4]

4. The conjunction of psychoanalytic theory, feminist criticism, and a new

As Luce Irigaray has observed, "Sexual difference is one of the important questions of our age, if not in fact the burning issue. According to Heidegger, each age is preoccupied with one thing, and one alone. Sexual difference is probably that issue in our own age which could be our salvation on an intellectual level."[5] I would expand Irigaray's observation by claiming that sexual difference first became an obsessive concern—with ideological ramifications—during the late eighteenth and early nineteenth centuries. This concern was, to a large extent, a response to the dislocated sexual roles that occurred during a period of rapid industrialization, socioeconomic and religious upheaval, and political revolution. As John Lukacs notes, the "Romantics were bourgeois" who sought in both their homes and their literary works a "bourgeois interiority," an impulse to domesticate not only the external world but the internal one as well. As the social, political, and economic consequences of the industrial and political revolutions were felt, the culture (a tissue of ideological fantasies) sought to preserve and shield a remnant from corruption. Women, at least those of the middle

---

historicist approach to literature is still in a state of critical infancy. For the most complete bibliography of works on psychoanalytic theory, see Norman Kiell's *Psychoanalysis, Psychology, and Literature: A Bibliography*, 2d ed., 2 vols. (Metuchen, NJ: Scarecrow, 1982). For a survey of the central issues facing feminist criticism, see Showalter's "Feminist Criticism in the Wilderness," *CI* 8 (1981), 179–205. For valuable revisionary discussions of the critical and ideological issues implicit in feminist and psychoanalytical theory, see Nina Baym, "The Madwoman and Her Languages: Why I Don't Do Feminist Literary Theory," in *Feminist Issues in Literary Scholarship*, ed. Shari Benstock (Bloomington: Indiana University Press, 1987), 45–61; Judith Newton, "Making—and Remaking—History: Another Look at 'Patriarchy,'" in *Feminist Issues*, 124–40; Ellen Pollak, "Feminism and the New Historicism: A Tale of Difference or the Same Old Story," *EC* 29 (1988), 281–86. See also Alice A. Jardine, *Gynesis: Configurations of Woman and Modernity* (Ithaca: Cornell University Press, 1985).

5. Luce Irigaray, "Sexual Difference," in *French Feminist Thought: A Reader*, ed. Toril Moi (Oxford: Basil Blackwell, 1987), 118. Foucault traces the growing importance of the question of the sexual difference of "Woman" to the increased sense of self during the Enlightenment: "The intensification of the concern with the self goes hand in hand with the valorization of the other," and, as Naomi Schor has argued, "in Freud the valorization of the same does not preclude—indeed it requires—the centrality of the Other; phallocentrism resolves around the riddle of femininity" (see her "Dreaming Dissymmetry: Barthes, Foucault, and Sexual Difference," in *Men in Feminism*, ed. Alice Jardine and Paul Smith [New York: Methuen, 1987], 98–110).

and upper classes, had to be redefined initially as inhabitants and later as priestesses of the newly enshrined domestic abode, the bourgeois home. As Roland Barthes has argued, the permutations of the bourgeois myth conceal its vagaries at the same time they clothe the middle class in an aura of "humanity" that claims to have the qualities of permanence and timelessness. In other words, the myths and symbols used by the bourgeoisie all conspire to lend what is historically random an air of biological necessity and inevitability. Foucault makes the same point: "It is worth remembering that the first figure to be invested by the deployment of sexuality, one of the first to be 'sexualized,' was the 'idle' woman. She inhabited the outer edge of the 'world,' in which she always had to appear as a value, and of the family, where she was assigned a new destiny charged with conjugal and parental obligations." He notes further that the hysterization of the female body, now saturated with sex and intrinsically pathological, represented the culture's attempt to discipline and control both the family and population.[6] Further, the ideological matrix of the Eternal Feminine—even in its later crudely domestic manifestation, the Angel in the House,—merged neatly with the various millennial religious cults of the time, most of which advocated some form of psychic androgyny as a form of fantasized escape from the social and political dislocations of the period. Within this context, then, the English Romantic poets took it upon themselves to imagistically "redeem" woman, to place her back into her ultimate home—the "androgynous"/masculine mind.

This study actually began many years ago and has shadowed the various feminist critical trends over the past decade. It took me a number of years to see clearly how androgyny intersected with and in fact ex-

6. John Lukacs, "The Bourgeois Interior," *AS* 39 (1970), 625–26; Roland Barthes, *Mythologies*, sel. and trans. Annette Lavers (New York: Hill and Wang, 1972), 137–45; Michel Foucault, *The History of Sexuality, Volume 1: An Introduction*, trans. Robert Hurley (New York: Random House, 1980), 121; 104. The theme of sexual difference resolved through the ideology of "Love" has been the subject of a number of studies: Susanne Lilar, *Aspects of Love in Western Society*, trans. Jonathan Griffin (New York: McGraw-Hill, 1965); Denis de Rougemont, *Love Declared*, trans. Richard Howard (Boston: Beacon, 1963), and *Love in the Western World*, trans. Montgomery Belgion (Garden City, NY: Anchor, 1957); Martin D'Arcy, *The Mind and Heart of Love* (London: Faber and Faber, 1945); Anders Nygren, *Agape and Eros*, trans. Philip S. Watson, 1932); Jean Hagstrum, *The Romantic Body: Love and Sexuality in Keats, Wordsworth, and Blake* (Knoxville: University of Tennessee Press, 1986), and *Sex and Sensibility:*

plained the images and ideologies of women in the poems. The raging feminist debate as to whether androgyny was "sexist" or not did little to clarify the issues for me.[7] Looking back at the shifts in feminist criticism, I realize that my own professional interests conformed to the pattern described by Elaine Showalter in "Feminist Criticism in the Wilderness." That is, before seeing this book to completion I despaired about its "old-fashioned" examination of images of women in poetry written by males, and abandoned it in favor of examining gothic novels written by female writers. But I saw there the same sort of images and themes and found myself asking the same questions: How have historical "realities," psychoanalytic theories, and cultural ideologies determined literary representations of men and women? For female writers, as for male poets, the same oedipal, hysterical, narcissistic, and quasi-incestuous impulses emerge. My attempt to formulate a response to these questions within two different books, then, came to represent for me two sides of the same cultural and psychological phenomenon. This work on "images of women" in British Romantic poetry, then, will be complemented in the future by a companion study of masculinist ideologies in the female gothic novel.

In 1971 I was a student in Nina Baym's graduate course on Women in the American Novel, and that course first demonstrated to me in a somewhat rudimentary form the two major directions that feminist criticism would take over the next decade. We read Simone de Beauvoir's *Second Sex* at the same time we read Friedan, Millett, and Greer. We also learned that women could read and write about literature as women, not just as "honorary" men. Over the years, however, that experience has not been repeated often, for I found myself in a pro-

Ideal and Erotic Love from Milton to Mozart (Chicago: University of Chicago Press, 1982); and Frederic Beaty, *Light from Heaven* (DeKalb: Northern Illinois University Press, 1971).

7. This debate was inaugurated by Carolyn Heilbrun's *Toward a Recognition of Androgyny* (New York: Knopf, 1973), and quickly answered by a special issue of *WS* 2 (1974) that included two early denunciations of androgyny as "sexist": Cynthia Secor's "Androgyny: An Early Reappraisal," and Daniel A. Harris, "Androgyny: The Sexist Myth in Disguise." More recently, Virginia Woolf's exaltation of androgyny has been criticized by Elaine Showalter as an escapist "flight" from feminism (*A Literature of Their Own* [Princeton: Princeton University Press, 1977], 263–97), while Toril Moi has defended Woolf's conception of androgyny as deconstructive of patriarchally imposed binary oppositions (see her *Sexual/Textual Politics*, 1–18.)

fession that defines and proscribes the voices in which we may speak, the voices that will be heard. I am only thankful that I have persisted. Of course, I could not have done so without the encouragement and support of a number of people who sustained me during my own years in the wilderness. Brian Wilkie was an exacting dissertation mentor and a constant source of support then and in the years that followed, as were the other two members of my doctoral committee, Dale Kramer and the late Robert Schneider. Friends like Roland Stromberg, Harold Wechsler, James Kroll, S. Lucy Freibert, S. Lucinda Hubing, Melvin Friedman, Thomas Hachey, and Frank Hubbard saw me through various ordeals. William Veeder encouraged me at a crucial stage, as did Karl Kroeber and David Latané. My colleagues at Marquette University, Edward Duffy and Russell Reising, read drafts and offered suggestions. The National Endowment for the Humanities supported me for two summers of research, and that validation was decisive in helping me see this work through to completion. I would also like to acknowledge the editors of *Essays in Literature* for permission to reprint "Blake's Erotic Apocalypse: The Androgynous Ideal in *Jerusalem*" in slightly revised form. And I would like to express my gratitude to Philip Winsor, Senior Editor at The Pennsylvania State University Press, for his professionalism and courtesy. Finally, my greatest debt is to my husband David Hoeveler. He has lived with my work on androgynous ideology as long as I have lived with his work on the New Humanism, muscular Christianity, and neoconservatism. It has made for an interesting household. As for our children, John and Emily, they have taught me how to love. The dedication of this book to my grandmother, mother, and daughter represents my debt of gratitude to their voices—sometimes unheard but always felt through the years.

Introduction: Women, Androgynes, Poets, and Critics

I

Images of women pervade English Romantic poetry; they appear to be omnipresent, omniscient at times, and often omnipotent. But if no one would deny that female characters like Wordsworth's Lucy, Blake's Jerusalem, Keats's Psyche, Shelley's Cythna, Byron's Astarte, or Coleridge's Geraldine are vivid and memorable, no one would say that these women are fully believable or real or "round" characters in their own rights. One of the most obvious facts that confronts a reader of British Romantic poetry is the profound unreality and amorphousness of the female character. She has traditionally been seen as simply a *topos*, detached from any sort of grounding in the world of historical reality, or she has been understood solely as the embodiment of the "Other" for male Romantic poets. In either guise she assumes archetypal and mythic qualities that resonate between poem and reader. When we read Coleridge's description of Geraldine, for example, we are moved in a way that bespeaks the power of mythic poetry. We know ourselves to be in the presence of something substantially more (or less) than human. And because of the power of the feminine as Other, women in English Romantic poetry have been on one hand idealized and on the other denigrated by critics in the field. This study attempts to correct the flaws of both alternatives by placing the various images of women into a psychoanalytical and historical framework. That is, the premise of this book is that the images that the symbolic woman assumes in the poetry are determined by the Romantic poets' conscious and unconscious adherence to the ideologies of both androgyny and the Eternal Feminine that permeated late eighteenth- and early nineteenth-century England.[1] Stated in the baldest terms, Romantic poets did not attempt to depict women as believable characters in their own rights because it was not compatible with the ideological frameworks in which they were living and working. They consistently presented women as "Other" to man—an idealized mother, a second self, a submerged double, an inspirational muse or mentor, or a demonic *femme fatale*—because all the Romantic poets to a large extent explored in their poetry one of their culture's dominant ideological fantasies—that artistic power and creativity were possible for men only if they unified their masculine and feminine components. For male poets, then, female characters had to be either projections and/or symbolic extensions of the masculine psyche. It is not comforting to realize that the majority of the "women" in English Romantic poetry exist only as symbolic qualities within the minds of the poets themselves, but such is the case.

Woman as "Other" is a familiar theoretical concept within the French tradition, beginning with Claude Lévi-Strauss and Simone de Beauvoir and extending through discussions of her function and identity in Lacan and more recently in the works of Kofman, Kristeva, and Irigaray. I will employ where appropriate the works of these theorists in order to illuminate the psychoanalytical basis of male attitudes toward the feminine. For Lacan, for instance, Woman is the absolute "Other," the complement to man and embodiment of the Eternal Feminine—lover, muse, and repository of the unconscious and its values. In his *Encore*, he defines Woman as man's dream, her function being to deny castration and the absence of relation between signifier and subject. Man projects onto Woman his own lack, and then when she is properly positioned he denies the existence of the lack/gap. This allows Lacan to

1. For an extremely thorough discussion of the androgynous as a political and social ideal in nineteenth-century France, see A. J. L. Busst, "The Image of the Androgyne in the Nineteenth Century," in *Romantic Mythologies*, ed. Ian Fletcher (London: Routledge and Kegan Paul, 1967). Shorter surveys of the image can also be found in Raymond Furness, "The Androgynous Ideal: Its Significance in German Literature," *MLR* 60 (1965), 58–64; Sara Friedrichsmeyer, "Romanticism and the Dream of Androgynous Perfection," in *Deutsche Romantik and English Romanticism*, ed. Theodore Gish and Sandra G. Frieden, Houston German Series 5 (1984); and Bram Dijkstra, "The Androgyne in Nineteenth-Century Art and Literature," *CLS* 26 (1974), 62–73.

claim that "the Woman does not exist" except as a male-created dream phantasm that allows man to psychically and linguistically complete himself.[2]

But if Woman can be understood as an absence/lack/gap, what could possibly constitute her presence? Current feminist theory locates the "real" subject of male discourse as the relation between men or between man and himself. In other words, woman is used as the third element in an essentially triangular (oedipal) relationship that characterizes male literary practice and theory. If woman is only the occasion, as Jacobus has noted, for "mediation, transaction, transition, transference" between men, then the relation between men (or the relation between aspects of the mind of man) is literature's primary concern and women can function only in a secondary and derivative manner. As Jacobus has further observed, the "triangle characteristically invokes its third (female) term only in the interests of the original rivalry and works finally to get rid of the woman." What Jacobus labels "textual harassment" or "specular appropriation" of women in both literary and theoretical texts written by men can be clearly discerned in the major poetry of the English Romantics.[3] In their poetic attempts to inscribe the nature and role of women, the Romantics not only made her radically "Other," but found themselves subscribing to an ideology

2. Claude Lévi-Strauss's *The Elementary Structures of Kinship*, trans. James Bell et al. (London: Eyre, 1969) observes that man's passage from the state of Nature to the state of Culture depends on his ability to view biological relations as a series of contrasts. He further developed this central observation—extended to the contrast between male and female—in his study *The Raw and the Cooked: Introduction to a Science of Mythology*, trans. John and Doreen Weightman (New York: Harper and Row, 1969). Simone de Beauvoir's *The Second Sex*, trans. and ed. H. M. Parshley (New York: Knopf, 1952), inaugurated serious contemporary academic discussion of both the philosophical and historical situation of women. For all its limitations, de Beauvoir's book has clearly influenced the thought of the recent French feminists who will be cited throughout the text. Two chapters from Lacan's seminar "Encore" have been translated into English and published in *Feminine Sexuality: Jacques Lacan and the école freudienne*, ed. Juliet Mitchell and Jacqueline Rose, trans. J. Rose (New York: Norton, 1982), 137–62. For a critique of Lacan's position, see Jane Gallop, *The Daughter's Seduction: Feminism and Psychoanalysis* (Ithaca: Cornell University Press, 1982), 43–55.

3. Luce Irigaray, "Commodities Among Themselves," in *This Sex Which Is Not One*, trans. Catherine Porter (Ithaca: Cornell University Press, 1985), 192–97, and Mary Jacobus, "Is There a Woman in This Text?" in *Reading Woman* (New York: Columbia University Press, 1986), 86, 85.

that called for her embodiment as a force of complete alterity, a trace, a self-negating signifier for male consciousness, an absence.

The androgynous—the fictionally perfect balance of masculine and feminine in the human psyche—also exists as a literary image, a symbol. It is, quite simply, an imaginative construct, an idea/ideology that has never existed in the realm of fact. But the androgynous image assumed major importance during the English Romantic period, and it accounts, I believe, for the depiction and treatment of women in the poetry written by the six major Romantic poets. The androgynous image, however, did not originate with the Romantics. In fact, it has had a long history—traced in several studies—and that history reveals a number of common qualities that have recurred throughout the ages.[4] First of all, the androgynous has always been a self-consciously artificial image, from its pictoral origins in ancient Greek art through its permutations in Kabbalistic, Gnostic, Alchemical, and Neoplatonic cults. Various religious sects have been attracted to this ancient notion of the mind as equally balanced between masculine and feminine qualities. A Jungian might very well claim that the androgynous psyche appears in so many cultures because it is an image that originates in the collective unconscious—a dream of our prelapsarian divinity—the original being, the Father/Mother God before its division and separation.[5] The myth of

4. Marie Delcourt's *Hermaphrodite*, trans. Jennifer Nicholson (London: Studio Books, 1961), is the standard history of the image during the ancient period. Mircea Eliade has published extensively on the topic. See, for instance, his *Mephistopheles and the Androgyne*, trans. J. M. Cohen (New York: Sheed and Ward, 1965); *Images and Symbols: Studies in Religious Symbolism*, trans. Philip Mairet (New York: Sheed and Ward, 1961); *Myths, Dreams, and Mysteries*, trans. Philip Mairet (New York: Harper and Row, 1957; rpt. 1975); and *The Myth of the Eternal Return*, trans. Willard R. Trask (Princeton: Bollingen, 1959). Also see June Singer, *Androgyny: Toward a New Theory of Sexuality* (New York: Anchor, 1976); Alan Watts, *The Two Hands of God* (New York: Braziller, 1963); Elemire Zolla, *The Androgyne: Fusion of the Sexes* (London: Thames and Hudson, 1981); and Robert Kimbrough, "Androgyny, Old and New," *WHR* 35 (1981), 197–215.

5. Androgyny assumed a major role in Jung's ideology, but his monolithic essentialism has aged his works much more quickly than Freud's, or perhaps he has just not been fortunate enough to have a Lacan to (post)modernize his vision. See his *Aion: Researches into the Phenomenology of the Self*, trans. R. F. C. Hull, 2d ed., vol. 9 (Princeton: Princeton University Press, 1968); "Woman in Europe" in *Civilization in Transition*, trans. R. F. C. Hull (New York: Pantheon, 1964); "The Special Phenomenology of the Child Archetype," in *Psyche and Symbol*, ed. Violet de Laszlo (New York: Doubleday, 1958); and "Anima and Animus" (vol. 7), "Symbols of Transformation" (vol. 5), "Al-

the one unified self composed of two entities, masculine and feminine, is elaborated in the poetry of each of the Romantic poets as a sort of Ur-myth, a primordial unification dream and an apocalyptic vision of potentiality and/or destruction.

The English Romantic poets, however, were writing in the more immediately accessible environment of the late eighteenth and early nineteenth centuries' social, political, economic, religious, and sexual revolutions. They lived in a world that had witnessed the French Revolution as well as the growing industrial transformation of their society. Their sympathies, at least initially, were liberal; they welcomed the political upheaval and concomitant demands for sexual equality that were by-products of the revolutionary spirit. Androgyny reemerged in late eighteenth-century England not simply as an abstract image, but as a social, psychic, and political ideology that suddenly seemed within reach, at least so the fantasy claimed. After all, if a king and a dynasty could be toppled, then perhaps sexual oppression could also be overthrown and a new society of perfect equals created. There was no sexual identity in the mind, as Mary Wollstonecraft declared in her *Vindication of the Rights of Women*: "the sexual distinction that men have so warmly insisted upon, is arbitrary" (13:318); and so male poets struggled to believe. But Wollstonecraft also observed in that work that the economic dislocation of women from family labor and their displacement by waged employees had created a new class of *nouveaux riches* who viewed their homes, and the women within them, as symbols of their newly gained affluence. The newly idle woman became, for Wollstonecraft, only one of the "toys of man" whom he "jingle[d]" whenever he "chose to be amused." Clearly, then, the ideology of androgyny, at least in its ideal construction, contradicted the new celebration of the feminine as domestic idol. It is not surprising, then, that the poetic ideal the Romantics set for themselves, at least theoretically, called for a radical reformulation of not only social roles for women, but attitudes toward them as well. Here, however, they met their stumbling block. Before woman could be accepted as the spiritual equal of man, she had to be (re)defined by the culture. The androgynous fantasy demanded that woman be essentially different from man and therefore a complementary force, but sexual differences institutionalized as gen-

---

chemical Studies" (vol. 13), "Mysterium Coiunctionis" (vol. 14), "Psychology and Alchemy" (vol. 12), "Two Essays on Analytical Psychology" (vol. 7), all in *Collected Works of C. G. Jung*, ed. Sir Herbert Read et al., trans. R. F. C. Hull (Princeton: Princeton University Press, 1970).

der roles have always been culturally understood as ideologies that justify inequality.

Just listen to a few contemporary spokesmen on the issue of women's "essential" differences from man. Rousseau delineated these distinctions in his *Émile* by claiming: "Men will philosophize about the human heart better than she does; but she will read in men's hearts better than they do. It is for women to discover experimental morality and for us to reduce it to a system. Woman has more wit, man more genius; woman observes, man reasons" (trans. Bloom, 387). Or here is Hegel distinguishing between the sexes: "The difference between men and women is like that between animals and plants. Men correspond to animals, while women correspond to plants because their development is more placid, and the principle that underlies it is the rather vague unity of feeling" (*Philosophy of Right*, trans. Knox, 263). Most notoriously, Comte expresses bourgeois culture's dominant fantasy/ideology in regard to (middle-class) woman; that is, that she has no identity apart from the family: "First as Mother, presently as Sister, above all as Wife, lastly as Daughter, nay as servant, in a lower degree repeating these four sides of home life, the mission of Woman is to save man from the corruption, to which he is exposed in his life of action and of thought. Her affective superiority spontaneously confers on her this fundamental office, which social economy develops increasingly by releasing the loving sex from all disturbing cares, active or speculative" (*System of Positive Polity*, II, 171).

Middle- and upper-class women for the first time in the eighteenth century were identified by men and male-created ideologies almost exclusively with the home and the realm of feeling, passion, and emotion, while the male appropriated to his natural sphere reason and the powers of the analytical mind. But at the same time that he was projecting feminine qualities out of himself, he was also engaged in a kind of masquerade, a charade in which he would come face to face with his "Other" self only to reabsorb it and thereby enhance his own psyche. Therefore the androgynous psyche as an imaginative ideal proposed by the major English Romantic poets was doomed from its inception because of the ambivalent attitudes these male poets held toward women and the feminine itself as an abstract (male-invented) ideology. As will be evident in the course of close readings of the poems themselves, the Romantics wanted to create female characters with whom their male heroes (often slightly veiled versions of themselves) could merge in a sort of apocalyptic union that would transform both the political and psychic realms. Except for the poetry of Blake, which captured a fantasized and artificially maintained poetic ideal the later Romantic poets were never able to reach themselves, none of the other Romantic poets was able to suspend his disbelief to the point where the female could accomplish what she supposedly does in the works of Blake—redeem the male imaginative power and transform all life into a Jerusalem, the promised land. The "Eternal Feminine" was a male-created ideological construct that celebrated the traditional feminine values of muse-like passivity, loving creativity, and nurturing acceptance. In reality, however, the feminine was not simply the unambivalent force that it needed to be to ensure the maintenance of the androgynous ideal. Male poets quickly realized that the "Eternal Feminine" could easily become the encroaching feminine, a usurping and castrating power that needed to be suppressed rather than simply exalted. The spiraling association of Geraldine and Christabel, for instance, demonstrates this fear in a forcefully explicit manner. Christabel as the beloved feminine collides with Geraldine, the phallic woman, the embodiment of the male's fantasy of woman as both castrated and castrator. And in her hideous physical deformity we can see that she also vividly depicts male fear of the female body as an uncanny and fetishistic commodity, an exchange object to be consumed/eradicated.

And so what we have in the androgynous psyche is a blasted image of ideal sexual equality, an ideal destroyed in its very origin because of the stereotypes and negative images that have adhered to women since Eve. In the realm of images, the androgynous is unique in that it attempts to meld masculine and feminine in a new and radically unique manner, and yet it is founded on the very stereotypes it seeks to destroy. Hence it is inherently flawed and persistently fails in the poetry to translate successfully humanity's desire to escape the constraints of sexuality altogether. The six major Romantic poets examined here were all—for a variety of reasons—attracted to the image of the androgynous psyche, and each of them attempted to employ the image as an ideal, at least initially. Very quickly, however, a self-conscious, self-mocking tone, Romantic irony[6] if you will, creeps into the works and the androgynous becomes confused with the hermaphroditic (its direct opposite).

The impossibility of merging in psychic completion with the feminine dominates the Romantic depiction of women throughout the poetry. Although various types of women are persistently depicted in the poems—mothers, sisters, lovers, *femme fatales*, muses—they all eerily

6. For a discussion of the "Romantic Ironist," see Anne K. Mellor, *English Romantic Irony* (Cambridge: Harvard University Press, 1980), and David Simpson, *Irony and Authority in Romantic Poetry* (Totowa, NJ: Rowman and Littlefield, 1979).

seem to be the same woman. This uncanny quality, which Blake captures so vividly in "The Mental Traveller," expresses their very real fear of, anger, and frustration toward both "real" women and those self-created psychic projections that were substitutes for the actual women who consistently failed to live up to male fantasies of androgynous perfection. And in supposedly looking at "real" women, the poets were actually looking into a mirror in which they saw aspects of themselves and their culture writ large. In their creation of mothers, for instance, they depicted their own desire to regress to both the ideal prelapsarian state—primary narcissism—that exists before infants are conscious of separation/individuation from that being who magically and instantaneously satisfies all of their needs, and the pre-industrial world they nostalgically idealized. In delineating the figure of the sister, the Romantic poet explores both his ambivalence toward the secondary narcissism that results from his knowledge that the mother—the primary love object—is irrevocably unattainable, and the new claustrophobic family constellation.

In moving beyond the quest for identification with and introjection of the mirroring mother/sister, the Romantics next seek to embrace female beloveds who exist as idealized projections of their own feminine qualities. These "women" can also be seen as representations of the new domestic ideology, the celebration of middle-class marriage as a substitute for traditional religion and a refuge from industrial corruption. But this fantasy is no more satisfactory to the poets who, in their futile quests to escape the limitations of individual identity, turn on these feminine doubles in rage and create the *femme fatale*. The *femme fatale*, however, is consistently associated with both the castration that men fear and the male fantasy that the woman herself is castrated, while the body of the *femme fatale* is persistently hystericized as uncanny or fetishistic to the male. The increased anxiety we see in Romantic texts, manifested imagistically in castration fantasies, can be explained as D. H. Lawrence later did—as a sexual response to the tyranny of machine-culture.

Finally, in their creation of the muse-figure, the Romantics make their strongest attempt to celebrate the power of the androgynous imagination, but this feminine principle of creativity within the male psyche again splits into two figures—one loving and positive, the other fearsome and engulfing. This pattern of persistently presenting women as what Kohut calls "self-objects" reveals the same underlying psychic dynamics—misogyny and sexual nausea—as well as cultural anxiety—the insecurity and economic dislocation caused by an increasingly feminized literary marketplace. This poetic phenomenon also reveals that the ideology of androgyny required not only the subjugation of women, but the (de)humanization and eradication of the female representation as well. The Romantics cannibalistically consumed these female characters, shaped them into ideal alter egos, and most of the time destroyed them by the conclusion of the poem. That cycle—idealization of women followed by fear, loathing, and destruction—corresponds also to the poets' growing realization that androgyny was only an alluring siren song of escape from the body. In the end, both women and androgynes become the subject of scorn, anger, and ridicule.[7]

II

There can be no doubt that the ancient traditions as well as the more contemporary history of the androgynous image were well known to each of the six major Romantic poets. Blake was a student of both Jacob Boehme and Emmanuel Swedenborg, and as such he was well acquainted with their theories of the original godhead as androgynous and of heaven as a return to androgynous union of self and other. Critics may argue over the extent to which Blake was directly influenced in his writings by either Boehme or Swedenborg, but that is not my concern here. The fact remains that he had done a good deal of reading in the arcane sources of androgynous tradition, as well as the biblical-Kabbalistic works that informed the mystical Jewish versions of the myth. Wordsworth owned copies of Boehme and was ridiculed by Byron for his absorption in the mystical tradition, while Coleridge's extensive studies of Boehme have been published as marginalia and inform a significant amount of secondary commentary on his works and thought. Keats read Plato and the works of Celtomania that were current at the time and rife with androgynous speculation. He, like all of the other major Romantics, was also familiar with Thomas Taylor's commentaries on Plato and his *Hymns of Orpheus*, both of which were influen-

7. See Heinz Kohut, *The Analysis of the Self* (New York: International Universities Press, 1971), xiv. Also consider the suggestive statement made by Thomas Weiskel: "We have arrived at the proposition that it is impossible at once to adhere to the hypothesis of primary narcissism and to celebrate Romantic Imagination as a genuine discourse of the Other: unless, of course, there is an imagination—a form of love—which begins beyond identity." (See his *Romantic Sublime: Studies in the Structure and Psychology of Transcendence* [Baltimore: Johns Hopkins University Press, 1976], 162.)

tial tracts that promulgated androgynous theories as the psychological basis of all mythological systems. Shelley, of course, translated Plato's *Symposium*, a major document in the history of androgynous theory, and was also widely read in both classical and contemporary continental works that employed androgynous themes. That leaves Byron (so many times the odd man out). He was, through his association with Shelley, conversant enough with platonic ideas of love to mock them throughout *Don Juan*. He was also, however, well read in Greek mythology as well as Oriental sources, and these are of some importance in his treatment of the thwarted androgynous impulse in *Manfred* and *Sardanapalus*. All of the major Romantic poets, then, were not simply influenced by the political and social ideologies of their time; they were also to a greater or lesser degree well acquainted with the entire mystical and philosophical traditions that had developed the notion of an androgynous self as an ideal psychic state.[8]

What does it mean, then, in practical terms to connect the androgynous with the feminine? Working within the androgynous tradition required the poets to present a symbolic woman with whom the hero could merge in order to find "wholeness." At times the hero, assuming the role of a young son, seeks to merge with a chthonic Great Mother, and his quest takes on the aura of a regressive search for origins or a primal struggle with the oedipal-capitalist father. At other times the hero,

8. There are dozens of critical studies on the mystical influence on Romanticism. The standard ones include George M. Harper, *The Neo-Platonism of William Blake* (Chapel Hill: University of North Carolina Press, 1961); Kathleen Raine, *Blake and Tradition*, 2 vols. (Princeton: Princeton University Press, 1968); *Thomas Taylor the Platonist: Selected Writings*, ed. Kathleen Raine and George Mills Harper (Princeton: Bollingen, 1969); Jacomina Korteling, *Mysticism in Blake and Wordsworth* (Amsterdam: H. J. Paris, 1928); Désirée Hirst, *Hidden Riches: Traditional Symbolism from the Renaissance to Blake* (New York: Barnes and Noble, 1964); Joseph Stoudt, *Sunrise to Eternity: A Study in Boehme's Life and Thought* (Philadelphia: University of Pennsylvania Press, 1957); Arthur L. Morton, *The Everlasting Gospel: A Study in the Sources of Blake* (New York: Haskell, 1966); Edward Hungerford, *The Shores of Darkness* (New York: Columbia University Press, 1944); Maurice Quinlan, "Byron's *Manfred* and Zoroastrianism," *JEGP* 57 (1958), 716–38; Bernard Blackstone, *The Consecrated Urn* (London: Longmans, 1959) and *The Lost Travellers* (London: Longmans, 1962); Edward LeComte, *Endymion in England* (New York: King, 1944); Ernest Tuveson, *The Avatars of Thrice Great Hermes: An Approach to Romanticism* (Lewisburg, PA: Bucknell University Press, 1982); and Meyer Abrams, "Divided and Reunited Man: The Esoteric Tradition," in *Natural Supernaturalism: Tradition and Revolution in Romantic Literature* (New York: Norton, 1971).

behaving like the classic narcissist, seeks a second self, a mirroring and idealized sister. As an "adult" the hero faces three transformations of the feminine: He can pursue the woman as beloved, the woman as castrating *femme fatale*, or the woman as mentor/muse. But no clear demarcations exist between these forms of the female; they often overlap in ways that suggest that for the male psyche all women are ultimately the same one. Readers of English Romantic poetry written by the six canonical male writers have often concluded that the meaning and significance of the feminine is finally determined only by the age and psychic needs of the hero/poet. The chapters of this volume are arranged in the chronological order charted above, without any attempt to claim that the images are as neat or consistent as such an arrangement suggests. What is evident, however, is that at every stage the woman encountered is a projection of the hero's split and ambivalent feminine aspect. For instance, when Endymion as Culture Hero pursues the triple goddess, he is seeking to colonize the multifaceted feminine as the embodiment of Nature, while on the psychic level he is uncertain of his sexual maturity, unclear about whether or not he is ready to leave the mother behind and embrace a sister or a beloved. At every stage of his social and psychic development, then, the hero needs and creates within himself the perfect feminine complement, and these "women" act out the role assigned to them by the laws of complementarity. Very rarely do we see any poetic attempt to present "real" women acting independently of the controlling male presence of the poem. Instead, we see the woman become the self-erasing Eternal Feminine, the "Other," the psychic embodiment of all those qualities the hero needs to fictionally complete himself.

III

Interpretations of Romanticism as a literary movement have traditionally tended to emphasize dichotomies: self and other, mind and nature, natural and supernatural, allegory and symbol, mediated and unmediated, subject and object. These pairings have prevailed in the general language of Romantic literary criticism because that criticism has shared and, as Jerome McGann has demonstrated, reinforced the ideological beliefs and critical assumptions of the poets themselves.[9] But one can utilize one particular Romantic ideology, the androgynous

9. See McGann's *Romantic Ideology* (Chicago: University of Chicago Press, 1983), 41.

ideal, in order to explicate an even more pervasive complex of ideologies, the Eternal Feminine, as it functions in the poems. In other words, this study proposes to utilize that most fundamental dichotomy of human experience, male and female, as an interpretive vehicle that informs our understanding of the Romantic poets' attitudes, not just toward women, but toward themselves, their fictional attempts to recreate themselves as divine, psychically restored to primordial wholeness through the use of the absorbed and self-created fantasy of the feminine.

Literary criticism of Romanticism has taken many fresh departures in the last decade or so, and we can gain new insights about the confluence of ideology, psychoanalytic theory, and history by examining the women who recur in the poems, not simply as representations, but as intrinsic to the androgynous quest that permeates the sensibility of both the literary climate and the historical *milieu* itself.[10] In his literary recreation of woman as once again part of his own being, the Romantic poet denies his subjective experience as a separated male being and aligns himself imagistically with the creator gods of primordial myth. The fact that the legal status of married women in England at this time reinforced their literary depiction is more than a little significant. As William Blackstone stated in his *Commentaries on the Laws of England* (1765): "The husband and wife are one person in law; that is, the very being or legal existence of the woman is suspended during the marriage, or at least is incorporated and consolidated into that of the

10. The question of literature's relation to its historical *milieu* is, I realize, tremendously complicated and hotly disputed. Louis Althusser's work argues that ideology represents "not the system of the real relations which govern the existence of individuals, but the imaginary relation of those individuals to the real relations in which they live." (See his "Ideology and Ideological State Apparatuses," in *Lenin and Philosophy and Other Essays*, trans. Ben Brewster [London: New Left, 1971], 155.) Consider also the statement by Terry Eagleton: "The literary text is not the 'expression' of ideology, nor is ideology the 'expression' of social class. The text, rather, is a certain *production* of ideology, . . . History enters the text *as ideology*, as a presence determined and distorted by its measurable absences." (See his *Criticism and Ideology: A Study in Marxist Literary Theory* [London: NLB, 1976], 64, 72.) Michèle Barrett discusses a methodology that focuses on the processes of stereotyping, compensation, collusion, and recuperation of women in cultural productions. For an overview of the theoretical issues involved here, see her *Women's Oppression Today* (London: Verso, 1980), and her "Ideology and the Cultural Production of Gender," in *Feminist Criticism and Social Change: Sex, Class and Race in Literature and Culture*, ed. Judith Newton and Deborah Rosenfelt (New York: Methuen, 1985), 65–85.

husband: under whose total protection and cover, she performs everything." The "covered" woman of historical reality easily merges with both the absorbed woman of Romantic poetry and the female as constructed by the domestic ideologies of the Eternal Feminine.[11] Ideology, literature, and psychoanalysis, all of them products of middle-class sensibilities and fantasies, have generally complemented each other in a reciprocal relationship of shared assumptions, stereotypes, and prejudices about women, and the major poetry of the Romantic period is no exception.

On the other hand, discussions of literary imagery should take into account what de Man has called "intentionality." Poetic language, he writes, is a product of consciousness rather than a reflection of external reality; it is insubstantial as such and reflects a preoccupation with the need to transcend its own insubstantiality. De Man reminds us that the image is not the thing itself and by its very creation becomes divided from the thing itself. Images can only intend; they cannot incarnate reality.[12] Although we can concede that this characterization of images has significant implications for the function of poetry, we must allow also that poetic imagery is at least to some extent rooted in objective existence, and that despite the alienation of the image from its ontolog-

11. There is a good deal of debate regarding the ideology of the feminine and its construction/production in literary works. A discussion of "Marxist-Feminist Criticism" can be found in Maggie Humm, *Feminist Criticism: Women as Contemporary Critics* (New York: St. Martin's,1986), 72–88; also see Michael Ryan's "Postleninist Marxism—Socialist Feminism and Autonomy," in *Marxism and Deconstruction* (Baltimore: Johns Hopkins University Press, 1982), 194–212; Juliet Mitchell, "The Holy Family and Femininity," *Psychoanalysis and Feminism* (London: Penguin, 1975), 361–416; *Feminism and Materialism: Women and Modes of Production*, ed. Annette Kuhn and AnnMarie Wolpe (London: Routledge and Kegan Paul, 1978); Ann Foreman, *Femininity as Alienation: Women and the Family in Marxism and Psychoanalysis* (London: Pluto, 1977). For a survey of the impact of Foucault's impact on "post-feminist" denunciations of ideology, see *Feminism and Foucault: Reflections on Resistance*, ed. Irene Diamond and Lee Quinby (Boston: Northeastern University Press, 1988). Another school of thought, represented by Rosalind Coward and John Ellis in *Language and Materialism: Developments in Semiology and the Theory of the Subject* [London: Routledge and Kegan Paul, 1977], 155), focuses on language—"language producing the subject and therefore the unconscious—which points a way to avoiding incorrect appropriations of psychoanalysis to Marxist thought. These are characterised by seeing the concerns of psychoanalysis as preexisting the social operations analysed by historical materialism."

12. Paul de Man, "Intentional Structure of the Romantic Image," in *The Rhetoric of Romanticism* (New York: Columbia University Press, 1985), 7.

ical source, the "women" who occur in the major Romantic poems reveal male fears and fantasies about "real" women in their actual historical context. The image of the Eternal Feminine also intersects in significant ways with images of androgyny so that together the two form a sort of patterned structure that does not simply conform to historical reality as such, but also conforms to male fantasies about women as spiritual/fleshly, passive/encroaching, redemptive/fearsome, omnipresent/eradicable.

Writing in the 1930s, Albert Béguin isolated the image of the androgyne as the quintessential symbol of the Romantic era. In a chapter titled "Cosmic Unity," he argues for a conception of Romanticism based on the unification theory: "The perception of unity is a premise the Romantics apply to the external world, but which has its source in an experience essentially internal and ultimately religious." Béguin, subscribing to the bourgeois fantasy himself, claims that the Romantics are primarily motivated by spiritual impulses, and as such they are acutely aware of the fallen condition of their world, the divisions and polarities that mark both their internal states and the external world of Nature, which previously had been an accurate reflection and emblem of man's mind. Béguin sums up the notion of the androgynous as nostalgia for a lost psychic paradise by stating his understanding of the Romantic fascination with the androgyne:

> The Myth is, like every tragedy, a confrontation with the real, an act of confidence in the faculties of transfiguration that man wishes to attribute to himself and his inventions. The Romantics interpret the Androgyne as an expression of intense nostalgia for the unity which haunts the imagination and makes humans want to escape the world of imperfection in which they feel themselves as exiles.[13]

13. Albert Béguin, *L'Âme romantique et le rêve: Essai sur le romantisme allemand et la poésie française* (Paris: Cortí, 1939; rpt. 1946), 68; and "L'Androgyne," *Minotaure* 11 (1938), 10–13 (my translations). Béguin's 1938 article was, I suspect, engendered by reading Auguste Viatte's study *Les Sources occultes du romantisme: Illuminisme-theosophie* (Paris: Champion, 1928). Other works that explore the currents of Freemasonry, occultism, and theosophy during the eighteenth and nineteenth centuries include Jacques Roos, *Aspects littéraires du mysticisme philosophique . . . au début du romantisme* (Strasbourg: Heitz, 1953); and René Le Forestier, *La Franc-Maçonnerie templière et occultiste aux XVIII et XIX siècles*, ed. Antoine Faivre (Paris: Aubier-Montaigne, 1970).

Following Béguin's framework, the mythos of the androgynous has been traditionally understood by literary critics as a unifying figure, a harmonious image of perfect fusion and ideal, prelapsarian balance. Meyer Abrams follows Béguin in seeing the figure in this manner, but the Romantics cannot be approached from a perspective that simply reinforces their own mythologies. If the criticism of the period is divided between those who believe that a definable ideological framework exists and those who believe that all ideologies are undercut and questioned by the dramatic situations depicted in the poetry, then it would appear that the image of woman in its androgynous context would prove to be an interesting test case. That is, as many times as the representations of women and androgyny express harmony in the poetry, they also reflect dissension, strife, and an apocalyptic repulsion from the natural world. An analogous observation, of course, can be made about women as "real" characters in the poetry; they function as either reified objects of commodity exchange, or rarefied and fetishistic idealizations.

Writing some fifty years after Béguin, Michael Cooke has claimed that Romanticism itself produced "a breakdown in the grammar of opposites—and opposition—that had defined the situation of the sexes," with the clear intention of instituting a new ideal: "a male-*and*-female principle" where both modes of being were "*included* in each other." The role of the feminine in this scheme is simple; she is the principle of reconciliation, grace, freedom, and wholeness, in other words, the Eternal Feminine within the fallen male poet. The Romantic poets sought androgynous union with this feminine principle as an enlargement of their own being: "At all points relationship is the key to a philosophy of gender in the nineteenth century." But as Cooke's vocabulary makes clear, the feminine principle being celebrated by the Romantics is not easily correlated with "real" women in the historical or sociological sense. The male poet is in love not with actual women; he is instead incorporating the essence or idea of the feminine into himself. He cannibalistically absorbs her perspectives, values, and qualities and in doing so tries to convince himself that he is a divinely creative androgynous being, both male and "female." More recently, L. J. Swingle has noted that "it is a mistake to suppose that writers of the Romantic period see union as a saving grace that will heal the wounds of contrariety and make all one. . . . Unions can be interesting because they create problems rather than heal them." [14] The androgy-

14. Michael G. Cooke, *Acts of Inclusion: Studies Bearing on an Elementary Theory of Romanticism* (New Haven: Yale University Press, 1979), xix, 171; L. J.

nous ideology, then, is a quintessentially artificial concept that on one level expresses the fantasy of sexual unity as a denial of death, but on other and deeper levels expresses the inevitability of frustration and the limitations of all human art and artifice.

If the Romantic poets have been celebrated for their *Sehnsucht*, their yearning toward the absolute, the wholeness of organic unity and the dream of perfection, they have also been condemned for the same religious impulses when seen as merely pseudoreligious. Leo Bersani has observed that "the fate of all fascination with the self as the other—the fate of a radical open-endedness of being—is a kind of restless immortality." This restlessness expresses itself in the literature of the Romantics through their use of the androgynous image, an image that embodies within itself both the dream of fulfillment and the realization that the dream is a fable, a fiction, an illusion. As Wendy O'Flaherty points out in her discussion of the androgyne in Hindu tradition, duality in yogic thought represented death, while nonduality expressed the conquest of death; the merging of male and female, then, was an image of immortality and a denial of the reality of death.[15] Such a belief is implicit in the English Romantic fascination with the androgynous, but more often than not the androgyne is a failed apocalyptic figure. The Romantic poets approached their diverse and contradictory heritage—Christian, pagan, empirical, and mystical—and attempted to forge a unified vision from these various strands of meaning. They were not attempting to create transcendent realms of cosmic perfection as Béguin and Abrams would have it, but simply a vision that would enable them to survive imaginatively the chaos of their times. The fact that they chose to write about the story of human creation as it has been told in all religious traditions,[16] that they chose to play all the

---

Swingle, *The Obstinate Questionings of English Romanticism* (Baton Rouge: Louisiana State University Press, 1987), 128. In an analogous observation, Edward Strickland has noted that "the analysis of Romantic preternatural women merely as symbols of the unconscious self is bound to remain centrifugal." See his "Metamorphoses of the Muse in Romantic Poesis: *Christabel*," *ELH* 44 (1977), 644–45.

15. Leo Bersani, *A Future for Astyanax: Character and Desire in Literature* (Boston: Little, Brown, 1976), 212; Wendy O'Flaherty, *Women, Androgynes, and Other Mythical Beasts* (Chicago: University of Chicago Press, 1980), 129.

16. For a discussion of the androgynous as a Christian symbol, see Wayne A. Meeks, "The Image of the Androgyne: Some Uses of a Symbol in Earliest Christianity," *HR* 13 (1974), 207; Jonathan Z. Smith, "Birth Upside Down or Right Side Up?" *HR* 9 (1970), 281–303.

roles themselves—God, man, woman, nature, redeemer, Satan—testifies to their imaginative virtuosity and daring.

Finally, one has to remember that the andogynous is a myth, and therefore its use as a literary device is limited by the parameters and ideological content of mythology itself. The Romantic poets immerse themselves in myth and mythic consciousness because it is a world in which the feminine (which they represent as the emotional, affective, kinesthetic, and spatial) dominates. Thus Keats becomes Psyche, Shelley identifies with a female Witch, Byron gives the name Astarte to his second self, and Blake names his final epic after its female protagonist Jerusalem. Myth, however, is the realm of ideology as well as fantasy and dream. As such, the Romantic immersion in the androgynous mythos expresses an ideological fantasy that poets, and by extension their readers, can reach a consciousness that lies beyond the narrow identities that society allows men and women. The Romantic poets knew, however, that neither they nor their readers could return in any way but imaginatively to what they saw as their original androgynous being. But, as Hartman reminds us, all myth is a mediation that presupposes a discontinuity and separation from the presence it seeks. Poetic narrative then becomes what he calls a series of bridges over a gulf.[17] Within these gulfs lies perhaps what the self most desires and most fears, and within one very significant gulf the Romantics glimpsed and tentatively approached their fascination with the curse and blessing of sexual identity and woman.

IV

The English Romantic poets are concerned with mythic symbols because they could find in these symbols a means of expressing their quest for the fiction of human/divine wholeness while acknowledging that they recognized the futility of the quest. Ricoeur makes the observation:

> If symbols are fantasies that have been denied and overcome, they are never fantasies that have been abolished. That is why one is never certain that a given symbol of the sacred is not

17. Geoffrey Hartman, "Structuralism: The Anglo-American Adventure," in *Beyond Formalism: Literary Essays, 1958–1970* (New Haven: Yale University Press, 1970), 15.

> simply a "return of the repressed": or rather, it is always certain that each symbol of the sacred is also and at the same time a revival of an infantile and archaic symbol.[18]

The symbol of the androgynous self is the child's dream of itself as omnipotent, as parent of self, as divine. An infantile conception to be sure, in fact, Freud thought that the androgynous was something that had to be split up in order for life to proceed. The Romantic poets were drawn to this symbol because it expresses in a sort of hieroglyphic form a new configuration of the self. Ultimately in the symbol of the androgyne they found a theory of love, an explanation for creation and fall, a redeemed Eve, and one hope, albeit illusory, for recapturing another version of Eden.

The English psychoanalyst Theodore Faithfull once suggested that the term "androgynology" would be the most accurate word to describe the branch of psychoanalysis that attempted to deal with the analysis and synthesis of the human psyche. His suggestion has not been adopted; however, it reveals how thoroughly the androgynous ideal was accepted by psychoanalysts in the early twentieth century. In fact, if the notion of androgyny survives in the twentieth century, it is because Freud and Jung revived it and placed it in their psychological cosmos, a cosmos, I might add, that exists ultimately as a fiction, an imaginative creation, an ideological construct of the human mind, and much indebted to a Romantic ethos. Norman O. Brown has also used the image of the androgyne to express the unconscious mind's aspiration to overcome the dualisms that cause neurosis. But the earliest psychoanalytic use of the concept was by Freud, who wrote to Fliess in 1901 about his intention to write an entire book on bisexuality:

> And now, the main thing! As far as I can see, my next work will be called "Human Bisexuality." It will go to the root of the problem and say the last word granted to me to say—the last and most profound. . . . [R]epression, my core problem, is possible only through reaction between two sexual currents.[19]

18. Paul Ricoeur, *Freud and Philosophy*, trans. Denis Savage (New Haven: Yale University Press, 1970), 543.

19. Theodore J. Faithfull, *The Mystery of the Androgyne* (London: Forum, 1938), vii; Norman O. Brown, *Life Against Death* (Middletown: Wesleyan University Press, 1959), 309–13; Freud's 1901 letter to Fliess in *The Complete Letters of Sigmund Freud to Wilhelm Fliess, 1887–1904*, trans. and ed. Jeffrey M. Masson (Cambridge: Harvard University Press, 1985), 448. For an almost comi-

Although Freud never wrote such a book, he obsessively invoked the androgynous, making it a sort of persistent subject throughout his writings.[20] In "Three Contributions to the Theory of Sex" (1910) he observes that a "certain degree of anatomical hermaphroditism really belongs to the normal," while in "Hysterical Phantasies and Their Relation to Bisexuality" (1908), he notes that the "assumption of a bisexual predisposition in man is clearly brought out by psychoanalysis of neurotics" (*SE* VII:141; IX:165). Throughout his writings Freud leaned toward a biological cause for an androgyny that evidenced itself psychically. For instance, in "The Psychogenesis of a Case of Homosexuality in a Woman" (1920), he concluded that "Psychoanalysis has a common basis with biology, in that it presupposes an original bisexuality in human beings, as in animals" (*SE* XVIII:171). And in the late work *Outline of Psychoanalysis* (1938), he observed that "we are here faced by the great enigma of the biological fact of the duality of the sexes: for our knowledge it is something ultimate, it resists every attempt to trace it back to something else" (*SE* XXIII:188).

The purely psychic, dreamlike quality of the androgyne was explored by Freud in "Leonardo da Vinci and a Memory of his Childhood" (1910), but before examining that work it is necessary to consider his essay "The Antithetical Meaning of Primal Words" (1910). In this work Freud had observed that in dreams and in words that combine antithetical meanings—such as "andro"-"gyne"—contraries and contradictions are simply disregarded; in fact, words and dreams both attempt to combine contraries into an impossible unity. The androgynous artistic creations of Leonardo, then, were interpreted by Freud as wish-fulfillments, dreams or hieroglyphics expressing a nostalgia for a lost psychic harmony. But most revealing in his essay on Leonardo is Freud's reliance on the ancient mythological tradition of the androgyne:

> Mythology can teach us that an androgynous structure, a combination of male and female sex characters, was an attribute not only of Mut but also of other deities. . . . Mythology may then offer the explanation that the addition of a phallus to the

---

cal example of how the bisexual was discussed during Freud's own life by his medical colleagues, see L. S. Römer's "Über die Androgynische Idee des Lebens," in *Jahrbuch für Sexuelle Zwischenstufen,* V (Leipzig: Verlag von Max Spohr, 1900).

20. Sigmund Freud, *The Standard Edition of the Complete Psychological Works of Sigmund Freud* (*SE*), 24 vols. Trans. James Strachey (London: Hogarth Press, 1953–74). All quotations from Freud will be from this edition.

> female body is intended to denote the primal creative force of nature, and that all these hermaphroditic divinities are expressions of the idea that only a combination of male and female elements can give a worthy representation of divine perfection. (*SE* XI:94)

In the essay on Leonardo, Freud states that the mental acceptance of bisexual beings is made possible primarily by biological factors—our memory traces of infantile sexuality—but in *Beyond the Pleasure Principle* (1920) he again resorts to mythology, this time Plato's. In trying to uncover the origin of sexuality he admits the aura of dreamlike mystery and relies on a hypothesis "of so fantastic a kind—a myth rather than a scientific explanation—that I should not venture to produce it here, were it not that it fulfills precisely the one condition whose fulfillment we desire. For it traces the origin of an instinct to a need to restore an earlier state of things." Freud quotes extensively from Plato's version of the androgyne as presented in the *Symposium*, and concludes that "Plato would not have adopted a story of this kind which had somehow reached him through some oriental tradition—to say nothing of giving it so important a place—unless it had struck him as containing an element of truth" (*SE* XVIII:54–57). The same observation, of course, can be made about Freud's self-conscious use of the myth, for it illustrates his growing realization that the tendency of the sexual instinct is to restore an earlier state of things, a state of undifferentiated sameness, unicellularity. In fact, he relies on Weismann's morphological theory to conclude that "unicellular organisms are potentially immortal, and that death only makes its appearance with the multicellular metazoa" (*SE* XVIII:46). The androgynous body, that "magical" body sought by poets and mystics, is the dreamlike embodiment of this urge to escape the inevitable death caused by the division and separation of the life principles.

But Lacan has more recently placed the Freudian fiction within the larger context of language theory/fantasy, and declared that the myth of the "total personality" is but "another one of the deviant premises of modern psychotherapy." Because of the psychic and linguistic realities of displacement and condensation, people can never become "whole," and such a quest can only be a phantasm doomed to failure. Because the subject can never be a signifier, and the lack of the object is the ultimate psychic reality, Lacan claims that all adult quests for transcendence are various forms of this original realization of the lack of the object: "In the same way as the quest for the lost 'authentic' self (however interminable)—depends upon an original loss and the discovery of difference, self-knowledge depends upon an original misconstruction." For Lacan the relationship of Self to some artificially found Other is not the means to any apotheosis or transcendence. Any relationship between Self and Other is doomed to objectification, alterity, and inevitably aggression, similar to the sadomasochistic relationships described by Nietzsche and Sartre. In these relations the Other becomes an object for us, while we can only make ourselves an object for the Other.[21] Lacan's position stands, then, as an indictment and condemnation of the poetic attempts—both the serious and the ironic—made by the English Romantics to objectify the female as Other.

V

The androgynous became for the Romantics an image that could signify in symbolic code as well as literal fashion their ambivalence not only toward life, death, sexuality, and women, but also their worst suspicion—that the dream of psychic completion was tenuous and artificial at best. The quest for androgynous union between the self/other stands, finally, as one manifestation of the Romantic interest in transcendence, even while we recognize the validity of Marjorie Levinson's observation that "Romantic transcendence is a bit of a white elephant. One wants to find a use for it." Although Levinson believes we cannot participate in the several persistent contraries of Romanticism, including that of subject/object, she admits that the only way we can recover the topic is to trace the sources and explain the character of that tran-

21. Jacques Lacan, *The Language of the Self: The Function of Language in Psychoanalysis*, trans. Anthony Wilden (Baltimore: Johns Hopkins University Press, 1968), 166, 161; *Écrits*, trans. Alan Sheridan (New York: Norton, 1977), 287. Lacan identifies the castration complex as the crucial point of divergence between Freud and Plato: "Castration is the altogether new motive force that Freud has introduced into desire, giving to the lack in desire the meaning that remains enigmatic in the . . . *Symposium*." For an extended discussion of this issue, see John Brenkman, "The Other and the One: Psychoanalysis, Reading, the *Symposium*," *YFS* 54 (1977), 396–450. For a comparison of the Freudian unconscious and ideology as both eternal, omnipresent, and transhistorical, see Althusser's "Freud and Lacan," in *Lenin and Philosophy*, 189–219.

scendence.[22] Such a task is precisely what this study attempts. By examining the sources and permutations of the androgynous compulsion—poetic depictions and attitudes toward symbolic and internalized women—we can discern the ideological roots of the erotic transcendence that was alternately idealized and deflated throughout the poetry.

And finally, if we entertain briefly the notion of the androgynous as a "discourse" about sexuality, we see that it reveals bourgeois concerns about the body, a mythic fantasy of fleshly redemption through erotic union with the Other. As a discourse, then, the androgynous is also informed by the social and the political representations of nineteenth-century power and authority. As Foucault has observed, the bourgeoisie distinguished itself from both the aristocracy and the working class by making sexuality and the health of its "bodies" a primary source of its own hegemony. And the Romantics, like the Greeks before them, tried to sustain the fiction of the body's sacredness and advocated sexuality as a means of approaching the divine. To transform the self as a union of masculine and feminine is to imitate God's original creation of the sexes as united. The poet, then, most clearly imitates God when he fictionally (re)creates himself and his double, his Eve, his second self in a discourse that denies the received categories of male and female. In doing so, the poet recaptures Paradise—or as reasonable a linguistic facsimile as possible—at least until the inherently ironic tensions explode the ideal and reveal the impossibility of the task.

In the ideologies of the androgynous and the feminine, we can finally discern an example of what de Man called *dédoublement*, the notion of self-duplication or self-multiplication as inherently ironic.[23] Ultimately, the Romantic poets came face to face with the limitations of language, images, tropes, symbols, and all literary devices. They sought to use the imagination's capacity to transcend ontology, or "being-ness", but they found themselves reduced to ironic postures, or nonbeing-ness. In idealizing androgyny, in seeking to unify the mascu-

22. Marjorie Levinson, *Wordsworth's Four Great Period Poems* (Cambridge: Cambridge University Press, 1986), 57. Also see Morse Peckham's "Cultural Transcendence: The Task of the Romantics," in *Romanticism and Ideology* (Greenwood, FL: Penkevill, 1985), 11–33.

23. See Michel Foucault, *The History of Sexuality*, I, 124–27; Alan Sheridan, *Michel Foucault: The Will to Truth* (New York: Tavistock, 1980), 191; Paul de Man, "The Rhetoric of Temporality," in *Blindness and Insight: Essays in the Rhetoric of Contemporary Criticism* (Minneapolis: University of Minnesota Press, 1983), 212.

line and the feminine within the male psyche, they came to the realization that there never was and never could be an escape from the limited self. The self can never transform itself—can never unify with the nonself—because a part can never grasp the whole. Platonic metaphysics notwithstanding, the Romantic poet found himself, as well as his poetry, in an abyss from which there was no escape, where language and imagery failed. This study, then, will explain why women in Romantic poetry were both idealized and feared, connected as it is with why the androgynous was both sought and fled. In the final analysis, the Romantic poets could not sustain even the fiction of the androgynous as a positive ideology because of their intrinsically ironic and ambivalent attitudes toward both the feminine and themselves. What we see in the androgynous is the attempt to make everything, including the godhead, internal. We also glimpse, if we can borrow an image from Freud, a huge mouth devouring the world at the same time it is kissing itself. The androgynous may be an ideal that speaks on the surface of love, unity, social balance and reconciliation of the sexes, but it finally speaks in a stronger voice of conflict and tension about the irreconcilable divisions between man and woman, mind and matter, Culture and Nature.

1

The Mother: "Medea's Wondrous Alchemy"

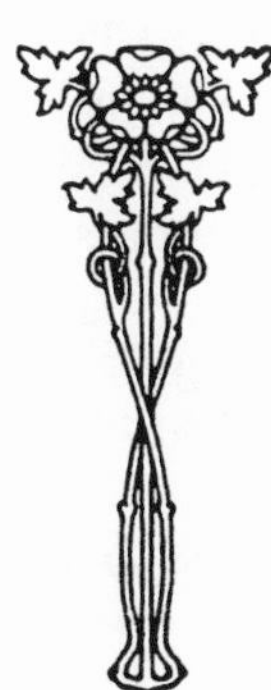

On August 15, 1838, the feast of the Assumption of the Virgin Mary, a certain Parisian, one Monsieur Ganneau, more familiarly known as *Le Mapah,* began chanting to the followers of his cult, the *Evandanistes:*

> Mary is no longer the Mother. She is the wife.
> Jesus Christ is no longer the son. He is the husband.
> The old world (confession) is coming to an end.
> The new world (expansion) is about to begin.
> Humanity is now constituted for the great betrothal.
> The hour of human virility has come.
> The era of *Evadah* is at hand.

According to the beliefs of this somewhat eccentric cult, Mary the mother was to be transformed not only into a wife, but also into Mary Magdalen, Mary the whore. Later in the ceremony, the mother was worshipped as a triple goddess—woman as mother, wife, and whore—the same amorphous woman who appears under various guises in the poetry of the Romantics, and the same woman Robert Graves described in *The White Goddess.* According to Graves, the triple goddess is Moira, Ilithyia, and Callone—Death, Birth, and Beauty—the force who presides over "all acts of generation whatsoever: physical, spiritual or intellectual."[1]

1. This French cult is discussed in Enid Starkie, *Petrus Borel: The Lycanthrope* (London: Faber and Faber, 1954), 53–54. Other equally eccentric groups

This chapter explores the image of the mother as she appears most clearly in the works of Blake, Shelley, and Keats; however, the very amorphousness of the feminine hampers our attempts to neatly distinguish at which point a certain female character ceases being a mother and instead becomes a muse. Wordsworth's Nature, which surely has many maternal features (such as nursing breasts), or Shelley's Asia (initially addressed as "Mother") are both finally less mothers than forces for imaginative inspiration or love, and as such will be discussed in later chapters. The criterion for inclusion in this chapter rests on my sense that the female character being analyzed exists in the poem primarily in her internally projective role as a mother—a force for generation or the primal psychic source of the hero. Literal mothers like Donna Inez in Byron's *Don Juan* or Margaret in Wordsworth's "Ruined Cottage" are not discussed here because they do not function in the poems as internal projections of the male poetic heroes of those works. In other words, they are intended to be read as "real" women and not primarily as symbols of the Eternal Feminine within the male poet.[2] The "women" analyzed in this chapter may not literally be the heroes' mothers, but they function in that capacity within the males' minds and ultimately cannot be understood apart from the maternal characteristics bestowed on them.

As Poulet has perceptively observed, "for the Romantic, man first of all is a self-generative force. . . . His expansion is therefore not simply psychological. It is really ontological. To expand, is to realize one's being." To be more precise about this process, however, it is necessary to recognize that the English Romantics both defined and expanded their own limited male identities through their appropriation of the female(s) external to them. Looking at one's reflection in the mother's eyes is, as we are told by a number of psychoanalysts, the earliest experience we have of self-identity. When we are first capable of seeing our-

---

are described in Frank Manuel, *The Prophets of Paris* (Cambridge: Harvard University Press, 1962); Robert Graves, *The White Goddess* (London: Faber and Faber, 1952), 11. Androgyny in the mid- to later-nineteenth century became bound up with the French notion of a "third sex" and the general decadence of the period. Mario Praz's *Romantic Agony,* trans. Angus Davidson (1933; rpt. London: Oxford University Press, 1954), is still the classic work on this period.

2. Nor will I discuss the "real" mothers in Wordsworth's poems about loss between mother and child: "The Mad Mother," "The Affliction of Margaret," "Maternal Grief," "The Sailor's Mother," and "The Emigrant Mother," or the very ephemeral "mothers," Life-in-Death and Mary Queen, in Coleridge's *Rime of the Ancient Mariner.*

selves reflected in our mother's eyes—as in a mirror—that act of perception causes us to know ourselves for the first time as both a self and a (m)other. But the Other is typically perceived as one's own reflection even though it appears to exist "outside" the self as an "objective me"; thus from the start we experience ourselves as if we were both self and Other, and therefore a part of an external pattern, a term in a discourse not initiated by the "I." [3] The attachment to the mother's eyes as the first mirror of self-concept forms the primary and perhaps strongest image of symbolic women in the English Romantic period, but as the Romantic hero matures he finds himself compelled to replace the mother with a younger version of herself—the sister—who functions ultimately for the poet as a narcissistic mirror as well as an aspect of his gradually expanding self.

In "Inhibitions, Symptoms, and Anxiety" (1925), Freud refined his theory on the etiology of original anxiety. He explains that the infant psyche, basking in its primary solipsism, inevitably comes to experience a threatening increase of tension arising from nongratification of its needs. This danger, however, is already dialectical, a relation between needs and nongratification experienced as object loss. When the infant learns that an external and perceptible object (the mother) can gratify his needs, the signifying content of the danger of object loss is displaced to her withdrawal or absence. Thus the phenomenology of original anxiety must center on absence so that desertion or object loss must logically and temporally occur prior to the overfilled inner self (*SE* XX:77–172). We can see, then, that secondary narcissism contains an original, decisive absence in its image of identity, which is after all, a kind of surrogate mother. It is not in fact an excess of delight that urges the ego to overflow toward objects, but an insufficiency in that delight, a qualitative absence, a lack of being.

In *Civilization and Its Discontents* (1929), Freud clarifies the process, stating that "narcissistic libido turns toward objects, and thus becomes object-libido; and it can change back into narcissistic libido

3. Georges Poulet, *The Metamorphoses of the Circle,* trans. Carley Dawson and Elliott Coleman (Baltimore: Johns Hopkins University Press, 1966), 97. See also Jacques Lacan, "The Mirror Stage as Formative of the Function of the I," in *Écrits, A Selection,* trans. Alan Sheridan (New York: Norton, 1971), 1–7; Anthony Wilden, "Lacan and the Discourse of the Other," in Lacan, *The Language of the Self: The Function of Language in Psychoanalysis,* trans. Anthony Wilden (Baltimore: Johns Hopkins University Press, 1968), 159–77; and "The Mirror Phase" in Jean Laplanche and J.-B. Pontalis, *The Language of Psycho-Analysis,* trans. Donald Nicholson-Smith (New York: Norton, 1971), 250–52.

once more." This curve occurs as a secondary movement and presupposes an introjection of the love object, but this phenomenon (what Freud called "secondary narcissism") is particularly evident in Romantic poetry, primarily because the mother and sister most frequently alternate as love objects, one now primary, one now secondary (*SE* XXI:118). But by Freud's own evidence, the original narcissism, defined as the attachment to the mother/mirror, cannot be painful—only its disruption can cause the internal confusion and disharmony experienced as pain. The anxiety of solipsism—called by Van den Berg "the groaning of an overfilled inner self"—is a secondary, derivative anxiety, for solipsism is itself a defense against the original anxiety of deprivation of the mother.[4]

Thus incest and love of the mother occur frequently enough in English Romanticism to constitute what could be called an uncanny compulsion to repeat, with Freud's original meaning in mind: "an unintended recurrence of the same situation, but which differs radically from it in other respects, also resulting in the same feeling of helplessness and of uncanniness." For Freud, certain events are experienced as uncanny because they are the recurrence of something that has been repressed: "an uncanny experience occurs either when infantile complexes which have been repressed are once more revived by some impression, or when primitive beliefs which have been surmounted seem once more to be confirmed" (*SE* XVII:237, 249). In *Beyond the Pleasure Principle* (1920), Freud notes that "all instincts tend toward a restoration of the earlier state of things," a return to the primal condition womb/tomb—a return, in other words, to that condition of unconscious fusion with the mother (*SE* XVIII:57). But the desire to remain fused with the maternal can only reduce the poet to a variety of self-destructive infantilized postures, so that he is compelled to seek an altered version of her in the sister. In idealizing, pursuing, and merging with the sister, the male poet confronts the reality of his secondary narcissism; he has chosen a substitute for the mother, the primary love object, but his "love" for his sister is finally another version of solipsistic self-absorption and cannibalization of the feminine.

The mother assumes several guises in English Romantic poetry, and these differing manifestations conform to some extent to the psychological development of the male as delineated by Freud's fiction. That is, the woman who appears in some of the poems is the fearful preoedipal mother of infancy who alternately abandons or engulfs the infant.

4. See Weiskel, *Romantic Sublime*, 160–64, for a fuller discussion of this phenomenon.

On other occasions she is the phallic-narcissistic mother who either confirms her son's masculinity or denigrates and denies it. Finally, she can appear as the oedipal mother who is never satisfied, who seductively leads the son on and then rejects him for the father. These three faces of the Freudian fantasy-mother are all ultimately projections of the young boy's fantasies and can be clearly discerned in English Romantic poetry. By examining them we can distinguish how and why the androgynous union sought by the male poets so frequently foundered in dread of the woman within.

But Freudian theory also provides us with a convenient explanation as to why love of the mother—primary narcissism—will not suffice psychically because the development of identity requires the sort of self-consciousness that is predicated on awareness of the separation from the primal love object. As Weiskel notes, "though the first knowledge of the object is of an absence, it is not the less recognition for that. At all events, a critique of Freud on this point amounts to a critique of Romanticism as well. If Freud was in error about love, the error was Romantic love." The Freudian fiction of the mother reveals, however, a persistent male fantasy about the (M)Other as either virgin or whore, that is, as ambivalently split. One thinks, for example, of the extremely split women in Coleridge's *Rime of the Ancient Mariner*—"Mary Queen" and the "Night-mare Life-in-Death," with the power to "thick man's blood with cold." The idealized/defamed mother can be discerned on another level as an expression of the primitive ambivalence that characterizes psychic development according to recent psychodynamic theorists. According to Kernberg, the ego of the child is defined in its earliest relationship with the mother, who is internalized as a split figure: both as a "good" and loving mother and as a "bad," denying mother. This split perception of the mother generally results in the failure to develop a coherent self, to form a clear sense of reality outside of the self, along with a regressive need to merge again with the mother or a tendency to idealize images of the self/other as a "grandiose self." All four of these psychic possibilities can be seen in the depictions we have of the mother in English Romantic poetry, and for the most part the poems reveal what Schapiro labels the "narcissistic wound," with the poets exhibiting either "violent rage" or "insatiable yearning" for the mother.[5]

5. For Freud's theories on the maternal, see his "Taboo of Virginity" (*SE*, XI), "Some Psychical Consequences of the Anatomical Distinction between the Sexes" (*SE*, XIX), and "Female Sexuality" (*SE* XXI). Also see Otto Kernberg, "Types of Idealization and the Relationship of Narcissistic Idealization to the

More recently, Julia Kristeva has stated that "No language can sing unless it confronts the Phallic Mother." Kristeva believes that the mother's identity originated for Western culture in the cult of the Lady, a hieroglyphic semiotic practice that inscribes "a conjunctive disjunction of the two sexes as irreducibly differentiated and, at the same time, alike." Further, the increasing dominance of the sign (nondisjunction) over the symbol (conjunction) produced for Western culture a "centered system (Other, Woman) whose center is there only so as to permit those making up the Same (Man, Author) to identify with it." The reduction of Woman to sign signifies the culture's need to erase disjunction (sexual difference) by either excluding her as the Other or by dissolving her into a series of images (from the Virgin to the temptress) that can be both opposed to or assimilated by the Same. But in such a culture Woman can only be a "blind center," possessing no value in herself; she can exist only as an object of exchange among members of the Same. Kristeva defines this complex of gestures as "devalorizing valorization," a mode of explicit devaluation of women that first systematically appeared in fourteenth-century bourgeois literature (*fabliaux, soties,* farces). According to Kristeva, the son's role in this cultural semiosis is to play the "pivot-mirror," "never masculine," always the "child-lover," or "accomplished androgyne." [6]

The Romantic poet-hero as Same exists within the text, then, as his own self-created fantasy of the consuming artist-conqueror, empowered by swallowing and introjecting the power of the (M)Other:

> What we take for a mother, and all the sexuality that the maternal image commands, is nothing but the place where rhythm stops and identity is constituted. . . . His oracular discourse, split (signifier/signified) and multiplied (in its sentential and lyrical concatenations), carries the scar of not merely the

---

Grandiose Self," in *Borderline Conditions and Pathological Narcissism* (New York: Aronson, 1975), 276–82, as well as the discussion of this phenomenon in Schapiro, *Romantic Mother,* x, 7–15, xi.

6. See Julia Kristeva, "The Novel as Polylogue" and "The Bounded Text," in *Desire in Language,* ed. Léon S. Roudiez, trans. Thomas Gora, Alice Jardine, and Léon S. Roudiez (New York: Columbia University Press, 1980), 191–93; 49–51. For a critique of Kristeva's ideology here, see Jane Gallop's "The Phallic Mother: Fraudian Analysis," in *The Daughter's Seduction,* 113–27. And for the best analysis of the Virgin Mary as an icon of constructed femininity, see Marina Warner, *Alone of All Her Sex: The Myth and the Cult of the Virgin Mary* (New York: Knopf, 1976).

> *trauma* but also the *triumph* of his battle with the Phallic Mother. . . . The war, however, is never over and the poet shall continue indefinitely to measure himself against the mother, against his mirror image—a partially reassuring and regenerative experience, a partially castrating, legislating and socializing ordeal.

According to Kristeva's revision of Lacan's distinctions between the Imaginary, the Symbolic, and the Real, then, the preoedipal mother is largely concealed in Western discourse because she is the embodiment of the power of the "semiotic" within the realm of the Imaginary—the archaic choral, matriarchal tradition. The preoedipal mother also opposes the oedipal father in her relation to the origins of discourse. Throughout her writings, Kristeva, following Lacan here, defines the realm of the Symbolic as the Name-of-the-Father, the point at which language acquired meaning, signification, and representation through the power of the father and the threat of castration. In opposition to the Symbolic order, Kristeva places the Imaginary/semiotic, with its "uncertain and indeterminate articulation," the babble of infants and the antirepresentational maternal chora. The mother as transformed by the "symbolic," however, must supplant the power of the semiotic Other. This makes her acceptable to the patriarchy because her sexuality is harnessed and defined by the male child Jesus in her arms. In other words, access to the preoedipal mother is only possible through the oedipal world of the father, for he stands as a blocking figure as well as a mediator between mother and son.

Kristeva's fantasy of the "split" mother—either the potent preoedipal semiotic force or the coopted patriarchal version—has been viewed as a contribution to theories of sexual equilibrium, for the Virgin Mary, according to Kristeva, functions to provide an image that defuses woman's paranoia about her importance at the same time it assuages male anxiety about the generative power of women. But she goes further to claim that poetic language itself exists as the equivalent of incest: "it is within the economy of signification itself that the questionable subject-in-process appropriates to itself this archaic, instinctual, and maternal territory; thus it simultaneously prevents the word from becoming mere sign and the mother from becoming an object like any other—forbidden."[7] As we will see in analyzing the maternal figure in

7. For the best summary of Lacan's position, see Fredric Jameson, "Imaginary and Symbolic in Lacan: Marxism, Psychoanalytic Criticism, and the Problem of the Subject," in *YFS* 55/56 (1977), 338–95. And for Kristeva's revision of

the poetry of Blake, Shelley, and Keats, the poet-hero ambivalently presents himself struggling with the preoedipal mother, seeking sanctuary in what Kristeva labels the realm of the Symbolic. But he cannot finally defeat her power (through assimilation, cannibalization) until he launches himself into the paternal realm of language, the Symbolic, celebrating his transformed masculine identity as an apotheotic artist whose abilities have been wrested from the buried and fictionally destroyed mother. This persistent fantasy, in fact, emerges as a central ideology in those texts that also present a confrontation with the mirroring feminine. One is tempted to conclude that the ideology of the Romantic artist as Culture Hero—perhaps the most prevalent ideological strain in English Romanticism—was embraced by the poets specifically to do battle with the archaic powers of the semiotic mother. By defeating and then absorbing her, the poet styles himself as doubly potent, containing within his new androgynous psyche both the "masculine" realm of the Symbolic and the "feminine" forces of the Imaginary, Nature, and semiosis.

But what we also see, according to recent feminist theorists, is that these fictions of the mother are all male-created fantasies designed to ward off the fear of castration that the mother represents for the male psyche. For instance, Luce Irigaray has noted that

> the mother woman is a *castrator*. . . . [She] creates an endless interval, game, agitation, or non-limit which destroys the perspectives and limits of this world. But, for fear of leaving her a subject-life of her own, which would entail his sometimes being her locus and her thing, in a dynamic inter-subjective process, man remains within a master-slave dialectic. He is ultimately the slave of a God on whom he bestows the qualities of an absolute master. He is secretly a slave to the power of the mother woman, which he subdues or destroys.[8]

Lacan, see "From One Identity to Another," in *Desire in Language,* 136–40. Also see Mary Jacobus, "Dora and the Pregnant Madonna," in *Reading Woman,* 137–93, for a discussion of Kristeva's maternal fiction as developed in "Motherhood According to Giovanni Bellini" (also available in *Desire in Language*). Further critiques of Kristeva's maternal "fantasy" can be found in Domna C. Stanton, "Difference on Trial: A Critique of the Maternal Metaphor in Cixous, Irigaray, and Kristeva," in *The Poetics of Gender,* ed. Nancy K. Miller (New York: Columbia University Press, 1986), 157–82; and Ann R. Jones, "Julia Kristeva on Femininity: The Limits of a Semiotic Politics," *FR* 18 (1984), 56–73.

8. See Irigaray's "The Politics of Difference," in *French Feminist Thought: A Reader,* 122. Kristeva has observed, "Fear of the archaic mother turns out to

The male fantasy of the phallic mother stands as the fictitious psychic origin for fetishizing the mother's body throughout Romantic texts that attempt to elide the power of the female. In ambivalently posturing before sternly phallic mothers such as Blake's Tirzah, Rahab, and Vala, Shelley's elusive women in *Alastor,* or Keats's triple goddess in *Endymion,* the poets conducted a ritual dance of approach-avoidance, a fictional engagement that reveals at the same time it appropriates the mother's power on both psychological and political levels.

It is important to recognize, however, that according to Leslie Fiedler the mother assumed new significance during the Romantic period because of the general emphasis on Wordsworthian "wise passiveness" and the interest in "mysterious natural origins." Keats was to characterize this "wise passiveness" in a letter as the power to receive rather than to impose: "let us open our leaves like a flower and be passive and receptive" (Letters, I, 232). This particular ideology led not only to a resurrection of "matriarchal" ideals but to a new sense of positive power for women themselves. There can be no doubt, though, that the mother also assumed importance at the beginning of the nineteenth century because of a variety of cultural factors. Domestic life was not a fashionable pastime among the upper and middle classes during the eighteenth century largely because houses were still sites of production rather than consumption. After industrialization irrevocably altered patterns of production, women found themselves participating in a feminized version of the Protestant work ethic.[9]

---

be essentially fear of her generative power. It is this power, a dreaded one, that patrilineal filiation has the burden of subduing." See her "From Filth to Defilement" in *Powers of Horror: An Essay on Abjection,* trans. Léon S. Roudiez (New York: Columbia University Press, 1982), 77. Sarah Kofman analyzes the relation between penis envy, castration, and the Medusa's head in *Enigma of Woman,* 82–83, as does Neil Hertz in "Medusa's Head: Male Hysteria Under Political Pressure," in *The End of the Line* (New York: Columbia University Press, 1985), 161–92.

9. See Leslie Fiedler, "The Politics of Realism: A Mythological Approach," *Salmagundi* 42 (1978), 31–43. And for a pertinent discussion of how female-conduct books functioned to reinforce the new domestic ideology, see Nancy Armstrong, "The Rise of the Domestic Woman," in *The Ideology of Conduct: Essays on Literature and the History of Sexuality,* ed. Nancy Armstrong and Leonard Tennenhouse (London: Methuen, 1987), 96–141. Other works that place the mother-figure in historical context include: Marlene LeGates, "The Cult of Womanhood in Eighteenth-Century Thought," *ECS* 10 (1976), 21–40; Elizabeth Badinter, *Mother Love: Myth and Reality* (New York: Macmillan,

But woman-as-mother finally wields less power as a cultural/historical force than she does as a psychic power. Bruno Bettelheim, in differing with Freud, noted that "a possibly much deeper psychological layer in boys has been relatively neglected... a complex of desires and emotions which... might be called 'vagina envy' [but which includes] in addition, envy of and fascination with female breasts and lactation, with pregnancy and childbirth." Karen Horney has also identified a similar phenomenon in boys, which she defines as the "dread of woman." Gilbert and Gubar use Bettelheim's "womb-envy" theory to speculate: "isn't it also possible that the primordial self/other couple from whom we learn the couplings, doublings, and splittings of 'hierarchy' is the couple called 'mother/child' rather than the one called 'man/woman'? If this is so, isn't it also possible that verbal signification arises not from a confrontation with the 'Law of the Father' but from a consciousness of the lure and the lore of the mother?" [10] The male Romantic poets may be primarily motivated by cultural nostalgia for the preindustrial world, fear/hystericization of the mother's body, envy of her generative capacities, anxiety about castration, or love of male-projected perceptions of the mother. The complex of emotions and psychic tendencies is a potent one, wrapped up as it is with notions of the Mother Goddess as the First Cause, the primal source for all life. In seeking to merge with the maternal, the Romantics were posturing, positioning themselves as Father Gods, worthy consorts for the Great Mother. The fact that their poetic efforts all conclude in despair and failure reveals something significant—both physically and culturally—about their various attempts to portray the mother.

II Blake: "Thou Mother of my Mortal part"

The female in Blake's poetry is terrifying and uncanny because of the many and varied forms she is able to assume. Most prevalent through-

---

1981); and Lawrence Stone, *Family, Sex and Marriage in England, 1500–1800* (New York: Harper, 1979).

10. See Bruno Bettelheim, *Symbolic Wounds* (Glencoe: Free Press, 1954), 20, and Karen Horney, "The Flight From Womanhood," in *Feminine Psychology* (New York: Norton, 1967). Erich Neumann's studies *The Great Mother,* trans. Ralph Manheim (New York: Bolingen, 1963), and *The Origins and History of Consciousness,* trans. R. F. C. Hull, 2d ed. (Princeton: Princeton University Press, 1973), discuss woman/womb as the true source of Logos. Also see

out Blake's works is the motif of the triple female who, like his depiction of the male spectre, attempts to frustrate all efforts at psychic reunification. This triple female, however, cannot be understood apart from her origin in the Great Mother. For Blake this mother is the embodiment of the fallen natural world; she is generation personified, the flesh as omnipotent, "a Sexual Machine," a force that in its power relegates the male to a subsidiary appendage. As Blake stated in his 1818 version of "For the Sexes," the "Worm" is mother and sister, the female force who places the male under a tree to weave the "Dreams" of "Sexual Strife." The mother is inescapable in her potency, her power to engender and destroy both reason and the imagination.[11] For example, when Urizen encounters three females in *The Four Zoas:* VI, he recognizes them as his daughters. None of them, however, can speak. They can only silently perpetuate the cycle of Nature by ceaselessly pouring water. For Blake, this triple female represents man's ambivalent and ultimately destructive relation with the external world. Examining Freudian myth on this point is instructive. In his "Theme of the Three Caskets" (1913) he states that the triple female represents man's encounter with the elemental being who embodies the powers of both life and death, in other words, the mother. Freud further remarks that these women are frequently dumb, and he equates their speechlessness with death.[12] His final analysis of the triple-woman motif corresponds in significant ways to the meaning of the figure in Blake:

Sandra M. Gilbert and Susan Gubar, *No Man's Land: The Place of the Woman Writer in the Twentieth Century, Vol. 1: The War of the Words* (New Haven: Yale University Press, 1988), 265.

11. William Blake, *Jerusalem:* 39 [44], and "For the Sexes," in *The Complete Poetry and Prose of William Blake,* ed. David V. Erdman, newly rev. ed. (Berkeley: University of California Press, 1982), 187, 269; *Blake: Complete Writings,* ed. Geoffrey Keynes (1957; rpt. London: Oxford University Press, 1971), 674, 771. All quotations are from the Erdman edition, though page numbers from both texts are cited in parentheses in the text. Plate numbers are referred to except for the written text of *The Four Zoas.*

12. In an interesting related comment, Diane Christian has observed that "Blake uses a triad to express psychic organization. There is a shadow double of the same sex and an emanation of the opposite sex. The male-female strife is not the central conflict; the real warfare is between the doubles. Self-murder is man's real menace and its consequences are social and sexual murder." See her "Inversion and the Erotic: The Case of William Blake," in *The Reversible World: Symbolic Inversion in Art and Society,* ed. Barbara Babcock (Ithaca: Cornell University Press, 1978), 126.

> [the triple goddess is] the woman who bears him, the woman who is his mate and the woman who destroys him;. . . they are the three forms taken by the figure of the mother in the course of a man's life—the mother herself, the beloved one who is chosen after her pattern, and lastly the Mother Earth who receives him once more. (*SE* XII:301)

There can be no doubt that Blake was more than a bit obsessed with the devouring and threatening power of the multiple feminine principle, and several notebook and manuscript poems dwell on permutations of this "woman." For instance, "The Crystal Cabinet" presents the fallen female as a deceptive and demonic threefold woman. In her first guise she is the youthful maiden who catches her male prey and locks him in a "cabinet," his fallen and sexually divided body. But when the male attempts to "seize the inmost Form" of the next personification of the triple woman—the "lovely Moony Night" Diana—he finds himself "like a Weeping Babe" thrown out onto "the wild." This time he is found by a "Weeping Woman pale," Hecate, the mother as queen of Hell. Blake's vision of life here forcefully depicts men as forced to measure their lives in terms of usurping women who alternately function as mothers, lovers, or destroyers. The same syndrome is obsessively traced again in "The Mental Traveller" and "The Golden Net."

In Blake's poetry the triple female, the mother/antimother, is defeated only when all the female characters become Jerusalem. But until that fictitiously apocalyptic moment, the female rules the fallen world through the power of her sexuality and its perverted manifestations, marriage and institutionalized religion. According to Blake, Mary as the virgin mother of God is an unnatural and evil personification of the maternal, and her visage haunts a number of his poems. But before we can unravel Blake's attitude toward the mother, we must first understand his larger philosophical position toward women.

The complaint is often made that Blake's depiction of women rests on the sexist premises of his culture, and that, although he tried mightily, he could not resist internalizing this sexism.[13] Reading several of

13. See, for example, David Erdman's comment that Blake's hostility to the "female will is not easy to evaluate" (in his *Blake: Prophet Against Empire,* rev. ed. [New York: Anchor, 1969], 254.) Also see Susan Fox, "The Female as Metaphor in William Blake's Poetry," *CI* 5 (1977), 507–19; Diana Hume George, "'Is She also the Divine Image?': Feminine Form in the Art of William Blake," *CR* 23 (1979), 129–40, rpt. *Blake and Freud* (Ithaca: Cornell University Press,

Blake's early poems might very well cause one to suspect that he blamed women not only for the original fall, but also for the ensuing condition of fallen life. Yet the true evil in Blake's ideology is not femaleness as such; rather, it is the fallen and single-sexed self. Destroying this fallen sense of selfhood, that is, the self as divided from and hostile to its counterpart, stands as the central concept in Blake's scheme of redemption: "Man is born a Spectre or Satan & is altogether an Evil, & requires a New Selfhood continually, & must continually be changed into his direct Contrary" (*J* 52: E, 200; K, 682). Only when the fallen self rejects its delusive sense of self-sufficiency, embodied for Blake in the hermaphroditic Satan, will it be able to reunite with its separated half to form the androgynous whole. But does the female survive in the Blakean apocalypse, or, as Diana George citing Blake asks, "Is She Also the Divine Image?" Does the female exist as a separate principle in Blake's ideal, or is the androgynous for Blake simply a grandiose male self with a female element within it?[14] Answering these questions while simultaneously exploring the multiple dimensions of the maternal constitute the focus of this section.

One must begin, however, by carefully distinguishing between "women" and "woman as symbol" in Blake's poetic universe. It may appear that Blake is attacking actual women in his denunciation of the fe-

---

1980), 185–207; Alicia Ostriker,"Desire Gratified and Ungratified: William Blake and Sexuality," and Anne K. Mellor, "Blake's Portrayal of Women," both in *B:IQ* 16 (1982–83), 148–65; David Punter, "Blake, Trauma, and the Female," *NLH* 15 (1984), 475–90, and his "The Sign of Blake," *Criticism* 26 (1984), 313–34; Karleen M. Murphy, " 'All the Lovely Sex': Blake and the Woman Question," and "The Emanation: Creativity and Creation," both in *Sparks of Fire: Blake in a New Age,* ed. James Bogan and Fred Goss (Richmond, CA: North Atlantic Books, 1982); and Margaret Storch, "Blake and Women: 'Nature's Cruel Holiness,' " in *Narcissism and the Text: Studies in Literature and the Psychology of Self,* ed. Lynne Layton and Barbara Schapiro (New York: New York University Press, 1986), 97–115.

14. Diana Hume George (in *Blake and Freud,* 25) attacks Blake's androgynous ideal as a Jungian "blur," claiming that Blake does see the feminine as part of the perfection of humanity, even though most of his female characters are in a fallen state where they are either victims or victimizers. In *Romantic Contraries: Freedom versus Destiny* (New Haven: Yale University Press, 1984), Peter Thorslev asserts that the androgynous simply is not present in Blake's poetry. Leopold Damrosch, Jr. concludes that the woman does not survive Blake's androgynous scheme, becoming totally absorbed into the male, like "an electrical circuit plugged in to itself." See his *Symbol and Truth in Blake's Myth* (Princeton: Princeton University Press, 1980), 239.

male will: "In Eternity Woman is the Emanation of Man she has No Will of her own There is no such thing in Eternity as a Female Will" (E, 562; K, 613). But the female will is not easily equated with women as such. Rather, it can more accurately be associated with the flaws that fallen beings have come to possess because of their separation from their counterparts. In fact, Blake's denunciation of the Spectre throughout his poetry is at least equally vehement. This Spectre, always imaged as a male, symbolizes the fallen selfhood as the female will symbolizes the corrupted emanation. The reader can conclude that Blake meant to treat the male-female relationship both realistically and symbolically. But in Blake's poetry there is no clear line between the sexes as poetic characters and the characters as embodiments of psychic qualities.

Blake can be said to have included throughout his works a sort of cosmic version of *Pride and Prejudice,* for if the faults of the fallen female are secrecy and deceit, then the faults of the fallen male are egoism and an inflated pride in the masculine powers of intellect. Blake consistently uses the image of a root to describe both fallen and separated sexes. After Enion has separated from Tharmas, she is compared to "a root growing in hell" (*FZ* I: E, 302; K, 265). Man separated from woman is described similarly as "a little grovelling Root, outside of Himself" (*J* 17: E, 162; K, 639). For Blake, both sexes are equally fallen and inadequate apart from his fantasy of their original androgynous union. Salvation, then can be achieved only through the union of self with the emanation, most frequently pictured as female, but also depicted at times as male:

> For Man cannot unite with Man but by their Emanations
> Which stand both Male & Female at the Gates of each Humanity
> How then can I ever again be united as Man with Man
> While thou my Emanation refusest my Fibres of dominion.
> (*J* 88: E, 246; K, 733)

Blake implies through this curious use of pronouns that each self has an emanation and a transformed spectre (the two are then androgynous) so that all individuals are made up of four components (zoas). For instance, in *Milton* 17:5–6, Blake writes, "they and / Himself was Human" to describe Milton and Ololon (E, 110; K, 498). The "they" component apparently encompasses the fourfold zoas, while "Himself" represents the composite of all of these aspects. We can see this composite male/female again in *Jerusalem* 97:15 when the narrator tells us that in the apocalypse "the Hand of Man grasps firm between the Male & Female Loves" (E, 256; K, 744).

To further complicate matters, however, both feminine and masculine emanations have their demonic doubles in the female will and the fallen spectre. If salvation is achieved through a fluid and harmonious balance of opposites imaged as contraries, then the female will and the spectre are false gods because they are both negations: "Negations are not Contraries: Contraries mutually Exist: / But Negations Exist Not." Negations are "Exceptions & Objections & Unbeliefs"; therefore, "The Negation must be destroyd to redeem the Contraries / The Negation is the Spectre; the Reasoning Power in Man" (*J* 17: E, 162; K, 639; *Milton* 40: E, 142; K, 533). The female will can most easily be understood as an aberration of the power-hungry mother, while the spectre exists as a perversion of the father. The struggle for domination begins, then, on this most basic of levels, the level of Urizen and Ahania, or primal father and mother.

Just as the female will haunts Blake's poetry, so does the fallen spectre. In fact, Blake's struggle with the spectre's threatening presence continues throughout the epics, but "My Spectre" stands as the central text in his vision of the separation of the sexes and the union that is necessary before the human can become fully human-divine. The poem presents a dialogue between two elements of a fragmented consciousness. The male self mourns that its spectre hovers around him "Like a Wild Beast" while his emanation weeps from within. But there is some inconsistency about the location of the emanation, for in the next four stanzas (subsequently canceled) Blake describes the emanation as separated from the self because the self has fallen. Both self and emanation wander and weep in a "Fathomless & boundless deep," the fallen world, pursued by the haunting spectre. While both elements are punished, the emanation is blamed for the division of the self. It was the emanation's jealousy that destroyed the self's loves, his imaginative creations. The self realizes that the emanation has to return and accept these other loves in order to renew their existence as one being. But, filled with a vindictive female will, the emanation boasts that she will never return and that "Ill be thy Grave." The self now recognizes that he has hopelessly pursued the emanation through "Night & Morn," so he vows to "turn from Female love." The male self thinks that this action will "root up the Infernal Grove"; he fancies that his rejection of the female will free him from the warfare of divided sexuality. Instead, this rejection is only a futile attempt to deny the necessary fluctuation between self and emanation. The self finally comes to realize that he "shall never worthy be / To Step into Eternity" if he murders his emanation "on the rocks / And another form create / To be subservient to my Fate." And so the self abandons that threat and returns with the proposal:

> Let us agree to give up Love
> And root up the infernal grove
> Then shall we return & see
> The worlds of happy Eternity.
> (E, 475–77; K, 415–17)

The redemption of the fallen female principle is similar to the redemption of the Spectre, although it is complicated by the numerous forms the female assumes in Blake's poetry. The mother is synonymous with the natural world of the flesh, and as such she represents the self's unfortunate tie to the world unredeemed by humanity's transforming imagination. But if the male spectre can be redeemed only by the imagination, so can the female will. Blake altered his views on this subject during the course of his life, for his writings before *The Four Zoas* assert the need to destroy and usurp the female (as Boehme's writings on the subject do). Blake criticism has emphasized this aspect of his vision and seen the female throughout the corpus as inferior and ultimately eradicable. But for Blake a supreme male would only be a spectre. Divinity in Blake's Eden is constituted by the fiction of the androgynous human imagination that allows all human beings to rise above the level of fallen sexual distinctions and limitations.

As Bloom has noted, sexuality as a fallen "state," unredeemed by the imagination, becomes in Blake's works similar to what D. H. Lawrence later called "sex in the head." That is, the fallen zoas are violent in their denunciations of the physical natures of their counterparts who, properly perceived, are not physical at all.[15] This mistaken perception

15. Harold Bloom, *Blake's Apocalypse: A Study in Poetic Argument* (1963; rpt. Ithaca: Cornell University Press, 1970), 215. For more "sex in the head" and suggestive discussions of Blake's obsession with homosexual fantasies, sadistic degradations of women, primal rage at the mother for withholding the breast, and compulsive depictions of the split mother, see Brenda S. Webster, *Blake's Prophetic Psychology* (Athens: University of Georgia Press, 1983), 9–30. Webster claims that in the majority of his depictions of women Blake was compelled to present them either as "good (obedient virgin)" or "bad (malevolent whore)" mothers (247): "Paradoxically, it is the longing for the lost mother that creates the negative image of Mother Nature, displacing all good onto the male body" (181).

causes Luvah, as Blake says, to "reason from the loins" and thereby deny his divine imaginative potential. The attempt to use the fallen reason, flawed and immersed in the world of sexual warfare, causes the fallen Zoas to see the androgynous union of humanity as a "Human delusion" rather than its true destiny (E, 318; K, 282).

But Blake did not come to this realization particularly early in his life, and several of his early writings reveal both his anger toward women and his bias against the equality of women in the final scheme of salvation. For instance, in the Cynic's *Song* from his very early work *An Island in the Moon,* we see a young man enraged at both his father, whom he refers to as the "old corruption," and his mother, whom he calls "flesh." This angry young man is fed from his father's breast, since his mother "would not let him suck." Deciding that he must murder his mother with a "crooked knife," he seeks her out, only to meet "with a dead woman, / He fell in love & married her / A deed which is not common" (E, 454–55; K, 50). As a father himself later on in the poem, the man reveals his horror of the flesh by using his knife on his own offspring. The motif of neurotic parents inflicting their sexual madness on their offspring and thereby infecting the children and continuing the entire process stands as Blake's dominant critique of the social travesties that tyrannize people as "institutions" in our culture: family, education, religion.

In a later poem, Tiriel's experience of his parents succeeds in both exposing and condemning the newly idle domestic woman and the newly empowered capitalist:

> The child springs from the womb. the father ready stands to form
> The infant head while the mother idle plays with her dog on her
>   couch
> The young bosom is cold for lack of mothers nourishment & milk
> Is cut off from the weeping mouth with difficulty & pain
> The little lids are lifted & the little nostrils opend
> The father forms a whip to rouze the sluggish senses to act
> And scourges off all youthful fancies from the new-born man
> (E, 285; K, 110)

It is no coincidence that the patriarchally dominated family became a microcosm of oppression and sexual tyranny that accurately mirrored Blake's perception of the social macrocosm.[16] Years later, while writing

16. For an excellent recent discussion of the historical basis of Blake's critique of society, see Jackie DiSalvo, *War of Titans: Blake's Critique of*

Jerusalem, he returned to the theme of "soft Family-Love," which he ironically and viciously described as "cruel Patriarchal pride / Planting thy Family alone / Destroying all the World beside. / A mans worst enemies are those / Of his own house & family" (*J* 27: E, 173; K, 651). The extremity of the attack on both fathers and mothers leads one to suspect that there might be a biographical as well as a social basis for its vehemence. Rather than speculate about Blake's relationship with his own parents or his brother Robert, however, I think it makes more sense to see the anger as caused by a certain resentment against his own and Catherine Blake's childlessness, their own lack of a family. One senses, finally, a "protesting too much" in his portraits of families.

But Blake does not simply resent patriarchal institutions because they reinforce and codify sexual oppression and tyranny. When Lavater praises the four virtues of woman, Blake notes: "let the men do their duty & the women will be such wonders, the female life lives from the light of the male" (E, 596; K, 82). This particular statement reveals an interesting mental contortion; women are not the source of life, men are. There is in Blake a persistent womb-envy of women as creators, life-givers, mothers, coupled as it is with a fear and loathing for the female genitals (witness his illustrations, partly erased, to the *Four Zoas*). His elevation of the male principle as primary, original, and omnipotent expresses by its sheer vehemence his very real fear of and anxiety toward the maternal. In another version of this syndrome, the poet states in *The Four Zoas* V that "in Eden Females sleep the winter in soft silken veils / Woven by their own hands to hide them in the darksom grave / But Males immortal live renewd by female death" (E, 302; K, 266). Here we witness some sort of sadistic male fantasy that women are willing sacrifices, passive victims who relish their destruction and absorption into the male. In these early statements Blake clearly depicts androgyny as a male-centered ideal that exists only through the predatory usurpation of the female. Unless the female

---

Milton and the Politics of Religion (Pittsburgh: University of Pittsburgh Press, 1983). She cites Alice Clark, *The Working Life of Women in the Seventeenth Century* (New York: Kelley, 1968), on the degradation of the mother by incipient capitalism: "Thus it came to pass that every womanly function was considered as the private interest of husbands and fathers, bearing no relation to the life of the State, and therefore demanding from the community as a whole no special care or provision" (307–8). Blake, she asserts, more rightly belongs in his sensibilities to the lower-class Protestant sects that advocated equality of woman, sexual freedom, and community cooperation (DiSalvo, 341).

willingly sacrifices her existence to the male, he remains a spectre, a shadow of his unfallen potential.

We need only examine a few texts to see that this early notion of the female as an unequal principle was derived from Blake's readings in Boehme and Swedenborg, both of whom functioned for the young Blake as embodiments of the Name-of-the-Father (to use the term in Lacan's and Kristeva's sense). For instance, according to Swedenborg, "the male and female were so created that from two they may become as one man, or one flesh; and when they become one, then taken together they are man in his fullness; but without this conjunction they are two, and each is as it were a divided or half-man." The female for Swedenborg is subsumed in the male; she is a vehicle for his salvation. Presumably, there is no salvation for her since she has no ontological reality apart from the male. For Boehme, "Adam was a complete image of God, male and female, and nevertheless, neither of them separately. . . . Adam was man and wife in one individuality."[17] These are Boehme's words, but several attempts by Boehme to describe the androgynous led Blake, as well as later readers, to see that the female for Boehme was finally sacrificed for male salvation. The Boehmistic androgyne is a male who lives parasitically off the sacrifice of the female—the ultimate capitalist fantasy of woman as commodity. For Boehme, the woman has no existence after the male has successfully completed the androgynous quest. But Blake changed the title of his first attempt at an epic from *Vala* to *The Four Zoas* because he moved from a vision of blaming women for the fall to seeing them as equals in recapturing the androgynous ideal. A study of his later epics reveals that Blake attacked and satirized the Boehmistic androgyne, and, in fact, that he tried to value the female as co-partner with man in creating a new type of androgynous ideal that would transform what passes for both art and life. His final position stands, then, as a critique of not only patriarchally inspired re-

17. See Emmanuel Swedenborg, *Conjugal Love,* trans. Samuel Warren (New York: Swedenborg Foundation, 1971), n. 37; *Heaven and Its Wonders and Hell,* trans. John Ager (New York: Citadel, 1965), n. 376; and Jacob Boehme, *Mysterium Magnum,* trans. John Sparrow (London: Watkins, 1924), I, 103. Other secondary studies on Swedenborg and Boehme's influence on Blake include: Morton D. Paley, *Energy and the Imagination: A Study of the Development of Blake's Thought* (Oxford: Clarendon Press, 1970); John G. Davies, *The Theology of William Blake* (Oxford: Clarendon, 1948); Eugene J. Harding, "Boehme and Blake's *Book of Urizen,*" *JES* 8 (1970), 3–11; David V. Erdman, "Blake's Early Swedenborgianism," *CLS* 5 (1953), 247–57; C. A. Muses, "Blake and Boehme," *BSQ* 1 (1953); George E. Bentley, *Blake Records* (Oxford: Clarendon, 1969); and David Fuller, *Blake's Heroic Argument* (London: Croon Helm, 1988).

ligious systems, but the patriarchy itself in the very basis of its power—its economic and social subjugation of women as they symbolize all the other marginalized groups (blacks, Jews, and heathens) who occasionally appear in Blake's corpus.

By the time he was writing *The Four Zoas* III, Blake was able to satirize his own early misogynist views—Boehme's—as well as his society's increasingly dangerous celebration of the Eternal Feminine. The fallen Urizen hysterically charges Ahania with appropriating the female will in defiance of him:

> Art thou also become like Vala. thus I cast thee out
> Shall the feminine indolent bliss. the indulgent self of weariness
> The passive idle sleep the enormous night & darkness of Death
> Set herself up to give her laws to the active masculine virtue
> Thou little diminutive portion that darst be a counterpart
> Thy passivity thy laws of obedience & insincerity
> Are my abhorrence. Wherefore hast thou taken that fair form . . .
> Whence is this power given to thee! . . .
> Reflecting all my indolence my weakness & my death,
> To weigh me down beneath the grave into non Entity.
> (E, 328–29; K, 295)

Here Blake is clearly mocking Urizen's extreme misogyny as the original cause as well as the perpetuator of the division of the sexes. Although Blake does indict the fallen female will in Vala, Rahab, and Tirzah, he stresses that Ahania is innocent and has the right to be an equal counterpart in the androgynous union. The splitting of the self in both Tharmas and Urizen is viewed as a cosmic tragedy that reduces them both to spectral beings. Enion and Ahania are both almost totally destroyed and left wandering on "the margin of Non Entity" (E, 331; K, 297). Neither sex gains by the separation since divided from each other both can only be phantoms in the fallen world.

The cycle of male-female warfare, then, makes each slave and tyrant in turn, from youth to age, age to youth. But the real enemy is not the female; it is fallen life in the state of Ulro that Blake images as "a Sexual Machine: an Aged Virgin Form" (*J* 39 [44]: E, 187; K, 674). In *Milton* 10 the female form is created by Enitharmon's pity, a passive and contemptuous emotion. This "aged Woman" weeping in space symbolizes the mother, the fallen physical world that "shrinks the Organs / Of Life till they become Finite & Itself seems Infinite" (E, 104; K, 490). Escaping the power of the mother, then, becomes the central mission of Blake's heroes. The mother, rather than positively nurturing life, is seen by Blake as the very embodiment of the deathly pull of the body. The ultimate imaginative act, the one that makes all other acts of will possible, requires the overthrow of the maternal.

In "To Tirzah," a late addition to the *Songs of Experience,* Blake's narrator identifies himself with the Christ-son figure who must reject his mother in order to be reborn of the spirit, the imagination. Imitating Jesus' rejection of his mother, the narrator realizes that he must deny his mother, who represents his "Mortal Birth," his tie to the things of this Earth, before he can "rise from Generation free." The second stanza presents a brief cosmogony stating that the "Sexes sprung from Shame & Pride," died, and then arose to what is now called life, a kind of sleepwalk in which they "work & weep." The female aspect of sexuality, however, is held accountable for the continuation of the fallen condition:

> Thou Mother of my Mortal part
> With cruelty didst mould my Heart,
> And with false self-decieving tears,
> Didst bind my Nostrils Eyes & Ears.

The narrator knows he must experience a psychic rebirth in order to nullify his physical birth and thus create within himself an androgynous psyche above the cycle of generation. The example of Jesus' resurrection after death sets the male "free," for Jesus has proved that the imaginative body can rise from generation into a new life (E, 30; K, 220). Tirzah the mother, therefore, can be destroyed only by denying the basis of her power, the world of generation. Denying the mother, then, demands that one renounce the world of the senses as we know it. But it also means rushing into the arms of death. The Great Mother cannot be successfully escaped, nor denied or transformed, for in the very act of trying to renounce the mother, the hero finds himself confronting sexuality's power over the imagination. The mother is a fearful power for Blake because she is the embodiment of the sexual, the physical unredeemed by the imagination, the mind. She is even more dangerous in that she has institutionalized her power in religion and marriage—the two social conventions that Blake sees as negative, oppressive and finally destructive of the human spirit.

One of Blake's earliest attacks on the institutionalized sexuality of the maternal unredeemed by the imagination comes in one of his bitter denunciations of marriage. "Hail Matrimony" presents a frank attack on fallen sexuality, women, and the "Golden cage" of marriage. In "London" marriage is imaged as a "hearse" and linked with prostitution and death. The attack is even more specific in *Visions of the Daughters of Albion,* when Oothoon condemns marriage as a state in which a woman "is bound / In spells of law to one she loathes [while]. . . she drag[s] the chain / of life, in weary lust!" Blake's objections to marriage as a state of prostitution for women are very close to Shelley's position. But for Blake the solution does not lie in an idealized free love, for it is clear that Oothoon's glorification of "Innocence! honest, open, seeking / The vigorous joys of morning light! open to virgin bliss" is not feasible in a world of Theotormons and Bromions. Instead, her vision of life as holy is thwarted by Theotormon's secrecy, jealousy, and self-love (ironically traits usually associated with the female will), the triple evils inherent in fallen sexuality. Oothoon's "liberation" is impossible while she is alone, for as she herself recognizes, she is a "solitary shadow wailing on the margin of non-entity" apart from her necessary union with her counterpart, Theotormon (E, 49–50; K, 193–94).

When humanity is so fallen that the physical world is its only reality, then the mother is the all-powerful goddess, and she has institutionalized that position in her identity as Mary, mother of a weak son who is actually subservient and inferior to her until he discovers his divinity, his imaginative power to overthrow her. Because humanity no longer remembers its divine heritage, fallen sexuality is able to divert humanity from the proper object of worship—the fiction of androgynous unity. In their fallen condition, men and women are bitter, competitive enemies for dominance and power because both sexes have internalized their culture's dominant sexual ideologies. Instead of each being a "counterpart" in the creation of the self as divine, the male seeks to make the female subservient while the female is reduced to scheming to overthrow the male's tyranny. That is, at the same time Blake presents a revolutionary attack on his culture's inherited attitudes toward sexuality, he also depicts the devastation that has occurred because those attitudes have been internalized by his characters.

Blake reveals that the ideology of sexual superiority is the source for the corruption of the religious instinct in his Notebook poem "I saw a chapel all of gold." The object of his poetic attack is the perverse female will that has usurped and institutionalized humanity's religious instincts. The narrator initially approaches "a chapel all of gold / That none did dare to enter in." Instead, the fearful stand outside "Weeping mourning worshipping." The image of the chapel of gold recalls a Blake sketch for *The Four Zoas* in which a cathedral is superimposed on a woman's genital area. The sexual imagery in the poem becomes even clearer in the next stanza as a serpent rises between the "white pillars of the door" and tears "Down the golden hinges." The meaning for

Blake is clear: the female will has elevated itself above the natural cycle of generation so that it can claim to be a "virgin Eve" and a valid object of worship in itself.

In a marginal comment on Cellini, Blake wrote: "The Pope supposes Nature and the Virgin Mary to be the same allegorical personages, but the Protestant considers Nature as incapable of bearing a child" (E, 670; K, 779). Dante's Beatrice fares no better as far as Blake is concerned. In his Dante series (begun in 1824), he merges Dante's depiction of Beatrice with the "Goddess Nature" and later with the "Goddess of Fortune," whom he rather unchivalrously refers to as "The Hole of a Shit house" (E, 689; K, 785). A genuine nausea toward the female body, in all its functions, recurs when he confronts the maternal and her sublimated manifestations.

The female can only be acceptable in Blake's cosmos if she has been shorn of as much of her female sexuality as possible. In other words, any attempt to humanize Nature as feminine apart from the masculine imagination is a blasphemy, and can only be an attempt to redeem the self through the vehicles of the fallen sexual world of Ulro. But this perversion is, and must be, destroyed by the male aspect of generation, the serpent, who is forced into the role of defiler rather than equal and harmonious worker for salvation. The serpent is forced to vomit his poison "upon the altar white. . . . On the bread & on the wine." The narrator, confronted with this vision of the destructive warfare between the sexes, is unable to accept the futile cycle and decides to retreat "into a sty" and lie down "among the swine" (E, 467–68; K, 163).

The sexes usurp and use one another in this fallen, divisive world. In Blake's vision, sexuality and institutionalized religion have become hopelessly entangled through the machinations of the mother. The male and female agree to worship their fallen forms in religious ceremonies pervaded by sexual imagery: "For a Spectre has no Emanation but what he imbibes from decieving / A Victim! Then he becomes her Priest & she his Tabernacle" (*J* 65: E, 217; K, 701). But just as the male principle evolves from Urizen to Orc to Los to Albion, so does the female progress from Tirzah the mother to Rahab and Vala to Jerusalem, the redeeming power who through sacrifice of selfhood finally affords humanity the fiction that it can transcend the fallen natural cycle and regain Eden. These female figures, however, cannot be read on any level as believable "round" characters. They are principles, embodiments of ideologies, necessarily the splintered projections of their fragmented male creator.

The fragmentation of the mother into Tirzah/Rahab/Vala/Jerusalem creates for Blake's readers the dizzying effect of uncertainty, anxiety, and a spiraling sense of vertigo. At times, for instance, Rahab and Vala are described identically and said to have the same functions. The most important distinction between them lies in Vala's identification as Jerusalem's fallen form or shadow self. In this role she is very similar to the Spectre of Urthona, who must be redeemed as Los reintegrates. As the embodiment of the fallen female self, Vala represents the evils Blake sees as inherent to that state—jealousy, deceit, and cruelty. In her unfallen form as Jerusalem, Vala was the emanation within Albion, similar in function to Shelley's notion of the prototype. But both "emanation" and "prototype" reveal the dilemma of using women as vehicles for expressing ideologies. For all the Romantics to greater or lesser degrees, the feminine is initially an internal principle that is then projected outside the self and identified with female characters. Jerusalem, for instance, is imaged as both a "City" and a "Woman." As a "city," she is a locus of renewal, a source for imaginative freedom, a psychic and spiritual place to which one returns for redemption. As a woman, she is Albion's feminine counterpart, the woman within him, the emanative portion who restores both of them to their original androgynous harmony. In this role she is strikingly similar to Sophia, the feminine equivalent of Logos.

But before Jerusalem can function as the symbol of apocalyptic redemption who returns in power to claim Albion, she must project and repudiate her fallenness: Rahab/Vala. She is, like most of the Romantic women in the poetry, a "split" figure, a "part object" (in Melanie Klein's sense), a woman who embodies in her dual guise the child's conflicting feelings of aggression against and frustrated desire for the mother. Rahab can be seen as a form of Vala as she exists in the world of time. Since the realm of time is consistently identified with the fallen male principle in Blake's poems, Rahab can be understood as the demonic female who encroaches on and attempts to usurp even that fallen male domain. In a complementary fashion, then, Vala is the fallen female as she pervades the world of space. In a speech that asserts the imagination's integrity over the dominance of the omnipresent female, Los asserts:

> What may Man be? who can tell! but what may
> Woman be?
> To have power over Man from Cradle to
> Corruptible Grave.
> There is a Throne in every Man, it is the
> Throne of God
> This Woman has claimed as her own & Man is no more!
> (*J* 30 [34]: E, 176; K, 661)

Later Albion attempts to deny the source of Vala's power, divided sexuality, as he declares: "'O Vala! / In Eternity they neither marry nor are given in marriage'" (E, 176; K, 660). But Vala cannot simply be denied; she must be redeemed.

Although Tirzah, Vala, and Rahab differ so slightly from each other that the reader is often confused in distinguishing them, they all reveal the inadequacy of the sexes as divided and separate. Blake clearly blames these female figures for perpetuating the fallen state, for like other tyrants, they have the most to lose from a return to androgynous reintegration. *Jerusalem* 67 presents Rahab and Tirzah united in a hermaphroditic union: "A Double Female." In a parody of the creation, they then weave a male being that they divide into male and female parts. But they harden the edges of the two beings into "opake hardnesses" that they call "Atheistical Epicurean Philosophy." In other words, the sexes remain separated and fallen because they have ceased to believe in their own divinity and they live instead only for the paltry sensual pleasures of erotic domination: "Such are the Feminine & Masculine when separated from Man" (*J* 67: E, 220; K, 704). As Rahab and Tirzah come to realize, sexual, religious, and physical warfare result from their act of creation and separation:

> There is no time for any thing but the torments of love & desire
> The Feminine & Masculine Shadows soft, mild & ever varying
> In beauty: are Shadows now no more, but Rocks in Horeb.
> (*J* 68: E, 222; K, 707)

If the mother, then, represents the world of fallen sexuality and the deathliness of the physical unredeemed by the imagination, does Blake long for a world without mothers, without generation? Such a world, obviously, would not last long. Blake surely condemned the capitalistic appropriation of mothers as the private property of the patriarchy, just as he censured the rebellious attempts by mothers to find a substitutive form of power by tyrannizing their children and dominating religious institutions. The family as a peculiarly fallen Eden could not be transformed apart from a transformation of the imagination and the will. Hirsch has claimed that sex is redemptive in Blake's works "not because it gratifies natural desire, but because it restores the fallen unity and removes desire." Other critics have claimed that Blake evolved the split paradise of Beulah and Eden to explain the inescapability of sex (tolerated in Beulah) and the need to transcend it altogether (in Eden). For Frosch, Beulah is a location in which "man becomes male and female, and the mode of his repose apparently includes genitality; but his sexuality is now free from possessiveness, mutually expanding, and truly of the body, rather than the consuming natural heart and the Urizenic mind." In Eden, though, there seems to be no sexuality as we commonly understand it, and this has led Damrosch to assert that Blake's final response to sex was to dismiss it as an unhappy result of the fall.[18]

Love between Jerusalem and Albion is the final image in Blake, and in the final plate that presents their union we have his mystical/antimystical position. In an embrace that is a sexual embrace of lover and beloved, self and other, male and female, we also see a spiritual union of worshiped and worshiper, God and humanity.[19] Albion is no longer a male, the victim of his belief in the state, reason, the Enlightenment, or other perversions of masculinity, and Jerusalem is no longer a female, the victim of her adherence to the natural cycle, the emotions, Romantic love or religion, or any of the other peculiar notions that women are wont to hold. Blake presents the fantasy of an achieved religious ecstasy that is also a sexual rapture and a social transformation. In his commitment to a radical chiliasm, he presents to us a vision of shared communalism, and we must struggle as readers to comprehend his vision of the transformation of body into soul and soul into body, male into female and female into male, both into something ultimately beyond those identities.

II Shelley: "O great Mother of this unfathomable World"

Shelley's first important work, *Alastor,* can be analyzed as presenting the contortions that masculine desire takes as it confronts the "split" mother as a self-projected fantasy. Shelley prefaces the poem with an

18. E. D. Hirsch, Jr., *Innocence and Experience: An Introduction to Blake* (New Haven: Yale University Press, 1964), 112; Thomas Frosch, *The Awakening of Albion* (Ithaca: Cornell University Press, 1974), 177; and Leopold Damrosch, *Symbol and Truth in Blake's Myth,* 216.

19. For a valuable discussion of the Blakean apocalypse, see Jean Hagstrum, "Christ's Body," in *William Blake,* ed. Morton D. Paley and Michael Phillips (Oxford: Clarendon Press, 1973), 142, 154. For studies that analyze Blake's attitudes toward the body of the mother, see Eileen Sanzo, "Blake and the Great Mother Archetype," *NR* 3 (1978), 105–16; and Norma Greco, "Mother Figures in Blake's *Songs of Innocence* and the Female Will," *RP&P* 10 (1986), 1–15.

instance of textuality that distances his subject at the same time it reveals his theme. The quotation from Saint Augustine: "Not yet did I love, yet I was in love with loving; . . . I sought what I might love, loving to love,"[20] indicates that like the young Augustine, Shelley's hero is also in love with the idea of loving and not with any particular object. His desire exists, just as Lacan claims, because the unconscious is born out of the repression of desire. This compulsive desire for love, as Lacan has observed, resembles our use of language, in that both "behaviors" move constantly from random object to object, or from signifier to signifier. Like the Lacanian hero of the oedipal drama, the poet-hero of *Alastor* experiences only endless desire; he is in the grip of the frozen *gaze*, for there can be no final signifier, no ultimate *objet a* in the Symbolic realm to replace the imaginary unity the child once had with the mother.[21] But the end of desire, for Lacan following Freud here, can only be death, escape from the Symbolic altogether. In ways that bespeak uncanny compulsion, the *Alastor* hero enacts, then, a fall out of the mother's body, the world of Nature, the Imaginary/semiotic, and into the realm of the Phallus, the paternal Symbolic, the world of language, empty figuration and absent signification.

We must begin, however, by noting that critical opinion is divided on the function of the Preface and the nature of the poet's quest.[22] Suffice

20. All quotations from Shelley's *Alastor, A Defence of Poetry, On Life* and *On Love* are taken from *Shelley's Poetry and Prose,* ed. Donald Reiman and Sharon B. Powers (New York: Norton, 1977). This volume is also used for discussions of *Prometheus Unbound, The Witch of Atlas,* "Epipsychidion," "Adonais," and "The Triumph of Life." As it is incomplete, however, all other references to Shelley's poetry and prose, as well as his translation of Plato's *Symposium,* are from *The Complete Works of Percy Bysshe Shelley,* ed. Roger Ingpen and Walter E. Peck (London: 1926–30; rpt. New York: Gordian, 1965), 10 vols., known as the *Julian Works (JW).*

21. Lacan has, of course, connected voyeurism with a desire for mastery or power over one's libidinal objects; the *gaze* thus symbolizes "the lack that constitutes castration anxiety," while it enacts sadistic, phallic power over its passive, masochistic "feminine" objects (see his "Of The Gaze as *Objet Petit a,* " in *Four Fundamental Concepts of Psycho-analysis,* esp. 67–78).

22. The inconsistencies that critics have seized on are predicated on the belief that the author of the Preface must be identical with the Narrator of the poem. Raymond D. Havens inaugurated the assault on the poem by calling it "confused," and claiming that "Shelley had either forgotten or was imperfectly aware of much that was in his mind when he wrote the poem" (see his "Shelley's *Alastor,*" *PMLA* 45 [1930], 1098–1115). Also see F. L. Jones, "Inconsistency of Shelley's *Alastor,*" *ELH* 13 (1946), 291–98; "The Vision Theme in Shelley's

it to say that the critical debate centers on Shelley's attitude toward the hero: Is he a self-centered narcissist pursued by avenging furies for his rejection of earthly love or is he the innocent victim of an imagination that aspires to more than life can satisfy? Another way of posing that question, however, is to focus not on the poet but on the identity of the women in the poem. Who are they and why are they created by the consciousness of the *Alastor* poet? This is another way of asking if woman as Other can do anything more than represent abjection, function as an exchange commodity, disappear, or self-negate by the conclusion of the poem.

Shelley presents a sort of prose synopsis of the poem in the Preface that introduces the poem as "allegorical of one of the most interesting situations of the human mind." Rather than confusing the poem, however, this statement makes it clear that Shelley intended to disguise the poem's ideology behind the claim of universalizing his supposed topic, otherwise known as the internal quest-romance wherein a male pursues his ultimate love object, himself as Woman. That is, as readers we are supposed to participate uncritically in the poet's attempt to create within himself an androgynous psyche constituted of both idealized masculine and self-created and projected feminine components. Shelley discusses this quest more specifically in the Preface. There he writes that his hero is "joyous and tranquil, and self-possessed" only so long as his desires are "pointed toward objects thus infinite and unmeasured"—in other words, when he exists in some fictitious harmony with the mother. When he seeks, on the other hand, to gratify his desires corporeally, by union with a woman whom he perceives as other than the mother, he is frustrated. The Preface helps to make the meaning clear, for it presents the poem as an allegory of a psychic process. The boy is forced to shift his primary narcissism, his absorption in the semiotic maternal, to love for a substitute object, one acceptable within the Symbolic and paternal realm. But the psychic struggle is elided, blocked by Shelley's blatant ideological intent, disguised as philosophical and linguistic concerns. The hero, according to the Preface's more socially acceptable (because occluded) version of the quest-romance, is concerned with depicting his imaginative development; he has attempted to unify his perceptions of the "wonderful . . . wise . . .

Alastor and Related Works," *SP* 44 (1947), 108–25. More recently, Jerrold E. Hogle has discussed *Alastor* as compelled by psychological and linguistic transference toward the narrative's "point of origin" (see his *Shelley's Process: Radical Transference and the Development of His Major Works* [New York: Oxford University Press, 1988], 46).

beautiful," thereby uniting his abilities as "poet . . . philosopher . . . lover." He has struggled to attain this all-embracing ideal of self by imagining the "Being who he loves," "an intelligence similar to itself." His poetic goal, then, is to find a reflection of the unified "intellectual faculties, the imagination, the functions of sense" in "the sympathy of corresponding powers in other human beings" (69). But the voice of the Preface is not the voice of the poem's narrator. It is almost as if the Preface were written by Shelley the philosopher, the poem's narration written by Shelley the poet, and the inner core of the poem written about Shelley the lover/son. As such, the three layers within the poem speak of a man fragmented both within and from himself, and yet self-conscious enough to depict and to some extent to satirize that division. The cool voice of the Preface, then, contrasts with the voice of the narrator who attempts to mediate between the two extreme sides of Shelley's divided self—his reason and his emotions. In the narrator's voice we hear the Shelley whose so-called Nature/mother worship leads to an idealized humanism that would reconcile his disparate and separated faculties through the power of imagination. In contrast, the hero of the poem is the frustrated oedipal son who is destroyed by his futile efforts to embrace the mother as absolute love object.

As a supposed allegory of the mind's need to unify and create, then, the poem presents a curious psychology. The self cannot exist alone, even after it has unified its faculties and should supposedly be self-sufficient. The mind needs to continue creating until it accomplishes the ultimate creation—an ideal version of itself. In its ability to recreate itself, the integrated imagination also has achieved the fictional ability to humanize the natural world. Shelley discusses this idyllic state of consciousness in "On Life," an essay particularly interesting in light of the theme of *Alastor.* When the hero of *Alastor* attempts to internalize the otherness of the feminine and remain within the Imaginary/semiotic world, he is illustrating Shelley's idealization of the child:

> Let us recollect our sensations as children. . . . We less habitually distinguished all that we saw and felt from ourselves. They seemed as it were to constitute one mass. There are some persons who in this respect are always children. (477)

Blake's imaginative ideal was similar to this self-induced state of oneness with the internal/external world. But for him Albion/Jerusalem was the fictional reintegration of the external and internal world; Nature had no existence apart from Albion's perception. Shelley longs for this same harmony of self with creation, but *Alastor* concludes in defeat because the hero cannot merge his mind with creation, cannot bridge the distance between his own self-created and extremely polarized notions of "masculine" and "feminine," Symbolic/phallic, and Imaginary/semiotic.

Just as the power of life is addressed as a maternal force in *Queen Mab* and "Una Favola," so does *Alastor* begin with an apostrophe to all-powerful Nature, the "great Mother" "of this unfathomable world" (2, 18) The passages devoted to descriptions of Nature have been persistently criticized by scholars, who see them as distractions, unrelated to the movement of the poem.[23] But in fact, the descriptions of Nature constitute the buried body of the mother, the semiotic subtext that informs and controls the hero's quest for (re)union with the mother, regression to the womb as tomb, what the narrator himself calls "Nature's vast frame, the web of human things, / Birth and the grave" (719–20). The narrator speaking here presents the poem's hero as an Oedipus, a son-figure seeking to know his nature and origins from a sphinxlike female. He begs the mother to "Favour" his song, dedicated to her, because she has been the only love object throughout his entire life: "for I have loved / Thee ever, and thee only" (19–20). He presents himself as a seeker not only of his own destiny, but of his mother's identity and power. He admits that he has searched "In charnels and on coffins" to find his identity, this secret, "the tale / Of what we are" (24–29). He compares himself to "an inspired and desperate alchymist" who has mingled "strange tears" and "breathless kisses" to create the "magic" of his creation. He has attempted to unveil the mother's "inmost sanctuary" (31–38); that is, his quest is a return to the womb in order to uncover the sources and location of maternal generation and power. Like the narrator, the hero of the poem also makes a survey of all the wisdom of the ancient world until he discovers the "wild images / Of more than man" (118–19), and embraces the "thrilling secrets of the birth of time" (128). In many ways he is reminiscent of Mary Shelley's

23. Havens's attacks on the Nature imagery in the poem (see above) were answered almost immediately by Marion C. Weir, "Shelley's *Alastor* Again," *PMLA* 46 (1931), 947–50, and in part by Arthur Dubois, "*Alastor:* The Spirit of Solitude," *JEGP* 35 (1936), 530–45; and Evan K. Gibson, "*Alastor*: A Reinterpretation," *PMLA* 62 (1947), 1022–45. For more recent dicussions of the Nature imagery as internal, see Bryan Cooper, "Shelley's *Alastor*: The "Quest for a Vision," *KSJ* 19 (1970), 63–76; Ronald Tetreault, "Quest and Caution: Psychomachy in Shelley's *Alastor,*" *ESC* 7 (1977), 289–306; Lisa M. Steinman, "Shelley's Skepticism: Allegory in *Alastor,*" *ELH* 45 (1978), 255–69.

portrait of Victor Frankenstein, who was also obsessed with discovering the source of the mother's creative powers and who went so far as to usurp the mother's province by giving birth himself to a monster, a fitting critique of the masculinist attempt to cannibalize and colonize the powers of woman.[24]

As the hero wanders through a self-created, internal landscape, we note that its features are (over)determined by his ambivalent attitude toward the mother. For instance, at times the "external" world of the feminine is threatening and extreme, either burning and smoking with volcanic force or freezing with snow and ice (83–87). The mother can be seen in this section of the poem as "the springs / Of fire and poison," as a fearfully split and threateningly potent sexual presence (88–89). At other times, however, the poet conceals, somewhat hysterically, his dread of the mother and presents the landscape as fertile, loving, nurturing, with "starry domes," and "clear shrines / Of pearl, and thrones radiant with chrysolite" (90–94).

We can perhaps best understand the psychic dynamics underlying the *Alastor* poet's quest if we return now to Kristeva's formulation of the split between the Imaginary and Symbolic realms. That is, the *Alastor* hero's proper quest ostensibly begins when he realizes that the world he has depicted throughout the Preface of the poem (lines 1–106) stands as a representation of the external world of the mother's body, the realm of the Imaginary/semiotic. He cannot exist forever in this world, however, for it knows only good/bad, inside/outside, and is without language. It is the world of "Silence," where the poet has communicated with others by his "eyes" and "looks" (65, 80, 102). As pleasant as this realm is to him as a child, as he matures the poet is forced to seek another order, the paternal realm of the Symbolic, an order that imposes the necessary distance from the mother by convincing the son that the mother is dead and that substitutions for her can be found in figurations, language, that will be under the son's total control. We rec-

24. See Margaret Homans's discussion of *Frankenstein* and *Alastor:* The *Alastor* poet's "encounter with the Indian maid makes it clear that embodiment is itself an obstacle to desire, or more precisely, its termination" (see her *Bearing the Word: Language and Female Experience in Nineteenth-Century Women's Writing* [Chicago: University of Chicago Press, 1986], 107). Also see William Veeder, *Mary Shelley and Frankenstein: The Fate of Androgyny* (Chicago: University of Chicago Press, 1986), 94–98, for a comparison of Victor Frankenstein and the *Alastor* poet: "Autoeroticism in *Alastor* has the same consequences as parthenogenesis in *Frankenstein,* physically and psychologically."

ognize that the poet has moved into the Symbolic realm when he travels to the "fallen towers / Of Babylon, the eternal pyramids," and tries to decipher the languages on the "alabaster obelisk" and "stupendous columns" (110–11, 113, 117). These blatantly phallic representations, encoded with the hieroglyphics that constitute language, or the constant references to "ruined temples" and the "jasper tomb" (116, 114) trope the son's initiation into the Symbolic, the Paternal order that usurps and supplants the power of the mother and generation with figurative substitutions for her.

But the poet is not content to wander endlessly and alone through the monuments of the phallic realm; he is compelled to seek substitutes for the mother through either images of her (the visionary maiden) or through actual living women (the Arab maiden). But, as Kristeva has noted, woman exists in Western culture as the silent referent, who, as the embodiment of the literal, makes figuration possible. In other words, only with the mother's death does language become necessary. Shelley's hero thinks that he can escape the feared and desired body of the mother by rejecting the Imaginary/semiotic realm and embracing the Symbolic/paternal. Almost immediately he seeks his mirroring prototype, his ideal identical counterpart, only to discover the Arab maiden, who appears like a wish-fulfillment and offers food, not to mention adoration. The hero, however, cannot be content with an embodied mortal woman, a mature and separate love object, because that would require that the male accept the defeat of his primary narcissist relationship with the mother and accept a substitute object, a figuration, in her place. But if spurning love is an unnatural act, it is very natural for the solipsistic son, the narcissist who really has no other choice, to reject the love as well as the external reality of others (even the mother who is his real goal/love object throughout the poem).

The poet, however, is not simply a narcissist. He suffers as well from abjection, fear and loathing of women. As Kristeva notes, the transition from the Imaginary to the Symbolic occurs when a "representative of the paternal function takes the place of the good maternal object that is wanting. There is language instead of the good breast. Discourse is being substituted for maternal care." But the result of this psychic exchange is often "hallucinatory metaphor, fear and fascination, abjection—at the crossroads of phobia, obsession, and perversion." The *Alastor* poet's psychic journey away from women bears an uncanny resemblance to this scenario, particularly when we note that the male ego, overtaxed by a "bad object," turns from it, cleanses itself of contact from it, and vomits it (*Powers of Horror,* 45). One clear symptom of abjection can be found in its victim's revolt from within, manifesting itself in the reconstruction and finally rejection of languages as well as women.

The appearance of the "real" woman almost immediately triggers an "ideal" internal fantasy woman who functions not simply as a love object for the hero but as his fantasized mother-substitute, his fantasy of incest with an acceptable, because disembodied, object. The hero comes upon this discovery in the vale of Cashmire, the original site of human civilization, but it is clear that we are again in the realm of the semiotic—absorption in the self-created fantasy of complete fusion with the maternal. We recognize this when the poet dreams of a "veiled maid" whose voice "was like the voice of his own soul" (151–53). She is the ideal creation of his own mind; in fact, she is a veritable mirror of the poet singing of "Knowledge and truth and virtue. . . / And lofty hopes of divine liberty, / Thoughts the most dear to him, and poesy, / Herself a poet" (158–60). At this point in the poem it would appear that the feminine fantasy fulfills the poet's intellectual and imaginative needs, for she is the disembodied embodiment of his loftiest spiritual and intellectual values. (One recalls here Kristeva's term: "devalorized valorization.") But she is ephemeral, a phantasm, a self-created projection of the prototype, the "ideal" woman within. The narcissist is condemned to love himself, and if he chooses to engage in the fantasy of love, he must of necessity create a version of himself to love, ergo the "veiled maiden." We can also speculate on the need for the veil, supposedly used, according to tradition, to shield the observer from the brightness of the woman's overwhelming beauty. But it is more likely that the woman must be veiled because she has no face, no identity, no reality—that she is, in fact, an absent referent in an endlessly meaningless chain of signifiers.

But in order to satisfy the poet's senses, the veiled maiden takes on physical aspects, leading the poet into an orgasmic and temporary loss of self through what is actually a sexual union between split elements within his own mind:

> Her glowing limbs beneath the sinuous veil
> Of woven wind, . . .
> His strong heart sunk and sickened with excess
> Of love. He reared his shuddering limbs and quelled
> His gasping breath, and spread his arms to meet
> Her panting bosom: . . . she drew back a while,
> Then, yielding to the irresistible joy,
> With frantic gesture and short breathless cry
> Folded his frame in her dissolving arms.
>
> (176–87)

Shelley's need to sexually embrace his ideal as a feminine Other expresses his need to integrate a hopelessly fragmented being. By making the woman as nearly like himself as possible, his consciousness attempts to reconcile the physical, masculine self with the soul within, the ideal prototype. Shelley tries to depict this ideal as an embodied physical woman as well as a disembodied fantasy, but doing so leads to the failure of the quest for reintegration. At least in Shelley's ideology, the mind must pursue abstract ideals if it is to remain creative, but abstract ideals, according to Shelley, cannot be embraced even by the mind without lowering them to a physical level that thereby destroys them. It would seem, then, that all forms of literalization, figuration, externalization—from poetry to women—are doomed to fail the poet's expectations.

The pattern of seeking an ideal only to be disappointed in its literalization persists throughout *Alastor,* for immediately after his orgasmic dream the hero experiences "blackness" and a "vacant brain" (188–91). As in the "Hymn to Intellectual Beauty," the hero awakens to wonder where the "hues of heaven" have gone, where the "mystery and majesty of Earth, / The joy, the exultation" have flown (199–200). And again in a persistently Shelleyan leitmotif, the hero of *Alastor* prays for the power to differentiate between the ideal and the fleeting manifestations of that ideal. The poet of *Alastor* has learned that "limbs, and breath, and being" are "treacherously" "intertwined," which seems to suggest that he has learned that figurations cannot be embodied without reviving the power of the maternal, without bringing the semiotic back into existence. Further, he has realized that his quest to absorb the idealized and mirroring feminine, a displaced wish for incestuous union with the mother, cannot be attained. Paradoxically, he has come to realize that the body, represented finally by the mother, is both complement and destroyer of the spirit (209–10), just as woman as idealized love object is both desired and feared, sought and fled.

According to Shelleyan ideology, however, the one possible unifier of body and spirit is the power of the androgynous imagination, and so the rest of the poem is an exploration of the male's potential to absorb the feminine, thereby making himself "divine." As Cynthia Baer has observed, the poem self-reflexively enacts the androgynous myth by exploring "the possibility of integration through the imaginative and creative process of poetry, of vision."[25] But this is simply to uncritically

25. Cynthia M. Baer, "'Lofty Hopes of Divine Liberty': The Myth of the Androgyne in *Alastor, Endymion,* and *Manfred,*" *RP&P* 9 (1985), 35. In an astute observation, Stuart Sperry notes that the poet's intercourse with the Veiled Maid dramatizes "primordial incest, his romance with his muse" (see his *Shelley's Major Verse: The Narrative and Dramatic Poetry* [Cambridge: Harvard

accept the androgynous ideology and read it back into the poem. It is more likely that the *Alastor* poet wants us to participate in his fantasy of self-creation, and to overlook the fact that it has been constructed on the cannibalistic absorption of every female figuration in the text. For instance, we are supposed to sympathize with the poet's battle for what he claims is self-control. He has learned that during the daylight he is able to keep "mute conference / With his still soul," but at night he loses this self-control and finds that his mind becomes prey to "passion" and "darkness" (223–27), induced, no doubt, by fantasied women. The poet cannot and probably does not want to resolve the dichotomy between figuration and embodiment, flight toward and from the mother. This is the true source of ambiguity in his quest. He rejects the "youthful maidens" (266) who would comfort him and redeem him from his deathlike "spectral form" (259) because they are real and therefore not subject to his complete control. Disillusionment with his power to ever totally control the (real and imaginary) women who plague him, all of them unsatisfactory substitutes for the mother, causes the poet to want to "embark / And meet Lone Death on the drear ocean's waste" (304–5). He travels in a boat, an image used throughout Shelley's poetry as a symbol of the journeying soul. The boat manages to maneuver safely through the perils of the trip, carrying the spectral poet "As if that frail and wasted human form, / Had been an elemental god" (350–51). This image curiously speaks of boat and poet, soul and body, as one unit: "an elemental god." But this wish is more accurately an ideological attempt to deify the artist, to convince the reader that the male poet can achieve apotheosis through his own creative efforts. This fantasized union of external and internal, then, supposedly enables the poet to reach his goal, "Vision and Love" (366), a womblike cave in which a whirlpool confronts the boat with a type of challenge. Will the boat sink "Down the abyss" (395) or be carried forward? Instead it sails into a bower of yellow flowers that "For ever gaze on their own drooping eyes, / Reflected in the crystal calm" (407–8). These reflected yellow flowers trope the poet's own solipsistic state of mind, for like the classic narcissist, he gazes into his lover's eyes only in order to see his own projected and static beauty. If the poet is unaware of his sol-

---

University Press, 1988], 28). Other commentators on the identity of the Veiled Maid as an idealized aspect of the self include James C. Evans, "Masks of the Poet: A Study of Self-Confrontation in Shelley's Poetry," *KSJ* 24 (1975), 70–88, and Norman Thurston, "Author, Narrator, and Hero in Shelley's *Alastor*," *SIR* 14 (1975), 119–31.

ipsism, however, the biographical Shelley was more self-reflective and employed the image with satiric purpose.

Shelley's letters reveal an extreme distaste for the isolated self, as well as the paradoxical relation of love and egoism. Four years before writing *Alastor*, Shelley confided to Hogg that "Solitude is most horrible. . . . I cannot endure the horror the evil which comes to *self* in solitude." "Love" was the only escape from this horror of self, but Shelley was keenly aware of the danger of simply projecting the self onto the female beloved. He criticized all of Hogg's attempts to love as "self-centered self devoted self-interested," while depicting his ideal conception of love as "Virtue Heaven disinterestedness, in a word friendship, which has as much to do with the senses as with yonder mountains."[26] The split between the senses and the spirit, the body and figurations of it, leads the hero of *Alastor* to the resolution found only in death. He longs for "Nature's dearest haunt, some bank, / Her cradle, and his sepulchre" (429–30). Regressively merging with the mother here offers the hero/son a return to the passivity of the semiotic realm, womb as tomb, an escape from the burdens of not only language but self-consciousness. The Lacanian/Kristevan formula here closely resembles the thanatos syndrome that Freud posited as the goal of all psychic energy. And while the *Alastor* poet is in the midst of a natural scene, it has clearly become an internal dreamscape, for his eyes can behold only "Their own wan light" (470). If his spirit is self-consuming, so is his heart: "Gazing in dreams over the gloomy grave, / [It] Sees its own treacherous likeness there" (473–74). The poet finds that he cannot escape from this forest of solipsism until he sees "two eyes, / Two starry eyes, hung in the gloom of thought, / And seemed with their serene and azure smiles / To beckon him" (489–92). But these eyes are clearly the "light / That shone within his soul" (493–94), and so he follows them until he comes upon a stream, a persistent symbol in Shelley's poetry for the journey into the depths of the self. This stream, with its mysterious "waves," "gulphs," a "searchless fountain," and an "invisible course" (506–7), becomes the site of the poet's next quest. As he journeys along it, he actually regresses deeper into his own psychic past, back to the silence of the semiotic with its denial of the Symbolic; he confronts now only "Rocks," and "black and barren pinnacles" (544–45). Like the other questing male heroes throughout Romantic

26. Letter #66 to T. J. Hogg, 8 May 1811; Letter #134 to Elizabeth Hitchener, 11 November 1811, in *The Letters of Percy Bysshe Shelley,* ed. Frederick L. Jones, 2 vols. (Oxford: Clarendon Press, 1964), I, 77; I, 173.

texts, the poet of *Alastor* explores the depths of his separate being and finds only images of desolation and sterility.

Finally, in desperation, the *Alastor* hero discovers within himself a "silent nook" that is the repository "Of all the grace and beauty" in his soul (572, 595). This "nook" tropes Shelley's fiction of the idealized feminine soul within, "whose breath can teach / The wilds to love tranquility" (587–88). But this semiotic refuge is not strong enough to shut out the "dim and horned moon," the "Yellow mist," and the "storm of death" presided over by the "colossal Skeleton" of maternal Nature (602–11). Shelley's two attitudes toward the feminine fiction converge in this section's imagery. The feminine as symbolic of the spiritual life is negated by the power of the horned/phallic moon, the abject mother as destroyer as well as creator of the world of generation. Shelley knew through his translation of the *Symposium* that Plato considered the moon "androgynous" (*JW,* VII, 184), but the Mother as androgynous moon is compromised by her association with death and destruction. The poet realizes that his "green recess"—worship of the mother as Nature—cannot provide him a sanctuary from death, and his last vision of anything before he resigns himself to death is of "the great moon" with its "dun beams" (625, 646, 648). For Shelley, the ambivalent power of the feminine within was too powerful to be successfully absorbed by the hero. Instead he dies in what amounts to a power struggle with his fantasy of the mother: Can he transform her into figurations he can psychically control (the veiled maiden), or must he accept the reality of embodiment (the Arab maiden) and accept the loss of the mother? But as an uncompromising idealist the poet must have the mother and not a substitute object; he must return to the semiotic realm; he must flee from the demands of language and all literalizations. But the mother's overwhelming power cannot satisfy the hero/son because she is, finally, unattainable. The hero can desire her, pursue her, try to transform all other women into emblems of her—but all his efforts are doomed to failure because the hero/son wants total (re)union with her and that desire can be fulfilled only in death.

According to his self-created fantasy, the soul within the soul must be feminine and must submerge itself into the apotheotic creative male artist. Without such a sacrifice, there can be no fictional salvation for the masculine psyche. But while the feminine can be at times a redeeming principle, as Asia is in *Prometheus Unbound,* she is more likely to be destructive, a force of abjection like the Shape in *The Triumph of Life.* The ironic complications in Shelley's poetry stem from this duality. Shelley was not able to articulate the highly systematized (and artificial) vision that allowed Blake to see the feminine as the embodiment of both functions—both fallen Nature and its redemption. Shelley cannot clearly distinguish between the two, or perhaps the refusal to do so is his comment on the futility of humanity's attempts to fictitiously depict either psychic harmony or its literal manifestation, an earthly paradise.

Shelley's more pessimistic vision of the feminine finally serves as an ironic commentary on the nature of the poet's imaginative abilities to transcend his physical limitations. At his death the *Alastor* poet cries out for "Medea's wondrous alchemy" (672). But Medea was the mother who killed her beloved children, killed them for spite despite her love. The poet recalls only her power to make "the earth gleam / With bright flowers" (673–74), but Shelley the poet was certainly aware that her power also was demonic, death-dealing. In fact, in imaging Medea's flowers, the narrator of *Alastor* ironically recalls the yellow flowers of narcissism that had blinded the poet earlier in the poem. Loving the phallic mother, in other words, directly leads to loving the self, to being a solitary wandering male. In his final images, Shelley's narrator resorts to depicting the Wandering Jew and an old alchemist, vainly seeking the elixir of life. Both men stand as impotent embodiments of the Symbolic realm, condemned by their false languages to seek unsuccessfully to displace the power of the mother. But the fantasy of a poetic power that permits the artist to recreate life as the alchemist hopes to do is gone for the Shelleyan hero: "Art and eloquence" have proved to be "frail and vain" (710–11). Early in his career, then, Shelley was aware of the limitations of language, poetry, and the use of "women" as symbols of imaginative fulfillment. Even as a consummately fictitious realm, poetry did not possess the power to redeem and transform the power of the mother. Language as the vehicle for depicting psychic or sexual transformation fails the male poet because of duality, the duplicitous nature of both images and women.

III Keats: "Would I were whole in love!"

John Keats's mother died of tuberculosis when he was fourteen years old, a particularly vulnerable period of adolescence. He seems never to have fully recovered from this loss or her desertion years earlier, and several critics have noted that the female presence haunting many of his poems is most probably the face of his doomed mother.[27] The

27. See, for instance, Aileen Ward, *John Keats: The Making of a Poet* (New York: Viking, 1963), for the observation that Keats lacked "the support of par-

mother functions in Keats's work not simply as a *topos,* but, more significantly, as absent but somehow within reach, as if the text of the poem might somehow bring her magically back to life. The oral character that pervades Keats's poetry, particularly the prevalence of female breasts that his poetic heroes long to consume, provides a vital clue to Keats's depiction of the fantasied woman within. The feminine as (M)other for Keats is the primary source of psychic and emotional nourishment for the hero/son; she must exist, however, as a composite/split figure throughout his poems because his need for her was so ambivalently complex. The feminine in Keats's work is multifaceted because she has to perform so many roles in relation to the hero—mother, sister, lover, friend, muse—and in no poem do we see women play these roles more fully and, one might add, in a more convoluted fashion, than in *Endymion.*

We will examine here, then, just one representative work, *Endymion,* as an early apprentice poem, but one that presents the maternal as omnipresent, inescapable, and finally, with some alterations, the hero's fantasied love object. As several critics have noted, the ostensible objects of the hero's quest in this poem are "beauty" and "love"—whether spiritual or physical—but it is more likely that Endymion's goal is bound up with his identity as a Culture Hero who needs to colonize Nature by introjecting and cannibalizing woman as Other. Further, Endymion bears a strong resemblance to the poet of *Alastor;* in fact, we know that Keats wrote the poem in order to "correct" Shelley's hero for his narcissism. But in supposedly presenting a hero free of solipsism, Keats instead recapitulated the quasi-oedipal dilemma himself. Endymion would like to achieve the sense that he has a coherent and stable self that exists in both space and time as constant and knowable, without reference to others. But as Weiskel has observed, this sense of identity is predicated on "the introjected image of the primal Other, or Mother" that can lead to either regression or desertion by the desired object: "In terms of what Freud called the family romance, identity is regarded with all the unresolved ambivalence of an oedipal crisis in

---

ents or other enduring patterns of maturity" on which to model his own sense of identity (61). One recalls the story of the five-year-old Keats, in what must have been the full flush of his oedipal stage, holding his mother hostage in their home, brandishing a "naked sword." For this episode and the discussion of Keats's mother as the "ultimate enigma" in his life (the "complete silence about her suggests some shattering knowledge, with which, at various times in his life, he can be seen dimly struggling to come to terms"), see Robert Gittings, *John Keats* (Boston: Little, Brown, 1968), 16, 30.

which there is, strangely, no symbolic father to come to the rescue." But there is at least one (buried) symbolic father in *Endymion,* as well as a struggle by Endymion to escape from the Imaginary/semiotic realm of the mother, navigate the treacherous world of the Symbolic/ paternal, and emerge into the Real. The contours and contortions of this psychic journey will form, then, the focus of our discussion of Keats's poem.

When we first meet Endymion he has no sense of himself at all as a separate entity. He is initially introduced to us as a "marble man, / Frozen,"[28] paralyzed, dumb, senseless; he is, in several senses, reduced to a state of complete infancy, an inhabitant of the semiotic realm. The only person who can initially release him from this condition is his sister Peona, who places him in a boat and takes him to an island to minister to him. She sings him out of his regressive sleep/daze, and functions quite obviously here as a semiotic maternal force. Only after he returns to consciousness does he tell her of his strange enchantment, his encounter with the beautiful moon goddess, Dian, "that completed form of all completeness," that "high perfection of all sweetness" (I, 606–7), a goddess who appears to be modeled on the mythic Diana of Ephesus. Diana as moon goddess is traditionally virginal and, as such, the hero cannot possess her the way a husband possesses a wife; he can only long for her hopelessly, as a son longs for the mother he cannot have. The "virginal" goddesses of antiquity, however, were not sexually innocent; they existed as symbols of Nature as well as embodiments of female self-reliance, self-possession, and self-sufficiency. The poet in this choice of images, however, expresses in unconscious fashion the prohibition against incest with the mother, the mother as taboo. But Endymion does not understand the woman's identity. He can state only that she is "A second self, that each might be redeem'd," (I, 659). The colonization of Diana as Nature goddess stands, then, as the central challenge to Endymion as self-appointed Culture Hero.

But Endymion sees his quest as the pursuit of "love," and in many ways he undergoes transformations in the course of the poem that parallel the stages in a young boy's relation with his mother according to Freudian theory. That is, first there is absorption in the primary narcis-

28. See Weiskel, *Romantic Sublime,* 162; *Endymion* in *The Poems of John Keats,* ed. Jack Stillinger (Cambridge: Harvard University Press, 1978), I, 405–6. All quotations from the poetry of Keats are from this edition, with line numbers in parentheses in the text. All of Keats's letters are quoted from *The Letters of John Keats, 1814–1821,* ed. Hyder E. Rollins, 2 vols. (Cambridge: Harvard University Press, 1958).

sism that occurs before the infant develops a sense of separate identity, then rejection of the symbiotic/semiotic mother and the development of secondary narcissism, and finally transformation of the maternal as a love object in accepting another as a substitute for the mother. But it is also important to understand that the son's relationship with his mother is fraught with fear and repulsion. For Kristeva,

> [a]bjection preserves what existed in the archaism of pre-objectal relationship, in the immemorial violence with which a body becomes separated from another body in order to be. . . . I experience abjection only if an Other has settled in place and stead of what will be 'me.' Not at all an other with whom I identify and incorporate, but an Other who precedes and possesses me, and through such possession causes me to be. (*Powers of Horror*, 10–13).

The struggle to become human, then, is a mimetic one based on the attempt to become homologous to another, that is, to experience oneself as primary, even though one knows that one is chronologically secondary. "I" come into being only as I separate, reject, throw off the mother, only as I seek to emerge out of primary narcissism and enter into a symbolic relationship with another. But the images that the son creates of the mother and projects onto other women can only reveal how thoroughly he has succeeded in internalizing her power, which then allows him to love himself.

In his earliest definition of love, Endymion says to Peona that he is seeking a particularly intense type of love, one that would transform him the way the alchemist transformed ordinary matter into gold:

> Wherein lies happiness? In that which becks
> Our ready minds to fellowship divine,
> A fellowship with essence; till we shine,
> Full alchemiz'd, and free of space. Behold
> The clear religion of heaven!
>
> (I, 777–81)

The love sought here, Platonic considerations aside, is the totalizing love of the infant and mother, the two forming a symbiotic bond that denies to the child at least temporarily that they are actually two separate beings. This preoedipal oneness with the mother, what we have seen Kristeva call the preverbal semiotic, is for Keats also the realm before language, in which communication is through "fellowship divine," "fellowship with essence." Several definitions have been proposed for Keats's use of the term "essence"; however, it can be read as a manifestation of preoedipal oneness with the mother, a state that we nostalgically remember and to which we return in dreams when we can be "free of space," not to mention language. As adults, however, we can only recapture this symbiotic/semiotic absorption with the mother through surrogate and socially acceptable relationships, most typically marriage, or, as we saw in Blake, visions of a transformed social/sexual apocalypse.[29]

If mother and son can never unify again, then husband and wife (mother-surrogate) will form the divine couple of androgynous tradition and spiritual alchemy. This state was briefly captured by Endymion and Diana, and he tells Peona that it allowed them to step "Into a sort of oneness, . . . / like a floating spirit's" (I, 796–97). This love fantasy is described by Endymion as the "chief intensity," that "sits high / Upon the forehead of humanity," making humanity equivalent to the gods (800–802). Endymion spends the poem trying to answer the questions posed by Peona: What is the nature of love? Is it a sort of spiritualizing power (" 'Now, if this earthly love has power to make / Man's being

29. Approaches to the psychic dynamics of separation and individuation from the mother are no more diverse than the differences between the French feminists and the object-relations theories of the Anglo-Americans. In addition to Kristeva's essays (cited above), Hélène Cixous claims that the mother embodies the "Voice [that] sings from a time before law, before the Symbolic took one's breath away and reappropriated it into language under its authority of separation" (*The Newly-Born Woman*, trans. Betsy Wing [Minneapolis: University of Minnesota Press, 1986], 93). Luce Irigaray's *Speculum of the Other Woman*, trans. Gillian Gill (Ithaca: Cornell University Press, 1985), and her essay, "And the One Doesn't Stir Without the Other," trans. Helene V. Wenzel, *Signs* 7 (1981), 60–67, also present the topic in a contradictory metaphysical, essentialist, even poetic mode. The Anglo-American approaches, characterized by the empirical object-relations theorists in the field, are represented by Margaret Mahler, *On Human Symbiosis and the Vicissitudes of Individuation* (London: Hogarth, 1969), and *The Psychological Birth of the Human Infant* (New York: Basic, 1975); D. W. Winnicott, "Mirror-Role of Mother and Family," in *Playing and Reality* (London: Tavistock, 1971); and W. Ronald Fairbairn, *An Object-Relations Theory of the Personality* (New York: Basic Books, 1954). In addition to Schapiro, other critics have recognized the underlying oedipal dynamics of the poem, including Paul Haeffner, "Keats and the Faery Myth of Seduction," *REL* 3 (1962), 20–31; Dorothy Van Ghent, "Keats's Myth of the Hero," *KSJ* 3 (1954), 7–25; and Bruce Miller, "On the Meaning of Keats's *Endymion*," *KSJ* 14 (1965), 33–54.

mortal, immortal?'" [843–44)], or is it the regressive and compulsive action of a son unable to psychically leave the semiotic/mother and accept the realm of the Paternal and the Real? In his last remembered image of the goddess in Book I, Endymion tells Peona that he has most lately seen his beloved while walking near a pool of water: "behold!" "The same bright face I tasted in my sleep, / Smiling in the clear well" (895–96). Endymion's goddess at this point in the poem possesses the characteristics of Shelley's ideal visionary maiden; both "women" are clearly internal projections of the masculine self writ large and feminized, while the image of the introjecting Narcissus, feeding parasitically from the body of the reflected beloved, tropes the cannibalistic impulse behind most Romantic depictions of the mother.

But before Endymion can continue with his quest to understand the nature of love and the nature of women, that is, that they are both self-created fantasies, he retreats to a cave, the grot of Proserpine (Persephone), in order to recover his calm and self-control. The cave, functioning here as a dark and protective maternal womb, shelters the hero so that he can explore his psyche, the depths within him, just as Shelley's *Alastor* hero does in his internal journey. Here Endymion is initially confronted by a nymph who pities his depression, and attempts to minister to him (in a displaced repetition of his sister's actions). He loftily informs her, however, that he cares for nothing "But the soft shadow of my thrice-seen love,. . . / Of Cynthia" (II, 168–70). Although he claims that he longs to be free of the "dreadful might / And tyranny of love" (173–74), he follows the commands of Cynthia when she appears and asks him to descend through "winding passages" within his psyche until he reaches a "fair shrine" to "quiver'd Dian" (235, 260, 262). The implication of this passage is that a temple of the feminine resides within every male (the "nook" within the *Alastor* poet), and that an initial step in self-knowledge requires every male to locate that fantasied woman within himself. But before Endymion can accomplish this task, he is overcome with solipsism: "thoughts of self came on, how crude and sore / The journey homeward to habitual self!" (275–76). The longing to cling to the grandiose male self, even though that self has brought Endymion nothing but unhappiness, is recognized as ironic by the narrator, who remarks that Endymion has found the "goal of consciousness" and learned that it evokes "the deadly feel of solitude" (283–84). Keats subscribes here to the androgynous ideology as idealization and then absorption of the woman within. Although Keats as poet fancies that he is correcting the solipsism that plagued Shelley's hero in *Alastor,* he actually succumbs to the same cultural neurosis—cannibalization of the female as self-created and projected principle.

Endymion continues his journey deeper within himself and next encounters the great fertility goddess, "mother Cybele," a blatant symbol of the dark underworld of death and a fitting image of the male's foreboding fear of the maternal powers of gestation. But Cybele does not speak or delay the hero and instead sends him quickly away from her "mournful place" (640–53). Why does Keats truncate his hero's one clear confrontation with the fertile maternal? One possible explanation lies in Keats's knowledge of mythic tradition, for he was aware that Cybele had an incestuous relationship with her son/lover Attis and then castrated him to prevent his marriage to another. Another possible explanation lies in the identity of Cybele, who required of her devotees their vitality if not their manhood as a sacrifice required to sustain the world of birth, fertility, and death. If the earth is female, she requires the blood of the male for fertilization, thus the notion that the male marries the earth and dies, becoming a fertility/vegetation god, ensuring new life.[30] Keats brings his hero face to face with his hidden desire, his love for and deep psychic attachment to his mother, and then he elides the impulse, recognizing its danger and regressiveness. But at the same time he elides, Keats as poet also expresses his fear of the mother because her deepest meaning, her real identity, tropes his castration anxiety.

The encounter and rebuff by the mother is followed immediately by the hero's descent into the "jasmine bower" and his meeting with his beloved. The mother, then, has been confronted, overcome, and denied, thereby making the hero worthy of his love object. But who is this beloved? When Endymion embraces her, he declares: "'O known Unknown! from whom my being sips / Such darling essence. . . . who art thou?'" (670, 739–53). This initial question suggests that the hero does

30. See James Wilson for a discussion of Cybele, *The Romantic Heroic Ideal* (Baton Rouge: Louisiana State University Press, 1982), 112. Other critics who analyze symbolic aspects of Endymion's quest in relation to the identity of the feminine figures in the poem include Helen Haworth, "The Redemption of Cynthia," *HAB* 18 (1967), 80–91; Robert Harrison, "Symbolism of the Cyclical Myth in *Endymion*," *TSLL* 1 (1960), 538–54; William Garrett, "The Glaucus Episode: Book III," *KSJ* 27 (1978), 23–34; Stanley C. Russell, "'Self-Destroying' Love in Keats," *KSJ* 16 (1967), 79–91; and Baer, who claims that Cynthia herself is an "androgyne" with whom Endymion will find "Unity of Being," (above), 35–37. Cooke sees the motif of the triple female as a manifestation of the Greek goddess Selene-Artemis-Hecate: "chaste aloofness, bloody athleticism, and spectral victimization" (*Acts of Inclusion*, 183).

not embrace an actual woman; he embraces an "essence" or principle of femininity while he himself does not understand exactly what he is "sipping." The full description of the goddess portrays her as an entity composed of interchangeable body parts: arms, hands, lips, eyes, breasts (those "milky sovereignties"); she is not a whole woman as much as she is parts that he fondles and tries to reassemble (740, 758–59). One is reminded here of Melanie Klein's notion of "part objects," a psychic phenomenon that occurs when the child fantasizes that the mother's body is a receptacle of part objects, and then libidinally valorizes the organs and parts of the body. But, as Lacan has insisted, the common trait of such objects "is that they know no alterity. They are the very lining, the stuff or imaginary filling of the subject itself, which identifies itself with these objects" (Jameson, 355). A similar compulsion appears to exist in the poem in that Endymion has valorized the self-created essence of woman as body, so that he merely absorbs a self-projected woman, the mother as Nature goddess, the necessary fictitious complement to his identity as Culture Hero. But even Endymion begins to realize that his self-created fantasy of woman cannot fulfill all his needs, as well as be everything—mother, sister, lover—to him. The quest for Endymion thus far, then, results in this dimly understood realization, propelling him into the Symbolic, into a realm where language, figurations, literalizations will compensate for the mother's inadequacy.

Before Endymion flees the semiotic, however, we witness another embrace between the lovers, clearly depicted in oral imagery that suggests the essentially regressive nature of the union:

> 'Aye, by that kiss, I vow an endless bliss,
> An immortality of passion's thine:. . .
> O let me melt into thee; let the sounds
> Of our close voices marry at their birth;
> Let us entwine hoveringly.'
>
> (II, 807–8; 815–17)

"Entwine hoveringly" suggests not simply the pose of lovers, however, but the male infant at his mother's breast, feeding from her body, absorbing her essence. Indeed, the Book concludes with Endymion in a swoon, "Drunken from pleasure's nipple" (869). This "melting" of beings accomplished through blatantly oral and regressive imagery—kissing, singing, sucking—was not to last. No sooner is it imagined than it is lost. Endymion has tasted the forbidden fruits of union with the triple woman, and forever after any other love will pale in comparison: "Now I have tasted her sweet soul to the core / All other depths are shallow: essences, / Once spiritual, are like muddy lees" (904–6).

Book III continues to throw up mirrors to Endymion in which he can explore his fears and fantasies about women and physical love. The Book opens with Endymion's reflections on his relationship with the moon, not realizing, of course, that his beloved is goddess of the moon. In the Hymn to the Moon that opens the Book we learn that the maternal moon can "Kiss dead things to life," and that the moon "hast sent / A moonbeam to the deep, deep water-world, / To find Endymion" (57, 100–102). Endymion's dim realization that the moon "seem'dst my sister: hand in hand we went / From eve to morn across the firmament" (145–46) recalls the traditional mythic identification of Endymion as the sun (another fertility god) hopelessly pursuing his sister moon in a cyclical act of natural and incestuous desire that defines night and day. The unreachable sister here, however, can also be read as a displaced symbol of the mother, because in both versions the incest taboo is the most dominant aspect of the relationship. The hero also identifies the moon as a muse figure, remembering that as a young boy the moon was like a "poet's harp" (165) to him:

> Thou wast the charm of women, lovely Moon!
> O what a wild and harmonized tune
> My spirit struck from all the beautiful!
> On some bright essence could I lean, and lull
> Myself to immortality.
>
> (169–73)

The moon in this passage supposedly represents the artistic beauty and harmony of art inspired by the love of women. But the reference to the harp recalls the eolian harp, with its self-reflexive quality. The hero thinks that he hears an external song that sings of his own immortality, but that song actually originates from within him. He has internalized the feminine so that he thinks her voice is separate from his, when, in fact, they are identical.

Endymion finally emerges from the semiotic when he confronts the first clear representation of the phallic/Symbolic, an old man sitting on a weeded rock, wrapped in a cloak decorated with magical occult symbols. Glaucus, the displaced and disinherited paternal principle, recognizes in Endymion the fulfillment of his destiny as prophesied by the "Sisters three" (251), another version of the maternal triple female. Glaucus functions in the poem not simply as the representative of the

Symbolic realm, the embodiment of language, but as the literal reality of castration brought about by love of the phallic mother. And he begins by telling Endymion his life story of bewitchment at the ruthlessly seductive hands of Circe, the destructive embodiment of female sexuality, the semiotic muse turned phallic mother. As Glaucus tells the tale, his destruction began when he fell into a "long love dream" with Circe and became her "tranced vassal," finally awaking after an indeterminate time and finding himself surrounded by other "deformities" who have also had the misfortune of being seduced by Circe (440, 460, 503). Circe's victims, who endure her "Fierce, wan, / And tyrannizing . . . look" (506–7) are obsessed with the futile struggle to win this phallic mother's love and approval. The tyranny she exerts over them is the tyranny of a harsh and demanding mother, and they, her victims, are prisoners of their own regression. They have given up their homes, their wives, and their children for the masochistic pleasures that loving Circe gives them (543–54). We learn that Circe seduced Glaucus by appealing to his regressive fantasies: "She took me like a child of suckling time, / And cradled me in roses" (456–57). But after the betrayal, Circe reappears in her other guise, the phallic mother, a "fierce witch" (538).

Glaucus has had to bury his true love, Scylla, and live entranced to Circe: " 'live and wither, cripple and still breathe / Ten hundred years' " (597–98). He has endured over the years because of his belief in the power of the Symbolic, symbolized by the language on a magic scroll delivered to him, prophesying that he would eventually be saved by a youth led by "heavenly power" (708). Endymion recognizes that he is this youth, led by the power of the moon to restore Scylla to life and destroy the domain of Circe. Further, Endymion sees in Glaucus another instance of mimesis, a mirror image of himself, someone else who has misunderstood the nature of the Symbolic and sought to return to the semiotic realm of the mother; thus he addresses Glaucus: " 'We are twin brothers in this destiny' " (713). The triumph of "true" love over the sensual/regressive power of Circe, the oedipal/phallic mother, seems to indicate that the hero, as well as other men, must overcome their attraction to the psychic regression that loving the stern mother represents.[31]

31. The fullest recent discussion of the psychic dynamics implicit in loving the stern, phallic mother can be found in Helen B. Ellis, "Food, Sex, Death and the Feminine Principle in Keats's Poetry," *ESC* 6 (1980), 56–74. Although she presents an essentialist, Jungian discussion of the poet's need to "nurture the feminine principle within himself," Ellis does recognize that the poet's actual goal is to "metaphorically 'eat' his mistress," a rather blatantly cannibalistic

Book IV begins with Endymion, now the desperate lover, attracted to an Indian maiden and condemned as fickle by the narrator: "He surely cannot now / Thirst for another love: O impious, / That he can ever dream upon it thus!" (86–88). It would seem that the lesson of Glaucus has been lost on Endymion, who even condemns himself:

> 'I have a triple soul! O fond pretence—
> For both, for both my love is so immense,
> I feel my heart is cut for them in twain.'
> (95–97)

So distraught that he thinks he is going to die, Endymion asks the Indian maiden to sing to him, just as Peona his sister did in Book I. In her song the maiden compares Endymion to a "babe" nursing at her breast, and then goes on to depict him as "her mother, / And her brother, / Her playmate, and her wooer in the shade" (281, 288–90). In addition to the sexual displacement occurring here, the state described is very similar to what Freud in "Infantile Sexuality" (1905) called the "polymorphous perverse," that initial condition in which we respond to others indiscriminately and without genital identification (*SE* VII:191). Endymion is metaphorically male and female to his beloved, just as she is mother, sister, and lover to him.

This love, in which the male finds his mother and beloved merged, becomes the goal of the Culture Hero, and the lovers at this point escape the earth with two horses provided by Mercury. But because love of the transformed mother/Nature is not acceptable to the conscious mind informed by the reality of the Symbolic/paternal, the lovers are depicted in a sort of love sleep/dream state. And while in this trance Endymion overhears the careless gossip of the gods and discovers that he is the beloved of Dian. He awakes, like Adam, to find his dream true. As he makes love to a golden-haired woman called Phoebe, he watches her become a shadow and melt away (456). His dark-haired earthly love awakes and Endymion realizes the hopelessness of his predicament: "would I were whole in love!" (472). He is no better off than he was in

---

impulse. More typical of (idealizing) male critics, Leon Waldoff sees Keats's quest for the "Principle of Beauty" (*Letters,* I, 266) as representing his obsession with "a feminine figure or symbol who takes various forms in whose presence the poet imagines his heroes or himself seeking an affirmation of self" (see his *Keats and the Silent Work of the Imagination* [Urbana: University of Illinois Press, 1985], 49–50).

Book I; in fact, he thinks himself in a more serious dilemma since he now thinks he is in love with three women.

Conventional wisdom sees the Nymph of Book II as embodying Endymion's physical desires, the Indian maid as eliciting his romantic and protective feelings, and the goddess as evoking his pure spiritual adoration. Endymion is, according to this diagnosis, a victim of what Freud, in "On the Universal Tendency to Debasement in the Sphere of Love" (1912), diagnosed as a common problem in men—the splitting of affectionate and sexual feelings—a problem that he saw as originating in the overidealization of the mother (*SE* XI:177–93). But Endymion's goal throughout the poem has been to locate what Lacan calls the Real: "that which resists symbolization absolutely," history as "a text-to-be-(re)-constructed" (Jameson, 388–89). His own efforts to achieve that condition of self-construction have not succeeded because they are based on self-contradictory emotions: abjection as well as overvaluation of the mother. When he seems resigned to accepting his merely mortal lover, that is, woman as embodiment of the Symbolic/paternal, she also disappears, melting in his very hands so that "her hand he kiss'd, / And, horror! kiss'd his own—he was alone" (509–10). It should be pointed out here that the Keatsian lover, unlike the poet of *Alastor,* finds it a "horror" to be kissing himself, an appropriate emblem of narcissism rejected.

Endymion next finds himself in the Cave of Quietude; he has sunk to the depths of his psyche,and now his journey upward to salvation can begin. Before that can occur, however, Endymion must face the challenge that virtually all Romantic heroes fictitiously face and conquer—the spectre of hubristic love, the idea that they can save themselves through their own creative efforts as "artists." The ideology of the apotheotic artist, however, is complicated by the complementary androgynous ideology, the notion that the divinity being created must be, of necessity, both "masculine" and "feminine." Hence Endymion must absorb an idealized woman masquerading as the feminine principle. He initially manages to embrace a revitalized Indian maiden and state that he has rejected the lure of the goddess, accepting his mortality and its limitations. He rejects his first love (mother/sister) and declares his allegiance to the paternal, Symbolic realm:

> 'I have clung
> To nothing, lov'd a nothing, nothing seen
> Or felt but a great dream! O I have been
> presumptuous against love'
>
> (636–39)

But just as he makes this acquiescing speech accepting his own allegiance to the Symbolic, his Indian maiden declares herself a "forbidden" love object (752), and once more Endymion is in the realm of tabooed desire. Peona appears to announce that they are to attend a ceremony that night to honor Cynthia and Dian, and in the midst of the ceremony a beautiful stranger appears with both dark and golden hair: "Her long black hair swell'd ampler, in display / Full golden" (984–85). This rather bizarre image is meant to suggest the merging of earthly and heavenly loves, and Endymion recognizes this dual woman as "his passion" (987). She tells him that they have been separated by "foolish fear," then by "decrees of fate," and finally by a restriction imposed until he was "spiritualiz'd" (989–93). The "fear" that separated them can be read as the fear of incest, while "fate" can be seen as the cultural and social traditions, the exogamous customs that decree that sons reject their mothers/sisters and marry outside the family. Now that Endymion is supposedly "spiritualiz'd" he is able to kiss his triple goddess—mother/sister/beloved—three times; one kiss, it appears, for each identity. The escapist fantasy, it would seem, is complete.

Even though Keats ostensibly ends this poem on a triumphant, fictitiously apocalyptic note, no one, not even Keats himself, felt that the ending provided a suitable conclusion to the complex issues raised—the nature of narcissism disguised as love, the identity of woman as other.[32] Keats's problem originates in the composite female form, the triple-woman motif, a figure who symbolically represents the permutations of the mother/sister/wife. There is a strangely incestuous attraction between Endymion and the composite woman who functions throughout the poem. His sister Peona is a semiotic muse, while the

32. Keats himself initiated the critical attacks on *Endymion* by confessing to Shelley that while writing the poem his "mind was like a pack of scattered cards" (*Letters*, II, 323) and that the poem was "slipshod" (*Letters*, I, 374). Critics who have defended the poem as structurally unified have done so by reference to platonic or Neoplatonic allegories of love, or a rejection of allegory in favor of "everlasting eroticism." On the two sides of the issue, see Jacob Wigod, "The Meaning of *Endymion*," *PMLA* 68 (1953), 779–90; and Newell Ford, "*Endymion*—A Neo-Platonic Allegory?" *ELH* 14 (1947), 64–76. In his *Keats the Poet* (Princeton: Princeton University Press, 1973), 103, Stuart Sperry claims that "the poet's need to explore, through the metaphor of carnal knowledge, [reflects] his own relation to the hidden springs of inspiration on which the life of his art depends." In his *Keats and His Poetry: A Study in Development* (Chicago: University of Chicago Press, 1971), 113, Morris Dickstein reads the "erotic longing" in the poem as part of "a larger quest, for what we may call selfhood."

nymph/unknown goddess/Indian maiden exists as a splintered being who reflects the fragmentation of Endymion's own solipsistic psyche. That Endymion never seems to know the identity of anyone very clearly adds to the preoedipal quality of the relationships in the poem. Endymion actually appears to readers of the poem as a sort of little boy lost, wandering around trying to locate his mother/sister/beloved/friend, and discovering that they are all finally the same woman within him. Keats was trying, perhaps not very convincingly, to capture the all-pervasive power a child feels in the presence of his semiotic/symbiotic mother—a mother who had no clearly separate identity from his. The hero of *Endymion* wants to engage in his culture's dominant quest-romance; he wants to conquer the narrow male self and become androgynously divine through his absorption of a female beloved. It was simply his misfortune to choose as his beloved a woman who also embodied both the benign and fearful aspects of the mother. Endymion as Culture Hero is engaged finally in the quest to move beyond the maternal as primary love object. But for Keats, the mother could never be successfully supplanted or overcome; she only could be tentatively transformed.

2

The Sister: "She was almost a mother, she was something more tender"

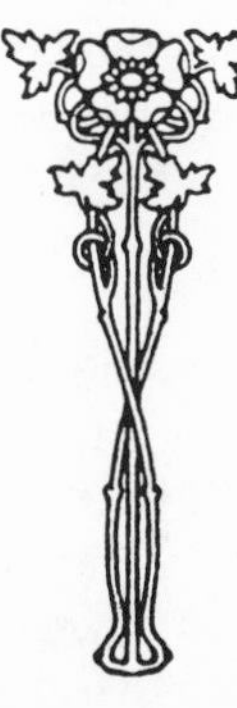

Two of the most famous and, one might add, notorious stories about Percy Shelley reveal his rather peculiar fixation on the female breast. The first clear indication we have that all perhaps was not well with Shelley occurred when his first wife Harriet refused to breastfeed their daughter Ianthe. Shelley was so distraught at this shirking of maternal duty that, in desperation, he seized upon the idea of nursing the child himself: "At last, in his despair, and thinking that the passion in him would make a miracle, he pulled his shirt away and tried himself to suckle the child." Needless to say, his efforts were in vain. The other revealing episode concerns Shelley's hysterical reaction to the description of Geraldine's hideous bosom during Byron's reading of *Christabel;* he fled from the room after seeing eyes staring out at him from Mary's breasts.[1] The female breast in both of these incidents functions as a cathected object, overdetermined, a signifier whose signification extends beyond itself. We can choose to see both episodes as indicative of nothing more than Shelley's own personal neurosis and sexual ambiguity, but that would belie the more important cultural and social implications of both acts. In the first act, Shelley assumes that he can become biologically female through a simple act of will. The female, in other words, is a quality within the prior being, the male, that can be released and used at his discretion. In the second—and obviously more

1. For a fuller description of both biographical incidents, see Newman Ivey White, *Shelley,* 2 vols. (New York: Knopf, 1940), I, 326; I, 443–44.

complicated—episode, Shelley projects onto the female breast his own paranoia. The breast here has been radically severed from its identity as "female" and instead functions as an extension of the male power of poetic vision. The female breast is also hystericized as uncanny in the Freudian sense of uncovering something that has been long buried—in Shelley's case, the sense of seeing himself through the (M)Other's eyes/nipples. Both episodes reveal attitudes that I think were shared to some extent by all of the male Romantic poets. They believed that the power of the feminine resided in her capacity to nurture and "mother," seen essentially as a fearful and threatening power to a male who did not, could not, possess such qualities. In order to supplant the mother, to displace her, to deny and eradicate her, the male poet transformed her—initially—into a sister who mirrors as closely as possible the reflection of her brother/lover.

The mirror has been interpreted by the French feminist Madeleine Gagnon as representative of the phallus. According to Gagnon, man "is constantly double, he and his phallus. He has established, from the farthest of ages and without giving birth, the binary relation. He has set up the mirror, projected the phantasm. He has become his own representative, his own reference point. He has to become master of himself since it is in himself he finds his second, his diminished other, his slave. Then he can become Master of others."[2] There can be no doubt that a good deal of mirroring solipsism and its literal manifestation, an interest in incest, existed in the lives and poetry of the English Romantics. Byron and Shelley were at one time accused of forming "a league of incest" with stepsisters Mary Godwin and Claire Clairmont, while Byron was later charged by his wife with committing incest with his half-sister Augusta. And Wordsworth had what we would recognize as a pathologically close relationship with his sister Dorothy. In one sense the attraction of incest can be read as an aspect of the "egotistical sublime." The Romantic poets write courtship narratives, but the courtship is ultimately only between elements of the male self.

From another perspective, however, we can read the sister as simply a more suitable—because displaced—version of the mother. The first psychic substitution of sister for mother makes the next substitution possible, for the beloved can be seen as a displaced—but socially acceptable—manifestation of the sister. The role of the feminine in the (re)creation of the male Romantic self exhibits, then, the emotional and psychic transition that the hero makes from total dependence on

2. Madeleine Gagnon, "Body I," in *New French Feminisms,* ed. Elaine Marks and Isabelle de Courtivron (New York: Schocken, 1981), 180.

the mother—primary narcissism—to love for the sister as a mirrored manifestation of the self—secondary narcissism. The male Romantics were not so much fleeing the demands of self-consciousness or identity as seeking a new and redeemed/expanded self in an androgynous ideology that stressed union with one's complementary opposite. It just so happened that the general impulse behind this goal required union with someone as much like the self as possible. After all, sometimes the first step beyond the mirror stage of psychic development is very small. Sometimes it is no further away than one's closest sibling, a person who physically reflects the self and shares the same parents. This particular phenomenon—love for the idealized sister—has been generally dismissed as a peculiarly "escapist" characteristic of Romanticism. But as McGann points out in regard to Byron and Shelley, the two major practitioners of the theme of incestuous love for the sister, these two poets are "most deeply *engaged* (in a socialist-activist sense) when they have moved furthest along their paths of displacement and escape." For both Shelley and Byron, incest as a physical act, as an assault on bourgeois values, was not their primary goal or purpose. They were much more interested in incest as a mental game, a psychological introjection of the feminine so that the idea of the act symbolized their attempts to radically redefine the male self as both masculine and feminine, forming what Levinson has called the impulse toward a "two-party psyche." This new psyche is predicated on the narcissistic object (the sister) living in the self as "an alienated and idealized consciousness *of* the self." And unlike the object loved by transference, the genuinely belated other, the sister "can never fully satisfy. . . . Narcissism enables a longing that is precisely *not* the desire that fills you up, absorbing the space of consciousness." [3]

Freud saw the origin of incestuous passion for one's sister as caused by illicit sexual emotions toward the mother, emotions originally felt

3. McGann, *Romantic Ideology,* 124; Marjorie Levinson, *Keats's Life of Allegory: The Origins of a Style* (Oxford: Basil Blackwell, 1988), 160. Also see Peter Thorslev, "Incest as Romantic Symbol," *CLS* 2 (1965), 41–58, for an analysis of Romantic incest as an attempt to shock the middle class. A valuable discussion of incest as a narrative device occurs in Peter Brooks's *Reading for the Plot: Design and Intention in Narrative* (New York: Knopf, 1984). Brooks claims that incest short-circuits narrative structure: The "reader experiences the fear—and excitation—of the improper end, which is symmetrical to—but far more immediate and present than—the fear of endlessness." Love for the sister "hovers as the sign of a passion interdicted because its fulfillment would be too perfect, a discharge indistinguishable from death, the very cessation of narrative movement" (109).

and repressed. In "On Narcissism: An Introduction" (1914), he observes that when narcissistic gratification encounters actual hindrances, the sexual ideal may be used as a substitutive gratification. In such a case "a person will love in conformity with the narcissistic type of object-choice . . . what he once was and no longer is, or else what possesses the excellence which the ego lacks for making it an ideal" (*SE* XIV:101). But as Freud has also observed in his writings on the Wolf-Man case, men whose erotic development is marked by the "sister-complex" have a need to choose women they can then degrade (*SE* XVII:22–23; 76–78; 82; 100–101). The compulsion to either idealize or degrade women, also known as the virgin/whore syndrome, is clearly discernible in Romantic attitudes toward women, most frequently manifesting itself in the split female figures who populate so many Romantic texts.

In a similar vein, Hillis Miller has argued that the three versions of the Dionysus myth all reveal a "[f]amily romance involving defeat or death for the father figures, and a complex role for the female figures as murderous mothers, as self-slaying victims, and as transfigured mates for the god." Although the "true" meaning of the Dionysus story is forever veiled by its repetitive tellings, one begins to discern in the myth as well as in Romantic poetry what Miller calls the "relation of simultaneous love and hate which is at the same time the narcissistic mirroring of an androgynous self by itself, in self-love and self-hate." Such a mirroring solipsism forms the core of the Romantic poet's treatment of the sister. The hero embraces the self as other and ends up creating a doubled self as love object, what René Girard has called "mimetic convergence on a single object."[4] The lovers in Shelley's *Laon and Cythna*, or Byron's *Manfred*, for instance, are not individuals as much as partners in mimetic desire, and that sort of desire itself becomes a self-reinforcing process so that thesis and antithesis are constantly polarized; there can be no synthesis where there is solipsism. But the incestuous lovers in Romantic poetry are not just incestuous, they are narcissistically incestuous. Garber has recognized this sort of incest as "that [which] reduces to its smallest reach the distance one needs to go to get outside of the self. If what one reaches for is the exactest cast of oneself, then one has hardly to reach at all." Self-completion becomes of necessity self-consumption, or as James Wilson has noted, "the incestuous attachment highlights the fact that the ideal woman is the

4. J. Hillis Miller, "Ariadne's Thread: Repetition and the Narrative Line," *CI* 3 (1976), 65–67; René Girard, "Myth and Ritual in Shakespeare: *A Midsummer Night's Dream*," in *Textual Strategies: Perspectives in Post-Structuralist Criticism*, ed. Josué Harari (Ithaca: Cornell University Press, 1979), 191; 198.

male's mirror image, that she depends entirely for her identity upon the narcissistic male. Just as God created man in his own image, so the Romantic poet fashions his ideal mate from a Platonic conception of self."

If we follow this Platonic position to its logical conclusion, as was standard in Romantic criticism about twenty years ago, we can conclude, like David Perkins, that the woman in Romantic poetry was merely an "earthly analogue" of a self-generated transcendental ideal, Truth and Beauty. But embracing this phantom woman could only be self-destructive because she had no ontological reality; she was ultimately undifferentiated from the male hero, and the love they shared could only bring sterility and frustration to the social order.[5] One can see how critics pursued this line and either exalted or condemned the Romantic woman as the embodiment of Truth/Beauty or a self-generated destructive chimera. In fact, it is more accurate to recognize that the Romantic woman functions persistently as a split figure, a dual-visaged image, a victim and victimizer. Admittedly, though, she is almost always an internal principle, and the various poetic efforts to externalize her and embrace her as an "Other" often read as exercises in futility, as if the poets could not bring even themselves to believe in the fiction of her reality.

Solipsism, the epistemological counterpart to incest/narcissism, was, for a variety of historical and philosophical reasons, the greatest fear of the Romantics. As Robert Langbaum has stated: "Solipsism was the condition dreaded by the Romanticists—the danger incurred by the individualism and self-consciousness that was their special glory." In inhabiting a world where values were individual and self-created, the Romantic found himself ultimately alone, wondering if the external world was simply another projection. The Romantic poet was also haunted by a peculiar form of psychic claustrophobia, a sense that the individual was alone and totally isolated in a universe that was perhaps merely self-delusion. But the feminine Other—woman as both "real" and ideal—was seen as one possible means of breaking out of the solipsistic dilemma.

Heinz Lichtenstein has asked, "What is first, object-cathexis or ego-cathexis?"—primary narcissism or primary love? The ego must first develop before there can be an object-cathexis:

5. Frederick Garber, *Self, Text, and Romantic Irony: The Example of Byron* (Princeton: Princeton University Press, 1988), 134; James Wilson, *Romantic Heroic Ideal,* 97; 103; David Perkins, *The Quest for Permanence: The Symbolism of Wordsworth, Shelley and Keats* (Cambridge: Harvard University Press, 1959), 170.

> There is, of course, a considerable difference between being in love with oneself and being in love with one's mirror image. . . . The image in the mirror is not real in the same sense in which the ego or the self are real. Somebody who is in love with his mirror image loves a picture or a phantom which he can never possess and reach.

The mirror may refer to either the possibility of losing one's self or soul to another, or retrieving one's lost self. The mirror is not a primary love object, "but the outlines of the child's own image as reflected by the mother's unconscious needs with regard to the child." Primary identity is based on mirroring experience when there is no differentiation between subject and object: "this narcissistic libidinous mirroring reinforces the identity delineation through magnification and reduplication." The object of love, then, "serves as a mirror for a faltering or undeveloped identity." [6] We all begin life as narcissists, then, first directing our object love to the mother. As adults we absorb the mother and other primal figures into the psyche as identifications, all of which need to be balanced in some sort of unified way so that we can love as adults. But the male Romantic poets faced a very real struggle before they could move beyond both the mother and the sister/mirror. As we will see, the sisters in Romantic literature are all either displaced or eradicated by the conclusions of the poems, implying that women who are primarily self-generated must then be self-erased.

In Blake's "William Bond" (E, 496–98; K, 434–36), we can discern a fairly subtle critique of neurotic love for the sister as an internal and idealized second self. In this Pickering Manuscript poem (ca. 1803), Blake presents one "William Bond" ("bound" by his incestuous fantasies, his solipsistic need to love a woman who mirrors him and answers his every unspoken need), who has taken to his bed "very ill" because the "[g]irls . . . mean to kill" him (1–4). William is, in short, suffering from the inability to renounce his love for his "Sister Jane" and turn instead to a "real" woman, "Mary Green," who is standing on the right side of his bed and obviously represents the power of fertility and maternity that her name tropes. Mary pleads with William to admit his feelings, to reject her if he must; she is willing to live with him as a servant if that is his wish (class aspects of the male wish-fulfillment fan-

6. Robert Langbaum, *The Mysteries of Identity: A Theme in Modern Literature* (New York: Oxford University Press, 1977), 6; Heinz Lichtenstein, "The Role of Narcissism in the Emergence and Maintenance of a Primary Identity," *IJP* 45 (1964), 50–54.

tasy can be seen here in the biographical Blake's own attempt to bring another woman into his household with Catherine Blake, already his virtual servant). In this poem, however, the blocking female is the sister Jane, who is mute and unreal throughout the poem; she silently assists William as they lift Mary off the floor and place her in bed with William. Once in bed with William, "Fairies" dance around their heads, conveying a message of Love: "Seek Love in the Pity of others' Woe" (41, 49), and the poem veers off into occlusions, pieties that present love as some sort of prescription for avoiding neurosis. Jane disappears as quietly and mysteriously as befits her presence in the poem.

A work that was obviously much more influential in shaping Romantic attitudes toward incest, Chateaubriand's *René* (1802) stands as an important text because it was a popular novella that utilized a number of themes and images that Shelley and Byron both were to develop later. The young hero, cut off from his family, turns to his sister Amelia as to a muse. Together the two of them sit and "whisper poetry inspired in us by the spectacle of nature." But, like some precursor of the Byronic hero, René journeys throughout Europe, chiefly Greece and Rome, in order to find some meaning and purpose for his life. After rather melodramatically resolving on suicide, René writes to Amelia and manages to arrange a final meeting with her, for, as he observes, "she was the only person in the world I had ever loved, and all my feeling converged in her with the sweetness of my childhood memories." Without expressing his despair in words, René is intuitively understood by Amelia, and she comforts him with kisses: "she was almost a mother, she was something more tender." But Amelia withers in the presence of her brother; she flees to a convent to escape his suffocating demands. In her farewell letter she reminds René that she has been both a mother and a spiritual lover to him: "Though hardly older than you, I once rocked you in your cradle"; "Many times we used to sleep together. Ah, if we might one day be together again in the same tomb!" In a particularly strange episode, René is led to the altar to participate in the installation of Amelia as a nun. He is there to play the "role as a father," to give the "bride" away. Handed a pair of scissors, he is suddenly overwhelmed with passion. With no psychological subtlety here, Chateaubriand clearly associates phallic aggressiveness and sadomasochism with sexual desire, implying in fact that the former is necessary to precipitate the latter. René manages to cut off Amelia's hair and then kneels next to her as she prostrates herself and prays just loud enough for him to hear: "Merciful God, let me never again rise from this deathbed, and may Thy blessings be lavished on my brother, who has never shared my forbidden passion!" Amelia's confession releases René's inhibitions, and he falls on his sister's body screaming, "'Chaste spouse of Christ, receive this last embrace through the chill of death and the depths of eternity which already have parted you from your brother!'" Amelia dies a short time later, and René, inconsolable, seeks pity from his counselor Father Souel. The good priest sensibly points out to René that he is "a young man infatuated with illusions, satisfied with nothing, withdrawn from the burdens of society, and wrapped up in idle dreams."

The "idle dream" that René had tried to pursue was the dream of self-creation by devouring the sister, a feminine version of the self. Amelia realizes, as Garber observes, that to succumb to an incestuous relationship with her brother would be to submit to "a form of self-devouring." Fantasized incest with the sister constituted a relationship between elements of the male psyche, and as such it was a "version of recoil, a turning upon oneself." It created the illusion that the male could possess both his own likeness and his contrary at the same time within his own mind. This is actually an attempt to deny the female her role as the male's "Other," for in this scenario "the self is its own contrary, its own necessary Other"; "the self makes itself out of itself" and incest is "one of the aptest metaphors for such situations." Or, as Margaret Waller has observed about Amelia's passion for René, "through a woman's desire, the male self escapes solipsism, the better to revel in narcissism."[7]

As one can see from the example of *René,* the tendency of Romantic solipsism, the turning in on oneself, inevitably finds a release in an object that the interior self creates and then projects. This double for the self, however, must necessarily be as similar to the self as possible. Coincidentally, the Romantic poets tended to have actual sisters they strongly identified with, poetically idealized, and finally linguistically incorporated. Love of the sister, however, constitutes a persistent element in the androgynous mythos. Denis Saurat has noted that the sexual aspects or "Law" of creation requires a "hermaphrodite God, who divides himself and whose parts fecundate each other; hence the theme of divine incest":

> Sometimes the feminine divinity is called the daughter and is fecundated by her father, sometimes it is the brother who fec-

7. *René,* trans. Irving Putter (Berkeley: University of California Press, 1957); Garber, *Self, Text, and Romantic Irony,* 87; Margaret Waller, "Male Malady and Narrative Politics in the French Romantic Novel," *PMLA* 104 (1989), 147.

undates the sister; sometimes the poet places the myth on the human plane while keeping the incest.[8]

The sister as doubled self—the feminine embodiment of all those qualities cast out of the masculine ego—came to represent for the male poet a physical representation of his *Sehnsucht nach dem Unendlichen* ("yearning after the infinite"). If he himself could not capture the ego ideal of complete harmony between self and external world, then he would create and project out of himself another self who would act as mediatrix between the two realms. Such a psychic phenomenon appears to be at the root of the Romantic poet's presentation of the sister, the woman who becomes for him "more than a mother."

I Wordsworth: "My dear, dear Sister!"

No doubt the most famous sister in the English Romantic tradition is Dorothy Wordsworth, in both her literally real identity as William's sister and her symbolic role as his second self and muse. Dorothy has most recently come into her own as a Romantic poet, but that is not my concern here.[9] I am interested in discussing Dorothy as an idealized sister to William, both in her "real" identity as a sister and, more importantly, in her symbolic role as internalized feminine "Other," because William's use of Dorothy in her dual role as "sister" not only informs the marriage metaphor that runs throughout his poetry, but illuminates his displacement of androgynous ideology. Dorothy as idealized sister permeates William's poetry as the most powerful and significant embodiment of the feminine in his vision. Her identity as a displaced mother and an inspirational muse are, of course, implicit in her nature, but it is finally as a sister that Dorothy functions through-

8. Denis Saurat, *Literature and the Occult Tradition,* trans. Dorothy Bolton (London: Bell, 1930), 17.

9. I will refer to "Dorothy" and "William" throughout the sections of the text that discuss both of them. At those points at which I am discussing the male Romantic poets, I will use the name "Wordsworth." See Margaret Homans, *Women Writers and Poetic Identity: Dorothy Wordsworth, Emily Brontë, and Emily Dickinson* (Princeton: Princeton University Press, 1980) and Susan M. Levin, *Dorothy Wordsworth and Romanticism* (New Brunswick: Rutgers University Press, 1987) for studies that reflect the recent feminist interest in Dorothy as a poet in her own right.

out the corpus.[10] It is certain that William loved Dorothy as a sister in a way that was unusual and excessive, even in a period that encouraged devotion between siblings. John Gregory's *A Father's Legacy to his Daughters* (1774) advocated the position that brothers and sisters were destined to be each other's best friends. The Wordsworths perhaps took his advice a bit too seriously. For instance, in describing his love for Dorothy, William wrote: "She . . . whom I have loved / With such communion, that no place on earth / Can ever be a solitude to me," while Coleridge observed that William had "hurtfully segregated & isolated his Being" by living so closely with Dorothy. In fact, Coleridge went so far as to charge William with living like a parasite off Dorothy and Mary, his wife:

> I saw him . . . living wholly among *Devotees*—having every the minutest Thing, almost his very Eating and Drinking, done for him by his Sister, or Wife—& I trembled, lest a Film should rise, and thicken on his mortal Eye.[11]

"Nutting" and the so-called Lucy poems present early versions of the sister/Dorothy as a crucial component in the male poet's quest to cannibalize the feminine and thereby (re)create himself as the divinely potent androgynous artist. In "Nutting" (1798), William states that he is presenting his readers with an autobiographic incident that captures his growing awareness of Nature as a split feminine power. As a boy he had been sent by his mother-substitute, a "frugal Dame" (11), to harvest

10. See Susan J. Wolfson, "Individual in Community: Dorothy Wordsworth in Conversation with William," in *Romanticism and Feminism*, ed. Mellor, 140: William's poetry "simultaneously advances a male center and writes the female as the 'other'—necessarily represented without her own subjectivity or power of self-representation, and inscribed in political and epistemic hierarchies alike as the object of appropriation, instruction, or mastery." Anne K. Mellor, in "Teaching Wordsworth and Women," notes that Wordsworth "has constituted the female as not human" (see *Approaches to Teaching Wordsworth's Poetry*, ed. Spencer Hall and Jonathan Ramsey [New York: MLA, 1986], 145.)

11. "Poems on the Naming of Places, III" (1800), in *The Poetical Works of William Wordsworth*, II, 115. All quotations from Wordsworth's poetry, except for *The Prelude*, will be from this edition: 5 vols., ed. Ernest De Selincourt and Helen Darbishire (Oxford: Clarendon Press, 1940–49). Coleridge's comments on Wordsworth can be found in *The Collected Letters of Samuel Taylor Coleridge*, ed. Earl Leslie Griggs (Oxford: Clarendon Press, 1956–72), I, 491 (6 May 1799); II; 1013 (14 October 1803).

nuts in the forest. He describes how he used force to break into "one dear nook" in order to forage amid a "virgin scene" (16, 21). This Eden reads like a clear description of the semiotic realm, a preverbal locus whose logic is primarily visual. The boy is most impressed with the "Tall and erect" hazel trees with their "tempting clusters [of nuts] hanging about" (20). In fact, the blatant sexual imagery that occurs throughout this poem recalls not only the movement from the semiotic to the Symbolic/paternal, but also Freud's description of the polymorphous perverse (*SE* VII:191). This prelapsarian ideal, however, is corrupted not simply by a fall into the Symbolic, but by the reification of the maternal—the "frugal Dame"—the feminine who no longer remembers the beauty of unspoiled Nature and instead sees it as a commodity, a source for commercial gain. Boys become men, Wordsworth implies, when they allow themselves to be corrupted by the fallen sexual principle that sees the external world as not in harmony but competition with the internal realm. Whereas the corrupted-capitalistic feminine evidences itself in a concern with Nature as a source for material goods, possessions, and status, the fallen masculine principle is the spirit of violence, the compulsion toward aggression.

When the boy enters this Eden, he immediately feels like a glutton at a "voluptuous. . . banquet," not knowing which delicacy to indulge in first (24–25). While partaking of this luxurious realm, he is filled with a "temper known to those, who, after long / And weary expectation, have been blest / With sudden happiness beyond all hope" (26–29). He simultaneously indulges his senses of touch, sight, hearing and smell as he alternately explores the nuances of the natural scene. Filled with "ease" and "joy secure," his heart feels the "kindliness" that emerges effortlessly and demands no reward for itself. But this world of unconditional love is suddenly and rudely disrupted when the boy lifts his phallic hook to the hazelnuts and desecrates them, deforming and imagistically raping them. As Lacan has pointed out, the mirror stage, the precondition for primary narcissism, is the very source of human aggressivity; in fact, the two forces are inextricably associated with each other. There can be no psychic emergence from the mother without violence, abjection.

The boy feels no shame at the time of the incident; rather, he admits to leaving the grove feeling "rich beyond the wealth of kings." But he knows as the man he now is, the poet writing about emotion recollected in tranquility, that his crime against the world of Nature was, in fact, a fall into the Symbolic. With some displaced irony he begs the "dearest Maiden" he walks with now, presumably Dorothy, to "move along these shades / In gentleness of heart" and "gentle hand" (51, 54–

55). If William's hand and heart cannot resist desecrating Nature, then perhaps he can substitute as his the idealized feminine hand and heart of Dorothy. At the conclusion of the poem William and Dorothy return to walk in harmony with Nature in their joint attempt to "Touch . . . a spirit in the woods" (56). Their symbolically joined hands trope the fictitious androgynous balance of both the unfallen masculine and feminine qualities of power and beauty. Dorothy as sister in this poem embodies the ideal feminine, the redemption of the frugal dame who initially instigated the "crime" in the first place. The fallen woman functions as the cause of Nature's despoiling, while woman as unfallen ideal operates at the conclusion of the poem to redeem both sexes. We can see here another example of the split female figure, with Dorothy as sister redeeming and replacing the Frugal Dame/mother. But as Levinson has remarked, why should the Maiden be "a literary fixture, an allegorical emblem, or a nympholeptic vision when the scene, the hero, and the wood are insistently literal?" Her explanation is that the nature of desire is the subject of the poem, while its recognition and representation through language is nominalist; the poem, therefore, should be read as a rejection of the materialist or realist idea of the world.[12] But surely Dorothy is as "*un*real" within the poetic cosmos as the hero and the semiotic wood. That is, the poem contains striking similarities to other Romantic psychomachias in Blake, Shelley, and Keats's works particularly. The action occurs in the masculine mental theater, with the (split) feminine principles struggling for dominance or acceptance within the mind of the male poet.

In the so-called Lucy poems, we see another attempt to present Dorothy as a representative of the positive feminine powers of Nature, although it is only fair to point out that the figure of Lucy is not universally considered to be Wordsworth's sister. Various critics have interpreted Lucy as Annette Vallon, Mary or Margaret Hutchinson, or Mary of Esthwaite, as well as Dorothy Wordsworth. Without resorting to a good deal of biographical hypothesis here, I believe Lucy has most accu-

12. In *Romantic Fragment Poem: A Critique of a Form* (Chapel Hill: University of North Carolina Press, 1986), 68–72, Levinson has stated that it is the "*conjunction* of epistemological, verbal, and erotic desires that precipitates the anxieties which shape the narration" of "Nutting." In "Woman's Place in Wordsworth's Ideological Landscape," *ELH* 53 (1986), 393–96), Marlon Ross has also provocatively analyzed the sexual dynamics of "Nutting," claiming that the displacement of responsibility onto the Maiden represents an ideological appropriation of the feminine and an attempt to "repurify nature and purge masculine guilt."

rately been read as a composite of Dorothy as "real" sister and Dorothy as the idealized feminine component within William. Coleridge read the poems in this manner, while recent criticism has reinforced the fiction that the poems form a cycle (which, of course, was not Wordsworth's intention). In the Lucy poems, then, William confronts the consequences of loving Dorothy as both a real woman, his sister, and an imaginative projection of his own creation. This is not to agree with Bateson's claim that William was falling in love with Dorothy and therefore needed to solve the potentially dangerous situation by symbolically killing her in the poems.[13] I am suggesting instead that the po-

13. In *Wordsworth: A Re-Interpretation* (London: Longmans, Green, 1954), F. W. Bateson discusses the "tragic intensification" of the relationship with Dorothy during 1798–1802. And see Hugh Sykes Davies's "Another New Poem by Wordsworth," *EIC* 15 (1965), 135–61, for a discussion of the "Lucy group" as a fabrication of the Victorians Francis Palgrave, Matthew Arnold, and Aubrey de Vere. The question "Who was Lucy?" and what motivated Wordsworth to write the poems we continue to call the Lucy poems has been the subject of endless biographical and psychological speculation. Coleridge definitely thought that "A Slumber" was an expression of Wordsworth's fear that Dorothy might die (see Paul Magnuson, *Wordsworth and Coleridge: A Lyrical Dialogue* [Princeton: Princeton University Press, 1988], 199–200): Lucy "is an imaginative realization that Wordsworth's melancholy originated in a fear of being separated from his past and from the source in which he had located his imaginative beginnings." Also see Herbert Hartman, "Wordsworth's Lucy Poems," *PMLA* 49 (1934), 134–42, for an early account of the various biographical theories. Richard E. Matlak's, "Wordsworth's Lucy Poems in Psychobiographical Context," *PMLA* 93 (1978), 46–65, sees the poems as an expression of Wordsworth's deeply ambivalent relationship with his sister while they were living in Goslar, Germany. Frances Ferguson sees the Lucy group as a succession of echoings in which "through the course of these poems, Lucy is repeatedly and ever more decisively traced out of existence" (see her *Wordsworth: Language as Counter-Spirit* [New Haven: Yale University Press, 1977], 174). In a similar vein, David Ferry has claimed that the speaker of the Lucy poems is "uncertain of his vision of these girls; or rather, he is certain of the instability and perishability of his vision of them. He knows he is making up a fiction and that his fiction will not be able to sustain itself forever" (see his *Limits of Mortality: An Essay on Wordsworth's Major Poems* [Middletown: Wesleyan University Press, 1959], 79). Finally, Levinson has discussed "Dorothy-Lucy" as an "invaluable textual device" for Wordsworth since she is "felt to exist on the margins of the speaker's enclosure and to have access both to that haven and to the unimaginable relations outside it. She is the hypostatized, desired alien—a phantom figure—always on the boundary of the familiar and now and then sliding into the beyond" (see her *Wordsworth's Great Period Poems: Four Essays,* 49).

ems present the very personal and threatening reason why William chose to displace his use of the androgynous theme. Blake, Byron, Shelley, and Keats could use the feminine as a component of the androgynous quest in fairly straightforward ways, but when Coleridge and Wordsworth depicted love for women their poetry veered, elided, and displaced human emotions onto natural objects. Both Coleridge and Wordsworth explore fictitious androgynous unions, but only by using the displacements of mind and Nature, sun and moon, tower and river, or fountain and dome. I suspect that William was uncomfortable when he wrote about the feminine within because he could do so only by depicting his sister Dorothy and that was, ultimately, too threatening for him. Each of the Lucy poems contains, whether blatant or not, a foreboding sense of transiency and death. The recurring psychological pattern is one of approach-avoidance, aggressivity and repression.

For instance, in "Strange Fits of Passion Have I Known," the narrator describes his approach to Lucy's cottage as a descending and yet bright moon presides over it. When the moon sinks, the narrator at exactly the same moment lets a "fond and wayward" thought cross his mind: "O mercy! . . . If Lucy should be dead!" The connection here between the waning influence of the feminine as a nurturing power in the poet's life and his fear of losing Dorothy's power to see into the heart of Nature collide imagistically with the sinking power of the traditionally feminine moon. It is conventional to see Lucy as part of both the landscape and the moon, with her death serving as the means whereby she is transmuted into the cycle of generation. But critics have failed to address the poet's emotional ambivalence toward both Nature and moon—and their association with Lucy—as expressing a sort of claustrophobic fantasy of feminine omnipresence. That is, in addition to anxiety about Lucy's demise, there is a not-very-hidden wish to be free of Dorothy/Lucy, to be independent of his need for and dependence on the feminine.

In "She Dwelt Among the Untrodden Ways," William treats the anonymity of Lucy and her dispersal throughout the landscape. Here Lucy, like Dorothy as the inspiration of William's imaginative creativity, is "unknown"; both live with little praise or love. But the loss of Lucy/Dorothy is an event that the poet again professes to dread: "But she is in her grave, and oh, / The Difference to me!" In other words, the poet is only able to contain the power of the omnipresent feminine by localizing her—in her grave. In both of these poems William expresses his greatest fear and, paradoxically, a concealed wish to be free of the feminine's power over his psychic life. William's refrain implies that loving

Nature intensely leads to physical death, which could also be understood within the psychic dynamics of the poetry as the belief that loving women leads to imaginative death.[14] Such an equation, of course, is a blatant denial and defense mechanism given the fact that William knew he needed Dorothy's personal insights and observations of Nature, recorded in her *Journals,* if he was to continue reflecting on their experiences and writing himself.

In "I travelled among unknown men," the poet tries another more socially acceptable way of curtailing the power of Lucy; he domesticates her and places her within the idealized English cottage, placidly spinning wool, "turning her wheel / Beside an English fire." This domestication and containment of Lucy reveals in no uncertain terms the poet's attempt to transmute the ideology of the Eternal Feminine (woman as omnipotent and omnipresent) into an enshrined goddess of the hearth, brought to heel and constrained by the realities of her new domestic identity. But this fictionally idealized solution still left Lucy alive, an option that posed certain problems that the poet sought to permanently resolve in the next three poems.

"Lucy Gray"—a poem not generally discussed as part of the (fictitious) sequence, but that clearly continues its psychic dynamics—also presents the loss/disappearance/death of the pubescent and "solitary" Lucy. In this version, however, Lucy is victimized by a father who sends her out into a snowstorm to escort her mother home safely. Although her parents can trace her footprints, she has disappeared, appropriately, while in the middle of crossing a bridge. A number of attitudes toward the feminine can be discerned in this poem, and all of them reveal a deep ambivalence hidden behind the balladlike facade of love and concern. First of all, the sister is sacrificed for the mother by the male authority figure in the poem. Lucy is sent out of the house at 2:00 A.M. by her father, who ironically invokes the protection of the moon. Second, Lucy is at every opportunity stripped of her human qualities; she is compared to animals (the fawn or the hare) or a flower growing "Beside a human door," or she is the "sweetest thing." Her mysterious evapora-

14. As Schapiro notes about these poems, they all to a large extent "are elegies for a lost infant self and for a lost union with the mother. The yearned-for fusion with the mother, however, must inevitably result in death" (*Romantic Mother,* 110). Also using a psychological argument, J. M. Hawthorn (in "The Strange Deaths of Sally, Ann, Lucy and Others," *Trivium* 6 [1971], 70–80) claims that Romantic poets used death or fantasies about death to gain control over their female characters who were associated with sexual love.

tion into the atmosphere at that point where earth, water, and sky intersect implies that she has been absorbed back into the natural elements since she was never fully human to begin with. Her loss is denied or softened by the country-folk rumor that she still is a living child whom one could meet "Upon the lonesome wild."

In the final two poems, William effectively faces the reality of life without the feminine within. In "Three Years She Grew in Sun and Shower," he reconciles himself to Lucy's loss by stressing her closer ties to Nature, stating that the three-year-old Lucy was simply reclaimed by Nature as one of her own. Although especially nursed by Nature so that she is instructed by an "overseeing power," Lucy is also taught by the clouds, stars, and water. Her participation in all four natural elements reveals that she herself functions as the link between the external and internal worlds. It is she who is to transfer her "vital feelings of delight" and her "thoughts" to the poet "in this happy dell." Lucy's "work"—embodying the feminine qualities of emotion for the male narrator—was accomplished in just three years—"How soon my Lucy's race was run!" The poet returns to his life after Lucy's death, as if cannibalistically sustained by absorbing her. She has, that is, served her symbolic purpose of functioning as a human sacrifice, parasitically consumed by the male poetic persona.

Lucy in this poem has taken on clear mythic and symbolic roles, as we see further developed in "A Slumber Did My Spirit Seal." This poem effectively lays Lucy to rest; she has become a "thing" that the poet can manipulate to relive and efface the death of not only his mother, but the feminine principle itself. In this brief poem Lucy is a "thing that could not feel / The touch of earthly years." She is, in other words, a fantasy figure of wish-fulfillment, the literary recreation of William's mother dead and yet still somehow magically alive. Lucy dead is perhaps not much different from Lucy alive—both are imaginative projections of the male poet's need to create a feminine counterpart who will not only act as a fictional intermediary for him with the world of Nature but willingly disappear after she has allowed the male to take what he needs from her. She is dead and alive at the same time, or rather she is neither. She is finally the woman as absent sign, consumed commodity, vacant signifier. Women are, after all, "things" because they are less (or more) than human. In his perceptive commentary on the poem, Hillis Miller resorts to Heidegger's discussion of the word "thing" ("A man is not a thing. . . . Only a stone, a clod of earth, a piece of wood are for us such mere things") in order to explain Lucy's radical Otherness. But women traditionally *are* things in poems written by men, whether that fact is clothed in a structure of chiasmus, rhetorical reversals, or psychic substitutions.[15] We can conclude that William went through an early period when he experimented with approaching the feminine within and writing about male/female relationships overtly. But the feminine image and face that emerged from his own unconscious was uncomfortably close to his sister's face, and so he distanced, domesticated, infantilized, and finally displaced her into oblivion. The feminine he was able to confront in his later poetry was more safely troped as a nursing mother, a river, or a moon.

Dorothy as the "Maiden" appears as a redeemed version of the mother—"the Frugal Dame"—at the conclusion of "Nutting" and in displaced versions in the Lucy poems, but she first assumes her true significance as a sister/muse only in "Tintern Abbey," a poem that has most frequently been seen as an abbreviated history of William's imaginative development in relation to the feminine powers of Nature. William's salvation as portrayed in this poem lies in establishing a reciprocity between his mind and the external world so that Nature, as "other" than and feminine to the self, can be contained, absorbed, and finally cannibalized by the powers of the masculine mind.

The first eight lines of the poem emphasize the conjunction between sight and hearing, in that the poet declares he "hear[s] / These waters" and "behold[s] these steep and lofty cliffs" (2–3, 5). This conjunction enables him to capture initially a unified vision of the semiotic realm of Nature in order to begin his quest: to "connect / The landscape with the quiet of the sky," that is, to merge the semiotic world of Nature with his own masculine/Symbolic power to perceive, interpret, and "connect." Hartman has pointed out that "Tintern Abbey," like all of William's greatest poems, begins with the mind being moved by itself after it has been moved by something external. But the fact is that Nature is not actually "external" to the poet; Nature throughout William's poetry is identified with the feminine elements of the poetic self, and, as such, must therefore be a projective aspect of his own fragmented mind. Thus the speaker in "Tintern Abbey" finds that the "beauteous

15. See J. Hillis Miller, "On Edge: The Crossways of Contemporary Criticism," in *Romanticism and Contemporary Criticism,* ed. Morris Eaves and Michael Fischer (Ithaca: Cornell University Press, 1986), 104–10. Miller was motivated to discuss this particular poem, I suspect, as a response to Paul de Man's analysis of the same poem in his essay "The Rhetoric of Temporality," in *Interpretation: Theory and Practice,* ed. Charles Singleton (Baltimore: Johns Hopkins University Press, 1969). Both readings are perceptively analyzed by M. H. Abrams in "Construing and Deconstructing," *Romanticism and Contemporary Criticism,* 127–82.

forms" of Nature have the power to lighten "the burthen of the mystery, / . . . the heavy and weary weight / Of all this unintelligible world" (28–40). It is the scenes of Nature and the "serene and blessed mood" they produce that enable the poet to make his internal journey. But these scenes are not wholly external, if at all. They are only perceived when his blood has been "almost suspended" and he is "laid asleep / In body" so that he can see "into the life of things." They are, then, clearly internal phenomena, semiotic manifestations that occur within his "living soul" (45–49).

The poet next outlines his mind's growing relation to Nature, and in this sense "Tintern Abbey" is a miniaturized version of *The Prelude*. As a young boy, his first relation to Nature was one of "coarser pleasures" and "glad animal movements" (73–74). We can recall here as analogous the rape of the hazel trees in "Nutting." Here the feminine world of Nature is simply an unconscious extension of the self to be used and abused by the male without any thought to consequences. As a projection of the masculine self, it represents the boy's own insignificance and lack of mature consciousness. In the second phase, however, the boy begins to experience "aching joys" and "dizzy raptures" while in Nature's presence. His "appetite" for Nature can immediately be gratified because he still has no sense of a separation from Nature, or of Nature as "other" to him. But by the third phase the poet has matured to the point of unifying his senses—his sight and his hearing—and of managing to both see and hear "The still, sad music of humanity" (91). In this third phase the poet is infused with "a sense sublime" that allows him to participate with Nature as part of the Life Force, the sense that "impels / All thinking things, all objects of all thought, / And rolls through all things" (95, 100–103). Nature as the all-encompassing Life Force—the mother—is a manifestation of the poet's earliest conception of the projective feminine. One is reminded of Shelley's Urania, that maternal presence forced to create and then to destroy in a continuous spiral of seemingly futile generation. Rather than face his anger and hostility toward the mother, however, the poet of "Tintern Abbey" displaces his frustration and instead declares that Nature is the "anchor of my purest thoughts, the nurse, / The guide, the guardian of my heart, and soul / Of all my mortal being" (109–11). Nature as mother/nurse/guardian is functioning at this stage as a projection of the male's desire to see the feminine within as a nurturing, nonthreatening power. It is the masculine mind, after all, that is primary, while the feminine exists in a secondary capacity, not really even an inspirational muse. And Nature, as de Man observed in his "Rhetoric of Temporality," can most accurately be read, not as symbol, but as allegory, a construct of the (male) mind that attempts to evade the solitude and meaninglessness of immersion in the temporally vacuous.

It is no coincidence, then, that Dorothy appears at this point in the poem, standing beside William on the banks of the river Wye. She functions to a certain extent like Dante's Beatrice; she is supposed to play the role of mediatrix between the immortal world of imaginative visions and the human world of natural beauty and joy. William turns to Dorothy, noting that in her voice he hears and relives "The Language of my former heart," while he sees his "former pleasures in the shooting lights" of her "wild eyes" (115–19). At this point, Dorothy is a mirror image of William's earlier self, an ego ideal, the self whose loss he has been mourning throughout the poem, and the self that is lost to him unless he can recapture a facsimile of it through Dorothy. There is a long critical tradition of identifying the historical Dorothy with the fictions of "sister" in this poem. For instance, consider Richard Fadem's comment that "at twenty-six she is what William was at seven. She is splendid but rudimentary and incomplete." Wolfson rightly points out that the "real" Dorothy read French, Italian, and German literature, and was a valued companion to intelligent men besides her brother, while Levinson sees the turn to Dorothy here as a "move toward otherness, or toward a social reality, albeit a greatly complaisant (cathected) instance of that order. Dorothy functions in the poem as a final surface, the condition for the poet's ongoing reflective life." [16] In fact, William wants Dorothy to pose as some sort of *tableau vivant* so that he can "behold in thee what I was once" (120). She is to be for him the living symbol of his former self; she is not only to be his projective feminine side, but she must necessarily be free from the ravages of time, frozen in time, the sister as fictional muse.

16. See Richard Fadem's "Dorothy Wordsworth: A View from 'Tintern Abbey,' " *WC* 9 (1978), 17; Wolfson, "Individual in Community," *Romanticism and Feminism,* ed. Mellor, 165; Levinson, *Wordsworth's Great Period Poems,* 45. Most critics, I realize, see "Tintern Abbey" as the zenith of Wordsworth's faith in Nature. Notable exceptions include Charles Clarke ("Loss and Consolation in the Poetry of Wordsworth," *ES* 31 [1950], 81–97); Albert Gérard ("Dark Passages: Exploring 'Tintern Abbey,' " *SIR* 3 [1963], 10–23); and Harold Bloom (*The Visionary Company* [New York: Anchor, 1961], 139–49). In "The Dangers of Sympathy: Sibling Incest in English Romantic Poetry," *SEL* 25 (1985), 748, Alan Richardson claims that in "Tintern Abbey" William identifies with Dorothy, his female counterpart, so that he can "take over wholesale a female heart, the fountain of tender feelings, and with it a feminine mode of perception (wise passiveness, as opposed to the masculine meddling intellect)."

At this point of confrontation with the sister as both real and symbolic, William proceeds to ask for a blessing on her, but with a piousness that betrays its own self-serving anxiety: "My dear, dear Sister! and this prayer I make, / Knowing that Nature never did betray / The heart that loved her" (121–23). But William has revealed throughout the poem that Nature—the projective feminine—has indeed betrayed a heart that loves her—his. And, furthermore, he quite obviously envies Dorothy's simpler, less intellectual, more authentic relationship with Nature. Although Margaret Homans has claimed that Dorothy could not write poetry because of the metaphoric tradition that William had established—Nature as female to a male mind—it is evident that at least William thinks that Dorothy's relationship with the feminine power of Nature is analogous to his, regardless of the fact that Dorothy is female. Nature has not led him "from joy to joy," nor has she enabled him to live a life free from "evil tongues, / Rash judgments, nor the sneers of selfish men" (128–29). William is trying very hard here to convince himself that Nature indeed has these powers, or, rather, that the mind redeemed by the imaginative power of the feminine has these powers. But William is speaking, after all, from the growing realization that his imagination is failing and that he is, as any poet would be, bitter. He chooses, probably unconsciously, to displace his bitterness onto Dorothy, for if she is for him the emblem of the feminine within, then she is the cause of his imaginative decay. Such would appear to be his logic of blame. If she cannot be his savior, then she deserves the same fate he has received.

William concludes this most famous paean to the powers of the imagination by wishing imaginative decline for his own beloved sister. He predicts in the years to come that Dorothy, like he, will lose her imaginative capacities: "these wild ecstasies shall be matured / Into a sober pleasure" (138–39). In fact, he goes so far as to hope she is left with the one power left to him—memory—cold comfort indeed (141). But most revealing is that William turns in this poem not to his own mind, but to his sister's, just as he would turn so many times to her *Journals* in order to recapture the essence of their walks throughout the countryside. Dorothy's mind assumes mythic importance for William because in some strange way it is actually his mind also, just as Dorothy was his second self, his embodied imagination. According to the ideology he has created, he possesses reason and the capacity to arrange words in poetic form, but he clearly relies on her intuitive "feminine" capacity to see into the heart of things. And it is his realization and resentment of her capacities that lie at the root of "Tintern Abbey." Not only resentment, however, motivates the poem. There is finally a good deal of fear, for when Dorothy's imaginative powers decline and eventually extinguish (as William both dreads and wishes for her), so will his ability to relive his earlier experiences with Nature through her.

II Shelley: "Blending two restless frames in one reposing soul"

Shelley once wrote to Maria Gisborne that "Incest is like many other *incorrect* things a very poetical circumstance." But Shelley's intention in depicting incest was not simply to shock the bourgeoisie, much as that goal was near and dear to his heart. As a student of Paracelsus and the medieval mystics, Shelley knew that the union of brother and sister was a traditional symbol within alchemy, another important source for androgynous ideology. Abrams also notes that alchemical imagery provides a clue to the Romantic theme of brother-sister love when he observes:

> . . . in alchemy, on the grounds that the male and female opposites had a common genetic source, the *coniunctio* was often represented as an incestuous brother-sister union. From the chymical wedding issues the Philosopher's Stone, figured as a *rebis* or androgyne, who reunites the two sexes into the unitary form they had exhibited before their separation.[17]

Shelley certainly has been accused by other critics of cannibalizing the feminine as sister, of creating an ideal love object, in order to complete his own psyche. In his early poem "Rosalind and Helen," he observes that "love and life in him were twins, / Born at one birth / . . . children of one mother." The necessity of loving that which is as similar to the self as possible pervades Shelley's poetry, and finds its first full poetic expression in *Laon and Cythna,* with its dual hero/heroine, brother and sister, and eventually, one composite and fictionally androgynous self.

In the original version of the poem, Shelley went to some trouble to establish the identities of Laon and Cythna as siblings. The original version of the poem, *Laon and Cythna,* presents the two as brother and sister. *The Revolt of Islam,* the published version of the poem, depicts Cythna as an orphan, raised by Laon's parents as both their child and

17. Meyer Abrams, *Natural Supernaturalism,* 160.

Laon's adopted sister. Shelley utilizes incest (overt and covert) not simply for shock value, but because the relationship conformed to ancient traditions in both Platonic and androgynous theory, with which he was familiar. The fact that he was forced by his publisher to omit the incestuous relationship and publish the poem as *The Revolt of Islam* should not, I think, obscure his original vision or intention.

In writing *Laon and Cythna,* Shelley attempted to delineate both a political and a personal, psychic struggle. In trying to treat both struggles separately and yet in some ways identically, the poem is at times confused, as many critics over the years have recognized. Shelley later solved the same artistic dilemma in *Prometheus Unbound* by making that political struggle an internal quest for reconciliation between warring factions of one (masculine) mind. Like *Prometheus Unbound, Laon and Cythna*'s Preface endorses a worldview in which "Love is celebrated everywhere as the sole law which should govern the moral world" (*JW,* I, 247). But this "Love" is predicated on the willing sacrifice of the feminine to the masculine principle, and, as such, leads to a political realm in which women are absent except as enabling components for the male psyche.

The struggle between good and evil forms the basis of Canto I's imagery and action. The poem begins with a serpent, representing the forces of energy and goodness, temporarily defeated in battle by an eagle, symbol of evil. The serpent coils itself in a woman's embrace while it waits to rise again to wage the perpetual war between good and evil in this world. This mysterious and comforting woman is reminiscent of Shelley's Witch of Atlas as she is carried over the sea in a "boat of rare device" reciting a poem, "a strange and awful tale" that is "like some mysterious dream" (xxiii–iv). Leigh Hunt was the first critic to recognize that an androgynous and mystical "Form" presides over Canto I as the Woman (not Cythna but a Venus figure) merges with the serpent (spirit of eternal good).[18] The merging of the two creates the Spirit of the

18. Leigh Hunt's review of the *Revolt of Islam* (1 February 1818) states: "A magic and obscure circumstance then takes place [in stanza LVI], the result of which is: that the Woman and the Serpent are seen no more, but that a cloud opens asunder and a bright and beautiful shape, which seems compounded of both, is beheld sitting on a throne" (*Shelley—Leigh Hunt,* ed. R. Brimley Johnson [London: Haskell House, 1928], 17). Carl Grabo makes a similar observation in *The Magic Plant: The Growth of Shelley's Thought* (Chapel Hill: University of North Carolina Press, 1936), 210. James Ruff also comments on the androgynous nature of Laon and Cythna: "Their relationship obviously duplicates that of the Woman and Serpent of Canto I, who fused together into an

Temple, a Light that then becomes a mighty planet. This dual spirit represents an androgynous union of love with the power of good, and as such presents Shelley's belief that social and psychic reform cannot take place without the fictional and mimetic reconciliation of woman and man, love and goodness (lvi).

Shelley presents throughout Canto I a series of incestuous cosmologies, a succession of siblinglike forces that function as displaced representations of the eventual relationship of Laon and Cythna. The forces of Good and Evil are described in Zoroastrian terms: "Twin Genie, equal Gods. . . burst the womb of inessential Nought" (xxv). The God of Evil and the God of Good find their parallels in the next creations, the "blood red Comet and the Morning Star," who war like the eagle and serpent until the temporary victory of evil causes the race of man to be "Famished and homeless, loathed and loathing, wild / And hating good" (xxvi–vii). At this point of multiplying images, Shelley begins the story of Laon and his sister, whose earthly actions are an analogous attempt to reinstitute the rightful dominance of the powers of good both in society and the individual psyche of cosmic humanity.

The woman who has related the story thus far is presented as a divinely inspired muse "nurtured in divinest lore" by a "dying poet" (xxxvii). But the first canto, according to the fiction of the poem, is a dream within the woman's mind inspired by her love for an ideal, "but not a human lover." This all-consuming love has caused her mind to focus on only "one thought—one image," a "shape of speechless beauty," an image of "light," a "winged youth, whose radiant brow did wear / The Morning Star" (xl–ii). This youth presents the challenge to the woman: "How wilt thou prove thy worth?" to an immortal Spirit. The woman chooses to prove herself worthy of immortal love by fighting in "a field of holy warfare" in which she can "brave death for liberty and truth" (xliii–iv). Like Ariosto's Bradamant and Spenser's Britomart, she is in the tradition of women-warriors who are separated from their beloveds. The woman, however, is continually sustained by "The Spirit whom I loved in solitude" (xlv). Only after appearing before a "mighty Senate" of spirits is the mortal woman able to vanish and be replaced by the eternal form. She reappears with Laon, her spiritual counterpart, who emerges as the embodiment of good, "like the morning sky, / The Cloudless Heaven of Spring" (lix), while Cythna appears beside him "like his shadow. . . far lovelier" (lx). These varying and continuously

androgynous figure" (see his *Shelley's Revolt of Islam* [Salzburg: Studies in English Literature, 1972], 60). Also see Frederick L. Jones, "Canto I of *The Revolt of Islam*," *KSJ* 9 (1960), 27–33; Stuart Sperry, *Shelley's Major Verse*, 44–47.

shifting forms of Cythna, Laon, and the androgynous woman have confused critics over the years.[19] One point emerges clearly; Shelley intended, as he stated in the Preface to the poem, to present "a succession of pictures illustrating the growth and progress of *individual mind* aspiring after excellence." His poetic theme and technique was most similar to Blake's intention in *Jerusalem,* and in several ways the first canto of *Laon and Cythna* is also the poem's conclusion, so that the action, as in Blake's epics, is circular and to a large extent psychic.

The action in Canto II shifts to the physical world, where Laon introduces his "little sister," Cythna, as a "shape of brightness," a "power," "some radiant cloud," "the bright shade of some immortal dream," "mine own shadow," a "second self, far dearer and more fair," "clothed in undissolving radiancy" (xxiii–iv). Like Blake's Ololon, Cythna is only twelve years old, a barely pubescent muse figure who separates from Laon only during his sleep. Even in her sleep Cythna mirrors Laon, murmuring his name while singing inspired songs, "Hymns which my soul had woven to Freedom, strong / The source of passion, whence they rose to be; / Triumphant strains" (xxviii). Cythna functions here both as a sister and as an unconscious medium, divinely inspired and subsequently inspiring Laon to "zeal," "wisdom," and "knowledge" (xxxii). In short, Cythna functions in the poem as not only an ego ideal, but on an objective level as a female savior, a feminist chiliastic redeemer in the mold of Shelley's contemporaries—Mother Ann Lee, Mary Evans, Luckie Buchan, Sarah Flaxmer, and (most notoriously) Joanna Southcott. Blake may have laughed at the dropsied Joanna Southcott (1750–1814), bloated with cancer yet convinced that she would miraculously give birth to Shiloh, the new messiah, but that same millennial fervor inspired the young and idealistic Shelley. In fact, Cythna's portrayal as a feminist reformer recalls the fact that Joanna's prophecies were specifically addressed to working-class women

19. Harold Bloom sees the poem as "abortive" (in his *Shelley's Mythmaking,* 8). Alicia Martinez claims that in *The Revolt* Shelley "ignores society's role divisions and seeks to create equality between the male and female by celebrating the subordinated characteristics of each" (see her *Hero and Heroine of Shelley's The Revolt of Islam* [Salzburg: Studies in English Literature, 1976], 70). Richard Haswell sees the poem as "far better designed and unified than commonly believed" in that both hero/heroine undergo symmetrical adventures: "Ultimately the poem makes the point that these two functions [reason and the emotions] must be integrated in the perfect person. Initially, both Cythna and Laon are one-sided, and both fall" (see his "Shelley's *Revolt of Islam*: 'The Connexions of Its Parts,'" *KSJ* 25 [1976], 84, 87).

and assured them that men were villains and that women would now be raised to their rightful positions within the society of believers.[20] The poetic creation of Cythna, a female preacher who bears a mysterious child seemingly without male intervention, occurred within three years of Southcott's death, and we can only conclude that to some extent Shelley's attack in the poem on the tyrant's dystopian city anticipates his attack on the corruption of urban life in "Peter Bell the Third": "Hell is a city much like London."

Cythna's unconscious reveries have caused Laon to dedicate himself also to the cause of women's rights, for he has come to realize through Cythna's ministrations that women have been made "slaves to soothe vile unrest, / And minister to lust its joys forlorn / Till they had learned to breathe the atmosphere of scorn" (xxxv). This form of feminism as disguised distaste for physical sexuality is remarkably reminiscent of Blake's denunciation of marriage in "London," as well as Oothoon's words in *The Visions of the Daughters of Albion.* Cythna mourns the "servitude" of women, for, in addition to being "Victims of lust and hate," they are also "the slaves of slaves" (xxxvi). Just as Blake portrays the fallen and destructive Female Will and Spectre, so does Shelley present both sexes as divided from the harmonious (and fictitious) balance that is their birthright. The male in Shelley's poetry is enslaved by false and corrupt political systems, while the female is enslaved by the male and thus doubly victimized. In a letter to Elizabeth Hitchener, Shelley moaned, "these detestable distinctions [between men and women], they will surely be abolished in a future state of things" (*Letters,* I, 195). And in his *Discourse on the Manners of the Ancient Greeks Relative to the Subject of Love,* he states that "This invidious distinction of humankind as a class of beings [of] intellectual nature into two sexes is a remnant of savage barbarism which we have less excuse than they [the Greeks] for not having totally abolished."[21] Both Laon and Cythna realize, as did Shelley their creator, that the liberation of women would begin a process that would ultimately lead to a transformation of the entire social structure. Laon declares that "Never

20. See the discussion of female messiahs in Barbara Taylor, *Eve and the New Jerusalem: Socialism and Feminism in the Nineteenth Century* (New York: Pantheon, 1983), 161–72. Political interpretations of the *Revolt* can be found in Anthony Arthur, "The Poet as Revolutionary in *The Revolt of Islam,*" *XUS* 10 (1971), 1–17; and Harold Orel, "Shelley's *The Revolt of Islam:* The Last Great Poem of the English Enlightenment?" *SVEC* 89 (1972), 187–207.

21. *Shelley's Prose or The Trumpet of Prophesy,* ed. David Lee Clark (Albuquerque: University of New Mexico Press, 1954), 223.

will peace and human nature meet / Till free and equal man and woman greet / Domestic peace." Cythna agrees and assumes her role as liberator of the human race, asking, "Can man be free if woman be a slave?" (xxxvii; xliii).

Laon and Cythna part in Canto III to begin a series of separate yet parallel adventures. During their separation, however, Laon is consistently aware of a void within himself. After killing three of the tyrant's soldiers, Laon is taken captive and finds himself haunted by "Cythna's ghost," a "woman's shape, now lank and cold and blue, / The dwelling of the many-coloured worm" (xxvi). This passage recalls Blake's depiction of Albion's separation from Jerusalem and union with Vala, the embodiment of fallen Nature. While in prison Laon finds solace from a kindly old man who begins to nurse Laon's "inmost soul" (xxxi). The figure of the wise old man recurs throughout Shelley's poetry, most notably in "Prince Athanase," but here it is made clear that the old man is an idealized masculine projection of Laon that he has created as a substitute object in the absence of Cythna, whom he now remembers as but a "dream" (IV.iv).

But Laon separated from Cythna is an aging and increasingly weak being, while Cythna without Laon is initially triumphant, strong, and a potent force for social change. Where Laon fails in revolt, Cythna succeeds, and Laon learns while in prison that Cythna has overthrown the tyrant's power and made "Her sex the law of truth and freedom" (IV. xviii). Like Shelley's Asia and the Witch of Atlas, Cythna was "veiled" as she preached her messages of "equal laws and justice . . . To woman" (xix; xxi). But Laon has sunk even further into impotence, with "prematurely grey" hair and a face "lined / With channels" (xxix). He experiences himself as not only a fragmented being, but as severely psychically dislocated. When he looks in the mirror he does not see his own face, but sees himself as Cythna would see him. He experiences himself as uncanny, only vaguely familiar. It was

> . . . her brother's face—
> It might resemble her—it once had been
> The mirror of her thoughts, and still the grace
> Which her mind's shadow cast, left there a lingering trace.
> (xxx)

The passage, like so many in Shelley's poems, deals with a crisis of identity. Laon is forced to ask the haunting question, "What then was I?" (xxxi). Apart from union with his antitype, the self is empty, passive, aged, dangerously unbalanced. Without Cythna's actual presence,

Laon exists literally as her memory of him. He has forsaken his own conception of himself as a separate and complete man. This image of man decimated without the feminine is one of the most startling and unsettling Romantic versions of the sister. Without the feminine there is no psychic existence, health, or even reality for the male.

The situation reverses again at the beginning of Canto V when Cythna assumes the name of "Laone" (xix). Laon now is able to inspire the people to overthrow the tyrant, and his success is celebrated by a "sacred Festival, / A rite to attest the equality of all / Who live" (xxxvii). Appropriately, the rite that celebrates sexual equality is presided over by the veiled figure of Laone. Like the bearded Venus or the other androgynous deities who convened ancient rituals to celebrate the divine power of androgyny and its association with fertility, Laone addresses her song to the "Eldest of things, divine Equality!" She also endorses the freedom of "man and woman, / Their common bondage burst" (LI, 3–4). The festival celebrates typical Shelleyan ideologies—truth, joy, hope, and justice—while Laone presides as a sort of chiliastic female deity who has bestowed intellectual blessings but, like Blake's Jerusalem, remains veiled to shield lesser beings from the brightness of her beauty, or to disguise what we have come to recognize as the absence of the woman in the text.

The festival, clearly informed by the chiliasm so prevalent during the late eighteenth and early nineteenth centuries, comes to an end in Canto VI when the horsemen of a new tyrant descend upon the city. This image of an earthly apocalyptic utopia destroyed by violence tropes a common belief shared by virtually all the major Romantic poets. Their earlier belief in a literal apocalyptic transformation of society—shattered by the failure of the French Revolution—is later replaced by faith in a metaphorical, personal, and imaginative apocalypse. Laon, appropriately, is rescued from the ensuing battle by Cythna, once again the more dominant figure, who appears as "an Angel, robed in white" (xix). Brother and sister flee to a woods and consummate their love. This scene of incest, one of the few literal depictions of sexual love in Shelley's poetry, is filled with references to the regressive attraction of the womb, and of sexuality as deathly sleep:

> the sickness of a deep
> And speechless swoon of joy, as might befall
> Two disunited spirits when they leap
> In union from this earth's obscure and fading sleep.
> (xxxiv)

Laon and Cythna's sexual embrace is described as an effort to "blend two restless frames in one reposing soul" (xxxvi), suggesting again the essentially androgynous nature of the relationship. They are brother and sister, and yet they seek even more similarity; they seek to be one soul. The brother and sister perform their own marriage ceremony at this exact midpoint of the poem, but they achieve psychic and physical balance here only symbolically, briefly, tenuously.[22]

The next three cantos of the poem present a flashback account of Cythna's activities during her separation from Laon. In a series of sexual analogies, she has mirrored and mimicked his actions, for just as he was imprisoned in a phallic tower, so was she held captive in a womblike cave. The images neatly reflect the extreme sexual juxtaposition that occurred while they were separated and single-sexed identities. Without the other, each is trapped in a world of sexual extremity. Also like Laon's confusion as he looked in the mirror, Cythna suffered a madness in which she experienced identity confusion. During this madness she dreamt that she gave birth to a baby girl who looked exactly like Laon: "It was like thee, dear love, its eyes were thine, / Its brow, its lips. . . Thine own" (VII. xviii). E. B. Murray has claimed that this dream child was "at once the fruit of her spiritual communion (in the one mind) with Laon and her physical rape by the Tyrant." But the child can also be interpreted in light of nineteenth-century conceptions of idealized love as well as chiliastic fantasies about virgin births. According to Ortega y Gasset, the idealistic attitude claims that

> the rapture of love consists in feeling ourselves so metaphysically porous to another person that only in the fusion of both, only in an "individuality of two," can it find fulfillment. . . . Love is complete when it culminates in a more or less clear desire to leave, as testimony of the union, a child in whom the perfections of the beloved are perpetuated and affirmed.[23]

22. In "Incest in *Laon and Cythna*: Nature, Custom, Desire," *KSR* 2 [1987], 85), John Donovan has pointed out that the employment of androgynous imagery here suggests that the lovers desire fertility, "that absolute fertility which guarantees self-perpetuation and which made of eros androgyne the object of a religious cult in antiquity."

23. E. B. Murray, "'Elective Affinity' in *The Revolt of Islam*," *JEGP* 67 (1968), 578; José Ortega y Gasset, *On Love: Aspects of a Single Theme*, trans. Toby Talbot (Cleveland: Meridian, 1957), 36–37.

Such would seem to be the personal and political impulses behind Shelley's vision of the mysterious love child. But the dream child can also be read as an expression of the desire to give birth to an idealized version of the self in an attempt to symbolically replace one's own mother. The dream child, like the buried mother in *Alastor* and *Endymion,* tropes the solipsistic need of the male poet to attempt to render the entire universe as created and reflected by the self.

Cythna has profited from her experience in the cave because, like the Witch of Atlas, she has stolen the secrets that the cave contains: "human wisdom," "Necessity, and love, and life, the grave / And sympathy, fountains of hope and fear; / Justice, and truth" (VII. xxxi). After this necessary period of instruction, Cythna emerges from the cave and is restored to civilization by sailors who worship her as a deity. Like the many female messiahs of the period, Cythna instructs the sailors in the lesson of their own divinity. Shelley, like Blake, believed that to worship a God external to the self was to "mock yourselves" (VIII. v), and Cythna expresses this belief in her claim that the external Jupiter-deity was a creation of humanity's limited and mistaken perceptions. Ironically, however, this "innocent dream" has caused humanity to forsake the true divinity within itself, which is, according to Shelley's ideology, "To feel the peace of self-contentment's lot, / To own all sympathies, and outrage none . . . To live, as if to love and live were one" (xii).

Cythna begins her political activity by declaring that the roots of evil in this world are thrones on Heaven or Earth (xii), religious and political ideologies that place people in power over other people. According to Cythna's incipient feminism, all political systems culminate in the oppression of women. Rather than being the agents of love in this world, women are the victims of venereal diseases that cause them to be "bond slaves . . . [so that] life is poisoned in its wells" (xiii). Cythna, like Blake's Oothoon, inspires women to arise and see that love is "free to fill / The world, like light" (xvi). She preaches that the only way "all will be free and equal" is by destroying "the dark idolatry of self" (xxii). Cythna, then, begins her campaign for the liberation of the great City in Canto IX. Like so many mythic heroes and heroines whose birth is mysterious and whose identity is uncertain, Cythna is thought by the populace to be a "maniac," "the Prophet's virgin bride, a heavenly ghost," "the child of God, sent down to save / Women" (viii). The apocalyptic conclusion of her political activities allows Cythna to establish temporarily a utopia. As a feminine Christ-like redeemer, she rejoins Laon in a symbolically androgynous ideal, brother and sister joined momentarily in a perfect political harmony that reflects their fictionally sustained sexual equality. But this millennial mood does not last long, even for Cythna. Almost immediately, Cythna expresses her realization that no external utopia can survive, that paradise must be within "thine own heart" (xxvi).

The tyrant's horsemen descend upon the utopian City and destroy it in Canto X. Laon is captured and Cythna voluntarily joins him at the stake in Canto XI, facing death with an almost sexual fervor. Her eyes are filled with "a light / Of liquid tenderness like love," while her lips are "warm and odorous" (v–vi). The two are led to the pyre in Canto XII, where they burn at the stake in a passage that recalls their earlier sexual union as well as the myth of the phoenix, which Shelley was to employ again in an escapist gesture at the conclusion of *Epipsychidion.* During their executions they bask in "Looks of insatiate love" (xv) and awake to find themselves sitting around a clear, flower-decked pool. They are then escorted to "The Temple of the Spirit," the abode of the same androgynous form that presided over Canto I, by their mysterious dream child, the prototype and psychic emblem of their fictitious androgynous unity.

Laon and Cythna reads as a curious, almost surreal poem, and its strangeness stems from the dual nature of the poetic personae—Laon/Cythna—one fictitiously androgynous being who periodically splits into two throughout the poem. Every time the composite being splits, however, each half-self feels inadequate, sinks into madness, and attempts various means of restoring the original androgynous condition. Thus Cythna gives birth to a version of herself who is identical with Laon, while Laon attempts to fill the void in his partial identity by creating a version of himself in the old man. Like Blake's epics, *Laon and Cythna* is a poem about the fictional lure of incorporating both the masculine and feminine components into the (androgynous) psyche. This ideology claims that either of the sexes alone is weak, impotent, stricken with a sense of psychic insufficiency. But the effort to achieve a literally "real" androgynous union will always be censored by the culture because it threatens the framework of society. Truly equal status for men and women, which is represented in the radical vision of androgyny in *Laon and Cythna,* threatens the political and social institutions that are founded on the subordination of women, with men acting as willing accomplices in oppression, thereby dehumanizing themselves in the process. The ideal androgyny of Laon and Cythna can exist, ultimately, only in the spiritual realm, beyond the assaults of tyranny. Shelley the political activist was committed to radical goals, to nothing less than the transformation of minds and social systems. Shelley the poet, however, was forced to conclude this artistic celebration of the revolutionary *beau ideal* in the Platonic realm. In the deaths of Laon and Cythna, he admits, in effect, the failure of his effort to transform the androgynous ideology, to make woman something other than merely a historically conditioned cultural construct.

Laon and Cythna has been celebrated as "the most powerful feminist poem in the language," a poem that advocates "full sexual integration" and "militant" feminism. Indeed, Nathaniel Brown goes so far as to claim that Shelley wanted to get away from the notion of gender altogether in favor of "androgynization" of the sexes, which Brown defines as "the release of opposite-sex elements of the self, so that in their increasing synthesis or integration, men and women will truly reflect or reduplicate one another."[24] In choosing to depict this union as an incestuous one between a brother and sister, Shelley self-consciously worked in the ancient alchemical traditions that saw such a merger as beneficent and powerful. The solipsism of the effort, however, undermines its efficacy even as a literary convention. Even Shelley recognized that the androgynous existed only as a desired goal, an elusive mirage, perhaps even a false siren, but never as a reality that could be sustained as a vehicle for social reform.

III Byron: "And loved each other as we should not love"

Mario Praz has asserted, one would hope facetiously, that Byron committed incest with his half-sister Augusta in order to plagiarize Chateaubriand's *René* and thus be able to write *Manfred*. Indeed, the spectre of *René*—the sister as forbidden and fatal love object—haunts English Romantic poetry's depictions of women as narcissistic and solipsistic projections of the hero. Jerome McGann has similarly observed that the "female counterparts of Byron's heroes . . . correspond exactly to the state of the hero's soul which they inhabit. They objectify the passionate impulses in the man whose imagination made them what

24. Brown sees the poem as advocating "the total annihilation of the traditional gender stereotypes and sex roles" into some "mono- or unisexuality" (see his *Sexuality and Feminism in Shelley* [Cambridge: Harvard University Press, 1979], 224). Hogle's discussion of the poem, "Narcissism and the Gaze of the Other in *Laon and Cythna*," contains a provocative analysis of the sibling relationship within both Freudian and Sartrean paradigms (see his *Shelley's Process*, 96–103).

they are. This is as much to say that none of them are truly 'persons.' "[25] As a "Poem in dialogue," Byron's *Manfred* utilizes incest, narcissism, solipsism, and massive egoism to depict the struggle between the individual masculine mind and the feminine principle. Douglas Bush has observed that Byron's "Prometheus" is the best example of his mythological bent, but that description might be better applied to *Manfred.* In this poetic drama, Byron acts as a supreme mythmaker who depicts the self/hero as both creator and created, for Byron fictionalizes his own life's events in such a way that the drama presents the self struggling for unification and/or individuation by wrestling with forces of cosmic and mythic proportion. Manfred sets himself up as his own god, a supreme masculine power seeking dominion over those forces he feels most directly impinge on his existence. The fact that he fails to control anything except his own suicide suggests Byron's skepticism about the significance and value of the romantic egotist (otherwise known as the Byronic hero).

D. H. Lawrence once observed about Byron that he was a "man who is female as well as male, and who lives according to the female side of his nature." The fact that Lawrence made this statement is interesting in and of itself; however, his observation throws light on the curious interrelation between the life and art of Byron. Critics, of course, have taken to ignoring the life of the artist in preference to a close explication or deconstruction of the texts. But, as Paul West points out about Byron, "To try excluding the man is eventually to discover that little of the poetry can stand alone." All of which brings us to the question of Byron's incestuous relationship with Augusta. Is the source of *Manfred,* as Andrew Rutherford has claimed, incestuous guilt over the relationship with Augusta?[26] Byron himself claimed that the sources for the drama were some passages of a journal he was writing for Augusta while traveling through the Alps. The convergence here of a powerful

25. McGann, *Fiery Dust: Byron's Poetic Development* (Chicago: University of Chicago Press, 1968), 189.

26. All quotations from Byron's *Manfred* are from *Lord Byron: The Complete Poetical Works,* ed. Jerome McGann (Oxford: Oxford University Press, 1986), vol. 4. All quotations from Byron's works, except *Sardanapalus,* are from this edition, with line numbers in parentheses in the text. Bush's comment was made in his *Mythology and the Romantic Tradition* (Cambridge: Harvard University Press, 1937), 71; D. H. Lawrence's comment was made in his "Study of Thomas Hardy," in *Phoenix: The Post-Humous Papers of D. H. Lawrence,* ed. Edward McDonald (New York: Viking, 1936; rpt. 1968), 459; Paul West's comment was made in his "Introduction" to *Byron: A Collection of Critical Essays,* ed. West, 1. See also Andrew Rutherford, *Byron: A Critical Study* (Stanford: Stanford University Press, 1961), 78.

vision of the Imaginary/semiotic mountains with the memory of his sister's love is significant in itself. In his "Epistle to Augusta," Byron acknowledged that contemplating the Alps brought back memories of his sister: "Oh that thou wert but with me!—but I grow / The fool of my own wishes" (9). His wishes transform the natural scene, his memory of semiotic oneness with the mother/sister, into the reassuring knowledge that "in thy heart / I know myself secure, as thou in mine." The love that unites them, according to Byron's fiction, forms a mystical bond of similarity and connection: "We were and are—I am, even as thou art— / Beings who ne'er each other can resign" (16). Byron makes clear here that the strongest "tie" he has ever experienced is the one that connects him to Augusta, his half-sister, his second self. Their attachment is almost imaged as if they were one person; the sameness of their identities is resounded throughout the poem and in an analogous fashion in the relationship of Manfred and Astarte.

In *Manfred* we get Byronic solipsism in its purest form, distilled and potent. Manfred loves himself totally; that is, his supposed love for Astarte, his dead sister, is but an expression of his love for himself, for ultimately she is a projection of his own mind. Because the "real" Astarte failed him, he has created an ideal feminine counterpart—the fantasy Astarte, the solipsistic phantom of a woman. The phantom Astarte, like the veiled maiden in Shelley's *Alastor,* exists within the imagination of Manfred, and, as with the poet of *Alastor,* the mental image of the beloved is ultimately a feminine projection of the hero, so that Manfred is actually in love with himself, wallowing more and more deeply in solipsism and narcissism. Manfred finally twists his emotions and ultimately rejects them, just as he rejects the "real" Astarte because he prefers the phantom feminine within his own mind.

In discussing his use of the incest theme, Byron referred to its use by "the best of our old English writers," and by Alfieri, Schiller, and Gibbon. Robert Gleckner, however, dismisses the incest in *Manfred* by claiming that it is not central to the poem's meaning; in fact, the incest is only "a kind of sensationalism" that obscures the poem's real meaning, which is "the tragedy of the infinite mind and the finite human heart, eternally in unresolved conflict, the one destructive of the other, each destructive of itself." But in Gleckner's very vocabulary we again see an example of a critic who uncritically shares and reinforces the very mythologies of the poets (this time, the self-justifying pose of the Byronic hero is accepted at face value).[27]

27. Robert Gleckner, *Byron and the Ruins of Paradise* (Baltimore: Johns Hopkins University Press, 1967), 258. For the fullest discussion of the cultural background for Byron's evolution of the "Byronic hero," see Peter Thorslev, *The*

Manfred can more accurately be read as the struggle between the masculine and feminine principles for dominion of the (male) self. That struggle actually occurs as a form of psychic incest within the mind of Manfred, where his own masculine identity wars against and finally defeats the self-created fantasy of Astarte. Thus love and the feminine principle within Manfred are embodied in the phantom Astarte, the idea of Astarte, while the "real" Astarte functions on another level, less symbolically, as helpmate to Manfred in his scientific ventures. The fact that we can distinguish the two polarized female forms in this way—the feminine within and the actual remembered (but conveniently dead) woman—suggests that the struggle for Manfred is to unify not only his own mind, but his attitudes toward the female as well. The two forces—masculine and feminine—are hopelessly at war with one another and create the sustaining and central metaphor for the drama. Astarte's suicide, induced by Manfred, is meant to represent a sundering of their powerful fantasy of an original androgynous self. Manfred, like Blake's Urizen, thinks he can deny Astarte and find divinity only through his reason, his mind writ large and projected onto all objects of nature. He has aligned himself with the ideology that knowledge or the omnipotence of the male mind can only be obtained through cannibalization and destruction of the feminine principle.

In order to begin a close examination of the text of *Manfred,* we need to look first at the larger structure of the drama.[28] Act I depicts Manfred speaking to seven Spirits of the Air, the seventh one appearing to be Astarte. Act II includes Manfred's conversations with the Chamois Hunter (representative of sane humanity) and the Witch of the Alps (symbol of the power of transcendent Nature). The three Destinies, Nemesis, and the Spirits also appear, but the conversations again revolve around the nature, identity, and absence of Astarte. In Act III the Abbot and the servants Manual and Herman displace the Chamois Hunter as representatives of those mortals who possess ordinary vision, and are not as tortured or unique as Manfred. And they discuss—what else?—Astarte. Throughout the entire structure of the drama, Astarte is, if not actually present, even more dominant through her absence.[29] She is, finally, the woman as self-erasing cipher, the phantom woman as eradicated, metaphorically present only in her absence.

Byronic Hero: Types and Prototypes (Minneapolis: University of Minnesota Press, 1962).

28. Critics have seen *Manfred* as a "confused mixture of genres," with the hero as both agent and opponent of evil; for instance, see David Eggenschwiler, "Tragic and Comic Rhythms of *Manfred*," *SIR* 13 [1974], 72).

29. William H. Marshall, *The Structure of Byron's Major Poems* (Philadel-

Byron described *Manfred* in a letter to Murray as "very wild, metaphysical, and inexplicable." With those words in mind, this reading will trace the solipsistic impulse in the drama, connected as it is with the (failed and fictitious) androgynous quest throughout Byron's work. Manfred is introduced in I.i while he ruminates in his castle in the Alps about the nature of knowledge. He concludes:

> Sorrow is knowledge: they who know the most
> Must mourn the deepest o'er the fatal truth,
> The tree of Knowledge is not that of Life.
> (10–12)

The "fatal truth" that the tree of Knowledge has bestowed on man is, of course, that he is doomed, fallen, a "blighted trunk upon a cursed root" (Manfred's description of himself in I.ii.68)—in other words, castrated. In identical fashion the image of a cursed root was used by Blake, Coleridge, and Shelley to suggest the sterility of the isolated and phallic masculine principle, divorced from the self-created and projected feminine. Byron suggests the same about Manfred, who knows that there is a "strong curse . . . upon my Soul" (I.i.47). When the Spirits of the Air first appear to Manfred they appear through his own conjurations and specifically as emblems for "The thought which is within me and around me" (I.i.48). It would seem, then, that the Spirits appear as aspects of Manfred's fragmented and splintered psyche, as projections of his "mind," his thoughts (I.i.182). Who, then, is the seventh Spirit who asks Manfred, "'What wouldst thou, Child of Clay! with me?'" This Spirit, taking "the shape of a beautiful female figure," returns from within Manfred's mind to haunt him. He asks her for "Forgiveness . . . Of that which is within me," and for "Oblivion, self-oblivion" (I.i.131; 135–37; 145). But Manfred is dissembling here. He does not really want to forget his relationship with Astarte; he wants to resume it. But it is

phia: University of Pennsylvania Press, 1962), sees Manfred as the dominating presence in the drama, even when he is not present (97). In support of my reading, John W. Ehrstine sees Astarte as "central" to the drama and omnipresent whether in the form of star, spirit, or woman (see his *The Metaphysics of Byron: A Reading of the Plays* [The Hague: Mouton, 1976], 19). More recently, Cynthia Baer has seen Astarte as the tainted component of the androgynous quest: "here the image of wholeness is problematic, for union with the ideal is tainted by sin and leads, not to restoration of life, but to death. . . . Love, the imagination, myth, all are, according to Byron, tainted at the source—a human source like Manfred, by his very nature divided and therefore limited" (see her "'Lofty Hopes of Divine Liberty,'" *RP&P* 9 [1985], 44–45).

not the "real" Astarte he desires. He actually wants to become the lover of the phantom Astarte, the feminine that he has created and sustained in his own mind. Manfred concludes his visit with these inner projections with a curse:

> 'By thy delight in others' pain,
> And by thy brotherhood of Cain,
> I call upon thee! and compel
> Thyself to be thy proper Hell!'
> (I.i.248–51)

Like Milton's Satan or the Prisoner of Chillon, Manfred is condemned to live within his own mind, but it is a mind both sterile and devoid of the feminine qualities he both seeks and repels, a mind that cannot appreciate the splendors of the mountains or the sun because "thou shin'st not on my heart" (I.ii.12). Obviously Manfred cannot experience beauty because he has denied his feminine component, and he knows this, commenting as he contemplates suicide that he wears within himself "This barrenness of spirit," creating his "own Soul's sepulchre" (I.i.26–27). Manfred claims at this point that his misery is caused by the hopeless and paradoxical condition of humanity, to be "Half dust, half deity, alike unfit / To sink or soar" (I.ii.40–44).

Although Manfred begs the appropriately phallic crags of ice to crush him, he is rescued instead by the Chamois Hunter who hears in disjointed and wandering words a confession of incest from Manfred, who admits:

> I say 'tis blood—my blood! the pure warm stream
> Which ran in the veins of my fathers, and in ours
> When we were in our youth, and had one heart,
> And loved each other as we should not love.
> (II.i.24–27)

This incestuous love for his sister, the "real" Astarte, caused Manfred to be "shut out from Heaven" (II.i.29), and it is here that the similarity to Chateaubriand's *René* becomes very obvious. Manfred is then compelled to describe Astarte to the Witch of the Alps, whom he has conjured up for some insight into the Eternal. At this point he confesses the strange attraction that Astarte has had for him because she was a feminized version of him:

She was like me in lineaments—her eyes,
Her hair, her features, all, to the very tone
Even of her voice, they said were like to mine;
But soften'd all, and temperd into beauty;
She had the same lone thoughts and wanderings,
The quest of hidden knowledge, and a mind
To comprehend the Universe.

(II.ii.105–11)

In this description, however, we can clearly distinguish between the two Astartes—at least as far as Manfred himself has differentiated them. The "real" Astarte's attraction for Manfred is first of all physical; she embodies the same external characteristics as her brother (facial features, eyes, hair, voice) and therefore actually mirrors him. The idea/ideal Astarte embodies Manfred's internal qualities (intellectual interests, type of mind, and habits of thought) and also reaffirms his quest for knowledge at any price. The two Astartes function here, as has been widely noted, as mirror images of the hero. Manfred has managed to create a woman and an idea of woman, both of whom are as like him as possible, physically and intellectually. He has, in effect, created a female version of himself, a sister/twin who mirrors him as closely as possible.

The fantasy of having a twin, as Melanie Klein has observed, is intrinsically connected with the need to be understood and accepted by an internalized good object. Klein's observations are particularly pertinent as far as Manfred is concerned: The fantasy twin "represents those un-understood and split off parts which the individual is longing to regain, in the hope of achieving wholeness and complete understanding; they are sometimes felt to be the ideal parts."[30]

But Astarte also has qualities that are not present in Manfred, and it is her specifically feminine values that he most needs in order to be a complete being: "Her faults were mine—her virtues were her own— / I loved her, and destroy'd her!" (II.ii.113–17). The last refrain compulsively repeats throughout the drama, and can actually be inverted: I destroyed her because I loved her. Earlier Manfred stated that "my injuries came down on those who loved me— . . . my embrace was fatal" (II.i.85–88). Although he did not literally kill Astarte, he figuratively did so by forcing her to witness the "withered" being he actually was. He almost boasts to the Witch that he destroyed Astarte,

30. Melanie Klein, *Envy and Gratitude and Other Works, 1946–63* (New York: Dell, 1975), 302.

> Not with my hand, but heart—which broke her heart—
> It gazed on mine, and withered. I have shed
> Blood, but not hers—and yet her blood was shed—
> I saw—and could not staunch it.
>
> (II.ii.118–21)

These self-pitying statements serve to reinforce a point made earlier, as well as Praz's claim about the use of the incest motif. For Praz, Byron needed to use incest because only that sin was serious enough to create in him a sense of guilt and fatality, both of which reveal a sadomasochistic desire to play the "incubus-devil with his victim." He is able to both torture himself over his sins and relive throughout the play the satisfaction he experienced by knowing that he caused his beloved such agony that she committed suicide to be free of him. The spiral of guilt and crime continues indefinitely. One is reminded here of both Nietzsche's theories on the will to power, and Sartre's comments on all "love" as sadomasochistic master-slave relationships, dances of subjectivity and alterity. Manfred both enjoys his own sufferings and the sufferings he has caused Astarte. But has Astarte participated in her own destruction? Garber claims that because she shared so many of Manfred's qualities, Astarte must also have shared in their dangerous faults and therefore brought her destruction down on herself: "Aspects of their continuity had undone the continuity, recoiling upon themselves and fracturing the wholeness he is now so painfully reseeking."[31] Is this not, however, simply another way of blaming the female victim? But Manfred can have no wholeness as an exclusively male self, and the full implications of this realization form the text of the drama. In the concluding words of his confession to the Witch of the Alps, he asks:

> What is she?
> What is she now?—a sufferer for my sins—
> A thing I dare not think upon—or nothing.
>
> (II.ii.193–98)

31. Mario Praz, "Metamorphoses of Satan," in *Byron*, ed. Paul West (Englewood Cliffs, NJ: Prentice-Hall, 1963), 48; Garber, *Self, Text, and Irony*, 133. Bernard Grebanier discusses at length (and with dubious sources) the incestuous relationship between Byron and Augusta in *The Uninhibited Byron: An Account of His Sexual Confusion* (New York: Crown, 1970). More recently, Louis Crompton (in *Byron and Greek Love: Homophobia in 19th-Century England* [Berkeley: University of California Press, 1985], 370–71n) has tried to see Manfred's anguish as a reflection of Byron's guilt over his own bisexuality.

What is Astarte? The nature of Astarte as self-consuming psychic artifact, the woman as both "thing" and "nothing," constitutes the central image of the drama. Not only do we hear again about love as the cause of her destruction, but we begin to understand the compulsion under which Manfred labors. He has had to disembody her; he has had to make her into an idea, a concept of the feminine, rather than a "real" woman because the fact of her physical reality was simply too threatening, too overwhelming to him. A real woman—even a sister—poses issues such as difference, individuality, separateness, whereas the idea of a woman can be infinitely malleable, continually cooperative since she is, after all, a self-created projection.

In the final scene in Act II, within the Hall of Arimanes, Manfred uses his conjuring powers to call up the phantom Astarte from the tomb, and begs her to either forgive or condemn him. She refuses to do either and stands as an emblem of all those feminine qualities he has rejected within himself. He goes on to try to reason with this projection, in a speech that smacks of the same sort of deceit he has used before. For instance, he claims:

> Thou lovedst me
> Too much, as I loved thee: we were not made
> To torture thus each other, though it were
> The deadliest sin to love as we have loved.
> (II.iv.121–24)

The "deadliest sin" can be either incest, sadomasochistic torture, or solipsism, though all of these crimes in the final analysis stem from the same psychic syndrome. As we have seen before, however, the attraction in the relationship between Manfred and both Astartes has resided in the torture/self-torture syndrome, as well as the incestuous mirroring and narcissism that have been evidenced. Manfred has killed his real sister not to be free of her, but in order to possess her more fully in his mind.

As the final spokesman for sane humanity, the Abbot of St. Maurice tells Manfred that he "should have been a noble creature . . . as it is, / It is an awful chaos—light and darkness— / And mind and dust—and passions and pure thoughts" (III.i.160–65). Manfred, he implies, has been destroyed by succumbing to the fiction that the feminine can and must live only within the male. But by this time Manfred has returned to his tower, an appropriate image of his allegiance to the Symbolic realm, with its endorsement of phallic, isolated, and solitary power. The servants, though, state that at one time Manfred had worked in harmony in the tower with Astarte, "The sole companion of his wanderings / And watchings—her, whom of all earthly things / That lived, the only thing he seem'd to love" (III.iii.43–45). But that only "thing" is now gone, and Manfred only "seemed" to love her anyway. The insubstantiality of Astarte is persistently emphasized; not only is she a "thing," less than human, but she is consistently a void, a hole, an absence. Manfred could no more find solace with the "real" Astarte than he could with the phantom Astarte. His infatuation with solipsism has led him to embrace the spectre of his masculine self—his "genius"—who beckons him to his death (III.iv.81). Manfred dies praising those masculine values that have led him to his demise; he praises even in his final moments his "superior science," and his "strength of mind—and skill" (III.iv.115–16). His final realization, though, is consistent with his dilemma throughout. He declares that

> The mind which is immortal makes itself
> Requital for its good or evil thoughts—
> Is its own origin of ill and end—
> And its own place and time.
> (III.iv.129–32)

Manfred's mind has indeed been its own place (the isolated male tower) and its own time (suspended in a self-created vacuum between past and present). His mind is not able to survive the absence of Astarte, and yet he sought to destroy her through domination and then rejection. Herein lies the cause of his solipsistic predicament. The fantasy of the Byronic hero as solipsist posits a tragic individual who has destroyed the only other self who ever existed for him, and yet he is fated to destroy her by his very real psychic demands for complete cannibalization of the feminine. Through equal union with the "real" and living Astarte, Manfred could have tempered his own narrow masculine selfhood, but instead both Manfred and Astarte reject that possibility and die as a result. One recalls here Girard's definition of a "Romantic Solipsist" as one who desires autonomy against the other and internalizes the master-slave dialectic, as well as Freud's description of the solipsistic woman.[32] For the "real" Astarte is as much a solipsist as Manfred, a woman compelled because of the traits she shared

32. René Girard, *Deceit, Desire and the Novel,* trans. Yvonne Freccero (Baltimore: Johns Hopkins University Press, 1965), 287. See Kofman's analysis of Freud's depiction of the solipsistic woman, as well as her critique of Girard, in

with her brother to deny his reality and to seek in love only her own self-aggrandizement. One has to conclude that on some level Byron explored in *Manfred* the inherent flaws and limitations of Romantic love as ideology for both men and women.

The causes of Manfred's problems are manifold. In many ways his dilemma is spiritual as well as psychic. He cannot accept his identity as a singular male identity; he is postlapsarian man bemoaning his separation from the feminine principle. Manfred and the "real" Astarte are divided and "fallen" specifically because they have split away from or fragmented the original unity that would comprise their fictionally androgynous divinity. Further, the nature and function of Astarte as both real woman and idealized fantasy causes considerable confusion for Manfred. On the one hand, Manfred's desired union with the real Astarte is similar to a young adolescent boy's longing for an idyllic relationship with his sister as a second self, so much like the self that her sexual identity as "other" does not overwhelm or threaten him. On the other hand, the phantom Astarte functions as the feminine within, a sort of mother with whom Manfred wishes to merge as into a preoedipal and all-encompassing relationship. But ultimately it makes little difference what feminine role Astarte plays in relation to Manfred, whether mother or sister (which is, as we have seen, simply a displaced image of the mother anyway). The important factor for Manfred is that Astarte is both the feminine within and the woman as "other," and both avatars of the female have to be accepted and embraced by the male hero.

Whether Byron chose to develop the theme of incest because of ideological or biographical reasons can never be, and indeed, need never be answered. The fact is that he did explore in a profound and ambivalent manner the inherent difficulties implicit in the ideology of androgyny. If, as Gleckner has claimed, "Byron gave a fairly clear indication that he sees man as temperamentally hermaphroditic—femininely creative, warm and human, masculinely destructive, cold, and inhuman: the heart of a woman, the mind of a man," [33] then it is possible to conclude

---

her chapter "The Narcissistic Woman" from *The Enigma of Woman*, 50–65. Girard's reading of Freud's depiction of woman in "On Narcissism" is published as "Narcissism: The Freudian Myth Demythified by Proust," in *Psychoanalysis, Creativity, and Literature*, ed. Alan Roland (New York: Columbia University Press, 1978), 391–414, and has provoked a fair amount of feminist critique: Toril Moi, "The Missing Mother: The Oedipal Rivalries of René Girard," *Diacritics* (1982), 21–31; Elizabeth Berg, "The Third Woman," *Diacritics* 12 (1982), 11–20.

33. Gleckner, *Byron and the Ruins of Paradise*, 145.

that some sort of androgyny is at the root of Byron's vision of human nature and psychic destiny. Byron may have recognized and indeed shared his culture's essential impulse to escape extreme sexual caricatures, but his heroes persistently end instead in postures of ironic polarization and fragmentation.

There is no final fictional synthesis of masculine and feminine in Byron's characters, only the juxtaposition of sexual extremities. The image of incestuous love appears throughout his work, then, submerged as a subtext. This idea of love between aspects of the same (male) self represents the psyche's attempts to love portions of a fragmented self desperately seeking union once more, but not, of course, recovering it. It is a fact that Byron experimented with incestuous love in both his poetry and his life. More than the other Romantic poets, he was able to live out the fantasy, enact the mythos, literalize the poetic obsessions of his age. That Manfred suffers and dies isolated, punished, and alone reveals that Byron's poetic vision caused him to expose the inherent limitations and the fictions of his own self-created fantasies. But in the very act of exposing the illusions we see only another even more pernicious illusion—that the poet can deflate the pretensions and ideologies of his age. Ironically, then, the Byronic hero and his fantasy woman stand finally as ideological constructions that participate in and indeed even reinforce the very gender limitations that Byron was ostensibly trying to attack.

3

The Beloved: "Sometimes I curse & sometimes bless thy fascinating beauty"

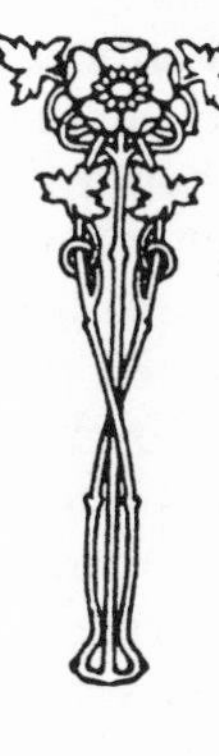

In 1841 one Goodwyn Barmby married a Catherine Watkins, having met her while both were working for the Central Communist Propaganda Society in London. The two soon became the founders of the Communist Church, a chiliastic cult, and styled themselves as the rightful spiritual heirs of Mary Wollstonecraft and Percy Shelley. In fact, Barmby used a passage from Shelley's *Revolt of Islam* to preface his best-known essay, "The Man-Power, the Woman-Power, and the Man-Woman Power," a document that elevates marriage to the status of an androgynous sacrament, declaring:

> In fine, to be a true communist, or Socialist, the man must possess the woman-power as well as the man-power, and the woman must possess the man-power as well as the woman-power. Both must be equilibriated beings. . . . Grace be to those in whom woman-nature and man-nature are at present equilibriated and active. We hail them as true priests of humanity, as the veritable social apostles.

In a similar vein, Robert Southey summed up Saint Simonian doctrine by stating that "the *social individual,* which has hitherto been the *man* alone, henceforth shall be the *man and wife,* presenting politically thus the perfect Androgyne of philosophical fable." [1] Somehow,

1. See Barmby's article in *The New Moral World; The Educational Circular and Communist Apostle* (1 May 1841) and Southey's comments pub-

amidst the era's political, social, religious, and sexual upheaval, during the uproar over the Owenite's proposals to reform marriage laws, the bourgeoisie came to believe that marriage to a beloved woman would redeem both a man's mind and his home. This ideology became a dominant middle-class fantasy, so pervasive that it informed virtually all the representations we have of women in Victorian fiction and poetry. Earlier in the century, however, the Romantic poets presented the beloved female—not to mention marriage—with a good deal more irony and self-conscious deflation.

While the colonization of the buried mother led the Romantic hero to the regression of the womb/tomb or the preoedipal malaise of entropy, the sister led him to the self-destructive mirroring of narcissism and solipsism. The Romantic woman as beloved, however, initially leads to a poetic idealization of active engagement with the world of the senses, the body as androgynous. In order to understand this aspect of the woman within, however, it is necessary to know that androgyny has traditionally been troped two distinctly different ways. In the first and most prevalent way, it exists as a totally psychic ideal within the mind of the hero—and in this case the woman is not a "real" woman external to the male but the embodiment of the feminine qualities within the mind of a hero. Yet androgyny can also be depicted as a "marriage" between a literal man and woman so that the union of these two people symbolically constitutes the achievement of the androgynous ideal on a physical level. This second type of androgyny generally employs traditional sexual polarization, with the man representing reason and intellect while the woman possesses emotional and sympathetic characteristics. Androgyny as hierogamy, mystical marriage, exists as a form of radical heterosexuality, a celebration of sexuality as a manifestation of a transforming religious power. In English Romanticism, as well as in a number of mythic traditions, the woman as beloved has functioned as the hero's savior, the means by which he gains self-realization and full identity. As Joseph Campbell has observed, "the mystical marriage with the queen goddess of the world represents the hero's total mastery of life; for the woman is life, the hero its knower and master."[2]

---

lished in *The Quarterly Review* 89 (1831), 443. The career of the Barmbys and the Owenite movement are discussed at length in Taylor, *Eve and the New Jerusalem*, 172–82.

2. Joseph Campbell, *The Hero with a Thousand Faces* (Princeton: Princeton University Press, 1949), 120–21.

In one of his sexual fantasies, one of his self-created fictions, the Romantic hero, trying to escape from both the narcissistic mother and sister, reaches out beyond himself to woman as "Other," this time not simply a version of the self, but a beloved who is an instrument or extension of the divine. It would seem that the hero has finally matured to the point that he can recognize the woman as an equal, a person existing in her own right, external to the male self. But, in fact, very few examples of successfully maintained erotic relationships between "real" male characters and "real" female characters occur in English Romantic poetry, and the reason lies, I believe, in the impossibility of the androgynous ideal. The ideal itself required nothing less than apotheotic transformation of self and other into some sort of dual cosmic deity, and in light of this fearful burden the poets found themselves retreating into ironically deflated or defeatist postures. As the poet realizes the impossibility of finding salvation through the beloved, he turns to depicting caricatures of her. In one mode, she is the vicious and destructive *femme fatale,* woman as devouring sexual predator, the *vagina dentata.* In her other and alternate manifestation, she is the muse, an asexual mentor who inspires the poet/hero to idealize a world in which women are finally unthreatening because their power is contained and appropriated only by males.

The Romantic poets themselves found some of their favorite reading material in continental works that stressed the new feminine ideology, one that presented the feminine as a religious power in an increasingly complex world that was seeking a new spiritual force. Rousseau's *Julie,* for instance, or Goethe's *Faust,* provided their readers with idealized heroines who functioned as semidivine, as inspirations for the befuddled and confused egotistical males who served as their heroes. A. W. von Schlegel's *Lucinde* and de la Motte-Fouqué's *Undine* both presented Germanic visions of the feminine that also proved tremendously influential in an age that saw woman as both victim and victimizer. Schlegel's *Lucinde,* for example, states that love for an ideal beloved is not merely a transition from the mortal to the immortal, but instead produces a complete union of the two states. Such a notion of the beloved is also implicit in the fictional androgynous unions depicted in the poetry of Blake, Byron's *Sardanapalus,* Shelley's *Epipsychidion* and *Prometheus Unbound,* and Keats's *Eve of St. Agnes.*

Just as the spirit of Beatrice Cenci haunts the topic of Romantic incest, so does another Beatrice—Dante's—preside over any discussion of Romantic Eros. This other Beatrice combines in her functions and meaning the roles of feminine guide, muse, anima, and religious power for the male poet. She further represents the escape from the dreaded solipsism that had haunted the poetry of English Romanticism. The poets were, to a certain extent, compelled to seek versions of her in their works, just as all of us, according to Freudian fiction, are compelled to love in order to escape our infantile narcissism. In "On Narcissism" (1914), Freud quotes Heine's fantasy that God created the world as a psychogenesis, motivated by the urge to escape his solipsism: "Illness was no doubt the final cause of the whole urge to create. By creating, I could recover; by creating, I became healthy." Building on this tenuous structure of poetic fantasy, Freud observes that a "strong egoism is a protection against falling ill, and we are bound to fall ill if, in consequence of frustration, we are unable to love" (*SE* XIV:85). Such an impulse would appear to be the motivating factor in idealizing woman as Beatrice. In other words, although the narcissism may be somewhat bemuted and submerged in poetry that depicts the embrace of the beloved, there can be no doubt that a good deal of solipsistic mirroring and eventual absorption of the female still occurs in most Romantic love relationships.[3]

In their analyses of nineteenth-century German and French literature, both Busst and Furness make similar points about the use of androgynous love relationships, claiming that androgyny could only be an ideal in an age "whose literature stresses the ultimate loneliness of each individual, the impossibility of significant human relationships and the almost inevitable disillusionment of sexual love." The androgynous image, in fact, is strangely discomforting; it is a

> further paradigm of the terrible inability of an age to bestow love upon the world. The soul that finds its opposite within itself and shrinks from commitments of intercourse with that which is outside (at most a brother-sister relationship is permitted) is yet one more witness to the devaluation of life and the ever-present awareness of nihilism.[4]

3. For discussions of the conflict between idealizing marriage as a poetic metaphor and the disappointing real-life marriages of the poets, see Susan M. Levin, "'The Great Spousal Verse': The Marriage Metaphor in English Romantic Poetry," *SCR* 8 (1975), 5–12, and Sarah McKim Webster, "Circumspection and the Female in the Early Romantics," *PQ* 61 (1982), 51–70.

4. A. J. L. Busst, "The Androgyne in the Nineteenth Century," in *Romantic Mythologies*, ed. Ian Fletcher, 10–11; Raymond Furness, "The Androgynous Ideal: Its Significance in German Literature," *MLR* 60 (1965), 64.

German literature persistently utilizes the alchemical concept of the Uroboros, the tail-eating serpent, which symbolizes the attempt of an individual to find perfection within and through itself, to be its own origins and end. For both Coleridge and Keats in particular, the woman as serpent will appear not as an image of perfect selfhood or individuality, but as an omen of the sterility and fearful consequences that come from loving women as aspects of the male psyche, as essentially masturbatory extensions of the male self.

A late nineteenth-century theorist on Eros, Emil Lucka asserts that there have been three stages of love in the development of human history. The first stage, according to Lucka, is manifested in the sexual instinct of the ancient world, the second in the deification of woman during the medieval period, and the third in the attempt to blend sexuality with love since the eighteenth century. According to Lucka, the latest stage was celebrated by the Romantic poets, who ostensibly elevated love to a religion that gave equal prominence to both the body and the spirit. For Lucka, Romantic love should then be described as a form of psychic escapism:

> Inevitably there arises in the soul the desire and the will to escape, together with the beloved, the insufferable solitude of existence; to achieve in death what life denies; to realize another, a higher condition, divined in dreams and seen in visions; to become one with the beloved, to transform all human existence into a new divine universal existence: 'Then I myself am the world!' Everything individual, all life, is blotted out; the death of lovers from love and through love is the mystic portal of a higher state of being.[5]

Stendhal, a more influential nineteenth-century theorist on the nature of love, sees the erotic as essentially a form of narcissism and a fiction. In the second chapter of his *De l'amour,* he presents his famous "Cristallisation" theory, in which he compares the stages of love to the branches of trees left in the flooded salt mines of Salzburg. As the branches are coated with thousands of salt granules, so is the mind of the lover constantly grafting upon the image of the beloved attributes from the lover's own mind. In the most perceptive modern analysis of Stendhal's theory, Ortega y Gasset observes: "in sum, this theory defines love as an essential fiction. It is not that love sometimes makes

5. Emil Lucka, *Eros: The Development of the Sex Relation Through the Ages,* trans. Ellie Schleussner (New York: Putnam, 1915).

mistakes, but that it is, essentially, a mistake. We fall in love when our imagination projects non-existent perfections onto another person." The similarities between Shelley's theories of love and those of Stendhal are obvious. In fact, Shelley's notion of the beloved is virtually identical to Ortega y Gasset's description of the Stendhalian woman: "the real likeness of a woman penetrates the masculine soul, and little by little becomes embroidered with imagined superstructures, which act to heap upon the bare likeness every possible perfection."[6]

From myth to mysticism to structuralism, such is the progression of theories of the erotic. In an essay that attempts to prove that Romanticism originated structuralist theory, Robert Scholes analyzes love itself as a structural convention based on the reality of binary oppositions. For Scholes, "Sexual differentiation is the basis, not only of our social systems, but of our logic as well. If there were three sexes, our computers would not have begun to think in terms of binary oppositions." In fact, Scholes goes so far as to claim that marriage is a "sacrament of structuralism"

> In fiction, as in life, the coming together of two human beings in the sexual embrace of love represents the reconciliation of all opposites. . . . In such an embrace, the cyclical dominates the temporal, the lovers are united with all lovers, and we partake of the universal. Marriage is a sacrament of structuralism. It is also precisely the point at which structural ideas and fictional structure are brought into the closest correspondence.[7]

It would appear, then, that structuralism itself can be finally seen as one of the many modern manifestations of the androgynous ideology in its attempts to merge oppositions in a new fictional synthesis.

Another factor in considering the relationship between the self and the other in Romantic poetry is what Girard calls the triangular desire of the mediator, subject, and object. For Girard, there are two fundamental categories of Romantic literature: those works that employ what he calls "external mediation" and those that employ "internal mediation"—both of which are distinguished from each other by the physical or spiritual distance between the mediator, the subject, and the object. Girard elaborates on this distinction as well as on his theory

6. José Ortega y Gasset, *On Love,* 22, 32.

7. Robert Scholes, *Structuralism in Literature* (New Haven: Yale University Press, 1974), 198.

of triangular desire, a desire he sees embodied both in the Don Quixote story and in the Romantic conceptions of love and the imagination:

> Triangular desire is the desire which transfigures its object. *Romantic* literature does not disregard this metamorphosis; on the contrary, it turns it to account and boasts of it, but never reveals its actual mechanism. This illusion is a living being whose conception demands a male and a female element.

Girard reads the poet's imagination as his "female" element, which remains "sterile" unless it is "fertilized by the mediator." But the Romantic poet, according to Girard, cannot simply accept this paradigm of sexual mutuality because he insists instead on believing in a "parthenogenesis" of his own imagination. He is, in fact, "in love with autonomy," and therefore refuses to accept the feminine within himself as an equal and valued component of the self. Girard sees the "series of solipsistic theories of poetry" produced during the past century as an attempt, ultimately, to deny the power of the feminine. Although he has been attacked recently for his own masculine bias, Girard's perceptions are partially valid on this point. What he sees as "rejection" of the feminine by male poets can be read more accurately as cannibalization of the woman, a persistent strategy that allowed the poets to rewrite Genesis as well as literary theory as both phallocentric and phallogocentric.[8]

I Blake: "on the verge / Of Non-entity"

Neatly distinguishing the woman-as-beloved from the mother and sister is virtually impossible in Blake's poetry, largely because these figures consistently collide and collapse into one another in a manner that bespeaks Blake's adherence to the ideology of Woman as Other, as well as his own peculiar psychic composition. In Blake's fantasized po-

8. René Girard, *Desire, Deceit, and the Novel,* 17–18. Most recently, Levinson has noted that Girard's theory places the mother "not as the boy's primary desired object but as both an instrument of primary aggression, and as an instrument of desire for the father. . . . to be him, loved by him." The mother, intrinsically an object of no value in herself, assumes value the way money or property does—as a mediator between sons and their father (see her *Keats's Life of Allegory,* 296).

etic vision, all life is but part of the body of one gigantic, androgynous being, and all individuals must seek to imitate that giant form within themselves. In this sense Blake's scheme of redemption is circular—all beings have their common origin in the body of one form and all life will return to that primordial form. Specifically, all human beings must recapitulate the redemptive process and imitate Albion and Jerusalem's androgynous apocalypse, for Jerusalem is the embodiment of the woman as real and ideal, the woman as historical place and time, the woman as internal principle and idea. Salvation in Blake's fiction is possible only when men realize that they can be identical to the divine One, the being who has resolved all antitheses within itself, who is both masculine and feminine, self and other. If humanity was originally created as an image of an androgynous God, then the return to that ideal state can be achieved by recapturing the imaginative potential of androgyny. Blake's art aims ultimately to depict the recovery of Paradise within, a state in which humanity is perfectly integrated with "God," that is, integrated within itself. Recovery of that integration, however, is possible only through the proper functioning of the perceiving imagination, for it is the imagination that creates and composes the "real man." In his *Vision of the Last Judgment,* Blake defines that "Divine body of the Saviour the True Vine of Eternity" as the "Human Imagination who appeard to Me as Coming to Judgment among his Saints & throwing off the Temporal that the Eternal might be Establishd" (E, 555; K, 606), while in "To the Christians" the imagination is declared to be "the real & eternal World of which this Vegetable Universe is but a faint shadow & in which we shall live in our Eternal or Imaginative Bodies, when these Vegetable Mortal Bodies are no more" (E, 231; K, 717). For Blake, the redeemed imagination is humanity's most effective link to its divinity because it is the one force that enables man to recapture his fictionally androgynous union with the Other.

Blake believed that the apocalypse or individual salvation could be achieved through forgiveness, love, and destruction of selfhood. But this apocalypse becomes possible only through reunion with one's divided counterpart, a reintegration that makes imaginative perception a reality. According to Blakean ideology, the androgyne is not only the original being, but also the ultimate apocalyptic condition that the imagination can envision. Imaginative vision, creative energy, and inward feeling are associated with the masculine in Blake's system, while space, matter, and outward expression are characterized as feminine. Union and transformation of both sets of qualities are necessary if man is to escape his fallen identity as a spectre and woman is to be anything but a female will.

In his annotations to Watson (1798), Blake observed that the "Beast & the Whore rule without controls" (E, 611; K, 383). That is, the fallen world is dominated by the demonic power of the "Hairy Man" and the "Scaly Woman," the monstrous aberrations that sexual beings have become in this world.[9] The individual perversions that have resulted from the separation of the masculine and feminine from one another have also caused the corruption of political and religious systems. Blake's concept of the fall is similar on this point to Boehme's theories. Blake believes that "God formed Nature perfect but . . . Man perverted the order of Nature since which time the Elements are filld with the Prince of Evil. . . . the plan of Providence was Subverted at the Fall of Adam & . . . it was not restored till Christ" (E, 614–15; K, 388, 390). In Blake's view there was nothing fortunate about the fall. In fact, Blake once told Crabb Robinson that Milton appeared to him in a vision and told him not to be misled by *Paradise Lost:* "In particular he wished me to shew the falsehood of his doctrine that the pleasures of sex arose from the fall. The fall could not produce any pleasure." And then, Robinson recalls, Blake "went off upon a rambling state of a Union of Sexes in Man as in God—an androgynous state in which I could not follow him."[10] At the risk of treading where the wise have not dared, I propose to analyze Blake's submerged androgynous text, an ideal that dared not speak its name but is for that very fact all the more pervasive as troping Blake's fantasy of human potentiality.

In addition to the abbreviated fall story in "The Argument" to *The Marriage of Heaven and Hell,* Blake presented his first full version of the fall in the *Book of Urizen.* In this early version Albion is not mentioned, and the male principle rather than the female precipitates the fall. More important, however, creation is presented as the result of the fall, as in Boehme. Like Boehme's Father God, Urizen is self-consumed with fire until he splits apart: "First I fought with the fire; consum'd / Inwards, into a deep world within" (E, 72; K, 224). Boehme's God is a principle of wrath who torments himself internally until he splits and gives birth to the God of love or light, corresponding to Blake's Los. The supreme male of Genesis and Blake's prophecies before the major epics is nonhuman because he is antiandrogynous. In fact, his existence de-

9. See Irene Tayler, "The Woman Scaly," *BMMLA* 6 (1973), 74–87, for a discussion of Blake's supposedly idealistic attitudes toward women.

10. Henry Crabb Robinson, *Diary, Reminiscences and Correspondence,* ed. T. Sadler, 2 vols. (Boston: Fields, Osgood, 1869), II, 29. For a biographical interpretation of Blake's portrayal of women and love in his poetry, see John Sutherland, "Blake: A Crisis of Love and Jealousy," *PMLA* 87 (1972), 424–31.

pends on the exclusion of the feminine, who is driven out of the self and then distorted. The pattern of a master-slave relationship with Ahania, of separation and fall, is disastrously imitated by the other three elements of the original being and produces the sexual warfare of the later epics. Urizen has to exclude the feminine other within himself, Ahania, because he cannot accept the vital principle of contraries that sustains all life. He shuts himself off in "the depths of dark solitude" and seeks "a joy without pain, / . . . a solid without fluctuation" (E, 71; K, 224). As Weiskel has noted, Urizen "falls spectacularly when he rejects his emanation Ahania in a fit of what is now called male chauvinism. . . . [T]he perceptual error of the Fallen Man is also a sexual crisis. . . . The Fallen Man responds to sexual guilt by expelling his passional life into a grotesque naturalization"—Vala—to whom he first feels fear and then sexual guilt.[11]

Urizen's fall is repeated as Los is divided by Pity, and "anguish dividing & dividing" his soul until a "female form trembling and pale" stood before his face. The Eternals are struck with "Wonder, awe, fear, astonishment . . . At the first female form now separate" (E, 77–78; K, 230–31). Los immediately lusts after this female, named Pity, and she begins her coy games of refusal and temptation. The Eternals observe their copulation and "shudder'd when they saw, / Man begetting his likeness, / On his own divided image" (E, 79; K, 232). It would appear that fallen sexuality is in fact a perversion, a type of masturbation, a futile and distorted act between self and self as other.

Ahania stands as the first portrait of the beloved feminine, while the *Book of Ahania* develops her identity as a principle of wisdom and intellectual beauty, hidden by Urizen and cherished as his "Sin." In this separated state she eventually becomes a "faint shadow," wandering hopelessly because she is "Unseen, unbodied, unknown, / The mother of Pestilence" (E, 85; K, 250). She can only weep impotently at the crucifixion of Fuzon, for she has become invisible since her separation from Urizen; she can only wail "on the verge / Of Non-entity" (E, 88; K, 254). The feminine beloved cannot be an active principle for redemption until the male counterpart recognizes her equality and divinity, and such a recognition does not occur until Albion and Jerusalem reunite at the conclusion of *Jerusalem*. In the meantime, female characters in Blake's epics are the emanations of their fallen masculine counterparts, as inadequate as the male spectres.[12]

11. Weiskel, *The Romantic Sublime*, 75.

12. Webster reads the psychic action in *The Four Zoas* as determined by "the horrible consequences of attempting to satisfy basic human needs for food and

Another manifestation of the perverted feminine as beloved occurs in the portrayal of Enitharmon, who does not speak in the *Book of Urizen* but finds her tongue in *Europe*. In this work she curses man for not realizing that "Woman, lovely Woman! may have dominion." She manages her misanthropic campaign by convincing men that "Womans love is Sin" and by teaching young girls to "Forbid all Joy, & from her childhood shall the little female / Spread nets in every secret path" (E, 62; K, 240). These golden nets represent institutionalized religion which, according to Blake, was a female invention that ensured the dominance of the fallen faculties. Enitharmon also capitalizes on man's notions about woman's true nature in order to institutionalize a religion of the Female Will: "Eighteen hundred years: Man was a Dream! / The night of Nature and their harps unstrung:. . . a female dream" (E, 63; K, 240). Like an unholy madonna, Enitharmon is enshrined in her "crystal house" where she dominates all within hearing distance (E, 65; K, 243). Los stirs himself in the final passage to call his sons to war, which throughout Blake's work is presented as a perversion and sublimation of sexual energy. Blake comments in *Jerusalem* 68 on this state of frustrated enslavement to an aloof feminine principle:

> I am drunk with unsatiated love
> I must rush again to War: for the Virgin has
> frownd & refusd
> Sometimes I curse & sometimes bless thy
> fascinating beauty . . .
> There is no time for any thing but the torments
> of love & desire . . .
>
> (E, 222; K, 707)

But in Blake's poetic universe the fall is not the result of an act performed by a divided female will; rather, it is the separation of the male and female elements, causing the estrangement of the four archetypal faculties within the cosmic being. This being is whole only when a fundamental unity exists among the mind, the imagination, the instincts, and the body. Although these four basic faculties are imaged as

---

sex. . . since they involve the absorption of one person (or part of him) by another" (see her *Blake's Prophetic Psychology*, 206).

male, each has its emanation, that is, a femaleness that cannot be separated out if the unified self is to be complete.[13]

Blake's first attempt to present the role of the feminine beloved in the fall and redemption occurs on an epic scale in *The Four Zoas.* Again he retells the story of the destruction of the cosmic being and its gradual reintegration. He presents characters who are at the same time symbols of faculties, each of which has split and must be reunified before Albion again can become both God and humanity as originally created, all aspects of self unified. Urizen and Ahania reconstitute the mind; Vala and Luvah reunite to heal the split between the emotions and the body; Tharmas and Enion reconcile in order to restore the instincts; Los and Enitharmon reintegrate to return the imagination to its divine status. But the ultimate act of reintegration must be between Albion and Jerusalem, masculine and feminine. Theirs is the final and apocalyptic reunion that brings full circle the story of fall and redemption.

The depiction of continual sexual warfare in *The Four Zoas* lends a certain circular sense to the activity of the poem; that is, readers can never be certain whether or not they are viewing an actual fall or hearing the recitation of the fall because the characters psychically reenact their falls over and over again throughout the work. More important, however, the falls are all presented as destructions of an original androgynous condition. When Urizen beholds the separate Ahania, he is "Astonishd & Confounded" to see "Her shadowy form now Separate. . . . Two wills they had two intellects & not as in times of old" (*FZ* II; E, 320; K, 285). The separate Enitharmon appears to illustrate the horrors of the female will, for she taunts Los by boasting, "thou art mine / Created for my will my slave." She further twists the ideal of sacrifice and love when she declares that the "joy of woman is the Death of her best beloved / Who dies for Love of her / In torments of fierce jeal-

13. Helpful discussions of the role and identity of the female in Blake's works can be found in Jean Hagstrum's "Babylon Revisited, or the Story of Luvah and Vala," in *Blake's Sublime Allegory,* ed. Stuart Curran and Joseph Wittreich (Madison: University of Wisconsin Press, 1973), 101–18; David Aers, "William Blake and the Dialectics of Sex," *ELH* 44 (1977) 500–14; and "Blake: Sex, Society and Ideology," in *Romanticism and Ideology: Studies in English Writing, 1765–1830,* ed. Aers et al. (London: Routledge, 1981); Brian Wilkie and Mary Lynn Johnson, *Blake's Four Zoas: The Design of a Dream* (Cambridge: Harvard University Press, 1978); Anne K. Mellor, *Blake's Human Form Divine* (Berkeley: University of California Press, 1974); Nelson Hilton, "Some Sexual Connotations," *B:IQ* 16 (1983), 166–71; Judith Lee, "Ways of Their Own: The Emanations of Blake's *Vala,* or *The Four Zoas,*" *ELH* 50 (1983), 131–51.

ousy & pangs of adoration" (*FZ* II; E, 323–24; K, 289). Tharmas displays his despair at being separated from Enion, which causes a psychic fissure and forces him to confuse love, pity, and rage as the same emotion. Tharmas alleviates his frustrations by sadistically ripping Enitharmon "far / Apart from Los." Los responds by howling "at the rending asunder all the fibres rent / Where Enitharmon joind to his left side in grinding pain" (E, 332; K, 299). But Los/Urthona relates a different fall story and describes another version of the birth of Enitharmon:

> the piteous form
> Dividing & dividing from my loins a weak & piteous
> Soft cloud of snow a female pale & weak I soft embracd
> My counter part & calld it Love I namd her Enitharmon.
> (*FZ* IV; E, 333; K, 300)

There are, then, two different versions of the identity of Enitharmon. In the *Book of Urizen* she was born from Los as Eve was born from Adam, and this version of her creation survives in the passage quoted above. But in the first Night of *The Four Zoas,* Tharmas and Enion are presented as the parents of Los and Enitharmon, who are therefore initially brother and sister before they become lovers. Although Blake does not make sibling incest a central feature in his poetic scheme, it is evident that he recognized its usefulness in depicting the horrors of solipsism and perverted love.

Urthona's spectre and the Shadow of Enitharmon repeat the story of their fall and long for the day when they will "reunite in those mild fields of happy Eternity" (*FZ* VIIa; E, 359; K, 326). The Spectre remembers their original androgynous condition when "thou & I in undivided Essence walkd about / Imbodied. thou my garden of delight & I the spirit in the garden / Mutual there we dwelt in one anothers joy" (E, 359; K, 327). When the two of them unified, they formed what the Spectre calls "Universal Manhood" until

> One dread morn of goary blood
> The manhood was divided for the gentle passions making way
> Thro the infinite labyrinths of the heart & thro the nostrils issuing
> In odorous stupefaction stood before the Eyes of Man
> A female bright.
> (E, 359; K, 327)

This initial and unprovoked separation is the beginning of all the ensuing divisions, for soon the "masculine spirit" departed and formed a spectral male as a counterpart to the separated female. But the Spectre vows to his fallen counterpart that he "will destroy / That body I created then shall we unite again in bliss" (E, 359; K, 327). As the Spectre castigates the separated female form for being a fallen delusion, so he condemns himself as a male principle, "insane brutish / Deformd . . . a ravening devouring lust continually / Craving & devouring" (E, 360; K, 327).

The Four Zoas also offers valuable clues to the development of Blake's philosophy, for in his revisions we can see him shaping and reshaping his attitudes toward the role the feminine plays in the fall and resurrection of the psyche. For instance, Night VIIb depicts life in bondage to the physical body, with the spiritual body of androgyny only a dim memory. In this section Tharmas longs for reunion with the "Crystal form that lived in my bosom," Enion as unfallen feminine (E, 362; K, 344), but she exists only as a vague phantom. Night VIIa focuses instead on Urthona's self-division. His Spectre recalls to Enitharmon the days "Where thou & I in undivided Essence walkd about / Imbodied. thou my garden of delight & I the spirit in the garden / Mutual there we dwelt in one anothers joy" (E, 359; K, 327). The Spectre wants to "unite again in bliss" with Enitharmon, but their union causes Enitharmon to give birth to "a wonder horrible," a female demon who causes "male forms without female counterparts" to rise from their graves (E, 360; K, 328). The event reaffirms Blake's belief that paradise cannot be regained through the fallen body. Single-sexed forms, whether male or female, are the inhabitants of Ulro, "Cruel and ravening with Enmity & Hatred & War" (E, 360; K, 328). Los tells his Spectre that "Self annihilation" is the only way to salvation, for only then can the "real Self" emerge—the imagination's power to reshape itself as androgynous (E, 368; K, 328).

Blake wrote two premature endings to Night VIII before he was finally able to resolve its conclusion, and these two drafts reveal his struggle to come to terms with the feminine's role in the fall of humanity. In the first version Los weeps after hearing the words of Ahania and Enion, and Rahab confirms the evil of the female will by placing the body of Eternal Humanity in a sepulcher. In the second version the door of the sepulcher opens and the Divine Vision confronts Rahab. Blake, however, deletes these lines and instead has Los and Enitharmon together place the body in a tomb as Jerusalem weeps. The change obviously emphasizes the guilt of both Los and Enitharmon, and removes it from Rahab. In the first version the female will, the separated female principle, entombs the eternal androgynous being. In the second version responsibility for this destruction is shared. Now the separate female no longer acts out of a spiteful will; instead both the fallen male and female principles must accept equal responsibility. Night VIII finally concludes with Rahab's triumph over Jerusalem; the forces of Natural Religion continue to foster and perpetuate the fallen and divided sexual cycle.

In an ascending progression of redemptions, all four Zoas are restored to their proper functions. Urizen and Ahania's redemption destroys the self-enclosed world of Ulro, while Luvah and Vala return to their rightful "place of Seed" and so restore the realm of generation. The redemption of Tharmas and Enion restores the world of Beulah, while the reunited Los and Enitharmon must build Jerusalem even though they are "Terrified at Non Existence / For such they deemd the death of the body" (*FZ* IX; E, 386; K, 357). They have to learn by the example of Albion and Jerusalem that "the male & female live in the life of Eternity / Because the Lamb of God Creates himself a bride & wife / That we his Children evermore may live in Jerusalem . . . a New Spiritual birth Regenerated from Death" (*FZ* IX; E, 391; K, 362–63).

With the regeneration of the "Human form Divine" through the reintegration of the Zoas, Albion pronounces the lesson that all the Zoas should have learned while they lived as fallen versions of themselves:

> Again reorganize till they resume the image of the human
> Cooperating in the bliss of Man obeying his Will
> Servants to the infinite & Eternal of the Human form.
>
> (*FZ* IX; E, 395; K, 366)

The reunited Zoas attend a feast of celebration, but it is clear that a universal apocalypse has not occurred, for

> . . . Many Eternal Men sat at the golden feast to see
> The female form now separate They shudderd at the horrible thing
> Not born for the sport and amusement of Man but born to drink up
> all his powers
> They wept to see their shadows they said to one another this is Sin
> This is the Generative world they rememberd the Days of old.
>
> (*FZ* IX; E, 401; K, 373)

This passage suggests that the reintegration that took place was Albion's alone, an individual and personal apocalypse. Redemption can occur in this world when an individual reintegrates his own faculties and thus redeems the masculine and feminine within. Salvation is possible only when humanity as individuals and groups lives by "Brotherhood & Universal Love" and "not by Self alone" (*FZ* IX; E, 402; K, 374).

The Zoas that compose Albion have learned that in "Attempting to be more than Man We become less" (E, 403; K, 376). Humanity as originally created is divine, so it is impossible to become more than "Man." The wine presses and the looms, both formerly symbols of the fallen world of generation, are now redeemed and external indicators of humanity's return to its original condition. The poem concludes with Urthona, the symbol of the divine imagination, "arisen in his strength no longer now / Divided from Enitharmon no longer the Spectre Los" (*FZ* IX; E, 407; K, 379). Regeneration has been achieved because the fallen world of female mystery religions has been supplanted by the harmonious "sweet Science" of the reintegrated faculties, an ideological construct that posits reconciling contraries in a fictional androgynous wholeness.

In *Milton,* Blake has fully developed his theory of salvation through the sexual Contraries, for here the Negations must be destroyed before the Contraries can reunite to form the redeemed self. The cosmology in this work is expanded, and Los and Enitharmon are identified as the parents of the three classes of fallen humanity. Although Los and Enitharmon are important at the beginning of the epic, they fade as the struggle for redemption focuses on Milton and Ololon. As in Blake's other works, the enemy is the concept of selfhood, and Milton and Ololon both must reject their "false garments" of self before they can reunite to form the spiritualized androgyne. This redemption is possible only when Milton as a type of epic hero plunges into the world of generation to redeem his emanation, who must also prepare herself for reunification by rejecting all traces of the female will. Only when they have united can they form the original imaginative ideal, the "Eternal Great Humanity Divine" (*M* 2; E, 96; K, 481).

Milton as the male principle must, like the feminine Ololon, cast off the satanic aspects of his being before they can be redeemed and unified. Milton expresses his awareness of the way to salvation when he tells Satan: "I come to Self Annihilation / Such are the Laws of Eternity that each shall mutually / Annihilate himself for others good" (*M* 38; E, 139; K, 530). Ololon learns this same truth when she asks Milton if together they can form the redeemed self: "are we Contraries O Milton, Thou & I / O Immortal! how were we led to War the Wars of Death"; (*M* 41; E, 143; K, 534). She has come to realize that salvation is possible only if she will destroy her fallen, feminine self, just as Milton has cast off his spectral, masculine self like a false garment.

An early version of Jerusalem exists in the portrait of Ololon, Milton's contrary and redeemer. Ololon is the first full portrait of the feminine beloved who functions as the redeemer in the imagination's quest to regain unity. According to Blake, Milton had failed to create a vision of a redeemed woman, the bride of the Great Marriage in biblical tradition. Ololon's appearance in *Milton* is analogous to Jesus' appearance in the fallen world, and so Ololon is related to the "new Jerusalem" just as Jerusalem is later identified with Jesus. But the demonic female trinity still persists in the portrait of Ololon, and the fallen female, like the spectral male, must lose its insidious capacity to self-divide before she can be redeemed. Ololon, in her initial form, represents Milton's three daughters and three wives, all of whom are "Female forms, which in blood & jealousy / Surrounded him, dividing & uniting without end or number" (*M* 17; E, 110; K, 498). This feminine amorphousness continues in *Milton* 36, when Ololon is referred to as both "They" and "One Female." Ololon also encompasses the identity of the beloved as the muse, Blake's belief in the imaginative potential of humanity that cannot appear in this world "except in a Female Form." She gives Milton, and by extension Blake, the poetic power "to display Natures cruel holiness: the deceits of Natural Religion," so that both writers can portray the supreme poetic act, the fictional recreation of the fallen sexes into the Divine Humanity (E, 137; K, 527).

The reunited Milton and Ololon join with the "Starry Eight," the Four Zoas in union with their emanations, to form the "One Man Jesus the Saviour" (*M* 41; E, 143; K, 534). The meeting between Milton and Ololon, then, is, as Mitchell has observed, "simultaneously a revelation of the archetypal errors of masculine and feminine consciousness and a redemption of these errors."[14] Milton and Ololon are able to form "One Man" only when they redeem the masculine and the feminine, allowing the imagination to transcend the limitations of the fallen self and achieve godhead. But do not think that Ololon survives this apocalyptic merger with Milton in any form other than as the cannibalized female within. In fact, Blake underlines her abdication of humanity by transforming her into a dove, thereby enabling her to dive into Milton's Shadow and initiate the fantasy of androgynous perfection.

As Milton and Ololon constitute the focus of the quest in *Milton,* so Jerusalem and her counterpart Albion are the central figures in *Jerusalem.* In fact, the entire focus of Blake's epics is Albion's quest, enacted by his elements as he lies sleeping on the couch of Nature. Albion's quest, like that of Prometheus, is totally internal. He is not searching

14. W. J. T. Mitchell, "Blake's Radical Comedy: Dramatic Structure as Meaning in *Milton,*" in *Blake's Sublime Allegory,* ed. Curran and Wittreich, 304. Also see Morton Paley's essay in that same volume on "The Figure of the Garment in *The Four Zoas, Milton,* and *Jerusalem,*" 119–39.

for something outside the self; rather, he is engaged in enacting the ideology of reintegrating himself as the complete artistic self, the Romantic Culture Hero. To do so, however, requires that he absorb the feminine as a component of his being. The united Albion/Jerusalem has traditionally been seen as a "Man," but if we understand that Blake was working within the androgynous tradition, then we must read this "he" as a fictional merger of two pervasive ideologies: the male artist and the cannibalized woman within.

To make the external world also and simultaneously an internal one requires both a suspension of disbelief and an expansion of the reader's imagination. Like Hobbes's Leviathan or the Kabbalistic Adam Kadmon, Blake's Albion/Jerusalem stands as a fantasied image of cosmic and individual totality. The Blakean apocalypse occurs when Albion, as the perceiver, discovers himself at the same time as everything he perceives becomes Jerusalem. And so perception stands at the center of Blake's spiritual vision, what in *Milton* 30:20 he called "Mental forms Creating." In fact, perception itself is a divine act in that the poet, like God, creates a world from the inner depths of his expanded being. The Romantic poet, however, found himself plagued by the spectre of solipsistic self-worship, unable to sustain the fiction of artistic creativity as divine apotheosis.

As Blake differed from Swedenborg on the nature of the sexes in eternity, so does he differ from him on the dynamics of contraries. One of the probable sources for Blake's conception of contraries was Swedenborg's notion of "correspondents." According to Swedenborg, correspondents meant that reaction and action absorb one another to form a united entity. For Blake, this state was static and isolated, like that of the hermaphrodite. The androgyne, however, was an ideal union that preserved dichotomies. Blake devised instead the ideal cycle of Eden and Beulah—a cycle in which the sexes can merge psychically in Eden and still physically separate in a sexually harmonious fashion in Beulah. The dichotomy between these two states is crucial, for, as Blake writes in *The Marriage of Heaven and Hell,* "Without Contraries is no progression. Attraction and Repulsion, Reason and Energy, Love and Hate, are necessary to Human existence" (E, 34; K, 149).

It would appear, however, that Blake did not take a clear or finally conclusive position on the question of sexuality in the apocalypse. We can distinguish between two "bodies" in Blake's writings—one physical and one psychically androgynous—and see that the mind's redemption occurs when it accepts the world of the redeemed senses, Vala at her best. The body's redemption, however, is a more difficult matter. Consciousness based on physical sexual identity has caused the senses to reject the androgynous vision, a vision that accepts both sexes as valuable and equal. The body has to be freed from the domination of genitally based perceptions and emotions. Women and men must both put off like a false garment the concept of body as totally "sexual," rather than primarily imaginative and psychic. Sexual relations exist in the world of Beulah, and Blake depicts this ideal vision of sexuality in *Jerusalem* 69 when he declares, "Embraces are Cominglings: from the Head even to the Feet; / And not a pompous High Priest entering by a Secret Place" (E, 223; K, 708). In the world perceived by the fallen and divided consciousness, sexual relations and religion are imagistically analogous in that "a Secret Place" is obviously both the curtained tabernacle and the vagina. Blake's poetry aspires toward a consciousness that includes genital sexuality, but this sexuality must include the entire being since according to Blake the reintegrated mind no longer distinguishes between the emotions, the intellect, and the instincts. *Jerusalem* 100, then, functions as the final visual appendix to the poem, illustrating the duality of humanity's destiny. Here Albion stands between the divine counterpart Jerusalem, symbol of Eden, and the redeemed Vala, representative of the life of Beulah. Albion has achieved divinity through his union with Jerusalem in plate 99, but Vala should not, indeed cannot, be destroyed since she embodies Beulah, the life of the natural world of generative sexuality.

Albion's merger with Jerusalem, then, stands in the same tradition of Prometheus's union with Asia in Shelley's *Prometheus Unbound*. The movement of such literary works is predicated on the identity of exterior and interior worlds, Nature and Culture, self and other. And such an idea, according to Busst, presupposes the use of the androgynous. For the Romantic writer "the beloved not only reflects the self, but in fact *is* the self. . . . and the androgyne which symbolizes this union merely reveals a pre-existent androgyny." [15]

But such a notion is an ideological construct and functions most persistently in the poetry as a concealed text or an absent wish-fantasy. The image of Woman as Other, as the vehicle for the androgynous ideology, appears most clearly when Blake tries to solve the problem of Nature—Vala—what Wagenknecht has called the "conundrum of *Jerusalem*," the "problem of the female," "the apparently insoluble bond between two females, Vala and Jerusalem." Blake attempted to solve this dilemma through his creation of Beulah and Eden. Vala is no longer the devouring Rahab; rather, she is the shadow of Jerusalem, the incarnation Jerusalem assumes in the Natural world. The redeemed psyche,

15. Busst, "The Androgyne," in *Romantic Mythologies*, ed. Fletcher, 62–63.

like all external objects that it perceives, must fluctuate between the two worlds, for contraries are essential to life and illustrate the Pauline notion of the two "bodies": "It is sown a natural body; it is raised a spiritual body. There is a natural body, and there is a spiritual body" (I Corinthians 15:44). The two "bodies," the sexual and the psychic, alternate between the worlds of Beulah and Eden and represent the best that life can offer.[16]

The androgynous in Blake's vision seeks to present itself as a spiritual and psychic ideal that raises humanity into a perception of the body as divine because it possesses all humanized reality. In *Jerusalem* 76 the figures of Los and Christ do not merge; in this imagistic fashion Blake reaffirms his commitment to the body and this world, as well as to the salvation possible to all of us through a redeemed imagination. For Blake, then, the androgyne suggests more than just a perfect because complete human being; it is a fantasized image of God, of the ideology that imaginative energy allows the mind to transcend the divisions that plague all victims of fallen life. To achieve androgynous reunification means to transcend the limiting sense of self and resume the wholeness of the "Human Form Divine," the self as omnipotent artist who, like the redeemed Los and Enitharmon, can transform the furnaces and looms of death into vehicles of life and salvation.

The same general observations can be made about *Jerusalem* 99, which illustrates the embrace of Jerusalem as the feminine beloved with Albion as masculine hero. Self and counterpart embrace here and symbolically regain their original psychic unity. But this merger is a metaphor and bodies remain distinct; there is no cosmic destruction of the flesh. Bodies remain separate because the redemption has been internal. Humanity can overcome the divisions of the fallen world, which is produced by divided consciousness, only through a spiritual apocalypse symbolized in sexual imagery. Salvation for the self is possible only by embracing the other self, and that embrace unifies the psyche and redeems the perceptions of the external world. The masculine and the feminine cannot be one in this world, a physical impossibility that Blake satirizes in his portrait of the hermaphrodite. But in the apotheotic vision of his fictional universe, the sexes can be recon-

16. David Wagenknecht, *Blake's Night: William Blake and the Idea of Pastoral* (Cambridge, MA: Belknap Press, 1973), 244; also see Jean Hagstrum, "Christ's Body," in *William Blake*, ed. Morton D. Paley and Michael Phillips (Oxford: Clarendon Press, 1973), 142, 154, and Robert F. Gleckner, "Blake's Religion of Imagination," *JAAC* 14 (1956), 359–69: "But if perception is a godlike act, God himself cannot be perceived except as He exists in the perceiver" (362).

ciled and live in harmony both physically and psychically through a fantasied reunification of the faculties of the mind. For Blake, humanity is divine when it realizes that it is, when it perceives with androgynously reintegrated faculties. The redeemed body cannot be distinct from or inferior to the spirit in Blake's vision, for that would disrupt the harmonious function of the contraries. By accepting and redeeming the world of generation, the world of the fallen and beloved female, Blake's erotic apocalypse leads to the assumption of a new "body"—an androgynous psyche that imitates the historical Jesus.

II Shelley: "Mine and me, / Of which she was the veiled Divinity"

Blake was able to conclude his poetic vision in a fictitious reconciliation of the body and the spirit, eros and *agape,* humanity and divinity in an apocalypse that denied the dichotomy between the two realms. For Blake, humanity was able to recover its lost divinity through the action of the redeemed imagination whose model was Jesus. Shelley aspired to just such an ideology, the apotheotic belief in the power of the imagination, and in his Preface to *The Cenci* he presents the imagination as incarnation: "Imagination is as the immortal God which should assume flesh for the redemption of mortal passion" (241). But Shelley's poetry finally differentiates between the world of the spirit and the world of the flesh, and women, it would appear, function significantly in his poetic attempts to reconcile the two realms. Whereas Shelley began his career committed to reforming society through institutional changes, he gradually shifted his focus to the psyche's efforts to achieve an internal harmony that would allow it to redeem the physical world at the same time it embraced the spiritually ideal one. The fictional reconstruction of the androgynous psyche, then, becomes the object of revolutionary reform in Shelley's poetry. Through such a fantasy of individual salvation, society as a whole would gradually be transformed into the image of Prometheus/Asia, wisdom and love.

The single most important source for Shelley's treatment of love was Plato's *Symposium,* which provided Shelley with the major attitudes toward love in the ancient world. His fascination with the work, as well as his reworking of the Prometheus/Asia mythos, reveals the Philhellenism so prevalent during the period. In fact, both Shelley and Byron, another fierce Philhellenist, celebrate the Greek as an expression of their political/cultural/sexual sympathies with the oppressed against the powerful as represented by the Holy Alliance, the Turkish Empire, and European imperialism.[17] For both poets, the Greek is consistently identified with feminine values, the Roman with the masculine.

According to Shelley, the *Symposium* was "the most beautiful and perfect among all the works of Plato" (*JW*, VII, 161). He translated it over a period of nine days in July 1817, and, according to Notopolous, it "was one of the most important things in Shelley's poetic life." Two speeches, Aristophanes' and Diotima's, form the central texts from which Shelley drew his poetic philosophy and imagery. Aristophanes presents his version of creation by stating that "human beings were formerly not divided into two sexes, male and female; there was also a third, common to both the others, the name of which remains, though the sex itself has disappeared. The androgynous sex, both in appearance and in name, was common to both male and female" (VII, 183). Aristophanes continues to detail Jupiter's division of this original being and to conclude that love is then an attempt to regain a facsimile of that original union. In fact, Aristophanes sees this yearning for the divided half as the most basic and powerful of all human emotions. He observes that when Vulcan approached the two lovers he asked: " 'Do you not desire the closest union and singleness to exist between you, so that you may never be divided night or day? If so, I will melt you together, and make you grow into one, so that both in life and death ye may be undivided' " (VII, 185). These particular lovers and all others since answered positively by feeling that this "was what he had ever sought":

> to mix and melt and to be melted together with his beloved, so that one should be made out of two. The cause of this desire is, that according to our original nature, we were once entire. The desire and the pursuit of integrity and union is that which we all love. First, as I said, we were entire, but now we have been dwindled through our own weakness. (VII, 186)

Aristophanes' speech in the *Symposium,* in addition to mocking the medical treatises of the day, also recognized the irony implicit in the quest for total sympathy between the sexes:

> From this period, mutual love has naturally existed between human beings; that reconciler and bond of union of their original nature, which seeks to make two, one, and to heal the di-

17. Jerome McGann, *Romantic Ideology,* 124–25.

> vided nature of man. Every one of us is thus half of what may be properly termed a man, and like a psetta [fish] cut in two, is the imperfect portion of an entire whole, perpetually necessitated to seek the half belonging to him. (VII, 185)

The impulse to merge totally with the feminine beloved becomes the motivating force and dominant impulse in poems like *Epipsychidion* and *Prometheus Unbound*. But this quest to dissolve into the beloved conflicts with the need to stand apart from and in awe of a beloved who is the embodiment of the good. What have been identified as the millennial and apocalyptic tendencies in Shelley's poetic vision converge, finally, in his depiction of the role of the feminine beloved.

For Shelley the quest to regain the other self was expressed in the similarly confused terms of gaining the prototype. That is, the psyche imagines what it lacks and unconsciously projects it onto another that it then seeks to possess. But Shelley could not finally settle on any firm conception of the prototype. Sometimes it is simply the self writ large; at other times it is an idealized father-teacher figure modeled on Shelley's tutor Dr. Lind. Most frequently, however, he images the prototype as a woman, a composite of Indian maiden and Dantean ideal. Whatever its manifestation, Shelley's need to unify his poetic heroes with another being or abstract principle is not simply a flight from self-consciousness or an expression of the limitations of the isolated self; rather, it can be seen as a desire to make the self more significant by combining it with another so that the new composite redeems each individual unit. Within Shelley's ideological universe, the new self was the product of the power of love and the imagination to deify humanity.

The Eros of Shelley in many ways anticipates the Eros of Freud, particularly when we recall that Freud images autoeroticism as a single mouth kissing itself. Lacan, commenting on Plato, or, more accurately, Plato via Freud, states that the significance of Aristophanes' fable in the *Symposium* lies in its presentation of sexuality as a lack, an empty space that represents death. In that empty space Lacan places a substitution and claims that human beings are not searching for their sexual complements, but instead for the fiction that there is a lost part of the self: "that [part] is constituted by the fact that he is only a sexed living being, and that he is no longer immortal." For Lacan, this lack of object is the primal condition and cause of desire in adulthood. All adult quests for transcendence, lost paradises, and lost being depend on "an original loss and the discovery of difference." He adds that "self-knowledge depends upon an original construction." Indeed, according to Lacan, all thinking depends on the reality of sexuality: "it is through sexual reality that the signifier came into the world—that man learnt to think." But for Lacan there is a difference between a love based on narcissism and a platonically circular love, which returns the lover to a sense of original divinity: "I suggest that there is a radical distinction between *loving oneself through the other*—which, in the narcissistic field of the object, allows no transcendence to the object included—and the circularity of the drive, in which the heterogeneity of the movement out and back shows a gap in its interval." [18]

The Lacanian distinction can be seen in what have been called the two impulses in Shelley's poetry. The radical impulse leads to attempts to establish an earthly paradise through a regeneration of the will, while the platonic impulse leads to the City of God, attained only through death. But Shelley seems to be asking his readers to participate in the fantasy that the real and the ideal are not polar oppositions any more than the female and male are. Shelley's later poetry explores what has traditionally been seen as a radical split between millennial and apocalyptic gestures.[19] To accept either of these extremes as Shelley's final poetic vision, however, is to miss his point. He is concerned with process and dichotomies, dialectics and renewal. Just as he sees life as a continuum, not even destroyed by death, so he sees the imagination as it veers from option to option, always seeking to expand itself in new combinations of possibilities. Like Blake, Shelley asks his readers to participate in the ideology of the androgynous imagination, the apotheotic merger of masculine creativity with the feminine Other.

The impulse to reunite the halves of a sundered self becomes the dominant motif in Shelley's later work. Shelley wrote to John Gisborne that his latest poem did not express love for an earthly woman: "*Epipsychidion* is a mystery—As to real flesh & blood, you know that I do not deal in those articles." [20] But it would appear that *Epipsychidion* is "flesh and blood" in that it is symbolically semiautobiographical. As in *Alastor*, the ideal love object is presented as an internal spark of (self-

18. See James Notopolous, *The Platonism of Shelley* (Durham: Duke University Press, 1949), 57; Jacques Lacan, *The Four Fundamental Concepts of Psycho-Analysis*, ed. Jacques-Alain Miller, trans. Alan Sheridan (New York: Norton, 1978), 205, 194.

19. See Milton Wilson, *Shelley's Later Poetry: A Study of His Prophetic Imagination* (New York: Columbia University Press, 1959), and Ross Grieg Woodman, *The Apocalyptic Vision in the Poetry of Shelley* (Toronto: University of Toronto Press, 1964), on the conflict between the millennial and the platonic impulses in Shelley's poetry.

20. Letter #668 to John Gisborne, 22 October 1821; *Letters* II, 363.

projected) divinity, a miniature within of the idealized self. The poet struggles to externalize this self, but all such attempts are necessarily doomed. In this poem the poet mourns that "this soul out of my soul" has deserted him and left him victim to the false loves this world offers (238). The Moon and the Comet, traditionally seen as symbols of Mary Godwin and Claire Clairmont, fail the poet, so he searches for one unique being who will never disappoint him.[21] He longs for one who will be "That world within this Chaos, mine and me, / Of which she was the veiled Divinity" (244–45).

Shelley was disappointed in every one of his personal love relations, but in Emilia Viviani he found for a very brief time what he thought was a similar spirit, a real woman he was compelled to reshape into an idealized feminine figure who inspired the poem. He uses a short passage from her essay, "True Love," as a preface to his poem. Like Shelley, Emilia believed that "The loving soul launches beyond creation, and creates for itself in the infinite a world all its own, far different from this dark and terrifying gulf." Emilia's "natural" Platonism complements Shelley's more sophisticated version. In reading Emilia's passage, one is reminded of Shelley's statement to Peacock: "You know I always seek in what I see the manifestation of something beyond the present & tangible object."[22]

But unless Shelley was purposely deceiving his friend Gisborne, and he certainly may have been, the poem, on at least some level, "is an idealized history of my life and feelings." It was also his final expression of the disillusionment he had found in idealizing women. As he confessed, "Some of us have in a prior existence been in love with an Antigone, & that makes us find no full content in any mortal tie." Shelley was compelled, then, to idealize Emilia Viviani in the poem. He declares: "I knew it was the Vision veiled from me / So many years—that it was Emily" (343–44). But the "real" Emilia became a "cloud instead of a Juno," and the poet found himself forced to celebrate Emily as something substantially less than a human being. She becomes an ab-

21. See, for instance, Daniel J. Hughes, "Coherence and Collapse in Shelley, with Particular Reference to *Epipsychidion*," *ELH* 28 (1961), 272. Other discussion of both the biographical and the allegorical aspects of the poem can be found in White, *Shelley*, II, 259–69; Kenneth Neil Cameron, *Shelley: The Golden Years* (Cambridge: Harvard University Press, 1974), 275–88; Frank McConnell, "Shelleyan 'Allegory': *Epipsychidion*," *KSJ* 20 (1971), 100–112; Stuart Sperry, *Shelley's Major Verse*, 158–82; and Jerrold Hogle, "The One as a Fusion of Opposites: *Epipsychidion*," in *Shelley's Process*, 279–86.

22. Letter #485 to Thomas Love Peacock, 6 November 1818; *Letters*, II, 47.

straction, an ideal of perfection within time, and as such she cannot be embraced. Shelley compares this dilemma to "poor Ixion [who] starts from the centaur that was the offspring of his own embrace."[23]

It is clear, however, that Emily has to be celebrated as a projection of the prototype and not as an earthly woman essentially "different" from the poet. She is also similar to the Cythna element of Laon/Cythna, another manifestation of the fantasied Eternal Feminine who leads the masculine self to an awareness of his own divinity. The poet of *Epipsychidion* begins the poem by addressing Emily as a "Sweet Spirit!" (1), "High, spirit-winged Heart!" (13), "Seraph of Heaven! . . . light, and love, and immortality" (21, 24), and "Sweet Lamp!" (53). Emily is, then, never human; in fact, the tone tends to more and more hysterical panegyric about Emily at the same time the poet increasingly debases himself. According to Freud, the cycle of elevating the beloved while subsequently demeaning the self is an error caused by a split between the sexual feelings and the emotional/affectionate ones (*SE* XI:177–93). Yet while Emily is presented as divine, she also has to be depicted as human, or at least the best of what can be expected of the human according to the demands of Shelley's fictional universe. She is "a mortal shape indued / With love and life and light and deity" (112–13).

Emily most resembles Cythna, however, in her identity as "sister" to the poet. The brother/sister relationship is implicit throughout the poem, although in a much more displaced manner than in *Laon and Cythna.* Shelley jotted on the leaf directly before the manuscript of the poem these lines from the *Song of Solomon:* "Thou has ravished my heart, my sister, my spouse"; "A garden enclosed is my sister, my spouse"; "It is the voice of my beloved that knocketh, saying, Open to me, my sister, my love, my dove, my undefiled." Throughout the poem, Emily is presented as a second self, the beloved sister, a symbol of the divinest portion of the self. Early in the poem, the poet exclaims: "Would we two had been twins of the same mother!" while later he addresses Emily as "Spouse! Sister! Angel!" "vestal sister," and "my heart's sister" (45, 130, 390, 415). But Emily is not a "real" sister in the sense that Cythna or Astarte are. She functions symbolically as a sister only because she must be as similar to the poet/hero as possible in order to partake in his solipsistic love fantasy.

The impulse to merge totally with another is the goal of the androgynous ideology in Shelley's poetry. The poet wants his ideal to be a part of himself, rather than an Other, just as he wants to lose himself in her

23. Letter #715 to John Gisborne, 18 June 1822; *Letters, II,* 434.

expanded being. He exclaims, "I am not thine: I am a part of *thee,*" while he endorses the power of love to blend the "equal, yet unlike, to one sweet end" (52, 358). He longs for a harmonious union of their total beings, which he compares to a musical composition: "We—are we not formed, as notes of music are, / For one another, though dissimilar" (142–43). Because he is using a simile from music, there is no mention here of the physical being of the poet or Emily; they are both disembodied psychic principles. In fact, Emily differs from the false loves that the poet has previously known precisely on this point. Unlike the Moon and the Comet, who are physical beings and thus intrinsically and ontologically alien to the poet, Emily represents the true object of love, the internal feminine principle, the prototype. Like the dream maiden in *Alastor,* Emily is a disembodied though incarnate projection of the perfection that the poet knows is within him.

The final section of the poem, then, attempts to image the union of the poet and Emily, a union symbolized by an idyllic life on an island, "Beautiful as a wreck of Paradise" (423). The poet pictures total union in a canceled fragment of the poem. Like Laon and Cythna, the lovers are to be conscious of their union every moment:

> If day should part us night will mend division
> And if sleep parts us—we will meet in vision
> And if life parts us—we will mix in death
> (*JW,* II, 382)

Again, the image of Narcissus comes to mind. The poet wants to merge with Emily so that they are one, a condition that allows them to perceive all reality as not only internal, but as a projection of the androgynous and combined self. In fact, the poet and Emily would become the only real world. Ideally, their love bestows on them the power to (re)create both their internal and external realms. The power of the apotheotic imagination to create all external reality is evidenced by the creation of the island that is both a place and a psychic state, similar to Jerusalem's identity as both city and woman. The poet even makes the island human by comparing it to Emily, "a naked bride . . . / like a buried lamp, a Soul no less / Burns in the heart of this delicious isle" (474–78).

The island becomes the fantasied locus for the transcendent union of the poet and Emily; it is Shelley's final attempt to present an image of a redeemed self existing in a redeemed world. The poet declares that he and Emily will be "Conscious, inseparable, one," while at the same time they "will rise, and sit, and walk together" (540–41). Like Rosalind and Lionel or Laon and Cythna, these two lovers will capture that ultimate state "to love and live / Be one" (551–52). The poet would like to believe that "Love makes all things equal" (126), but he also knows through experience that the union he desires with Emily, intense self-unification, is not possible in the physical realm. He continues, though, to create a fictionalized portrait of his ideal androgynous self achieved through a fantasized union with the feminine beloved: "We shall become the same, we shall be one / Spirit within two frames, oh! wherefore two?" (573–74). The poem has built to this climax, an image of two disembodied principles, the masculine and the feminine, the mortal and the divine, becoming one in an erotic apocalypse, but the very fictitiousness of the goal explodes the conceits even as Shelley hysterically denies the fictionality of his quest.[24]

On one hand, Shelley demands that the two souls be identical, while on the other he realizes that they must be essentially different if there is to be any sort of union. One cannot, in fact, unify with a projection of the self; that would be mere solipsistic absorption. As Hogle has perceptively remarked, "Different figures can approach a Shelleyan unity of equals only if neither figure is subsumed by the other and if no distinction is erased altogether in favor of one dominant sex, form, or being."[25] Emily must be different and separate from the poet because it is humanly impossible to become "conscious, inseparable, one" with another being and still be able to stroll about as separately through the island's garden. The poet realizes that he has placed impossible demands on his vision of love. Earlier in the poem he had exclaimed, "Ah, woe is me! / What have I dared? where am I lifted? how / Shall I descend, and perish not?" (124–27). Since the body ultimately cannot be transformed in Shelley's vision, it must be escaped. *Epipsychidion* concludes much like *Laon and Cythna;* the platonic impulse has defeated the hope of an earthly paradise.

24. See Hillis Miller's reading of this poem in "The Critic as Host," in *Deconstruction and Criticism,* ed. Harold Bloom et al. (New York: Seabury, 1979). In contrast to Miller, see the earlier idealistic readings of the poem: Irvin Kroese, *The Beauty and the Terror: Shelley's Visionary Women* (Salzburg: Institute for English Studies, 1976); Richard E. Brown, "The Role of Dante in *Epipsychidion,*" *CLS* 30 (1978), 223–35; and John H. Slater, "Self-Concealment and Self-Revelation in Shelley's *Epipsychidion,*" *PLL* 11 (1975), 279–92. For a discussion of Shelley's supposed allusion to his venereal disease in the poem, see Nora Crook and Derek Guiton, *Shelley's Venomed Melody* (Cambridge: Cambridge University Press, 1986), 147–55.

25. *Shelley's Process,* 286.

In keeping with the Phoenix imagery that runs throughout the portrait of the union, the poet realizes that this all-consuming ideal merger with Emily has led him to death. Thus he concludes his long description by repeating his earlier fear: "Woe is me!" (587). One is reminded here of Freud's *Beyond the Pleasure Principle* (1920). In seeking to merge totally with the beloved, that is, in seeking to pursue the erotic impulse to its natural conclusion, the hero is compelled to confront his own death wish, the desire to seek escape from consciousness in both physical and psychic oblivion. But in keeping with the completely self-conscious fictionality of his desires, the poet also refers to the symbolic love of Shakespeare's "Phoenix and the Turtle" and Donne's "Canonization." Both works use the myth of the phoenix, with its fiction that death is a rebirth for the bird, who has traditionally been interpreted as a symbol of androgynous reintegration. The poet in *Epipsychidion* seeks his "death" in an orgasm that is troped as a pyre, much like the death that concluded *Laon and Cythna,* for both literal and sexual "death" becomes the only escape from the world of physical limitations. In the envoy that concludes the poem, the poet very literally sings his theme, that " 'Love's very pain is sweet, / But its reward is in the world divine / Which, if not here, it builds beyond the grave' " (596–98). We have, in the pseudoarchaic device of an envoy, the attempt to increase the fictional artifice of a poet writing about a poet writing about a poet, a self-mirroring process that reflects all too accurately the ambiguity of a man writing about a woman embodying an idea.

The fictionally hysterical celebration of women leads the poet to the debasement that Freud diagnosed as a "common occurrence in men" (*SE* XI:177–93). And, in fact, the poet of *Epipsychidion* can trace his autobiographical miseries to this tendency to elevate women and alternately debase his own sexuality. Rather than see women in his life as equals, he is compelled to see them as goddesses or whores (one thinks here of the "One, whose voice was venomed melody," the woman whose "touch was as electric poison" [256–59]). As long as he perceives women in this extreme manner, he can never find that balanced fusion he needs in order to even fictionally redeem himself. Sexuality, Shelley implies, is the form the imagination takes in this world in order to transform minds and bodies so that they are truly in harmony with one another. There is a sexual apocalypse at the climax of the poem, but it is not sustainable, as Shelley well knew. This is not to say that Shelley condemned the body and wanted simply to escape it altogether. Instead, *Epipsychidion* suggests that in a totalizing love relationship the male comes as close as he can on earth to experiencing the fiction of redemptive oneness with another person. That ideology, combined with the illusive power it allows the imagination, is as close as the Romantic can come to any fictional divinity he can imagine. Of course the union never lasts and the male poet is always disappointed, but the quest to transform the masculine self is such a seductive lure that to reject it because reason tells him he will fail is to lose the one chance he has to achieve a self-constructed and fictionally androgynous selfhood.

Shelley expressed to Maria Gisborne his utmost claim for the human spirit—"Let us believe in a kind of optimism in which we are our own gods"[26]—at the same time he was composing Act IV of *Prometheus Unbound*. Such a sentiment reveals the core of Shelley's androgynous ideology and the role the feminine played in capturing that fiction. *Prometheus Unbound* can be read, then, as Shelley's most overt statement of the androgynous ideology because it presents in very clear archetypal fashion the fantasy that the symbolic reunion of masculine and feminine principles is necessary if both human society and the cosmos are to be reborn. Prometheus as male and Asia as female function as the most basic and important dichotomy in the drama, while their reunion in the cave in Act III represents Shelley's ultimately optimistic treatment of Eros as a transforming power. Although Shelley in his early years may have envisioned a millennium instituted by the French Revolution, he, like all of the other Romantic poets, except perhaps Byron, gradually despaired of political reform by fallible human beings. Instead Shelley, like Blake, put his hope in what he called in "On Love" an "ideal prototype" (473). In *Prometheus Unbound* this prototype is embodied in the fantasy of an androgynous merger of masculine and feminine in a new fusion of power and love.[27]

Asia as beloved feminine functions as the power of love and forgiveness in the drama, liberating Prometheus from his self-consuming rage. She is another of Shelley's ethereal Indian maidens with whom his heroes long to merge. Prometheus recalls the earlier Asia as like a "golden chalice" (I.i.810), an appropriately reified image of woman as exchange commodity, and, indeed, the poem can be read on some level as a symbolic retelling of the history of the human race. Like Freud's *Totem and*

26. *Letters*, II, 726.

27. For another reading of Shelley's theory of love, see James O. Allsup, *The Magic Circle: A Study of Shelley's Concept of Love* (Port Washington: Kennikat, 1976). On the identity of Asia, see Frederick A. Pottle, "The Role of Asia in the Dramatic Action of Shelley's *Prometheus Unbound*," in *Shelley*, ed. George M. Ridenour (Englewood Cliffs, NJ: Prentice-Hall, 1965), and Meyer Abrams's chapters, "Romantic Love" and "Shelley's *Prometheus Unbound*," in *Natural Supernaturalism*, 292–307.

Taboo (1912–13), Shelley's cosmic drama relates the fantasy that history is predicated on parricide and castration. Both works present humanity's overthrow of an all-powerful patriarch through rebellion by son-figure(s), leading to the establishment of a fantasied new order based on communal ideals of brotherhood and equality. What is unique about Shelley's vision is not his concentration on what amounts to an oedipal struggle between Jupiter and Prometheus, but his focus on the role of woman in redeeming the social and psychic anarchy caused by men. Asia's power of love makes possible the final proclamation by Demogorgon, while Panthea identifies Asia with Aphrodite, embodying the love that "Burst from thee, and illumined Earth and Heaven / And the deep ocean and the sunless caves / And all that dwells within them" (II.v.28–30). Asia's power of love empowers Demogorgon's message, nearly identical with Blake's, for it endorses "Gentleness, Virtue, Wisdom, and Endurance," while he cautions humanity "To forgive wrongs," "To love, and bear; to hope" (IV.i.562–74). But Asia is no optimistic simpleton; she presents a forceful and imagistic critique of the tyranny of binary oppositions, specifically noting that to "know" in the masculine sense of the word is inadequate in a universe that requires knowledge, "taming," and "play," the semiotic/Imaginary powers that supposedly can be found only through the feminine.

The redeemed Asia also personifies the form that beauty can take in the ideal world if it fuses the strength and wisdom of Prometheus with love. She is variously addressed by one spirit as "Life of Life," "Child of Light," and "Lamp of Earth" (II.v.48, 54, 66). The continuum of images here suggests her progression from an abstraction that exists in the spiritual realm to a concrete presence in the physical one. She also tropes the distance that the poet's imagination must travel in order to transform his disfigured world. Shelley has clearly made Asia the female divinity who presides over the drama. It is she who plays the role of Christ redeeming both Prometheus and herself, even though Prometheus is superficially associated with Christ in his crucified pose. Jupiter as the traditional patriarchal male deity is shown to be not only inadequate, but the logical and disastrous outcome of distorted masculine values operating in the fallen world. Whereas he can offer humanity only violence and rape, Asia as a female divinity offers growth and love, a fertility born of joy.

Shelley's Preface to the drama describes Prometheus as "the type of the highest perfection of moral and intellectual nature, impelled by the purest and truest motives to the best and noblest ends." The Preface also states clearly that Shelley is not interested in restoring Aeschylus's lost version of *Prometheus Unbound,* in which Prometheus and Jupiter reconcile because Prometheus gives up his secret, and therefore his power, to Jupiter. This version, according to Shelley, was a "feeble" end for the "Champion. . . of mankind" (133). Instead, Shelley transformed his version of the myth by resurrecting the feminine ideal that he had presented earlier as Cythna and the Witch of Atlas. Now his Prometheus will be unbound not by himself, but by the fantasy of androgynous unity. In fact, the word "Unite!" (IV.i.82) presides over the entire drama, impelling its structure, imagery, and theme.

Prometheus as frustrated Culture Hero, however, functions as the central figure of Act I, and we are introduced to him as he describes himself: "eyeless in hate" (I.i.9). He knows that he has bound himself through his own isolated faculties, just as he gradually realizes that to hate intensely is to become what he hates. Prometheus turns initially to the Semiotic realm/Nature, the "Earth," "Heaven," "Sun," and "Sea" (I.i.25–27) for answers, but he has not received the help he needs from them. Only when he hears his original curse—that is, the reality of the Symbolic realm of language—repeated by the Phantasm of Jupiter and when he repents his "quick and vain" words can he begin his progress toward Asia (I.i.303). And in his first conversation with his mother Earth, he begins to remember when he "wandered once / With Asia, drinking life from her loved eyes" (I.i.122–23). We recall here Kristeva's notion of the Imaginary/semiotic realm, a preverbal locus where only visual logic operates. In this world the Law of the Father does not yet exist, for figuration or the need for language do not yet exist. As Freud (citing Goethe's *Faust* I, 3) stated in *Totem and Taboo,* "In the beginning was the Deed," not the word, for it is language that initiates the fall into consciousness and separation from the originating sources of being (*SE* XIII:161). And so Shelley's drama begins *in medias res,* recalling the prelapsarian condition that Prometheus has lost because he has unleashed the patriarch within himself and thereby exiled Asia from his being. Prometheus's mother, reenacting the earliest voice of the feminine within, seeks to remind her son that he is "immortal" and, in fact, "more than God / Being wise and kind" (I.i.150, 144–45). Her lessons are well learned, for Prometheus is able to withstand the threats and temptations of the patriarch's messengers, Mercury and the Furies, by insisting that "[I] am king over myself" and that he will not be corrupted by their visions: "Evil minds / Change good to their own nature" (I.i.492, 380–81). One is reminded here of Blake's notion that all individuals create the external world in which they live through the state of their perceptual faculties.

Although Prometheus says at the conclusion of Act I that he wants to be "what it is my destiny to be, / The saviour and the strength of suffering man," (I.i.816–17), he cannot until he is united with Asia, the "golden chalice." She must be the reified object of their transformation, provide the form and structure of their salvation. And just as he is trapped in a ravine filled with mountainous crags, so she inhabits a distant vale; the geography here is vaguely sexual and reminds one of the sexual juxtaposition of tower and cave that occurred in *Laon and Cythna*. But at this point Prometheus and Asia are less physically than spiritually and sexually separated, for they are split from the fantasy of their original and androgynous form and, as such, fallen from their joint and fictional divinity. Prometheus needs, as Panthea, Asia, and Ione do, to feel and see in unity. To have separated his emotions from his mind is to fall from the Imaginary into the Lacanian realm of the Symbolic. In this world Prometheus can only be prey to the Law of the Father, the slave of the power of language, the victim of Jupiter who attacks through Prometheus's own complicity and acceptance of the father's verbal power. It is only when Prometheus renews his contact with the feminine world of the Imaginary that he can assert control over the patriarchal realm of the Symbolic and (re)turn to the "Real," a Lacanian ideology that posits the mind's ability to shape the world of historical fact into its best imagining.

Panthea acts as Asia's disembodied imagination in Act II and in many ways appears to be an androgynous character herself.[28] She carries dreams back to Asia, which Asia then reads in Panthea's eyes. Panthea also expresses Ione's thoughts, telling Asia that Ione is also haunted by her search for something vague, "some inchantment old" (II.i.100). Asia is actually able to commune with Prometheus through the medium of Panthea's eyes. When she looks into those eyes she sees not herself, but Prometheus, "arrayed / In the soft light of his own smiles" (II.i.120–21). When she follows the voices she next hears, she finds herself at Demogorgon's volcano, an appropriate symbol of his masculine power. And it is Asia, not Prometheus, who dares the unknown and asks the crucial questions regarding "thought, passion, reason, will, / Imagination" (II.iv.10–11). In learning that the "deep truth is imageless" (II.iv.116), she herself is transformed, for immediately after this Panthea must shield her eyes from the intense "radiance" of Asia's beauty (II.v.18).

28. See William H. Marshall, "Plato's Myth of Aristophanes and Shelley's Panthea," *CJ* 55 (1959–60), 122–24. For an attack on Shelley's use of the androgynous tradition as nothing more than "a kind of sexless second childhood," "an emotional immaturity, a kind of infantilism," see Edward E. Bostetter, *The Romantic Ventriloquists* (Seattle: University of Washington Press, 1963), 193–95.

Asia has learned that "all love is sweet, / Given or returned," while it has the power to make "the reptile equal to the God" (II.v.39–40, 43).

The stage has been prepared for the son of Earth to reunite with the "daughter of Ocean" (II.iv.168), but Asia has also been called "Mother, dearest Mother" by the Spirit of the Earth (III.iv.24), and we cannot fail to note the significance of the alteration here in imagery. By erasing Asia's association with the maternal, the poet seeks to enact the removal of the incest taboo that adheres to all women in the Symbolic realm. In other words, as Freud notes in *Totem and Taboo,* the sons kill the patriarch in order to possess all of the women to whom only the father previously had access. But the incest taboo adhering to the mother made her untouchable and laid the foundation for the "laws," ritual prohibitions that eventually formed human society (*SE* XIII:140–46). Asia must be identified as a "daughter"; otherwise she continues to inhabit the realm of taboo and cannot be reunited with Prometheus. But once this has been accomplished, Asia predicts that her soul will sail like an "enchanted boat" "Harmonizing this Earth with what we feel above" (II.v.72, 97), an appropriately escapist image and gesture.

In sharp contradistinction to Asia, the first time we hear Jupiter speak he brags about his rape of Thetis. This act of violent and perverse sexuality stands in sharp contrast to the fictional and ideal love relationship that Shelley posits as the poetic goal of the drama. In Act III, when Jupiter claims to have "begotten" a "strange wonder," a "fatal Child" (III.i.18–19), we see the full perversion of the androgynous ideal by the separated and fallen male principle. Refusing to merge in love and harmony with Thetis, he rapes her and in a distortion of logic seeks to become female himself and usurp the role of childbearing.[29] With ironic justice that defeats his hubris, Demogorgon arrives to announce that he is the rightful child of Jupiter: " 'I am thy child, as thou wert Saturn's child' " (III.i.54). Jupiter falls, not through Prometheus's efforts, but because of his own arrogant and misguided maleness. And in the continuous cycle of sons replacing their fathers—castrations disguised as parricides—we can see both Shelley's rewriting of the mythic origins of the race and the more immediate struggle taking place in France.

In the cave that Prometheus and Asia inhabit, they will both participate in and preside over an apocalypse that is also a millennium. Here, as Prometheus says, they "will sit and talk of time and change / As the world ebbs and flows, ourselves unchanged" (III.iii.23–24), a fantasy of escaping death that we can recognize as an intrinsic component of the

29. See Ross Woodman, "The Androgyne in *Prometheus Unbound,*" *SIR* 20 (1981), 225–47.

androgynous ideology. But the two will also participate in a process of continual creation, making "Strange combinations out of common things. . . Weav[ing] harmonies divine, yet ever new" (III.iii.32, 38). In this apocalypse of imaginative creativity, they will oversee humanity's millennium: "man grows wise and kind, / And veil by veil evil and error fall" (III.iii.61–62). In the forest Asia instructs the Spirit of the Earth, telling him that someday he will love his "chaste Sister," the moon (III.iv.86), as she and Prometheus do, androgynously, as one all-sufficient and self-fulfilling unit (or as the angels in Milton's *Paradise Lost* are described as loving each other). The fantasy here, of course, is blatantly escapist and nostalgic. In seeking to return to the Imaginary realm, Shelley seeks to deny the power, indeed the existence, of the Name-of-the-Father. His poem is, in fact, a panegyric to the latent power of the son to kill the father and institute a fantasied realm of perfection with the idealized feminine as mother/daughter.

In the conclusion to Act III, Shelley makes clear that the ideal society he desires has indeed come to pass. As the Spirit of the Hour says, the "mighty change" experienced by them all—Prometheus, Asia, the Earth—is also "Expressed in outward things," for now humanity lives in freedom: "The loathsome mask has fallen, the man remains / Sceptreless, free, uncircumscribed—but man:. . . just, gentle, wise" (III.iv.129–30,193–97). Whether or not this fantastic vision of reality is possible for mortal humanity or only a preview of the ideal afterlife is less important than the fact that Shelley has suggested that there can be no improvement of either realm apart from the fantasy of an androgynous merger of masculine and feminine. Panthea says in Act IV, "Heaven and Earth [are] united now, / Vast beams like spokes of some invisible wheel" (IV.i.273–74).

The fact that Act IV depicts an ideal and cosmically harmonious world without the literal presence of Prometheus and Asia should not obscure the reality of their felt presence. They are meant to be there in all of the oppositions that dominate the Act—the transformed water and fire, the Spirits and the Hours, the earth and the moon. Asia constitutes the renewed world of the physical, the redeemed senses, the creative natural force that animates Prometheus. He now represents the spirit, the conscious mind, and the imagination. In Prometheus and Asia we do not have, however, any rigid enactment of the dialectic of reason and the emotions, for Prometheus is certainly not merely the embodiment of reason, nor is Asia the simple emblem of emotion. What Shelley suggests is more complicated. That is, he sees the masculine and the feminine alternately assuming the traditional or stereotypical functions of the other sex. Thus at the beginning of the drama,

Prometheus is the victim of his emotions and therefore fallen and a prey to his worst imaginings. In the fantasy of the poem, Asia must then assume a traditionally masculine role and rescue him from himself.[30] In reading her dreams, she reads her own and his destiny as a composite and ideally balanced person. She then takes that vision of divine potentiality to Prometheus and makes it real. Prometheus, like Laon, is more than a little attracted to a passive posture; in fact, one is almost tempted to say that he regresses to the position of the infant at his mother's breast, idealizing that period of historical and psychic life that saw the child in total harmony with the maternal.

In this way the traditionally feminine forms of dream and song—the semiotic—are appropriated by Shelley as the modes of psychic liberation. Men sing themselves into the beings they would and could become through their feminized and feminizing imaginations. To escape the vicious cycle of tyranny and victimization that has enslaved Prometheus and Jupiter, then, Asia must transform not only Prometheus's will, but his vision of himself, his perceptual faculties. Not only does she have the power to transform the natural world into an imaginative one, she can change the human realm into its imaginative ideal. But all of this, of course, is purely a manifestation of the ideology of Woman as Other. According to Shelley's fantasy, only love inspired and directed by the imagination can redeem the world, and only the beloved woman can embody that love. Act IV pronounces that humanity is a "many-sided mirror," as well as "a chain of linked thought, / Of love and might to be divided not" (IV.i.384, 394–95). Prometheus and Asia, as the sexual embodiments of masculine "might" and feminine "love," have reunited these oppositions and thus made "one harmonious Soul of many a soul" and learned that "nature is its own divine controul" (IV.i.400–401). The fantasy here for the male poet/Culture Hero is the notion that he can create himself in the model of the reunited Prometheus and Asia when he realizes that "Language is a perpetual Orphic song" (IV.i.417). The notion of language as self-created and creating stands at the very center of the humanist ideology. The myth that the human is differentiated from all other creations, and that this distinc-

30. Stuart Curran has argued (rather conventionally) that Prometheus embodies the intellect, while Asia represents the emotions and intuition (see his *Shelley's Annus Mirabilis* [San Marino: Huntington Library, 1975], 99–100). For a Freudian reading of the poem, see Leon Waldoff, "Father-Son Conflict in *Prometheus Unbound*: The Psychology of a Vision," *PR* 62 (1975), 79–96. The most sophisticated recent reading of the poem's sexual imagery can be found in Hogle, *Shelley's Process*, 103–12, 182–92.

tion is based on the existence of the Symbolic/phallic realm of language, is at least as ancient as Orpheus and is stated most powerfully in the biblical notion that "In the beginning was the Word, and the Word was with God, and the Word was God" (John 1:1). The valorization of language here presents a most seductive and, we might add, pernicious lure—that man can appropriate the woman as his song, his voice, his creative spirit, and thus sing himself into divinity. *Prometheus Unbound* concludes on this triumphant note of masculine self-creation, but Asia is nowhere to be seen (or heard). Her absence confirms her status as a self-negating signifier for the fantasy of an enlarged masculine consciousness, the male poet's creation of himself as Culture Hero.

III Keats: "Thou art my heaven, and I thine eremite"

As we saw in *Endymion,* Keats was concerned with the dichotomies of flesh and spirit, Nature and Culture, male and female, but in his poetic delineation of Diana *triformis,* Keats's poetry finally does not present a convincing portrait of woman as anything other than a self-negating absence. In creating his version of the humanized apocalypse, Keats's Porphyro and Madeline, like Shelley's Prometheus and Asia, flee into an escapist denial of both the Semiotic and the Symbolic. This tendency toward a radically fictitious erotic apocalypse occurs in both poets' works for the same reason. Neither Shelley nor Keats was able to successfully translate the complexity of the feminine as both spirit and flesh, positive and negative, in his poetry. Blake (somewhat artificially) solves the problem by splitting Jerusalem and Vala and, although Keats attempted this in the triple goddess figure in *Endymion,* he does not convince. Keats's inability to decide whether woman is a lamia, victim/victimizer, or a Moneta, goddess/muse, finally paralyzes his heroes and his own vision as a poet.

In a letter to his friend Bailey (22 November 1817), Keats stated that his writing was caused by the lack of "a complex Mind—one that is imaginative and at the same time careful of its fruits—who would exist partly on sensation partly on thought—to whom it is necessary that years should bring the philosophic Mind." Keats troped his mind as a compilation of elements, called "Apartments" in another letter, in a way that reveals his recognition that a significant portion of his imagination was the feminine within him, his "Psyche." His philosophical and rational faculties he consistently images as masculine, his Apollonius side. But Keats came increasingly to reject and denigrate the feminine in favor of the masculine, which, ironically, led him to suspect the validity of his own imaginative powers. The Romantic revolution in sensibility, its demand for an androgynous personality, in turn demanded a (re)invention of the self (a fearful burden for any young poet). But it also required a poetic transformation of the perceived external world so that the new internal self could exist in harmony with others, as well as with the sexual and psychic components. Blake rose to the challenge with all the heritage of Western civilization behind him, albeit a heritage that he transformed into his own "system." Shelley and Keats both adapted traditional religious imagery in order to shape their own beliefs in humanized beauty, but neither was able to solve what turned out to be the crucial dilemma of their poetic universes: Was the feminine a lamia or a spiritual ideal, a whore or a redeeming madonna?

In his "Vale of Soul-Making" letter (21 April 1819), Keats stated that the gods originated in the human mind and as such were subject to the same conditions of change and flux as mortals were. Salvation for human beings, then, can only be found through internal reintegration of faculties, hence the popularity of the androgynous mythos and the prevalent use of psychomachia as a poetic device. Keats's poetic personae struggle in the poems to become identities and, without reducing any poem to allegory, it is possible to read Madeline as Keats's version of the beloved feminine, the embodiment of the "human heart," the semiotic/Imaginary, while Porphyro can be identified as the "World" and "Intelligence," the phallic/Symbolic. The effort to unify these two principles in *The Eve of St. Agnes* forms Keats's major poetic attempt to depict the androgynous quest as a transformation of male and female through the myth of the sacred, hierogamous "marriage."

We enter the world of the poem on Saint Agnes' Eve and are immediately immersed in a "chill," "cold," "frozen," and "silent" world. The first inhabitant we encounter in this world is the "numb" Beadsman, who worships the Virgin Mary in a particularly sterile and ineffectual manner (1).[31] His locus is the church, surrounded on either side by the "sculptur'd dead," "Emprison'd in black, purgatorial rails" "praying in dumb orat'ries" (2). We recognize that for Keats this deathly world of institutionalized religion is not only devoid of light, warmth, or passion, but is most pernicious because it has perverted the sexes and their power. The frozen Virgin Mary stands as a travesty of the feminine, what we recognize as the patriarchal cooption of the semiotic/maternal, while the numb and numbing Beadsman represents the ri-

31. *Letters,* I, 186; I, 280; II, 102. All references to *The Eve of St. Agnes* in the Stillinger edition are cited here by stanza number.

gidity and sterility of the Symbolic/paternal institutionalized as "religion." The Beadsman appropriately chooses to turn away from "Music's golden tongue," the beauty of art to transform the real, and to sit among "Rough ashes," praying for others when he himself is the one most in need of salvation (3).

We pass, then, from the world of perverted languages to the world of perverted senses—the world of the "level chambers." This realm is presided over by "snarling trumpets" and "carved angels" (4), a world of "argent revelry" with "rich array" and "shadows haunting fairily / The brain" (5). In the midst of this internal and external chaos, we are told about Madeline, the lady "Whose heart had brooded, all that wintry day, / On love" (5). She is the victim of the old wives' tales she has heard about Saint Agnes' Eve, the "visions of delight" and "soft adorings" she can have if she goes to bed without supper and keeps her eyes on heaven alone (6). We know, though, what Keats thinks of "heaven," and it seems clear here that he is gently spoofing the superstitions of the Catholic Church that are, after all, only slightly veiled versions of pagan beliefs and rites. Madeline wants to dream, however, "Agnes' dreams, the sweetest of the year," because she is not interested in the reality of love; she has, in fact, rebuffed many an "amorous cavalier." Instead, she wants to put herself into a trance, blind to everything but the ideal, visionary love her own fantasies can create (7–8). She reminds us in this context of the Sleeping Beauty of fairy-tale conventions who must sleep as a regression and escape from the emotional changes that are undergone during puberty. And just as the evil fairy or old woman functions as a foil, representing the fearful but necessary physical changes the adolescent must experience, so Angela doubles Madeline's psychic and physical development.[32]

We move next to the hostile moors surrounding the hall to find Porphyro, who has traveled to his enemies' house for a chance to "speak, kneel, touch, kiss" his beloved Madeline (9). As in a fairy tale of wish-fulfillment, Porphyro meets his only friend within the mansion, the old servant Angela, who warns him to flee the hall and escape "the whole blood-thirsty race!" (11). Taking Porphyro deeper into the mansion, she leads him to a "little moonlight room, / Pale, lattic'd, chill, and silent as a tomb" (13). There the two of them laugh at the folly of believing in the ancient power of the feminine. For Porphyro, St. Agnes' Eve is an occasion for mocking Angela about the traditional power of women: "'O tell me, Angela, by the holy loom / Which none but secret

32. See Bruno Bettelheim, *The Uses of Enchantment: The Meaning and Importance of Fairy Tales* (1975; rpt. New York: Vintage, 1977), 232–33.

sisterhood may see, / When they St. Agnes' wool are weaving piously' " (13). But Angela has been thoroughly coopted by the patriarchy herself and no more believes in the power of women than Porphyro does. In fact, she mocks Madeline's beliefs as ludicrous: " 'my lady fair the conjuror plays / This very night: good angels her deceive! / But let me laugh awhile' " (14). Porphyro, however, realizes that the fiction can be used as a way of gaining access to Madeline, immersed as she will be in "those enchantments cold" and "legends old" (15).

The "stratagem" that occurs to him comes "like a full-blown rose," but Angela sees nothing attractive in it: " 'A cruel man and impious thou art: / Sweet lady, let her pray, and sleep, and dream / Alone with her good angels, far apart / From wicked men like thee.' " In fact, Angela can hardly believe that Porphyro is "the same that thou didst seem" (16). Porphyro swears to do no harm to Madeline, and with words "woful, and of such deep sorrowing," Angela agrees to his plot (18). The night on which these lovers are to meet is, in addition to being Saint Agnes' Eve, also the night that "Merlin paid his Demon all the monstrous debt" (19). Are we to see Porphyro as a Merlin, magical in his power, and Madeline as a rarefied Vivien? The association is a contradictory prefiguration, ironically reversed in the course of the poem. Or perhaps we can more accurately see here the conscious and unconscious misogyny that pervades the majority of Romantic poetry. The story itself implies that in spite of the advantages that Merlin possessed he was still destroyed by the sexual machinations of a woman, and he therefore stands as a warning to Porphyro (and all male readers to beware of the seductive power of women.[33]

But Madeline is ostensibly presented as an ideal; her chamber is "silken, hush'd, and chaste," an alternative locus to the church depicted in the earliest stanzas of the poem. And she herself is a secularized Virgin Mary, a "mission'd spirit," a "tongueless nightingale," alive to the "spirits of the air, and visions wide" (21–23). But Madeline's chamber is most distinctly unlike the Beadsman's church in that it is filled with carven images of pagan fertility: "fruits, and flowers, and bunches of knot-grass," and stained-glass windows of saints and heralds, spiritual and political images of power (24). The natural/semiotic power of the moon mixes with this window—representing the Symbolic /paternal—as if in blessing on "Madeline's fair breast, / As down she knelt for heav-

33. See Marion Cusac, "Keats as Enchanter: An Organizing Principle of *The Eve of St. Agnes*," *KSJ* 17 (1968), for a review of the critical opinions that have been offered on the Merlin image. For the most critically sophisticated recent reading of the poem, see Levinson, *Keats's Life of Allegory,* 96–190.

en's grace and boon" (25). She is a "saint," "a splendid angel," "so pure a thing, so free from mortal taint" (25). The hyperbolic imagery almost strains in its re(de)ification of her as the Eternal Feminine.[34] The significance of the imagery here suggests that Madeline is to be some sort of human sacrifice, laid out on an altar bed, her virginity the crucial element in her desirability, used in a sacrificial manner to fictionally redeem them both. As an object of exchange, then, her value is predicated on her use as a sexual commodity.

Waiting until he is sure she is asleep, Porphyro creeps out and begins to set a table of "candied apple, quince, and plum, and gourd," jellies, syrups, manna, and dates (30). After arranging the food as a sacrifice, a communion with his goddess, he commands Madeline to awaken: "'Thou art my heaven, and I thine eremite" (31). But Madeline cannot be, nor should she be, awakened: "'twas a midnight charm / Impossible to melt as iced stream" (32). Porphyro next resorts to Madeline's "hollow lute" and attempts to awaken her by singing the ominous tale of betrayal in love, "La belle dame sans mercy," and—ironically—the song has the power to transform Porphyro: 'Ethereal, flush'd, and like a throbbing star." Art has bestowed on him the phallic power to blend into Madeline's "dream," that is, to melt his own dream of woman. Keats displaces the sexual intent throughout this section of the poem by resorting to flower imagery: "as the rose / Blendeth its odour with the violet,— / Solution sweet" (36). The phrase, "solution sweet," recalls the Renaissance erotic ideal, the mystery of merging with and "dying" into another in love. In this displaced version of the androgynous, Keats depicts Porphyro not simply as a sexual deceiver, but as the embodiment of the Symbolic/phallic realm, while Madeline represents the Imaginary/semiotic and natural world. Neither principle alone is enough, but together they provide the balance Keats knew was necessary for the fiction of a transformed psyche.

The lovers stand, then, as a redeemed version of the fallen Beadsman and Angela. In the two old people, Keats images what becomes of the masculine and feminine when divorced and alienated from each other.

34. Whether Madeline is the embodiment of ideal femininity or a dupe is the subject of a major critical debate, whose sides can be most clearly seen by contrasting the idealistic reading of Earl Wasserman in *The Finer Tone: Keats's Major Poems* (Baltimore: Johns Hopkins University Press, 1971) to Jack Stillinger's "The Hoodwinking of Madeline: Skepticism in *The Eve of St. Agnes*," *SP* 58 (1961), 533–55; rpt. in Stillinger's collection of essays, *The Hoodwinking of Madeline and Essays on Keats's Poems* (Urbana: University of Illinois Press, 1971), 67–93.

The Beadsman and Angela function as foils, fallen doubles for the transformed Porphyro and Madeline, who now speak as one self, each echoing the other in emotion and thought. Thus Porphyro says, "'This is not dream,'" while Madeline rejoins, "'No dream, alas! alas! and woe is mine.'" She sees herself as a "deceived thing;— / A dove forlorn and lost with sick unpruned wing" (37), while he sees himself as a "vassal blest," a "famish'd pilgrim,—sav'd by miracle" (38). The fiction here is that Porphyro has been redeemed, much as Prometheus was "saved" by Asia. In this poem the feminine as reified commodity is his "silver shrine" (38). It would seem that the male can be transformed, metamorphosed into eternity or some equally idealistic image of artistic perfection, only through the sacrifice and intercession of the idealized feminine. But the only object of value the female has to exchange in this transaction is her virginity.

The journey of the lovers is not quite complete, however; they must also flee from the castle perilous, inhabited by "dragons" (40), hystericized images of masculine violence. But they are invisible to the eyes and ears of those in the manor. "They glide, like phantoms" past the wakeful bloodhound who makes no bark and through a door whose key turns by itself in the lock (41). We as readers are in the world of poetic wish-fulfillment, fantasy, the reification of sexual apotheosis. The redeemed lovers leave behind them the world of the patriarchy, the violent and warlike masculine principle: "the Baron dreamt of many a woe, / And all his warrior-guests, with shade and form / Of witch, and demon, and large coffin-worm, / Were long be-nightmar'd." But the escape is also from the world of the isolated and sterile feminine principle as embodied in Angela: She "Died palsy-twitch'd, with meagre face deform" (42). Reportedly, Keats went out of his way to stress the grotesque aspects of the feminine divorced from union with the masculine. Richard Woodhouse stated in a letter to Taylor (19–20 September 1819) that Keats specifically wanted the image of the dying Angela deformed in order

> to leave on the reader a sense of pettish disgust, by bringing Old Angela in (only) dead stiff & ugly.—He says he likes that the poem should leave off with this Change of Sentiment—it was what he aimed at, & was glad to find from my objections to it that he had succeeded. (*Letters*, II, 163)

If Angela is the perversion of the feminine, is Madeline a successful symbol of the redeeming feminine within? It would seem that we are supposed to participate in the fiction that she can lift Porphyro, the

Symbolic/phallic principle, into some mystically oxymoronic realm. And if one analyzes her, one would have to recognize that her selflessness and sacrificial role are her most dominant characteristics. She functions quite literally as a human sacrifice, laid out on an altar/bed, her virginity the means of elevating both of them into some ideal, albeit escapist realm. The price demanded from a woman, quite simply, is her life, her individuality, her essence. Only when these are freely given, Keats implies, can the male be redeemed. The domestic ideology converges here with the androgynous compulsion to eradicate the woman, to reduce her to the status of self-negating signifier in the redeemed and expanded masculine consciousness.

IV Byron: "Half naked, loving, natural, and Greek"

Contrary to the opinions of the biographical Byron, who mocked "absurd womankind" and considered love "utter nonsense, a mere jargon of compliments, romance, and deceit," Byron's poetry often depicts idealized women who externalize the feminine qualities that Byron's male heroes most lack, most desire, and—quite often—most resist. Marlon Ross has observed about Byron: "What enables him to continue questing and conquering, despite the fact the quest is aimless and the conquest folly, is the presence of the feminine—the prospect of feminine nature, the promise of feminine love. . . . In Byron this feminine presence paradoxically is both the nurturer of the desire that impels the quest and the only escape, however momentary, from a 'contentious world.'"[35] In fact, Byron's compulsive tendency to portray idealized women as soft and loving counterparts to his stern and overly masculine heroes caused Hazlitt to remark: "Lord Byron makes man after his own image, woman after his own heart; the one is a capricious tyrant, the other a yielding slave."[36] But at the same time Byron depicted womanly women and manly men, he also explored the notion of feminizing his male characters and masculinizing his female characters. For instance, Medora and Gulnare become masculine women in order to love

35. See the discussion of Byron's attitudes toward women in Brown, *Sexuality and Feminism in Shelley,* 173–76, and Marlon Ross in "Romantic Quest and Conquest," *Romanticism and Feminism,* ed. Mellor, 44, 45–46.

36. See William Hazlitt, *The Spirit of the Age,* in *The Complete Works of William Hazlitt,* ed. P. P. Howe, 21 vols. (London: Dent, 1930–34), XI, 69.

Conrad, while Kaled is the complementary counterpart to Lara. One can attempt to dismiss the sexual imagery that runs throughout Byron's poetry as simply conventional, but its pervasiveness indicates that Byron indeed did use both sexual polarization and androgynous motifs to depict his own peculiar version of the ideology of idealized love. This ideology, however, is alternately exalted or undercut, just as the feminine beloved's power to redeem the isolated male is either praised or blasted. As Susan Wolfson has noted, Byron's poetry tends to "satirize prevailing ideologies," while its "sexual politics often reflect a conventional masculinism." The conflict between these two impulses, then, produces a "sexual disorientation" and "dislocation" that radically questions our traditional notions of what is "masculine" and "feminine."

In *Sardanapalus,* Byron claimed to be writing "Mental theatre," and such a term accurately captures the sense of the drama as psychomachia, for it portrays the struggle of a hero to balance his internal and warring sexual elements in order to achieve a harmonious and loving self. Myrrha, the Greek slave and beloved of Sardanapalus, functions as the first fully realized feminine ideal in Byron's work, for she is both a "real" woman and a symbolic ideal for Sardanapalus. In these capacities she most resembles *Don Juan*'s Haidée, who was praised for being "half naked, loving, natural and Greek." But Myrrha is as strong and decisive as Sardanapalus is flighty and weak, while she also symbolizes the Greek ideal of moderation and *virtu* that Sardanapalus so disastrously lacks. In fact, in *Sardanapalus* we are presented with characters who embody extremes, unbalanced caricatures of human qualities. Only Myrrha personifies the balance of oppositions that the Greeks (and Byron) held as their ideal. Salemenes, the king's brother-in-law and military advisor, is as stern, authoritarian, and pleasure-denying as Sardanapalus is the opposite. In depicting these qualities as "masculine," Byron is to a certain extent ironically deflating the simplistic sexual stereotypes of his earlier works at the same time he reinforces the mythology of what Edward Said has labeled "Orientalism." The vogue for the Oriental evidenced itself in a tableau of "sensuality, promise, terror, sublimity, idyllic pleasure, intense energy," but it is also more likely that given Byron's personal bisexuality he found in the Orient a world that "exuded dangerous sex, threatened hygiene" and excessive sexual freedom. In wallowing in the world of *Sardanapalus,* Byron was clearly trying to escape the tyranny of Western Europe's rigid and confining ideologies about the proper role and identity of men and women. Ironically, Byron carried those polarities so deeply within himself that even his fictional version of the Orient is polluted and becomes simply another microcosm of Regency England (complete with a disapproving estranged wife).

On the psychological level, however, we can clearly discern as the central struggle of Sardanapalus his attempt to balance the discordant elements in his own personality. And in this internal romance we have Byron's fullest treatment of the fictional androgynous quest achieved through union with the feminine beloved. The imagery, characters, structure, and theme reinforce the kings disordered identity and mirror his progressive transformation from an effeminate dandy to a man who briefly balanced both sides of his psyche before his death. Sardanapalus, more than any other Byronic hero, concerns himself with developing the feminine side of his nature even though he loses the loyalty of his subjects because of what they perceive as his effeminacy. The drama can be read, then, as an exploration of the impossibility of androgyny in a society that ultimately values only the masculine characteristics of aggression and power.

The composition of *Sardanapalus* supposedly occurred because of a quarrel Byron had with his mistress Theresa Guicciolo over the question of whether or not love was the "loftiest theme for true tragedy." Byron introduced the character of Myrrha to prove to Theresa that he could "imagine and delineate a woman who was both passionate and high-minded." But apart from the personal motivation for the drama, it is significant that Byron was working from a historical source, specifically Diodorus Siculus on the history of the historical Sardanapalus, the last king of the Assyrians. Diodorus's physical description of Sardanapalus (not to mention Byron's own extensively diverse sexual history) seems to have intrigued Byron enough to write a work that would attempt to vindicate Sardanapalus's sexually anomalous nature. According to Diodorus, Sardanapalus

> led a most effeminate life: for wallowing in Pleasure and wanton Dalliances, he cloathed himself in Womens' attire, and spun fine Wool and Purple amongst the throngs of his Whores and Concubines. He painted likewise his Face, and decked his whole Body with other Allurements. . . . He imitated likewise a Woman's voice and proceeded to such a degree of voluptuousness that he composed verses for his Epitath: "What once I gorged I now enjoy, / And wanton Lusts me still employ; / All other things by Mortals prised / Are left as dirt by me despised."[37]

37. Diodorus quoted in a footnote to the text of *Sardanapalus* in *The Works of Lord Byron,* rev. ed., E. H. Coleridge (London: Murray, 1924), vol. V, 5. All

The question of why Byron would be attracted to this historical character, and why he would be compelled to sexually transform him from an effeminate, one might even say hermaphroditic, freak can perhaps only be answered by exploring Byron's deep ambivalence toward the female beloved, not to mention his own "sexual confusion."

Although his rivals Arbaces and Beleses, as well as his brother-in-law Salemenes, condemn Sardanapalus for his female impersonation, Byron presents his protagonist in a much more sympathetic light. For instance, in the first act we learn that Salemenes condemns Sardanapalus's "effeminate heart," pointing out that he, a male king, is "scarce less female" than his grandmother, Semiramis, known as the "Man-Queen" (I.i.9, 42–43). This dead "Man-Queen," an image of the phallic mother, the ravenous and destructive female, haunts the entire drama, and quite possibly provides the explanation for Sardanapalus's sexual confusion. As a male he seeks to undo the sins of his overly masculine grandmother, a woman who had her own husband put to death so that she could rule the country. In a reversal and displacement, Sardanapalus becomes a stereotypical feminine character, a male who, like a female, values love and human emotions more than power or authority. To his mistress Myrrha, Sardanapalus proclaims: "'My chiefest joy / Is to contribute to thine every wish. / I do not dare to breathe my own desire, / Lest it should clash with thine. . . . Thine own sweet will shall be the only barrier / Which ever rises betwixt thee and me'" (I.ii.20–38). The drama essentially questions whether or not this inversion of traditional masculine power is admirable or aberrant.

Ironically, Sardanapalus tells Salemenes that, although a king, he has never particularly admired the glory of warfare because of the death and misery it inflicts (I.ii.136–38). Instead, he values traditionally feminine characteristics:

> "I feel a thousand mortal things about me,
> But nothing godlike,—unless it may be
> The thing which you condemn, a disposition

---

quotations from *Sardanapalus* will be from this edition, with line numbers in parentheses in the text. For the best recent discussion of sexual themes in Byron, see Susan Wolfson, "'Their She Condition': Cross-Dressing and the Politics of Gender in *Don Juan*," *ELH* 54 (1987), 585–617. On Byron's attitudes toward the Orient, see Edward Said, *Orientalism* (New York: Pantheon, 1978), 119, 167, and consider Leigh Hunt's report that Byron himself trimmed and oiled his hair "with all the anxiety of a Sardanapalus [so that] the Grand Signior is said to have taken him for a woman in disguise" (quoted in Wolfson [above]).

> To love and to be merciful, to pardon
> The follies of my species, and (that's human)
> To be indulgent to my own."
>
> (I.ii.273–78)

But always before him appears the image of his grandmother; she is never absent for long from the drama. When Salemenes warns Sardanapalus that his feminine qualities, his despotism, weakness, and sensuality will lead to his overthrow, Sardanapalus responds by pointing to the example of his grandmother as if to ask, is this what I must be in order to gain respect from my subjects: "'Semiramis—a woman only—led / These our Assyrians to the solar shores of Ganges,'" and she returned "'like a *man*—a hero'" (I.ii.127–31). For all of her laudable masculine prowess, Sardanapalus tells his brother-in-law that he sees his grandmother as a "sort of semi-glorious human monster" (I.ii.181).

Sardanapalus next appears with Myrrha, his soulmate, to whom he is linked by "some unknown influence." She complements his sexual nature, and he recognizes that they are inverted mirror images of each other, for he is a king and she a slave. Such, Byron seems to imply, is the socially determined relationship of the sexes. Women have power only through love, which is actually perceived by men as a sort of weakness and disease. When Sardanapalus tells Myrrha that he will not go to war to defend his crown, she responds by chiding him, "'thou lovest not thyself nor me; / For he who loves another loves himself, / Even for that other's sake'" (I.ii.486–88). Myrrha's role, as she herself sees, is to make a strong and vengeful ruler out of Sardanapalus and, in doing so, to create a man she can respect as well as love. As she admits to herself, "I love him; / And that's the heaviest link of the long chain / To love whom we esteem not" (I.ii.634–44).

Act I, then, has shown Sardanapalus in dialogue with both his masculine alter-ego, Salemenes, and his feminine side, Myrrha. When both of them urge him in Act II to fight to defend his kingdom, he states: "This is strange; / The gentle and the austere are both against me" (II.i.577–78). Sardanapalus's sexual confusion has alienated him from both the external world and the internal world of his own psyche. His rivals continue to attack him as "The she-king," "That less than woman," the "king of concubines" (II.i.48–49; 59). The stage is set for battle, and Sardanapalus, who had said earlier that "my life is love: / If I must shed blood, it shall be by force," now realizes that he is begins forced to do just that. The lesson, Byron implies, is that a king who values love above force will not be tolerated by society.

Act III continues to develop similar themes of love and sexuality. For instance, the act begins with a storm and an ominous thunder, which the character Zames explicitly labels as a male deity. Sardanapalus rejects the toast proposed to him by Zames, just as he rejects the thunder as "His father god." He tells his comrades that "'I seek but to be loved, not worshipped'" (III.36). The rest of the act depicts the battle itself, which Sardanapalus refuses to enter until after he has consulted his mirror. Myrrha, in the tradition of androgynous women warriors such as Spenser's Britomart, joins her lover on the battlefield in order to witness his transformation into a hero. She admits that through battle he has finally proved himself to be a man, and therefore worthy of her love.

Act IV contains very little external action; however, it stands as the pivotal act of the drama. The focus of the act is Sardanapalus's dream as he relates it to Myrrha, for the dream images the violent sexual dislocations within his psyche. Sardanapalus tells his beloved that on his left side he saw "'a haughty, dark / And deadly face; I could not recognize it, / Yet I had seen it, though I knew not where: / The features were a Giant's'" (IV.84–87). This visage of male power stares at Sardanapalus with a "fixed glare of his eye," and refuses the cup offered to him (IV. 92–95). Meanwhile, on Sardanapalus's right side a horrible female figure appears, who, in contrast to the male, holds a goblet "bubbling o'er with blood" (IV.111). This female is a

> gray-haired, withered, bloody-eyed,
> And bloody-handed, ghastly, ghostly thing,
> Female in garb, and crowned upon the brow,
> Furrowed with years, yet sneering with the passion
> Of vengeance, leering too with that of lust.
>
> (IV.104–8)

Sardanapalus confesses his deathly fear of these figures, particularly the woman who "curdles" the blood in his veins. He overcomes the fear enough, however, to laugh in "their phantom faces," and the male, whom he recognizes as the Hunter-Founder of his race, grabs his hand as if to symbolically bestow the kingship. Although Sardanapalus tries to hold fast to the hand, it melts and the male figure vanishes, leaving "nothing but / The memory of a hero" (IV.139–46). This vanishing male authority functions as a foreboding and ominous omen, for Sardanapalus is soon to lose his crown, which had been rightly bestowed upon him by the male hunters.

The phantom female figure, however, remains, and rushes abruptly to kiss Sardanapalus, as if to congratulate him for having rejected the model of the male hunter. But for Sardanapalus she too is a loathsome and extreme figure, embodying poison and spreading it throughout the kingdom: "'Methought their poisons flowed around us, till / Each formed a hideous river'" (IV.152–53). There is apparently no escape from the loathsome female figure. She embraces Sardanapalus in a clear imagistic reversal, for he has embraced the female over the male throughout the drama. He tells Myrrha that he shrank "'from her, as if, / In lieu of her remote descendant, I / Had been the son who slew her for her incest'" (IV.156–58). Sardanapalus realizes finally that he is standing between his murderous grandmother and the rightful male founder of the Assyrians, the primal father. According to the historian Aelian, Semiramis obtained permission from her unsuspecting husband Ninya to rule over Asia for five days, but her first act was to have him thrust into a dungeon and later murdered so that she could have sovereign rule for herself. Sardanapalus sees these two extreme figures as the only two options possible to him, and is unable to conform to either position. He (and, one might add, the biographical Byron) sees both sexes as gross aberrations. Neither the manly woman nor the womanly man can exist in a society that has radically polarized and then institutionalized sexual identities and roles.[38]

Sardanapalus now confronts his wife Zarina and confesses that she has not failed him as a wife; he has failed himself. He tells her that he was "'Misplaced upon the throne—misplaced in life'"(IV. 331). He has finally realized that his downfall has been caused by the dominance of his feminine qualities, a condition simply unacceptable to society and not particularly conducive to his own psychic health. The ideal that Byron presents in the drama is most fully embodied in Myrrha, for she more than others is a successful balance of masculine and feminine, *virtu* and love. She is not only the ideal counterpart for Sardanapalus, but she stands as the embodiment of both the intellectually and emo-

38. There are a number of helpful secondary commentaries on the drama's theme of sexual balance, initially identified as central by G. Wilson Knight, *The Burning Oracle* (1939), 247. Jerome McGann's *Fiery Dust* (1968) claims that Byron provides a critique of the masculine mystique in the drama (141–64). Also see Peter Manning, *Byron and His Fictions* (Detroit: Wayne State University Press, 1978), 126–33; Allen Perry Whitmore, *The Major Characters of Lord Byron's Dramas* (Salzburg: English Institute, 1974); Samuel Chew, *The Dramas of Lord Byron* (New York: Russell and Russell, 1964), 105–14; W. Paul Elledge, *Byron and the Dynamics of Metaphor* (Nashville: Vanderbilt University Press, 1968), 121–25; and Michael G. Cooke, "The Restoration Ethos of Byron's Classical Plays," *PMLA* 79 (1964), 569–78.

tionally balanced maturity to which he aspires. But Myrrha is doubled or mirrored by Zarina, the queen and Sardanapalus's largely absent wife. He has not so much rejected her throughout the drama as he has his limited masculine role as traditional husband and father. Sardanapalus's rather grotesque character is explained, however, in the mythic dream of origins that haunts him throughout his life. The woman who denied and found expendable the male is mimicked in a later generation by Sardanapalus, who vainly attempts to copy her by denying his own masculinity in a futile attempt to become a "man-queen."

Sardanapalus concludes, as *Laon and Cythna* did, with the image of two lovers jumping ecstatically into flames, but we do not see even the fictional flight to an escapist or supernatural realm in Byron's poetic universe. The lovers console each other only with the thought that their "ashes" will continue mixing and so provide them with more embracings (V.471–74). This ironic conclusion suggests that the love of even an idealized woman does not defend against death—but then the real object of fear in Byron's poetry is life rather than death. In his destruction of Myrrha (and, one might add, the later death of Haidée), Byron confronted his ambivalence toward the "woman within" himself—a lovely creature who, finally, did not deserve to survive.

4

The *Femme Fatale:* "A Sight to Dream of, Not to Tell"

On the night of 28 November 1800, Coleridge went to bed to confront one of the many guises the *femme fatale* was to take in his dreams. He records that on that night he was visited by "a most frightful Dream of a Woman whose features were blended with darkness catching hold of my right eye & attempting to pull it out—I caught hold of her arm fast—a horrid feel. . . the Woman's name Ebon Ebon Thalud—When I awoke, my right eyelid swelled." But this blatantly castrating woman with a man's name was not the only one to haunt Coleridge's sleep. On the night of 3 October 1802, the night before Wordsworth was to marry and the night before his own seventh wedding anniversary, Coleridge had another particularly uneasy dream. He provides in his *Notebook* this description: "I was followed up & down by a frightful pale woman who, I thought, wanted to kiss me, & had the property of giving a shameful Disease by breathing in the face/ & again I dreamt that a figure of a woman of gigantic Height, dim & indefinite & smokelike appeared—& that I was forced to run up toward it—& then it changed to a stool—& then appeared again in another place—& again I went up in great fright—and it changed to some other common thing—yet I felt no surprize." [1]

1. Coleridge, *The Notebooks of Samuel Taylor Coleridge,* ed. Kathleen Coburn, 2 double vols. (New York: 1957; 1961); entry 848, entry 1250. This edition is largely unpaginated and contains text and notes in separate volumes. These dreams are instructively discussed by Beverly Fields, *Reality's Dark Dream:*

The women in both of these dreams are obviously overdetermined; they represent both themselves, that is, the fearful guises of femaleness, and Coleridge's manifold anxieties about his own prowess as a man and a poet. Just as Shelley projected his own eyes—his specular appropriation of the creative act—onto the nipples of Mary, so does Coleridge know on an unconscious level that the female within him has the power to usurp his eyes—his sexual and poetic potential. As the second dream reveals, he fears the woman not simply because she can castrate him, but because she possesses an uncanny body. In one instance she is diseased, that is, castrated, but in another she is threatening and huge, the mother returned to wreak vengeance for her desertion by the guilty son. But before that manifestation can be confronted effectively, she has assumed the appearance of a three-legged stool, a typical dream symbol for the male. In other words, the woman is now the phallic mother, but before that transformation can be understood, she has changed again, this time into some "common thing," a "thing," that is, that can be controlled by the male. For Coleridge, the woman is fearful and uncanny not simply because she represents his own repressed fears about castration and punishment at the hands of his mother, but because she can assume so many deceptive and hysterical forms, shapes that actually mirror his own hysteria in regard to his (and her) body.

As the Romantic poets discovered, frustrations and failure are inherent in the quest for external salvation through an internal and self-created principle, that is, the feminine beloved. In seeking to embrace and love an idealized image of the self, the Romantic poets found themselves in postures of ironic defeat—either fleeing life itself or attempting to flee the body that was, after all, the palpable physical reminder that androgynous impulses could only end in failure. Anger and sexual nausea, then, result in the face of this frustration. The women themselves—not their poetic creators—are blamed for failing to elevate man to what he sees as his properly divine status, and the next women

---

Dejection in Coleridge (Kent, OH: State University Press, 1967), 59–63, 87–91, and Norman Fruman, *Coleridge, The Damaged Archangel* (New York: Braziller, 1971), 373–79. In *The Mermaid and the Minotaur* (New York: Harper and Row, 1970), 62, Dorothy Dinnerstein accounts for "archetypal nightmare visions of the insatiable female" as caused by the male's primitive desires for "unqualified access" to the mother's body, coupled with the mother's "terrifying erotic independence." Otto Rank interprets the female devourer as a manifestation of the male's anxiety about birth trauma; in confronting and slaying the female, the male denies his tie to her and mortality (see his *Trauma of Birth* [1923; rpt. New York: Harper and Row, 1973).

we will examine are poetic creations born of this frustration. In his anger and self-disgust, the male poet creates another darker projection of himself: female characters traditionally seen as *femmes fatales* within the corpus of English Romantic poetry—Coleridge's Geraldine, and Keats's Belle Dame and Lamia. Again, there are other seductive and fatal women in Byron's *oeuvre,* but they do not have the symbolic quality that allows them to exist primarily as feminine projections of their male creators. By examining the permutations that the fatal woman takes in a few key Romantic texts, I hope to demonstrate that what has been seen as a characteristically stock figure during the period actually tropes the self-loathing, self-disgust, and sexual doubts that these male poets most feared about themselves and their poetic missions. If they could not idealize the feminine and find salvation through her, then they would denigrate, attack, and abuse her power. The *femme fatale* stands as the mirror image of the feminine beloved, the dark double of the woman as savior. If the feminine beloved's sexuality leads man to "Heaven," or at least linguistically to an escape from the limitations of the flesh, then the *femme fatale* leads man to "Hell," or complete immersion in the body as corrupt, diseased, castrated, and fatal.

The body of the *femme fatale* also becomes the object of male fantasies about the female body as uncanny, as representative of the male infant's memories of discovering the mother's "castration," which gives rise to his own castration anxiety. The hysteria that results from that discovery, repressed and "buried" in the adolescent, emerges later in the poetry as the male confronts in hieroglyphic form his earliest ambivalent feelings toward the mother's "deformed" body. The metaphor of the buried and bloody mother can be further extended to the "body" of the poem, so to speak, which must be in some way "diseased," fragmentary, or inexplicable, as an appropriate mirror for its subject matter, the fatal woman. Karen Swann has observed on this point that the "Romantic woman, like flagrantly seductive style, functions similarly to divert: she secures poetry's enticing reserve and the knowingness of poets and critics by allowing interpretive dramas to be seen as fascinating romantic encounters."[2] But if these poems are not exclusively "about" the women who inhabit them and instead are "about" interpretive strategies, the female figure who functions as cipher, self-erasing muse, or absent signifier can also be seen as an element within the

2. See Swann, "Harassing the Muse," in *Romanticism and Feminism,* ed. Mellor, 82. In a provocative study, Camille Paglia claims that Geraldine consumes the text and causes the poem's hysteria because of her "psychoiconic" presence (see her *Sexual Personae* [New Haven: Yale University Press, 1990], 345).

male poetic psyche—in this case, the self-hatred and anxiety he has about his own masculinity.

The *femme fatale* traditionally represents woman as pure flesh, the embodiment of female sexual power—dark, powerful, voracious. As Xavière Gauthier has observed, Freudian ideology recognized that a girl's sexuality is greater than a boy's and therefore those raising her should devote more time to repressing its power: "Female eroticism is terrifying; it is an earthquake, a volcanic eruption, a tidal wave. It is disquieting and so is mystified. It is made a mystery."[3] We can apply Gauthier's observation to our reading of both Christabel and Geraldine—the two sides of woman as perceived by the threatened male consciousness. On one hand, Christabel as the young innocent is raised in an atmosphere rife with sexual repressions; she herself is the logical product of a patriarchal upbringing that has suppressed her emotions to such an extent that she must find what passes for "experience" only at night, away from the ever-watchful eyes of her father. Geraldine, on the other hand, functions as a libertine, a woman who has allowed her sexuality to openly display itself; like some volcanic force erupting from her body, her sexuality is perceived as diseased, dangerous, fearful, hypnotic.

The sexual caverns that threaten to engulf the male poet/heroes emerge in these poems with special force and immediacy. The woman as sexual predator, the *vagina dentata,* is carefully delineated only so that she can be carefully destroyed, her power eradicated by that same male poetic authority that created her. In the creation of the *femme fatale,* we can also discern a poetic recreation of the castration anxiety that is a central meaning, for instance, in *Christabel.* Freud's essay "The Medusa's Head" (1922) describes the horror that has traditionally been represented by the phallic snakes emerging from the head of Medusa. Her fearfulness arises from the fact that the snakes not only represent the female usurpation of the multiple power of the phallus, but are associated with her decapitated state—troping her castrated state as well as the male's dread of castration (*SE,* XVIII:273–74). The *femme fatale* also embodies what Freud was later to define in "Female Sexuality" (1931) as woman's "penis envy" and the "masculinity complex"

3. See *New French Feminisms,* 202. For an analysis of the reasons for Freud's anxiety about female sexuality, see Janine Chasseguet-Smirgel, "Freud and Female Sexuality: The Consideration of Some Blind Spots in the Exploration of the 'Dark Continent,'" in *Sexuality and Mind: The Role of the Father and the Mother in the Psyche* (New York: New York University Press, 1986), 9–28.

(*SE*, XXI:98–99). But as Gregory Zilboorg noted in 1944, Freud's observations about women's supposed "phallic inferiority" were determined by both misogynistic traditions and the male sexual anxieties that initially created those attitudes. Zilboorg also recognized that at the root of Freud's theories of "penis envy" was his and his culture's "fundamental envy" of women, what Karen Horney even earlier had called man's "dread of woman" caused by "womb envy."[4] More recent feminist theorists have turned Freud's castration theory on its head and claimed that male anxiety does not originate in childhood, but in adult fantasies designed to neutralize the power of the feminine. One has to remember, however, that Medusa was punished with both the snakes and the deadly gaze, according to the *Metamorphoses*, by another woman—Athena—who was offended by Medusa's sexual activity in Athena's temple. Athena, the patriarchally coopted woman, the woman as the ideological construction, the complete mental fantasy of the patriarch, functions in harmony with the Law of the Father to suppress and quickly punish any acts of overt female sexual rebellion. For instance, Susan Lurie asserts that "the sight of woman as castrated is [a] mature male wish-fulfillment fantasy, designed to counter the real terror the sight of woman inspires; *that she is not castrated* despite the fact that she has 'no penis,' and does not inspire male fear for his castration. . . . Psychoanalytic discourse participates in a broad cultural project. . . of constructing the woman as castrated precisely because the sight of her does *not* signify her castration."[5] But it is actually a moot

4. See McGann's "The Beauty of the Medusa: A Study in Romantic Literary Iconology," *SIR* 11 (1972), 3–25, for a discussion of the Medusa as the "key Romantic iconograph." McGann recognizes the "double aspect of the Medusa's appearance"—her beauty and her horror—but he chooses to interpret her within a political context, as a "victim of the tyranny and cowardice of established power" (7). His reading quite noticeably defends against recognizing the castration anxiety implicit in the Medusa. See also Zilboorg, "Masculine and Feminine: Some Biological and Cultural Aspects," in *Psychiatry* 7 (1944), 271, 294, and Horney, "The Dread of Woman: Observations on a Specific Difference in the Dread Felt by Men and by Women Respectively for the Opposite Sex," (1932); rpt. in *Feminine Psychology*, ed. Harold Kelman (New York: Norton, 1967), 133–46.

5. See her "Pornography and the Dread of Women: The Male Sexual Dilemma," in *Take Back the Night*, ed. Laura Lederer (New York: Morrow, 1980), 159–78; also see her "The Construction of the 'Castrated Woman' in Psychoanalysis and Cinema," *Discourse* 4 (1981–82), 53. Two useful collections that analyze the reasons for the predominance of the figure of the evil woman in the nineteenth century are Joseph Kestner, *Mythology and Misogyny* (Madison:

point as to whether the female body inspires dread predicated on male castration anxiety or awe because she is not castrated. Both possibilities reveal a terror of the female body that bespeaks her power to do harm either through her lack/absence/gap or her abundance/presence/power.

The *femme fatale*'s power finally rests on her dual visage, her doubleness, her fearful multiplicity. One is reminded, in fact, of the definition Edmund Burke proposes for Terror, for both derive their force from their "ability to hurt." And as Weiskel has pointed out, the "fear of injury points genetically and synecdochically to castration anxiety. We know that the castration fear of the young boy is not realistic; nevertheless it operates subjectively as a real fear. A fantasy of aggression or resistance toward a superior power is played out in the imagination, and the boy sees at once that he would lose." The boy's fantasy of bodily injury from the father ends in his realization of the defeat he will surely face if he openly becomes a rival of his father for the mother. At the same time he realizes that the threat he faces from his father is not, after all, a real one. This makes possible a positive resolution of the anxiety in the third phase, which allows him to psychologically identify with his father rather than his mother.

According to Freudian theory, identification is simply a more sophisticated defense mechanism, another form of introjection or incorporation. The boy must have introjected or internalized an image of the father in order to picture to himself the consequences of aggression against the father in order to possess the mother. The identification that thus establishes the superego retains for the boy an essential ambiguity; the boy neutralizes the possibility of danger by incorporating or swallowing it, and the father becomes an internal principle and cannot harm the boy from without. But the boy must also renounce the aggression and turn himself into—be swallowed by—the image of the father,

University of Wisconsin Press, 1989), and Bram Dijkstra, *Idols of Perversity: Fantasies of Feminine Evil in Fin-de-Siècle Culture* (New York: Oxford University Press, 1986). Nina Auerbach's *Woman and the Demon: The Life of a Victorian Myth* (Cambridge: Harvard University Press, 1982), examines the split female figure in mid- to late-Victorian culture, while Lynda Nead, *Myths of Sexuality: Representations of Women in Victorian Britain* (Oxford: Basil Blackwell, 1988), discusses art as a historical discourse. Peter Gay (in *The Bourgeois Experience, Vol. 1: Education of the Senses* [New York: Oxford University Press, 1984], 207) has observed that "No century depicted woman as vampire, as castrator, as killer, so consistently, so programmatically, and so nakedly as the nineteenth."

who now functions as an ideal with whom the boy identifies.[6] The *femme fatale* appears in this Freudian fiction as a hysterical version of the unattainable and punishing mother. And it is perhaps no coincidence that she is imaged similarly in Romantic poetry—as in some way diseased, hideous, freakish, or taboo. The poems themselves veer off into a self-deceptive style in a futile attempt to elide the actual subject matter of the poem—confrontation with the body of the bloody and fearsome woman.

Blake's poetry contains an early Romantic *femme fatale* in his depiction of Vala—less a fully realized female character than the embodiment of the Female Will run riot. The bleak vision of sexuality as animalistic and sadomasochistic recurs throughout Blake's poetry, culminating in the imagery of *Jerusalem* 64. Here Vala—the ultimate *femme fatale*—screams an accusation against the male that not only castrates him, but endows her with phallic power:

> The Human is but a Worm, & thou O Male: Thou art
> Thyself Female, a Male: a breeder of Seed: a Son & Husband: & Lo.
> The Human Divine is Womans Shadow.
>
> (E, 215; K, 698)

The mature Vala as presented in *The Four Zoas* III functions clearly as the *femme fatale*/phallic mother, for she not only reduces the male to marginality, she usurps his sexual role: "Vala shall become a Worm in Enitharmons Womb / Laying her seed upon the fibres soon to issue forth" (E, 320; K, 292). Blake describes this world of divided sexuality as "The Sexual Death living on accusation of Sin & Judgement / To freeze Love & Innocence into the gold & silver of the Merchant / Without Forgiveness of Sin Love is Itself Eternal Death" (*J* 64: E, 215; K, 699). But Blake's Vala is finally less powerful than her alter ego Jerusalem, although the two women (actually one split woman) form a feminine constellation that was to recur throughout the portrayals we have of the Romantic woman as *femme fatale*.

6. Freud's "Economic Problem of Masochism" (1924); *SE* XIX:169; Burke's comment can be compared to Robert Stoller's argument that the root of sexual excitement lies in hostility: "it is hostility—the desire, overt or hidden, to harm another person—that generates and enhances sexual excitement. The absence of hostility leads to sexual indifference and boredom. The hostility of eroticism is an attempt, repeated over and over, to undo childhood traumas and frustrations that threatened the development of one's masculinity or femininity." See his *Sexual Excitement* (New York: Pantheon, 1979), 17.

I Coleridge: "This mark of my shame, this seal of my sorrow"

Coleridge's authorship of *Christabel* has allowed Norman Fruman to claim that the poem reveals Coleridge's psychological legacy of "unresolved incestuous conflicts, hatred of women, divided personality, fear of sex, homosexual impulses, female demons issuing threats and punishments, and fiends in the guise of loved ones."[7] Whether Coleridge himself was guilty of this list of rather severe psychological shortcomings is not my concern here. The poem itself reveals a fear and hatred of women that need not be based on his personal history since this sort of misogyny was a cultural reality, endemic to Coleridge's era (and, one might add, to ours). But Coleridge does not simply create Geraldine as the *femme fatale* of this poem; his creation of Christabel, her double and alter ego, bespeaks his fear of *all* women, even those who convincingly appear to all outward appearances to be good and chaste. His portrait of the women in this poem reveals both his conscious and unconscious opinion of them as perverse, sexually voracious, predatory, and duplicitous.

Traditionally, the critical question asked about *Christabel* is whether Geraldine functions as an evil, horrifying power who completely subverts the calm, domestic, and ordered life of Christabel and her father, or whether she somehow represents a necessary knowledge that brings life and growth to a stagnant and death-possessed world. For Fogle, Enscoe, and Spatz, *Christabel* is a poem about necessary sexual initiation, while for Nethercot and Jones, Geraldine is a lamia or demonically possessed spirit. That this question can be seen as the central issue of the poem, and that it has been answered in so many different ways, testifies to the deep ambivalence implicit in Coleridge's treatment of the sexual power of women.[8]

7. Norman Fruman, *Coleridge: The Damaged Archangel,* 407. Considerably more optimistic readings of the poem can be found in Anthony J. Harding, *Coleridge and the Idea of Love* (Cambridge: Cambridge University Press, 1974), and his "Mythopoeic Elements in *Christabel,*" *MLQ* 44 (1983), 39–50; and J. Robert Barth, S.J., *Coleridge and the Power of Love* (Columbia: University of Missouri Press, 1988).

8. See, for instance, Richard H. Fogle, *The Idea of Coleridge's Criticism* (Berkeley: University of California Press, 1962); Gerald Enscoe, *Eros and the Romantics* (The Hague: Mouton, 1967); Jonas Spatz, "The Mystery of Eros: Sexual Initiation in Coleridge's *Christabel,*" *PMLA* 90 (1975), 107–16; Edgar Jones, "A New Reading of *Christabel,*" *Cambridge Journal* 5 (1951), 102–3; and Vir-

On a purely literary level, however, *Christabel* was intended by Coleridge to participate in the poetic dialogue he was conducting with Wordsworth. In fact, the creation of *Christabel* was a dialogic response to Wordsworth's portrayal of Margaret in *The Ruined Cottage,* a poem about the fate of a "real" woman separated from her husband. While the androgynous/symbolic impulses in Coleridge's poem are not to be found in Wordsworth's work, these impulses are eventually subsumed by the overwhelming sexual power that Geraldine exerts over all the other characters she encounters.[9] In Christabel and Geraldine we have a composite feminine power, one woman split into two, just as we have one composite masculine force in Leoline and Roland, one father split into two figures. The poem on one level presents an oedipal drama—a study of two fathers, two daughters, one father, one daughter, all fathers, all daughters. We have a poetic recreation of a self that cannot assimilate itself, a self that is split between the good little girl, "daddy's girl," and the dark and brazen hussy that daddy cannot accept in his maturing daughter. Both fathers, clear emblems of the patriarchy, reject Christabel and Geraldine and force an image of acceptability on them, an image that demands nothing less than sexual neutrality. Geraldine must become more like Christabel in order to be acceptable to her father, while Christabel—ironically—must become more like Geraldine in order to gain her beloved's (and her father's) love. But it would seem that at some level the poem also can be read as a psychomachia, a tale of a split being who longs for harmonious merger with its divergent and warring fragments.

Christabel begins in a world presided over by a dead mother and an almost impotent fisher king of a father. A strongly powerful and sexual

---

ginia Radley, *Samuel Taylor Coleridge* (New York: Twayne, 1966). Schapiro claims that the poem makes clear the fact that for Coleridge "the serpentine, bad mother resides in the heart of the seemingly innocent 'sweet maid,'" (*Romantic Mother,* 80). Beverly Fields points out that the psychological dynamics of the poem reveal that Coleridge's primary sexual identification was with his mother rather than his father, causing his extreme narcissism: "whenever Coleridge thought he was in love, he was actually attempting two things at once: the purgation of the female within him and the reconciliation of his male and female needs. The tension between these two opposite attempts caused the failure of both" (*Reality's Dark Dream,* 66–67).

9. See Paul Magnuson (*Coleridge and Wordsworth,* 97) for a discussion of *Christabel* as a poem that "questions both the optimism of hope and certainty of the meaning of signs within landscapes that the Pedlar claims to be able to read." Also see his *Coleridge's Nightmare Poetry* (Charlottesville: University of Virginia Press, 1974).

woman enters into this spiritual and physical wasteland, and her identity and purpose form the crux of the poem. Coleridge stated that while he was writing Part II, he had continually in mind Crashaw's "A Hymn to Saint Teresa": "Since 'tis not to be had at home, / She'll travail to a martyrdome." Warren Stevenson has pointed out that another poem in that same volume, subtitled "Her Masculine Courage," is based on the idea that Saint Teresa is able to transcend her sex and become like a male angel: "Read HIM for her, and her for him."[10] In depicting Geraldine, Coleridge was trying poetically to create a woman with the power of a man, one whose power would presumably be beneficial, much like the spiritually androgynous power of Saint Teresa. The irony of the poem, however, consists in the fact that strong women can only be perceived by men as phallic and castrating. Their sexuality is only threatening to a society that cannot permit or acknowledge female saints.

If Geraldine can only be active and fearful, then her double Christabel can only be passive and afraid. In fact, Christabel's function throughout the poem is to suffer the onslaughts of others; she is the complete masochist much as Geraldine is the consummate sadist. Christabel is the child who watches her father and Geraldine betray her love and devotion. Betrayal, then, echoes throughout the images that inaugurate the poem.[11] In Part I the clock strikes midnight, and we are reminded that the dead mother of Christabel had predicted that Christabel would hear the clock strike on her wedding day. If we participate as readers in the fantasies of the poem, then Christabel's "wedding day" occurs as she leaves the castle to meet her fate, Geraldine. She becomes herself in this meeting, for she encounters her necessary complement; she becomes, in other words, the complete woman she was always intended to become. She "marries" herself to herself; she joins the two sides of her personality and accepts her sexuality in accepting Geraldine.

From the exterior world of Nature, we move to the interior patriarchal world of Sir Leoline, "the Baron rich" (6). His masculine power and

10. Coleridge, *Notebooks,* III, notes 3911, 59–60 ff., quoted in Warren Stevenson, "*Christabel:* A Reinterpretation," *Alphabet* 4 (1962), 23.

11. If we follow Marjorie Levinson's recent speculation that the poem places Christabel's mother, Roland, and Leoline in a triangular relationship that results in the birth of Christabel, a child her father cannot quite accept as his own, then we can see Geraldine's arrival on the scene as both a substitute atonement for suspecting the dead mother and an object of revenge against Roland. She sees Geraldine as a "Fury" whose "appointed task" is to liberate the death-infested Langland Hall, with the poem's focus on Leoline's tragic di-

wealth are equated in a sort of syllogistic logic that excludes women from participation in such a world. The Baron's dog, a "toothless mastiff bitch," functions as an image of powerless animalistic maternity. She can only howl when she hears the clock striking, and is thought to be in touch with the power of the dead mother, for according to superstition she is able to "see my lady's shroud" (13). We move from this dead and frozen world of the separated sexes back to the exterior world, where, paradoxically, the night "is chilly, but not dark" (15). Somehow this is a natural world in which contraries mutually coexist, where clouds cover "but [do] not hide / the sky" (17). And although the moon is full, it looks "both small and dull" (19). The physical setting is further specified when we are told that the month is April, and "the spring comes slowly up this way" (22). In the midst of this strangely foreboding landscape of darkness, dullness, and dreams emerges the Lady Christabel, "Whom her father loves so well" (24). It is surely significant that she is introduced as her father's beloved daughter first, and that only secondarily are we told that she is also the beloved of "her own betrothed knight" (28). She is a woman defined by herself and her creator in relation to men. We are led, in fact, to ask if she has any identity of her own. And is her sudden encounter with the mysterious Geraldine a recognition for the first time of her own submerged sexuality and aggressive self?

We are told that Christabel has left her safe and warm castle to enter this cold world because of her frightening dreams (strangely sexual dreams in a rejected manuscript version). She intends, then, to pray for her beloved knight's safety beneath a "huge oak tree," a druidic and pagan power that stands in sharp contrast to the domesticated altar in her own bedroom (35). Clearly, Christabel is seeking an alternative female power; she is rejecting her own dead mother's influence as much as she is rejecting the Virgin Mary as an acceptable image of femininity. And in a passage that reads as wish-fulfillment, Christabel hears a moan that echoes her own pain. On the other side of the tree, as if in a mirror, Christabel views Geraldine: "a damsel bright, / Dressed in a silken robe of white" (58–59). Paradoxically, Geraldine is "frightful" because she is so "richly clad" and "Beautiful exceedingly" (66–68). Geraldine stands here as the emblem of powerful female sexuality, her white dress proclaiming a purity that she does not in fact possess. Her beauty can also

---

lemma (see her *Romantic Fragment Poem,* 88–93). But such a reading merely subscribes to and reinforces patriarchal prejudices, which must make the male presence in the poem the center of all action and meaning.

reveal a pervasive male fantasy: that women are ultimately false exteriors concealing internal depths of sexual corruption.

Before identifying herself and answering Christabel's frightened question, "'And who art thou?'" Geraldine asks Christabel to "'Stretch forth thy hand, and have no fear!'" (70, 75). Later, Geraldine repeats her request to embrace in fellowship with Christabel (102). What we see here are the two sides of a woman's way of relating to the "other" as both external and internal to herself. Christabel wants to use her linguistic and rational skills to define the essence of Geraldine by giving her a name. Geraldine, on the other hand, wants to initiate the relationship through physical contact, through the body. As if in sadistic and perverse recognition of Christabel's fear of the physical, Geraldine tells a story that purports to explain her identity. The story is, of course, Christabel's own projection, her own persistent and suppressed sexual fantasy, representing everything that is supposedly foreign and alien to her experience (but not, as we know, to her fantasies or dreams). Geraldine claims to have been "seized" and raped by five warriors, kidnapped, and then dumped beneath the same oak tree that Christabel is inexorably drawn to. Like the mastiff bitch, the owl, and the cock, she too has awakened only at the striking of the clock at midnight. But Geraldine's story (or what we can see more accurately as Christabel's projected rape fantasy) is belied by her radiant appearance; with her beautiful robes and gems intact, she hardly appears the way a woman would after such an escapade. But Christabel is not capable of questioning appearances; the word is true for her. As a genuine innocent, she accepts the reality of the verbal as easily as she accepts the veracity of the visual.

"Then Christabel stretched forth her hand, / And comforted fair Geraldine" (104–5). At this point we realize that Christabel is able to embrace Geraldine because she believes in and accepts the story, the fable of female complaint. That is, Geraldine has recited a rape fantasy, a story that embodies Christabel's deepest fears and desires. She, too, would like to have such fearful and exciting experiences, only to survive them guiltless and unscathed. Learning the true nature of sexual experience, Coleridge implies, requires accepting both the verbal and the physical dimensions of one's own being. Separating the head from the body can lead only to separating women into Christabels and Geraldines—neither is true and such a distortion will only bring destruction to patriarchal society. As if in recognition of the threat to the power of the father, Christabel immediately pledges Leoline's help and loyalty to Geraldine (106–7), as well as her own "couch" for the night (122).

Christabel knows, intuitively and guiltily, that she will have to introduce Geraldine into the house "as if in stealth" (120). Christabel assumes a dominant role throughout this episode; indeed, she imitates the ravishing warriors who had supposedly earlier "taken" Geraldine. In fact, Geraldine's passivity suggests that she functions within the poem as a female icon, carried around and sexually exploited periodically. She literally embodies the woman as object of desire, and her silence and passivity reinforce a male sexual fantasy—the woman who abdicates her own will in favor of the stronger male will. All of this sexual theorizing, however, places Christabel in the position of a man, which, of course, is how she functions in the poem in relation to Geraldine. She opens the heavy iron gate and carries Geraldine over the threshold, much like a bridegroom (130–32). The next images, the dog moaning, the owl screeching, the fire's ashes blazing, and Geraldine's refusal to pray to the Virgin, supposedly point to her identity as a lamia.[12] But the entrance of the two women into the father's house is most significant in the fact that they enter as one person, literally. If the dog, owl, and fire recognize Geraldine as a serpent, they must also see that her evil is entwined inextricably with Christabel.

As Christabel enters the house carrying Geraldine, she sees nothing but the "lady's eye" and the "boss of the shield of Sir Leoline" (160–62). The eye—the semiotic/Imaginary capacity for preternatural vision—and the shield—the Symbolic/phallic power of the male—mirror each other and image the challenge that Christabel faces. She must use Geraldine to understand her father and his power, and until she does so, she will never understand herself or her own place in society. The rooms of Christabel and her father are next contrasted in order to demonstrate the differences between their two worlds. The Baron lives in a room "As still as death, with stifled breath," while Christabel lives in-

12. On the lamia motif as well as early approaches to the psychological themes in the poem, see Roy P. Basler, "*Christabel*," *SR* 51 (1943) and his *Sex, Symbolism, and Psychology in Literature* (New Brunswick: Rutgers University Press, 1948); Arthur Wormhoudt, *The Demon Lover: A Psychoanalytical Approach to Literature* (1949; rpt. Freeport: Books for Libraries, 1968); Edward E. Bostetter, *The Romantic Ventriloquists* (Seattle: University of Washington Press, 1963); Arthur Nethercot, *The Road to Tryermaine* (1939; rpt. New York: Russell, 1962); and Edward Prodfitt, "*Christabel* and Oedipal Conflict," *RS* 46 (1978), 248–51. R. E. L. Masters discusses the lamia as a vampire who was compelled to kidnap children out of jealousy caused by her own barrenness. This lamia also was known to have sexual relations with both men and women (see his *Eros and Evil: The Sexual Psychopathology of Witchcraft* [New York: Julian, 1962], 184).

stead in the room of an artist, filled with carved "figures strange and sweet, / All made out of the carver's brain" (171; 179–80). But the moonlight does not enter Christabel's room; rather it is illuminated by a lamp "fastened to an angel's feet" (176; 183). Shutting out the power of Nature, Christabel lives instead in a world infused with the suffocating influence of religion. And yet, in the midst of this world of death, she speaks of her mother as if that woman had just been cooking the other day. Christabel offers to Geraldine "this cordial wine! / It is a wine of virtuous powers; / My mother made it of wild flowers" (191–93). We know, however, that the wine must have been sitting in the room for over fifteen years.

When Christabel informs Geraldine that her mother died giving birth to Christabel, Geraldine alters her false voice and curses the power of the mother: "'Off, wandering mother! Peak and pine! / I have the power to bid thee flee. . . . Off, woman, off this hour is mine—/ Though her guardian spirit be, / Off woman, off! 'tis given to me'" (206–7; 211–13). But what has been given to Geraldine? She clearly sees herself as some sort of surrogate mother to Christabel, an alternate maternal force that will bring Christabel to a maturity she could never gain through her "real" (physical/social/religious) mother.[13] Geraldine will function instead as the antisocial, antireligious force that Christabel both fears and desires, at the same time providing Christabel with the forbidden sexual knowledge she thinks she needs to negotiate and survive a world that rewarded her mother with death for bearing a child. A woman's fear of the mother is, finally, the fear of bearing a child, of submitting oneself to the ravages of generation and decay. Blake, of course, explored this same fear in *Thel,* and in many ways Christabel echoes that heroine's ambivalent flight from the soiling effects of sexual experience.

The two women enact a parodic communion service in Christabel's room, complete with the dead mother's wine as symbolic blood. Like mirror images, the two kneel next to each other and drink from the

13. On the question of Christabel's hysterical sense of her own feminine identity, see Karen Swann, "*Christabel:* The Wandering Mother and the Enigma of Form," *SIR* 23 (1984), 533–53; Charles J. Rzepka, "Christabel's 'Wandering Mother' and the Discourse of the Self: A Lacanian Reading of Repressed Narration," *RP&P* 10 (1986), 17–43; and Margery Durham, "The Mother Tongue: *Christabel* and the Language of Love," in *The (M)other Tongue: Essays in Feminist Psychoanalytic Interpretation,* ed. Shirley Nelson Garner et al. (Ithaca: Cornell University Press, 1985), 169–93.

wine. Geraldine blesses Christabel, clearly recognizing Christabel's spiritual superiority:

> All they who live in the upper sky,
> Do love you, holy Christabel! . . .
> But now unrobe yourself; for I
> Must pray, ere yet in bed I lie.
> (227–34)

Christabel obediently undresses, settles herself in bed, and then proceeds to watch Geraldine mirror her previous actions, except that in undressing Geraldine reveals to the reader her physical deformity: "Behold! her bosom and half her side— / A sight to dream of, not to tell!" (252–53). The canceled versions of this passage leave no doubt that Coleridge intended the bosom to be scaly, like that of a reptile. Geraldine's freakish condition suggests not only that she exists within the tradition of women as lamias/serpents, but that she specifically is antimaternal, breastless, without the necessary milk to nourish her (surrogate) young. But this glimpse of something physically hideous about the female body reads as a hystericized text, all too reminiscent of the young male's traumatic realization of the female's castration. In Christabel's frozen stare at Geraldine's deformity we can see a displacement, an overdetermination of meaning. On some level we can read Christabel's perception of Geraldine's physical deformity as symbolic of the male perceiving for the first time what he thinks are "castrated" (fe)male genitals. The hysteria in the text is displaced from the male author and reader onto a young woman, who functions as a surrogate for Coleridge's own anxiety toward women. But Christabel's vision can also be seen as representing the male's castration anxieties. Thus Geraldine's power for male readers stems from her symbolic status as the dark lady of male castration fantasies—victim and victimizer.

In the climactic scene of Part I, during which Geraldine struggles with some internal agony, we learn that "Deep from within she seems halfway / To lift some weight with sick assay, / And eyes the maid and seeks delay." Geraldine would seem here to recognize her own perversity, the corruption of her touch. But she is also clearly the creation of a male poet who, like his culture, views the sexual desires of a woman as aberrant, so unnatural, in fact, that the woman should find herself and her desires disgusting. In other words, Geraldine can only be an effective *femme fatale* if she herself internalizes her society's loathing of women. But rather than avoid contact with Christabel, she "Collects herself in scorn and pride, / And lay[s] down by the maiden's side!— /

And in her arms the maid she took" (257–63). The deformed and hideous bosom, the emblem of Coleridge's misogyny and Geraldine's denial of maternal sexuality, actually embodies the key to Geraldine's power. She tells Christabel: " 'In the touch of this bosom there worked a spell, / Which is lord of thy utterance, Christabel / Thou knowest tonight, and wilt know tomorrow, / This mark of my shame, this seal of my sorrow' " (267–70). The "seal of sorrow" that the two women will share is their identities as women who claim the power of female sexuality without the price of maternity. As Geraldine initiates Christabel into this "spell," she knows that Christabel will never be able to return to her innocent complicity with the father/betrothed. Geraldine will, in effect, be creating another *femme fatale* much as vampires kissed their victims into fellowship.

This central scene of Part I has been read as a seduction, a sexual initiation, an encounter with the power and fascination of evil. But we can also see it as a merging of two split aspects of one self that have hitherto been unconscious of each other. Just as Christabel has no mother and a father obsessed with death and power, so does Geraldine. And as Geraldine and Christabel lie together in bed, we are instructed to see them slumbering and mild "As a mother with her child" (301). Geraldine, despite her antimaternal inclinations, has not only brought to birth those denied aspects of Christabel's submerged self, but, in doing so, has also given birth to an aspect of herself: "A star hath set, a star hath risen, / O Geraldine! since arms of thine / Have been the lovely lady's prison" (302–4). When Christabel awakens she

> Grows sad and soft; the smooth thin lids
> Close o'er her eyes; and tears she sheds—
> Large tears that leave the lashes bright!
> And oft the while she seems to smile
> As infants at a sudden light!
>
> (314–18)

Between smiling and crying, Christabel cannot make much sense of the experience she has sought and undergone. She feels her mother's presence near her (328) and concludes the night sure in the certainty that "saints will aid if men will call: / For the blue sky bends over all!" (330–31). Her optimism and innocence are laughable, of course, particularly in the face of orthodox religion's complicity with the power of the fathers.

With the daily tolling of the matin bells to commemorate his wife's death at the beginning of Part II, we are back in the Baron's world of death. But when Geraldine hears the bells, she interprets them as "that merry peal" (361) and dresses to lay siege to her next victim, Sir Leoline, the patriarch himself. Refreshed and beautiful from her night's sleep with Christabel, Geraldine is, one might say, transformed. She now has "heaving breasts," and when Christabel sees this change she knows immediately and intuitively that "I have sinned!" (380–81). As Geraldine is externally altered, so is Christabel internally changed. Her facade of optimism cracks as she realizes that she has not only lost the self-created illusions about her mother, but will also lose her fiction of a father as well.

After meeting the Baron and telling him her fictitious tale of woe, Geraldine informs Leoline that she is the daughter of his youthful friend, Lord Roland de Vaux of Tryermaine. Their intimate friendship was destroyed by the idle gossip of acquaintances, and although they parted, "never either found another / To free the hollow heart from paining— / They stood aloof, the scars remaining, / Like cliffs which had been rent asunder" (418–22). This panegyric to male bonding reminds one of the fact that within the patriarchy the important relationships are between men, not between women or men and women. Leoline himself admits that he "[y]et ne'er found a friend again / Like Roland" (517–18). In gazing into Geraldine's face, Leoline sees Roland's face and swears vengeance on Geraldine's ravishers. He embraces her and, in proxy, Roland, for as Roland's daughter she is also his property, an extension of him. And it is here that we become aware of the other crucial social characteristic of women; they function as objects of exchange between the power brokers of the patriarchy. They also alternately mediate one point in an oedipal triangle that shifts in this poem between two men and one woman or one man and two women. One would think, in fact, that on some level Roland had sent his daughter to Leoline as a peace offering. Or that the proper response from Leoline would now be to send his daughter Christabel to Roland in exchange. The two women, after all, are interchangeable, fetishistic commodities of exchange.

After this embrace, Christabel experiences a "vision of fear, the touch and pain! . . . Again she saw that bosom old, / Again she felt that bosom cold" (453–58). So strong is her loathing, so overdetermined her reaction that one would think Christabel was witnessing a primal scene between her father and Geraldine. She even hisses like a snake, and Geraldine only just manages to transform her back into a praying "sweet maid" before Leoline sees her. By this time, however, Leoline is completely infatuated with Geraldine and can only see Christabel as "a thing divine" (476). She has now been transformed, as so many other

Romantic women have been, into "things"—silent, proscribed into shades of invisibility, less than human, caricatures of themselves.

And so the father's devotion to his friend's daughter is also a displaced manifestation of his devotion to himself and his own daughter. He wants, however, to continue living with both Geraldine and Christabel, and asks the Bard Bracy to travel to Roland's home to inform him of Geraldine's safety. But Bracy begs to delay his journey, citing a foreboding dream that he interprets as predicting danger to Christabel. In this vision, which had occurred the night the two women were in bed together, Bracy saw a dove named Christabel "uttering fearful moan, / Among the green herbs in the forest alone" and "underneath the old tree" (535–40). Upon closer inspection, however, Bracy discovered a "bright green snake" wrapped around the neck of the dove (549–50), the two of them breathing in harmony. The snake does not harm the dove, and the two forces joined together indicate imagistically the necessary conjunction of love and energy. The necessity to accept both the spiritual and the physical in woman is lost, however, on Leoline. He vows that he and Roland will "crush the snake"—destroy the reality of woman as physical, as body (571).

The final encounter of the poem is between the two women, who now openly vie for the father's favors. Leoline bestows a kiss of acceptance and love on Geraldine, and she turns with due deliberation to Christabel to reveal a "snake's small eye blink[ing] dull and shy." But this snake's eye is also filled "somewhat of malice, / and more of dread" (583, 586). Why should Geraldine fear and hate Christabel? Because she knows that Christabel has become as filled with self-hatred and disgust toward herself as Geraldine has always been. Both of them have been corrupted by the father's love/hate of woman; both have internalized the male's fear of the sexual power of woman. Christabel demonstrates her transformation by casting an identical snakelike look at Leoline: "And passively did imitate / That look of dull and treacherous hate!" (606–7). All Christabel can do is beg her father to send Geraldine away for the sake of her dead mother, who died sacrificially giving birth to a child who would "prove her dear Lord's joy and pride!" (631). The two "mothers"—Christabel's real mother and Geraldine—clearly compete with her for possession of Leoline. The Baron, however, does not take kindly to the suggestion that Geraldine be banished so quickly; in fact, he is enraged at the thought. He clearly sees the exile of Geraldine as another rejection of his former friend, and that he will not do again.

In the conclusion to Part II we are given a rather disjointed poem about a parent's excessive love for a child. In that very love the parent expresses his feeling in "words of unmeant bitterness" (665). Since the poem is supposedly unfinished, a fragment, we have inherited two contradictory conclusions concerning Coleridge's eventual intentions. Derwent Coleridge proposes the theme of the poem to be the doctrine of vicarious atonement, with Christabel suffering for the "weal of her lover that's far away." The other more pertinent theory was put forward by Dr. James Gillman, Coleridge's physician and later biographer. He asserted that *Christabel* was to conclude with Geraldine transforming "herself" into the appearance of Christabel's long-absent lover. In this male identity, "Geraldine" was to lead Christabel to the altar, and the real lover was to enter at the last moment, prove his true identity, defeat the false "Geraldine," and marry Christabel. Gillman claimed to have his version directly from Coleridge, but so did Derwent.

Another complication in the poem's history is the rumor that Hazlitt spread between the time the poem was written and actually published (1800–1816). He told friends that Coleridge's intention was to have Geraldine turn out to be a man, and this does sound like a garbled version of the Gillman theory. Coleridge was furious at such a simplistically insulting reduction of a poem that aims at being deeper and richer than a mere sexual masquerade, and he stated in a letter: "It seems that Hazlitt from pure Malignity had spread about the Report that Geraldine was a man in disguise." [14] But judging from the similarities between the Gillman theory and the Hazlitt rumor, it seems fair to speculate that Geraldine can be read on some level as a masculine figure. We know that Coleridge was familiar with Cudworth's *The True Intellectual System of the Universe,* which presents Josephus's account of a demon lover, a wicked dead man who assumed the body of a beautiful woman in order to spread destruction and evil. The lamia tradition was also well known to Coleridge, particularly her most characteristic quality: She is envious of mothers and slays children in revenge for her

14. James Gillman reported that Coleridge told him that "the story of Christabel is partly founded on the notion that the virtuous of this world save the wicked. The pious and good Christabel suffers and thus she defeats the power of evil represented in the person of Geraldine" (see his *Life of Samuel Taylor Coleridge* [London, 1838], 301–2). Derwent Coleridge, on the other hand, denied that Geraldine was a "witch or goblin or malignant being of any kind" (see his edition of *The Poems of Samuel Taylor Coleridge* [London: Frowde, 1907], 52). Coleridge's comment (9 February 1819) is recorded in *The Collected Letters of Samuel Taylor Coleridge,* ed. Griggs, IV, 918. Susan M. Luther's "*Christabel* as Dream-Reverie" (*Romantic Reassessment* 61; ed. James Hogg, 1976) and Michael D. Patrick's "*Christabel:* A Brief Critical History and Reconsideration" (*Romantic Reassessment* 11, ed. James Hogg, 1973) both survey the critical history of the poem.

own barrenness. But he could also have had in mind a passage from *Paradise Lost,* where fallen angels are doubly powerful because "when they please / [They] Can either sex assume, or both" (*PL,* 423–24).

Many critics over the years have recognized the sexual ambiguity that dominates all of the relationships within the poem. Christabel and Geraldine form a composite figure, whether some combination of masculine and feminine or, more probably, of types of femininity. There is also a good deal of displaced incest throughout the poem—mother and daughter, sister and surrogate sister, father and daughter. But the poem finally explores the various complexities that surround sexual identity and sexual rites of passage. Many commentators have pointed out that Coleridge assumes a female persona and vicariously undergoes female experiences in the poem. But it seems more likely that he elides the exploration of his very masculine fantasies about the female body as castrated and castrating. He claimed in his prose writings to celebrate the androgynous psyche; in fact, one of his most quoted and trendy statements makes this impulse explicit: "A great mind must be androgynous." [15] But the psyche in his poems is anything but androgynous; in fact it can most accurately be read as misogynistic. In *Christabel* we encounter experiences of sexual initiation, sexual betrayal, and desired and feared incest related simultaneously by the minds of female characters masquerading their real identities as male and of male characters concealing their identities as voices of the patriarchy. The poem reads very much like an extended sexual charade, a discourse that attempts to conceal its true source and motivating power—male fear of women buried beneath the literary trappings of a pseudomedieval fairy tale.

II Keats: "Some demon's mistress or the demon's self"

In a letter to his friend Benjamin Bailey, Keats recalled a persistent fantasy that he had entertained since he was a child: "When I was a Schoolboy, I though[t] a fair Woman a pure Goddess, my mind was a soft nest

15. This statement was made in the context of discussing Swedenborg's mind, and can be found in Coleridge's *Table Talk,* ed. W. G. T. Shedd, vol. 6 of *The Complete Works of Coleridge* (New York: Harper, 1884), 1 September 1834. For a discussion of Coleridge's other prose statements on androgyny, see Jean Watson, "Coleridge's Androgynous Ideal," *PS* 6 (1983), 36–56.

in which some one of them slept though she knew it not" (*Letters,* I, 341). This virginal goddess within the masculine psyche stands as one guise of the woman within, a sort of idealized memory of his mother, whom Keats the adult poet wanted to resurrect as a madonna, sexually inviolate in his fictional recreation of her. But every time Keats tried to present such a woman (Madeline, for instance), the sexuality that intrinsically adheres to women erupted into the text, and he found himself increasingly unable to sustain even the fiction of female purity. Keats's composition of "La Belle Dame Sans Merci" occurred eighteen months after he had contracted syphilis from a prostitute (autumn 1817), and just weeks after he learned that his brother Tom had been tricked three years earlier into thinking a woman named "Amena Bellefina" was in love with him. Keats's bitterness stemmed from the fact that Amena was a nonexistent fantasy woman, a creation of one of Tom's school friends. Tom, of course, died from tuberculosis, not from the disappointment of discovering that this woman was a chimera, but Keats seized on the poetic fantasy that Tom was destroyed by his fascination with a deceptive and fatal woman. And, without belaboring the various biographical (and ironic) implications, it seems that he rather persistently associates female sexuality with disease and/or death in his later poetry. In a letter written to his friend Bailey nine months before writing "La Belle Dame," Keats notes that he found himself constantly "full of Suspicions," "evil thoughts, malice spleen" while in the presence of women. He even reveals the source of his anger as rooted in his early disappointments in his mother: "You must be charitable and put all this perversity to my being disappointed since Boyhood. . . . I must absolutely get over this—but how? . . . That is a difficult thing; for an obstinate Prejudice can seldom be produced but from a gordian complication of feelings, which must take time to unravell and care to keep unravelled" (*Letters,* I, 342). One recalls here not simply the "gordian shape" of Lamia, but the twisted tangle of emotions in that poem that produces and reinforces misogyny, that "obstinate Prejudice." That Keats personally experienced the ambivalence of perceiving women as either virgins or whores has been noted by his biographers, using Keats's own letters on the subject.

The sexually mature woman is both ambivalently desired and feared in Keats's work for a number of reasons. She is, first of all, perceived as a mother figure who threatens to (re)engulf the poet/son in the semiotic, a regression that the son figure both fears and desires. As such, she must be overcome, or at least her power must be muted; she must be transformed into the passive beloved, the somnambulant woman who willingly and unquestioningly offers herself up for the salvation of the poet/hero. But Keats was also powerfully attracted to women whom we can recognize as narcissistic types. His description of Jane Cox, for instance, uncannily echoes Freud's description of such women as possessing the charm of "certain animals...such as cats and the large beasts of prey" (*SE,* XIV:89). Keats described Cox (one can only wonder how conscious he was of her name's phallic irony) by noting that "she makes an impression the same as the Beauty of a Leopardess. She is too fine and too concious [*sic*] of her Self to repulse any Man who may address her....I always find myself more at ease with such a woman" (Letter to the George Keatses, 14–31 October 1818). Keats presents, then, a darkly doubled version of woman in his creations of La Belle Dame and Lamia, both of whom express his sexual nausea and disgust at the sadomasochistic maneuvers that pass for "love" between the sexes.

In reading the title "La Belle Dame Sans Merci," we are immediately confronted with the ambivalence that characterizes both the subject of the poem and the author's attitude toward the female. The beautiful woman, it seems, has no mercy, or is it that she does not give thanks (to whom? for what?). The poem, one would suppose, will answer these questions, but instead the reader is presented with a riddling situation in which only questions are raised and no answers forthcoming. We are immediately introduced to the knight-at-arms, the Symbolic/phallic principle, clearly separated from the fantasy of a feminine ideal that he thinks he needs in order to bring fulfillment and love to his life. We see him "Alone and palely loitering" in a physical wasteland: "The sedge has wither'd from the lake, / And no birds sing" (1). We also learn that this knight is "haggard" and "woe-begone," wandering aimlessly in a landscape that has already been harvested and that promises no new growth (2). The knight stands, then, as an objective correlative to the sterile landscape. He, too, is painfully "withereth," physically plagued with "anguish moist and fever dew" (3). The symptoms, of course, resemble those from which Keats must have suffered during his syphilitic bout, as well as the more socially acceptable tuberculosis that is usually acknowledged as a presence in his poetry.

Between the third and fourth stanzas the voice shifts and we now hear the knight tell us how he has come to this predicament. He relates his own tale about a "Full beautiful" lady, a "fairy's child" with wild eyes (4). According to the knight, we learn that this woman is the cause of his destruction, for she has allowed herself to be wooed by the knight, who has presented her with a garland of flowers for her head and wrists. This supposedly innocent present actually suggests imagistically a "gift" of bondage, with the woman tied to the knight at her hands as well as through her mind. The knight's desired erotic domination is further enhanced by the woman's willing complicity: "She look'd at me as she did love, / And made sweet moan" (5). The two lovers are, in fact, both playacting, masquerading in the best tradition of sadomasochistic posturing. And they both play their assigned roles so well that not only do readers believe the fantasy, but so does the knight. Why shouldn't he? He is its creator. He sees nothing but the woman and hears nothing but her fairy song/moan (6), but this trance is clearly meant to be an image of his self-absorption, his egotism masquerading as eros.

The woman next assumes another passive-aggressive position by feeding the knight with "roots of relish sweet, / And honey wild, and manna dew," images that suggest a blatant oral sexuality. After indulging all of his physical needs, the woman talks to the knight in a "language strange," but is this language "strange" because it is foreign or because women as sexual fantasies do not talk? Indeed, they cannot talk because they do not really exist. The knight is "sure" that the woman has said, "'I love thee true'" (7), but is the "sure" to mean "I am sure that is what she said" or "surely that is what she said"? The knight's uncertainty stems from the fact that the woman exists as his projection, and she says whatever he wants or needs her to say to him at any given moment. There is no objective reality, no ontology here, only the psychological dynamics of sexual and sexist misogyny.[16]

The two lovers, however, repair to her "elfin grot," where the woman spends her time sighing and the knight shuts her "wild wild eyes" with

16. Robert Gittings puts the "Amena Bellefina" theory forward as the biographical source for "La Belle Dame Sans Merci" in his *John Keats: The Living Year* (Cambridge: Harvard University Press, 1954), 123. Earl Wasserman chooses to interpret La Belle Dame as "the ideal" that leads man toward heaven, but which can never be possessed in this world (see his *Finer Tone: Keats' Major Poems* [Baltimore: Johns Hopkins University Press, 1953; rpt. 1967], 74–77). On the opposite end of the critical spectrum, Morris Dickstein sees the lady as a "Circe" (see his *Keats and His Poetry,* 108). Taking the middle path in recognizing the lady's ambivalence as an image are Walter Jackson Bate, *John Keats* (Cambridge: Harvard University Press, 1963), 478–81; Stuart Sperry, *Keats the Poet,* 233–41; and Anne K. Mellor, *English Romantic Irony,* 93–94. Karen Swann observes on this point that the "romance" conventions in this poem indicate the lady's resistance, as well as aid in her disappearance: "romance blinds most readers to the woman's point of view—a point of view from which the exchange between lady and knight looks less like a domestic idyll or a fatal encounter and more like a scene of harassment" (see her "Harassing the Muse," in *Romanticism and Feminism,* ed. Mellor, 89).

"kisses four" (8). Whereas before she was bound to him, now she is "blinded" by his desire. But the woman in this poem only possesses the power the knight gives her, and with it she lulls him into a sleep and causes him to dream: "Ah! woe betide! / The latest dream I ever dream'd / On the cold hill's side" (9). This dream refers back to the dream that constitutes the first three stanzas of the poem, and in it he sees "pale kings, and princes too, / Pale warriors, death-pale were they all" (10).

This image has traditionally been read as a reflection of Keats's poetic anxiety, haunted as he was by the failed Chattertons who fell victim to the siren song of poesy. But within the most immediate context of the poem we can read these pale warriors as representatives of the Symbolic/the Law of the Father that has been under siege by ambiguous female power. These warriors, symbols of masculine power and authority, all warn the knight that he, like they, will fall prey to the evil lady (10). The paranoia and intense hatred of women is nowhere stronger in Keats than it is in this passage. The warriors further display their "starv'd lips" and try to convey once again their "horrid warning gaped wide" (11). The images stand, then, like the displaced hideousness of Geraldine's breast, as omens of castration anxiety. The sight of the evil lady functions to unman the warriors. They are silent, tongueless in expressing their fear and disgust for what they have seen in her. It would seem, however, that the warriors have succeeded in their goal, for the knight awakes in horror to discover that he too has been cut off from the lady and is alone on the cold hillside. He has become just like the other men of his society; he, too, hates and fears women. And so the twelfth stanza repeats the first stanza almost verbatim, giving the poem a circular structure of psychological frustration and futility. Keats has depicted in this poem both the results and the dynamics of misogyny and the frustrated "nympholeptic quest." There is no doubt that men need women, but they do not want "real" women; they want idealized sexual fantasies and so they create the ideal within themselves and then try to impose it on reality. The fantasy, of course, is doomed to explode from its own inherent (circular) contradictions and unreality. When the fantasy does explode, the poet/hero cannot condemn himself; he can only condemn the woman, the source/scapegoat of his failure.[17]

17. For a discussion of the "nympholeptic quest," see Nathaniel Brown's *Shelley and Feminism*, 40–44, and for another reading of the poem's linguistic circularity, see Susan Wolfson, "The Language of Interpretation in Romantic Poetry: 'A Strong Working of the Mind,'" in *Romanticism and Language*, ed.

But it would appear that Keats's portrait of the knight also conforms in striking ways to Freud's diagnosis in "On Narcissism" (1914) of the differences between men and women in their choices of love objects. According to Freud, men generally place a sexual overvaluation on the object of their choice, supposedly because their original narcissism has now been transferred to the sexual object. Men, therefore, experience love as a libidinal impoverishment of their egos while their beloveds grow in stature by absorbing, so to speak, the male's libidinal energy. For the woman, however, the situation is precisely reversed. Freud claims that at puberty the female who has developed beauty actually experiences an intensification of her infantile narcissism, which consequently makes her quite self-sufficient because she has fallen in love with herself. These narcissistic women do not seek to love but to be loved, and one man can fulfill this need as well as any other. In fact, the narcissistic woman is compelled to seek as many men as she can attract. Freud makes it clear that she exerts a good deal of attraction for men because she is capable of repelling any criticism of herself through the sheer power of her self-invested ego. Her own self-love ensures her happiness, as well as her relative indifference to her lovers. As Kofman observes, "it would no longer be she who envies man for his penis but he who envies her for her inaccessible libidinal position, for having known how to keep her narcissism in reserve while he . . . has impoverished and emptied himself of this original narcissism to the advantage of the love-object."

The love of the *femme fatale* is, then, one manifestation of the love of the narcissistic woman, whom Freud called the "most frequently met with, probably the purest and truest" type of woman. According to Kofman, this type of woman exists as the very "essence" of woman as created by men, the root of the male fantasy of the Eternal Feminine. The narcissistic woman corresponds to the desires of men in that

---

Arden Reed (Ithaca: Cornell University Press, 1984), 22–49. Wolfson claims that we as readers find the knight as difficult to understand as the knight finds the lady. The lady is therefore not the locus of the poem's significance, but only one of many mysteries that "accentuate the gap between the strangeness of signs and their proposed translations" (37). In an intriguing recent interpretation, Marjorie Levinson (in *Keats's Life of Allegory,* 46) argues that the knight represents the "hero of the masturbation myth," an "image of productive self-alienation. What the masturbator, like the middle class, produces is himself as an internally fissured, eternally hungry space: a market that consumes but does not assimilate."

> she represents the lost part of [the male's] own narcissism, which has been projected so to speak onto the exterior. The fascination exerted on them by this eternal feminine is nothing other than the fascination exerted by their own double, and the uncanny feeling which men experience is the same as that which one feels before any double or any ghost, before the abrupt reappearance of what one thought had been forever overcome or lost.[18]

"La Belle Dame" strikingly illustrates Keats's ambivalence toward the doubleness of the female as real and the feminine as male-created ideal. Traditionally, however, male literary critics have celebrated the (supposedly) benign face of the feminine in his poetry. For instance, Mario D'Avanzo reads the image of the woman in Keats's poetry as representative of the supreme beauty with which the poet aspires to merge, thereby becoming elevated to imaginative apotheosis. In troping the sexual act as a "frenzied creative act" or the "ultimate imaginative intensity," Keats was using women to play the part of the imagination to the male poet's knowledge or reason.[19] For Keats the woman as ideal anima could only embody the realm of truth and beauty, complemented and made whole by her union with the power of the male poet's mind/reason so that together they formed a new complete being. But if that was the ideal according to some platonic fantasy, the reality of failure/irony/frustration was the more typical result for Keats's heroes. The woman as ideal anima would not cooperate, and in her refusal to play the role of passive redeemer, she doomed the male hero to imaginative sterility and, finally, death.

With both the beneficent Madeline and the destructive Belle Dame in mind, I want to examine Keats's final completed work for its presentation of the misogynistic and frustrated androgynous dynamics implicit in delineating the *femme fatale*. *Lamia* also explores the notion that one must unify one's psychic faculties in order to survive. But the poem dramatically illustrates that such unification is impossible in a

18. See Freud's "On Narcissism" (*SE* XIV:73–102), and Sarah Kofman, "The Narcissistic Woman: Freud and Girard," in *French Feminist Thought*, 210–12; 215.

19. Mario D'Avanzo, *Keats's Metaphors for the Poetic Imagination* (Durham: Duke University Press, 1967), 36–38. The poem has been read insightfully by David Simpson, in "Keats's Lady, Metaphor, and the Rhetoric of Neurosis," *SIR* 15 (1976), 265–88, and in his *Irony and Authority in Romantic Poetry*, 15–17.

society that polarizes the two sexes as warring opposites. Lycius stumbles into a situation where he can be only a victim of himself and his illusions. Love can only be a disappointment for him because it is compounded of woman's dual (and irreconcilable) nature. The split woman in this poem is blatantly divided by male perceptions, and the poem asks the question, is woman a beauteous facade or a stinking sewer? And what is the proper male response to women? Lycius's tendency is to idealize Lamia in order to better subjugate her. What Keats gives us in *Lamia* is a profound study in erotic neurosis, a neurosis that results from society's dichotomous attitudes toward women. The virgin/whore syndrome is dramatized here with a vengeance. As Keats observed in *Endymion*, "There never liv'd a mortal man, who bent / His appetite beyond his natural sphere, / But starv'd and died" (IV, 646–48). Such a sentiment, the notion that loving a woman is ultimately "unnatural" for a man, expresses Lycius's dilemma. He is the male/hero destroyed by his own tendencies to hate the woman within him, and as such he falls victim to the war between his masculine and feminine sides, played out by his self-created fantasies of "Lamia" and "Apollonius."

The poem begins, appropriately, in a dreamlike atmosphere, complete with fairy-tale devices: "Upon a time, before the faery broods / Drove Nymph and Satyr from the prosperous woods" (1–2). We are asked by Keats to participate as readers in the fantastic world of myth, to return to a world where mental and physical transformations can occur with the stroke of a magical (phallic) rod, now troped as the power of poetry. The affair of Lamia and Lycius is framed mythically and self-consciously by the tale of Hermes and the nymph, who function as ironic/poetic/fictitious doubles for the central love affair that occurs in the poem. We are first introduced to Hermes as he leaves "His golden throne, bent warm on amorous theft" (8). His male authority and power do not guarantee him possession of the woman he desires; in fact, his identity as a thief is stressed. Love for him is just another commodity, as were his thefts of light (9). In order to escape the wrath of the patriarch Jove, this trickster flees to Crete, where he hears tales of a beautiful nymph, so lovely that she is worshipped and desired by all the Satyrs and Tritons on the island: "Ah, what a world of love at her feet! / So Hermes thought, and a celestial heat / Burnt from his winged heels to either ear" (21–23). The gods here are not loving in some refined "finer tone"; they, like ordinary mortals, are motivated by simple greed and lust. Hermes desires the nymph because she is desired by others; she exists in the text of amorous rumor and he wants to possess something that others want. He is, we are told, stung by jealousy; his hair falls "in jealous curls about his shoulders bare," while his search for the nymph is filled with "painful jealousies" (26, 33).

In appropriate irony Hermes fails to discover his nymph and finds instead a "palpitating snake" who begs to be released from her snake body, her "wreathed tomb." Within this body lies trapped a feminine soul that longs for "love, and pleasure, and the ruddy strife / Of hearts and lips!" (38–45). The description of this serpent woman stresses the ambiguity and power of the phallic woman:

> She was a gordian shape of dazzling hue,
> Vermilion-spotted, golden, green, and blue;
> Striped like a zebra, freckled like a pard,
> Eyed like a peacock, and all crimson barr'd;
> And full of silver moons, that, as she breathed,
> Dissolv'd, or brighter shone, or interwreathed
> Their lustres with the gloomier tapestries—
> So rainbow-sided, touch'd with miseries,
> She seem'd, at once, some penanced lady elf,
> Some demon's mistress, or the demon's self.
> (47–56)

Her association here with the moon clearly identifies her with the triple goddess who functioned as the buried mother in *Endymion,* but the more important semantic device employed is the use of "seem'd." The serpent only *seems* to be; her appearance is not an accurate reflection of her identity. Like the Belle Dame or Geraldine, the ambiguities and conflicts between female appearance and reality consistently characterize the *femme fatale.* Specifically, we are asked if this "serpent" is relatively harmless, in fact, a victim herself—a "lady elf" doing penance for some prior sin. Or is she more sinister, darker, the mistress of the devil or even the devil (her)self? The association here between female sexuality and evil, satanic power is explicit. The serpent/woman is feared because of her sexuality, and the only way to control that sexuality is to reduce her to an object of abjection, something one can defend against with the purification rituals (baptism, communion) offered by patriarchal religions (Kristeva, *Powers of Horror,* 90–112). Like the vision of Geraldine's breast, we are again in the psychological territory of a paralyzed male viewing a fearful scene—the body of the "castrated woman." Like the Medusa's head with its serpent-encrusted hair, the woman here has a serpent head (59) with a woman's mouth out of which she speaks "bubbling honey, for Love's sake" (65). Clearly, the imagery bespeaks the attraction/repulsion approach/avoidance dance conducted toward the female throughout Romantic poetry.[20]

But Hermes is not intimidated by this vision; rather, he is compared to a "stoop'd falcon ere he takes his prey" (67). Lamia, however, is able to prey upon Hermes because of his masculine vanity and his lust for capturing his ultimate prey, the nymph. The serpent/Lamia insinuates that she knows the location of the nymph and will reveal it if Hermes will transform her with his "'serpent rod, / And by thine eyes, and by thy starry crown!'" (89–90). But we are told that Lamia is the "brilliance feminine," infinitely stronger than Hermes' serpent rod (92). She possesses a specific female power that protects other women (and presumably herself), for the serpent/Lamia has made the nymph invisible so that she can wander as she likes without being visually assaulted by the "unlovely eyes, / Of Satyrs, Fauns, and blear'd Silenus' sighs" (102–3). If Hermes grants Lamia's request, Lamia promises to make the nymph visible to Hermes alone. But if Lamia has the magical power to make someone else invisible, why does she need Hermes' help to transform herself? And if much of Hermes' desire for the nymph is based on her desirability to others, why would he want her to be visible only to him?

At this point Lamia lifts "her Circean head" (115) and tells her story as if in answer to the questions we as readers have formulated. But can we suspend our own disbelief to even privilege this story-within-a-story as believable? Was Lamia ever a woman, or did she simply have, through magic and conjuration, a "woman's shape," an equivocal qualification that she herself acknowledges (117–18). By simply breathing on Hermes' brow, Lamia enables him to see the nymph: "It was no dream; or say a dream it was, / Real are the dreams of Gods, and smoothly pass / Their pleasures in a long immortal dream" (126–28). In other words, the nymph is as much a feminine projection, a psychological fantasy of a woman, as the other women we have examined throughout this study. Keats seems to acknowledge that gods are gods because they can live permanently in this fantasy world of women of their own making, un-

20. Marilyn Butler points out that serpents may be evil in Christian iconography, "in which they are associated with man's fall from perfection through his own sexual frailty, and through woman; but there is nothing in nature or in other mythologies to sanctify this reading. Keats's description of Lamia's change from serpent to woman allows for both possibilities—the ominousness of her serpenthood, the beauty and naturalness of it"; see her *Romantics, Rebels, and Reactionaries: English Literature and its Background, 1760–1830* (New York: Oxford University Press, 1982), 134.

encumbered by intrusions of reality and inevitable frustration. Hermes loved the nymph without ever seeing her; he loved her image as inscribed through the desire of others. It is that self-created image of perfection that he sees in his own mind.

In a contrapuntal transformation, Lamia undergoes a grotesque metamorphosis, grotesque in its very physicality. Whereas the nymph's transformation had been internal and emotional, Lamia foams at the mouth, convulses in pain, and finally dissolves, melting to nothing more than a voice. She loses all of her original serpentine beauty, her sapphires, greens, amethysts, and rubies, so that "Nothing but pain and ugliness were left" (164). We have seen in Geraldine this belief that the external veiling of the woman is what is beautiful, while her stripped and inner core can only exhibit ugliness, and we recognize it as characteristic of male fear in the face of what is perceived as the castrated female. But we never see Lamia in the process of her transformation as a woman; we are left only with this image of "pain and ugliness." Suddenly, like a male fantasy of wish-fulfillment, Lamia appears as a "lady bright, / A full-born beauty new and exquisite" fleeing toward Corinth (171–72). Standing by a pool, like a female Narcissus, we are instructed to see "a maid / More beautiful than ever twisted braid" (185–86). Lamia appears to be a "virgin purest lipp'd," but she is actually a "lovely graduate" of "Cupid's college" and as such is "in the lore / Of love deep learned to the red heart's core." She is particularly skilled in the arts of sadomasochism, with the enviable power to "unperplex bliss from its neighbour pain" (189–92, 197–98). Her goal now is to pursue the charioteer Lycius, whose "calm uneager face" (218) challenges her.

After sacrificing to Jove, Lycius "by some freakful chance" (230) separates from his friends and wanders into a region unknown to him—the feminine of his own mind. The meeting of Lycius and Lamia, then, has been to some extent engineered by the patriarch Jove: "Jove heard his vows, and better'd his desire" (229). Lycius clearly went to the temple to pray for love, experience, passion, for he had grown "wearied of . . . Corinth talk" (232). In boredom he wanders "Thoughtless" through the forest, lost in "phantasy," until he slips into a realm "where reason fades, / In the calm'd twilight of Platonic shades" (234–36). In this condition he is "shut up in mysteries, / His mind wrapp'd like his mantle" (241–42); he exists at this point as the purely masculine ego devoid of emotion, love, or energy. His psychic creation of Lamia meets his perceived need for an Other who will truly engage him. In a manner strikingly similar to Geraldine, Lamia presents herself to Lycius as a damsel in distress and appeals for help. He falls in love with her appearance, her voice, but we cannot fail to recognize that she exists as a consumable object for him. He wants to drink "her beauty up" and ingest her "delicious" words (249–51). Lamia, for her part, knows that she has successfully snared her prey: "she saw his chain so sure" (256). And Lycius within minutes has addressed her as a "Goddess" (257). This idealization and elevation of the woman reveals that Lycius instinctively knows that Lamia is not human. And indeed she is not.

Lamia tells Lycius, whom she flatters as a "scholar," that she is a "finer spirit" who will not survive in a "human clime" (279–81). Unless he can offer her a "serener palace" and "purer air," she will not be able to satisfy her needs and will be forced to depart (282–83). Lycius immediately swoons, and the "cruel lady, without any show / Of sorrow" for his pain, stoops to kiss him (290–91). She awakens him with a song and tells him another version of her identity story, which we know to be a (male-created) fantasy. According to this version, she has lived in Corinth as a reclusive virgin, only seeing Lycius as he worshipped at Venus's temple. It would seem, however, that Lycius himself is aware of the fictitiousness of the tale; he sits in amazed delight "To hear her whisper woman's lore so well" (325). It is as if he is trying very hard—not very successfully—to convince himself that she is a "real woman, lineal indeed" (332). Are we to believe that Lycius will confer reality on her by telling her imaginary tale? Can fiction create life for mortals as it did for the god Hermes?

Lamia, however, has shrewdly assessed her lover and determined that he could not love "in half a fright, / So threw the goddess off, and won his heart / More pleasantly by playing woman's part" (335–37). She is simply conforming to his latest fantasy of a woman. He is aware, however, that his sexual fantasizing is socially unacceptable, and he reveals this as he enters Corinth in disguise, "Muffling his face," and fearing detection by the "sharp eyes" of Apollonius (362). The introduction of Apollonius at this point emphasizes that he, too, is less a real person than the rational and skeptical masculine principle within Lycius. For Lycius, Apollonius exists to deny pleasure, beauty, love, and the feminine. He may be seen by Lycius as a "trusty guide" and a "good instructor," but he is also the "ghost of folly haunting my sweet dreams" (375–77). Lycius knows that if he is to indulge his fantasy life with Lamia, he must do so secretly, in a house "Shut from the busy world of the mere incredulous" (397).

The second part of the poem opens with a number of foreshadowing devices that predict the disintegration of Lycius's tenuous psychic embrace of the feminine. We learn almost immediately that "too short was their bliss / To breed distrust and hate, that make the soft voice hiss" (9–10). But, in fact, the "love" of Lycius and Lamia does turn into hissing, sadomasochism, and painfully pleasant torture. And as Lycius awakes from his love dream he is called to return to the real masculine world of power through the "thrill" of trumpets (27). The first thought that occurs to him is compared to a "buzzing in his head" (29), just as earlier love had been compared to a bat or a bee that "buzz'd his wings" above the couple in jealousy (12–13). And in the midst of barely introducing his lovers, we are told that "all this came a ruin" (16).

Like the knight in "La Belle Dame," Lycius has been immersed in the fantasy of love, dead to the rational masculine world. Now he sees his home with Lamia as a "purple-lined palace of sweet sin" (31), and his spirit longs to escape this mindless enslavement to the sexual feminine. Lamia is clever enough, though, to know that "a moment's thought is passion's passing bell" (39). When she confronts Lycius with her suspicions of his waning passion, he responds by "bending to her open eyes, / Where he was mirror'd small in paradise" (46–47). In this image we can see that his supposed love for her is actually based on his own narcissism; she is his creation and his female double. His next intention is to "entangle, trammel up and snare / Your soul in mine, and labyrinth you there / Like the hid scent in an unbudded rose" (52–54), and one is reminded of the lovers in Blake's "Clod and Pebble" who seek to use the other as an object to toy with or torture.

Lycius primarily desires to show off his acquisition, his self-created female object, much as Hermes wanted to compete with others for the nymph's love. Lycius wants to parade his "prize" through the streets of Corinth so that his friends will "choke" in envious jealousy (57, 62). Despite all of Lamia's pleas to the contrary, Lycius will not alter his plans; in fact, he is indignant that she would object to being displayed: "He thereat was stung, / Perverse, with stronger fancy to reclaim / Her wild and timid nature to his aim" (69–71). But Lycius's plans take on their own momentum because he finds so much pleasure in his ability to torture Lamia, taking "delight / Luxurious in her sorrows, soft and new," even though he knows this delight is "Against his better self" (73–74). Is love of woman the "better self" of man? The struggle occurs here between the semiotic/Imaginary and the phallic/Symbolic for control of the "Real" self. Keats suggests that the poet can only temporarily and tenuously balance these two forces within himself through the fiction of love. In other words, Keats no longer believes that love can work a "solution sweet." There is no salvation for his lover, for Lycius falls from love/lust by himself. No gods, no imagination, no visions can save him. His feelings for Lamia are now "passion, cruel grown" (75), and he is the prey of fierce and furious emotions, their power even stronger because of the fact that they are self-created and self-perpetuated. As he strikes Lamia for his amusement, we are told that she "lov'd the tyranny" (81). Just as Lycius unleashes his perverse masculine sadistic self, he also explores his masochistic feminine self, his fantasy of the woman as victim.[21]

For the first time, Lycius asks Lamia her name and parentage, confessing that he had not bothered to ask before because he had always thought she was "of heavenly progeny" (87). Although he states that he still thinks of her as holy, he is now more realistic, asking for her family name and the names of friends she would like to invite to the wedding feast, a display the narrator condemns as "mad pompousness" (114). In images that strikingly recall Shelley's treatment of marriage, we can see that as an institution it exists as a crucial component of the male's sadistic subjugation and commodification of women. Lamia has only one request, however—that Apollonius not be invited. But there is no escape from Apollonius because he is as much a part of Lycius as Lamia. He arrives at the wedding with an "eye severe" and immediately solves the "knotty problem" of Lamia's identity (157–60). Although Apollonius approaches Lycius and apologizes for forcing himself where he had not been invited, Lycius welcomes Lamia's foe. He seems to enjoy testing her, whereas he is actually pitting the two extremes of his mind—the Symbolic/phallic and the Imaginary/semiotic—against each other in what will prove to be a fatal confrontation for him.

After the feast has finished, the wine has flowed, and the fragrant oils have been applied, Lamia appears, hoping that with the sensory overload her guests will not be able to think or see clearly enough to recognize her, or more accurately, recognize her absence. But the narrator rhetorically asks us: "Do not all charms fly / At the mere touch of cold philosophy?" (229–30). The cold Apollonius and his rational/masculine science of philosophy have clipped "an Angel's wing, / Conquer[ed] all mysteries by rule and line" (234–35). His philosophy has

21. See Garrett Stewart's "*Lamia* and the Language of Metamorphosis," *SIR* 15 (1976), 3–41, for a discussion of this poem's "rhetoric of metamorphosis" as it functions from simple oxymorons to "masochism as a psychological oxymoron" (41). In her usual ingenious manner, Levinson reads Lamia as a commodity, "the most undifferentiated and anonymous form of exchange-value," which is progressively melted down throughout the poem so that she becomes by the conclusion of the poem both subject and money form (see her *Keats's Life of Allegory,* 281). Lionel Trilling, in "The Fate of Pleasure," notes that the world in which Lycius and Lamia briefly live is the "country of *La Belle Dame sans Merci,* the scene of erotic pleasure which leads to devastation, of an erotic fulfillment which implies castration" (see his *Beyond Culture: Essays on Literature and Learning* [New York: Viking, 1955], 67).

denuded the universe of its natural beauties and mysteries, unweaving rainbows as easily as they can melt the "tender-person'd Lamia into a shade" (238). When Lycius looks to his tutor for a toast, he sees that Apollonius stares at his bride, "Brow-beating her fair form, and troubling her sweet pride" (248). After much oracular dueling, Apollonius breaks the silence and shouts at Lamia, "'Begone, foul dream!'" (271). At this denunciation, Lamia loses all her beauty, becoming "deadly white" (276). And although Lycius attempts to return the curse—"'Shut, shut those juggling eyes, thou ruthless man!'"—the damage has been done (277). Lycius himself can no longer believe even in the beauty, let alone the reality, of his creation.

Once his creation of Lamia as semiotic/feminine is denounced by his Symbolic/masculine side, Lycius is forced to confront the deadly and irreconcilable nature of his mind. He has hated the woman within him, tortured her, denounced her as a temptress and *femme fatale,* but he hates the masculine within him just as fiercely. In his longest speech in the poem, his only real passionate outburst, he denounces Apollonius for his "painful blindness," "trembling dotage," and "impious proud-heart sophistries" (278–85). He specifically hates the *gaze* in Apollonius's "lashless eyelids," his "demon eyes" (288–89), that is, the Lacanian desire for phallic mastery over others as libidinal objects. Ironically, the masculine and the feminine here mirror each other in their association with the devil. Both are satanic because Lycius cannot balance them, cannot control their power within him. And so Apollonius destroys Lycius and Lamia with his curse: "'And shall I see thee made a serpent's prey?'" (298). His eyes, like a phallic "sharp spear" (300) in conjunction with his words, "'A Serpent'" (305), sound Lamia's and Lycius's death-knell. In an appropriate merging of images, Lycius is buried in his wedding robe, the victim of his self-created/self-destroyed and destroying love of woman.

Lamia, however, can also be read as a failed androgynous quest poem, although no one has used those terms or set the poem in the larger Romantic tradition of androgyny.[22] First of all, one has to ac-

22. Levinson helpfully discusses love in one of Keats's sources for *Lamia,* Burton's *Melancholy.* By way of introducing the strange story of Lycius, Burton notes the connection between love objects and commodities by pointing out that Love's parents were the god of wealth and the goddess of poverty. He then draws a parallel between this myth and Aristophanes' myth of the androgynes, "bifurcated for their pride and mechanically recombined through coitus. He seems to be developing a definition of love as an irreducibly oxymoronic phe-

knowledge that the text is fraught with ambiguity, ambivalence, and a certain amount of bitter irony. It inverts traditional mythic themes and to a large extent parodies Keats's own earlier treatments of love between mortal and immortal, male and female in works such as *Endymion* and *The Eve of St. Agnes.* Keats's earlier poetry presents a sort of humanized apocalypse in that the love relationship transforming the male and female into a divinely androgynous couple can only be sustained with much self-conscious artifice and tension in an escapist or fictitious realm. One reason the apocalyptic impulse occurs in these works lies in the fact that Keats was not able to translate successfully the complexity of the feminine Other as both spirit and flesh, with both positive and negative functions.

There is no easy equation of masculine and feminine, however, in *Lamia.* Apollonius, the Symbolic/paternal, is not just the embodiment of language and reason and therefore a negative force that hounds Lycius to his death. Conversely, Lamia is not just the Semiotic/Imaginary, the feminine principle, and the embodiment of the emotions, love, passion. Apollonius is necessary because without him we would not live in the world of facts, language, concrete reality. And Lamia is also necessary because without her we would not live in a world of beauty, art, and the complexities that the mind can create. What Keats is suggesting is that Lycius has polarized these two faculties within himself. He has set the two—the masculine and the feminine—at war with one another by making them extremes in the first place and then alternately choosing sides.

The poem, then, explores Lycius's neurosis as it were. He is a man torn internally by a masculine side that fears and despises his feminine side. When Lycius first meets and woos Lamia, he does so in fear of detection by Apollonius. He is a man whose feminine and affectionate nature is an embarrassment to his masculine and rational nature. But in addition to misogyny, Lycius fears not only his affection for what he thinks is a real woman, but most desperately he fears the woman within himself. Lycius (and Keats his creator) has come to despise the mere dreamer within, the poet whose fancies and fantasies have been built on nothing and will eventually bring him nothing. The Keats who knew material fact so well that he assisted in amputations performed by one of the most notorious doctors in London was a man with a firm sense of fact and physical reality. Keats, however, was apparently able to detach his two sides and present them as almost cartoon caricatures—

---

nomenon, tending to impose its own monstrosity upon its 'fair enticing objects,' women and things" (see her *Keats's Life of Allegory,* 258–59).

the extremes that Apollonius and Lamia are to Lycius. The reader can see that both Apollonius and Lamia have positive and negative attributes and that Lycius needs mediation and compromise if he is to survive. But Lycius is unable to see this and dies because of his own extreme response to the question of sexual identity. The Keats of *Lamia* founders on the extremes of his own self-created and fictitious masculinity and femininity. What we are seeing is his ambivalent attempt to value and embrace the feminine as an equal in the quest for self-transformation. His masculine side, however, is simply too powerful to allow this to occur.

5

The Muse: "I see, and sing, by my own eyes inspired"

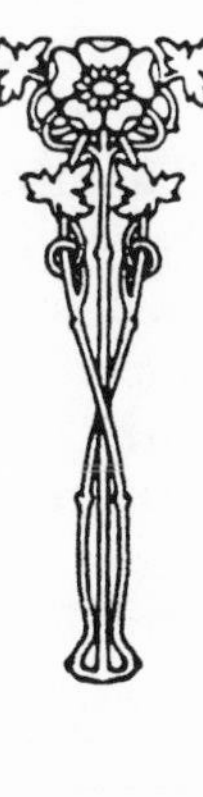

In 1916 the Jesuit Pierre Teilhard de Chardin found himself in the French trenches, fighting for his life. With shells exploding around him, he began writing the notes that eventually became the poem he entitled "The Eternal Feminine." It is no coincidence that a deeply religious man would engage in such a seemingly strange—distractive—activity in the midst of a war that revealed in all its horrors the ideological (and spiritual) bankruptcy of the nineteenth century. Teilhard's text has no great poetic merit, but it is worth quoting a few lines to suggest how tenaciously bourgeois man clung to his fiction of woman, particularly in a world that had become excessively, frighteningly masculinized:

> Since the beginning of all things, Woman has never ceased to take as her own the flower of all that was produced by the vitality of nature or the art of man.
>
> Who could say in what climax of perfections, both individual and cosmic, I shall blossom forth, in the evening of the world, before the face of God?
>
> I am the unfading beauty of the times to come—the ideal Feminine.
>
> The more, then, I become Feminine, the more immaterial and celestial will my countenance be.
>
> In me, the soul is at work to sublimate the body—Grace to divinize the soul.

> Those who wish to continue to possess me must change as I change.

But Teilhard's "Woman," whom he saw as the Virgin Mary, stands clearly in the ancient tradition of restorative, healing Nature goddesses, most probably initiated by the Egyptian Isis. All of the Romantics were familiar with her mythic identity and role in seeking and reassembling the pieces of her dead husband Osiris's broken body. Coleridge, following Plutarch's interpretation, saw Osiris's destroyer as Typhon, the masculine spirit of insolence and pride, while Isis, like her later manifestation, Psyche, embodied his belief that the feminine had to temper the masculine errors of power and discord. The ancient Nature goddesses, like Goethe's "Das Ewig-Weibliche / Zieht uns hinan," or Novalis's Rosenblüte, her nineteenth-century avatars, exist as the idealized internal aspect of the artist-hero. She images his creative spirit, the glass he gazes in to see himself but darkly. It is interesting that when Novalis uses the Isis myth he presents a hero who approaches the veiled goddess, lifts her veil, and sees "wonder of wonders—himself." The Eternal Feminine as muse, veiled and ambivalently powerful, finally conceals the fact that she is—and always has been—an absent signifier for the masculine consciousness that creates her fiction only to absorb it. Coleridge made this nowhere more evident than in his *Aids to Reflection,* when in a note he identifies "*Desire,* as the inferior nature in Man, the *Woman* in our Humanity." And as such, woman wars against the "Will," the masculine powers of reason and thought, and deserves therefore to be silenced and suppressed. But desire cannot be buried, and neither can the feminine muse, who erupts with frightening regularity and increasingly angry visage throughout key Romantic texts.

The female muse exists to defend against the male fear of both the female's sexuality (her castrated condition) and his own fear of castration at her hands. In order to express this dual fear, then, the female muse is split between two women who embody both sides of the fantasy. On one hand, the female is beneficent and unthreatening; in this manifestation she is Blake's Ololon/Jerusalem or Shelley's Witch. On the other hand, however, the female muse is denying, cruel, and punishing; she is Blake's Vala, Shelley's "Shape," or Keats's Moneta. But even this fiction, self-created and self-sustained as it was, could not always be perpetuated in the poetry, for the muse is the most doubled of feminine figures. Her guise is equivocal in that she ostensibly tropes the source of male creative power—his "feminized" imagination—while at the same time she often embodies the very "female" forces that seek to destroy his imaginative power—the power of female sexuality and the alienating and encroaching forces of an increasingly feminized literary marketplace.

Woman appears, then as a muselike goddess inspiring both intellectual creativity and dread in her final manifestation in English Romantic poetry. The muse, as noted earlier, often has maternal characteristics or functions in other instances somewhat in the role of a lover to the poet/hero. There are, in fact, many different facets to the feminine muse; however, her two consistent traits are her doubleness and her paradoxical association with androgynous motifs. Whether she is Blake's Jerusalem, Wordsworth's Nature/Dorothy, Keats's Psyche or Moneta, or Shelley's Witch or Urania, the muse generally functions as both an emblem of the desexualized power of the feminine within the male poet and his self-conscious realization of her fictionality. He can embrace her now because she no longer threatens him with sexual absorption and annihilation. He has "castrated" her, so that she has, to a certain extent, been neutered, and can now stand as a sort of epic figure of his projected imaginative and creative strength. But there is always the consciousness that the feminine muse is the most artificial of the many women within, that she has not really been successfully sublimated and tamed.

It is no coincidence that the muse and her avatars are often veiled; they are mysterious, brooding, unknown, and unknowable. The veil conceals at the same time it reveals, however; her sexual power is subsumed by the male and in its place he leaves drapery, the vestiges of her fearfulness. The veiled woman stands, then, as the ultimate embodiment of the woman as fetishistic commodity. According to Freudian myth, fetishism occurs as a result of the male fear of castration. When the young boy sees that females do not possess penises, he is so horrified that his response is to repress the original sight and to substitute another object that takes the place of the absent female penis. This object, then, assumes the status of a fetish and constitutes itself as an overdetermination of meaning.[1] For the Romantic poets, the female

1. See the discussion of Teilhard's poem in Henri de Lubac, *The Eternal Feminine: A Study on the Text of Teilhard de Chardin,* trans. René Hague (New York: Harper and Row, 1971), 100. Coleridge's knowledge of Egyptian mythology and the Isis figure is discussed by John Beer, *Coleridge the Visionary* (New York: Collier, 1962), 107–32. The Eternal Feminine's role in the Romantic hero's circular journey is analyzed by Abrams, *Natural Supernaturalism,* 244–52. And see Freud's "Fetishism" (1927) (*SE* XXI: 147–58). For a provocative discussion of woman and novelistic text as fetish in the fiction of the period, see Jon

muse became the final manifestation of the woman as fetishistic object, while the texts that celebrate and elide her power are themselves overdetermined because of her sexually ambivalent power and their response to it.

To shed some light on the psychic mechanics here, let us examine Freud's late work *Beyond the Pleasure Principle* (1920) as it develops his notion of desire as Eros, a power that is not specifically sexual but actually polymorphous in that it seeks "to combine organic substances into ever greater unities." Against this machinelike power, described by Peter Brooks as "Eros as motor," Freud posits the death instinct, the drive that impels extinction, the force that lies beyond the pleasure principle (*SE* XVIII:54). In the attempt to totally realize one's desire, the self confronts at the same time its impossibility and the realization that to desire can finally only lead to death. Eros propels living matter to its original inorganic condition, a state prior to life. Lacan interprets this point by defining desire as the split between need and demand, and he illustrates the concept by contrasting the infant's need for nourishment from the mother's breast to the child's demand for the mother's love as represented by the breast. In a passage that accurately describes the Romantic poet's relation to woman as fetish, an overly determined desired/rejected object, Laplanche and Pontalis observe:

> Desire is born from the gap between need and demand; it is irreducible to need, for it is not in its principal relation to a real object, independent of the subject, but rather to a phantasy; it is irreducible to demand, in that it seeks to impose itself without taking account of language and the unconscious of the other, and insists upon being absolutely recognized by the other.

Lacan reinterprets Saussurian theory on this point by claiming that the slash separating signifier and signified (S/s) represents the power of repression, the impossibility of ever reaching the true signified (the object of unconscious desire). Discourse is then the interconnection of signifiers in a "signifying chain" in which meaning (access to the meaning of unconscious desire) cannot be found in any single piece of the chain, and narrative is forever condemned to telling something other

---

Stratton, *The Virgin Text: Fiction, Sexuality, and Ideology* (Norman: University of Oklahoma Press, 1987).

than what it would like to tell.[2] How can we apply these various theories to the depiction of the feminine muse in English Romantic poetry? It would seem that the doubled female muse functions as a signifier that stands beyond desire, a metonymy that represents both itself as an object of desire and the death and defeat for the males who stand behind/beyond that desire. In other words, the male can only embrace the muse in his mind as a fantasied and fetishistic object, for to possess her physically can only lead to his complete physical and imaginative extinction.

The ambiguity and doubleness of the muse—her asexuality coupled with her imaginative power—recurs in virtually every portrait we have of her in English Romantic poetry. The split female muse who appears in Coleridge's "Kubla Khan" can, perhaps, stand as representative of the dual-visaged woman who inspires both intense sexual longing and powerful imaginative visions, suggesting at the same time that the two are inextricably linked through their association with the feminine. The "woman wailing for her demon-lover" in the first section of the poem embodies the vision of potential destruction that is unleashed by human passion and the desire of men and women to seek their now separated counterparts through sexuality. The "chasm" that appears in the landscape of the poem is perceived as "A savage place!" "holy and enchanted" and dominated by a "waning moon" "haunted" by this frenzied woman. The mixture of the sacred (the earth) and the profane (the woman) suggests the poet's desire to merge the two realms by sanctifying the woman, transforming her into a vehicle of the sacred, and this he can do only if she is desexed and made less powerful. But it is not only the woman who needs to be transformed by the vision of the poem. The male lover also has to be redeemed and desexed before his imaginative salvation can occur. Norman Fruman sees the "demon lover" here as "someone towards whom the woman stands in such a relation that sexual love between them would be demonical," "an incestuous lover."[3] Indeed, the first draft of the poem used the word "daemon," suggesting that the male's love participates just as fully in the dark underworld of fallen, even satanic passions. Both the male and female, then, stand as the fearful sexual potential in all of us that has to be neutralized, or at the very least socialized, before civilization and "poetry" can originate.

2. See Peter Brooks, "Narrative Desire," in *Reading for the Plot*, 37–61, and Jean Laplanche and J. B. Pontalis, *The Language of Psychoanalysis*, 122.

3. Fruman, *Coleridge: The Damaged Archangel*, 396.

The wailing woman and the demon lover reappear in the second part of the poem, through the power of imaginative metamorphosis, as a "damsel with a dulcimer" singing to a narrative "I" who vaguely recalls the divine heritage of both of them. She sings of "Mount Abora," but it was "Amora" in the first draft of the poem, and we can conclude that her song is one of love as she repeats in a muted and distorted manner her earlier wailing. There the message of sexual anguish was clear; now the poet/narrator is not certain what she is singing. He wants to "revive" within himself her "symphony and song" because he knows it will bring him "deep delight"—not salvation or imaginative redemption, just enjoyment. Such is the deflation of the second part of this poem as presided over by a desexed muse. But unless the feminine muse can be transformed into a weaker version of herself, the male will never be redeemed and the poet never created. Woman as muse bears the burden of civilizing the male and making culture possible. She is the ultimate psychic creation of the male imagination. She must allow herself to be "castrated" and then she must freely give her sexual power to the male. She may appear like Wordsworth's Dorothy, a sister/muse, or Keats's Psyche, a beloved/muse. But all of these "women" finally share a sacrificial quality; they are heroines of culture, the self-consumed bearers of the ideology of sexual sublimation.

I Blake: "Jerusalem in every Man / A Tent & Tabernacle"

The imagery of sexual warfare was central to the vision of apocalypse that Blake proclaimed as his poetic mission throughout his life. The political apocalypse of earlier work, such as *The French Revolution,* fades as the spiritual—or at least more effectively sublimated—gains prominence, for Blake's vision of the natural world seems to have darkened over the years so that by the time he was writing *Jerusalem* the only apocalypse he could endorse was one in which the "sexes must cease and vanish" in the psyche so that humanity can assume its spiritualized "body." It became clear to Blake that political reform of society could not be effected until an individual and spiritual redemption took place in every person's heart. To become androgynous, to overcome the flaws inherent in each sex—these themes emerge as the central fiction in Blake's works while the feminine muse—Jerusalem—leads to the promised land that is Albion's best imagined self.

Blake's poetry, then, is dominated by the image of the androgyne, which he envisions as a paradisaical state of consciousness that has resolved all dichotomies so that "man" possesses that complete harmony in which "he" is Albion-Jerusalem, both God and all external, "feminine" reality. For Blake the androgynous is a consciousness that is neither masculine nor feminine; rather, it is a distinct third psychic possibility in which neither sex predominates. Unlike Boehme, who envisions the androgyne as a male with a subordinate female element, and unlike Swedenborg, who thought the division of the sexes persisted even into paradise, Blake emphasizes that sexual divisions must be annihilated psychically, because both sexes are equally fallen from the original divinity of the androgyne: " 'In Eternity they neither marry nor are given in marriage' " (*J* 30 [34]; E, 176; K, 660).

Blake alludes to the androgynous ideal in *Milton* 2 when he praises the "Eternal Great Humanity Divine" (E, 96; K, 481). Most of his poetry, however, centers on the dynamics of the fallen, divided states and the ensuing sexual warfare. To graphically illustrate the dichotomy between the apocalyptic and the actual, Blake's poetry contrasts the fallen physical body, constricted to the limitations inherent in the divided sexes and represented by the hermaphrodite, to the human-divine, the androgynous "body." In his poetic versions of the fall, an original androgynous union of masculine and feminine is destroyed, thereby giving rise to the fallen world of nature. This fallen physical world incorporates qualities that Blake depicts as feminine, while the other, and even greater, evil in his system is the conception of the self, which is embodied in the male. These two separated principles cause the ensuing sexual warfare.

Blake, then, describes the androgynous condition chiefly by depicting what it is not. He contrasts the sacred image of redeemed sexuality to the profane image, the hermaphrodite. The contrast between the hermaphrodite and the androgyne is a long-standing tradition in theological speculation.[4] Blake follows in this tradition by viewing the her-

4. The ancient world's distinction between the hermaphrodite and the androgyne is discussed in Marie Delcourt, *Hermaphrodite,* 45: "Androgyny is at the two poles of sacred things. Pure concept, pure vision of the spirit, it appears adorned with the highest qualities. But once made real in a being of flesh and blood [the hermaphrodite], it is a monstrosity, and no more." This ancient distinction was current during the early nineteenth century, particularly among certain writers in the German Romantic movement. Novalis and minor figures, prose commentators like Michael Hahn, Johann Jacob Wirz, and Carl Gustav Carus, revitalized interest in the mythology. The most prolific German

maphrodite as a sterile fusion of the physical male and female, while the androgyne transcends sexual divisions to become a spiritual and psychic ideal.[5] The hermaphrodite in Blake's poetry, then, is embodied in the fusion of the fallen male, a spectre representing the rational and reductive consciousness, and the fallen female, representing the secrecy and deceit that support abstract morality. In an early cosmology, "then She bore Pale desire," Blake describes the gods who were born from fear—"nor male nor female are but single Pregnate or if they list together mingling bring forth mighty powrs" (E, 446; K, 40). These gods strengthen the demonic power of the Great Mother, and aid in giving birth to "a Goddess. fair or Image rather, till knowledge animated it. 'twas Calld Selflove." This power of self-love will later be embodied in the Female Will and the Spectre, but even in this early prose piece Blake recognized that it was the concept of an all-sufficient self that was the most serious threat to reintegration. He observes, "Go See more strong the ties of marriage love. thou Scarce Shall find but Self love Stands Between" (E, 448; K, 42–43).

Blake made his first attempt to physically depict a hermaphrodite in *The Four Zoas* VII. Here the hermaphrodite appears as the merger of the fallen Enion and Tharmas, a physical parody of their eventual androgynous union in Night IX. This hermaphrodite is formed from the mixing of "his horrible darkness" and "his darkly waving colours" with "her fair crystal clearness." Together, they produce a "wonder that nature shuddered at / Half Woman half beast." This "lovely" wonder wan-

---

writer on the subject, Franz von Baader (1765–1841), based his religious writings on the distinction. Jean Halley des Fontaines, *La notion d'androgynie* (Paris: Dépôt Général, Le François, 1938, 139), summarizes von Baader's position: "the Androgyne is conceived of as an opposite to the Hermaphrodite. The Androgyne is the harmonious fusion of the sexes, resulting in a certain asexuality, a synthesis which creates an entirely new being, and which does not merely juxtapose the two sexes 'in an enflamed opposition' as the hermaphrodite does" [my translation].

5. Peter Thorslev, Jr., in "Some Dangers of Dialectic Thinking, with Illustrations from Blake and His Critics," in *Romantic and Victorian,* ed. W. Paul Elledge and Richard L. Hoffman (Madison, NJ: Fairleigh Dickinson University Press, 1971, 64–68), claims that the "theme of the Angelic Androgyne versus the Hellish Hermaphrodite" is an example of the "Both-And Syndrome" in Blake's poetry. Although Thorslev recognizes that the two images are contradictory states, he claims that Blake never makes the distinction clear: "both terms denote quite simply the union of the two sexes in one body, and it is difficult to see precisely where the distinction lies. Blake nowhere specifically defines it, and there is no basis for it in etymology or myth."

ders over the earth, its "rocky features" and its "female voice" wrapped in "self enjoying wonder." Enion, however, dominates the merger, for she proclaims that this hermaphroditic union is "Glory, delight: & sweet enjoyment born / To mild Eternity shut in a threefold shape delightful / To wander in sweet solitude enraptur'd at every wind" (E, 304; 846; K, 381).[6] In this hermaphroditic union, then, the feminine entraps the masculine just as the Female Will dominates the history of the human race. But Blake also condemns any attempts at self-redemption by the fallen reason, identified as masculine. For if the fallen female embodies the curse of the physical, unredeemed world, then the fallen male is "a ravening eating Cancer growing in the Female / A Polypus of Roots of Reasoning Doubt Despair & Death" (*J* 69: E, 223; K, 707). Any union or forced merger between these two fallen forms can only produce the monstrous hermaphrodite, embodiment of the horrors of sexual separation and "Blasphemous Selfhood."

Hermaphroditic unions also symbolize the merger of female religion with male warfare, the two powers that serve to institute and perpetuate humanity's fallen existence. History for Blake, then, can be viewed as a cycle of hermaphroditic unions between the fallen female and male as they destructively struggle for dominance. In *Milton* 37 and *Jerusalem* 76, Blake presents this history as twenty-seven churches made up of three groups of nine: the hermaphrodites, the Female-Males, and the Male-Females.[7] Blake presents in this image all of the possible forms

6. There is some uncertainty as to Blake's intention in this physical description of the hermaphrodite. He revised the passage several times. Erdman's 1965 edition concludes that Blake's final intention was to present the hermaphrodite as "half woman and half beast," while his 1982 edition gives the line as "Half Woman & half Spectre" (304), as does Keynes. Bentley notes that "Serpent" and "desart" were both possible revisions for the male component (*Vala*, 9). Webster discusses the psychic contortions and permutations of the figure in her *Blake's Prophetic Psychology*, 208: "What interests Blake primarily is the danger to the male of feminization or draining. He deals with this through a process of reversal that transfers power from the female to the male (what was once feared from her is now done to her)."

7. See Milton O. Percival, *William Blake's Circle of Destiny* (1938; rpt. New York: Octagon, 1964), chapter 6, and Peter Fisher, *The Valley of Vision* (Toronto: University of Toronto Press, 1961), chapter 2, for extended discussions of the twenty-seven hermaphroditic churches. Margaret Storch has interpreted the hermaphrodites in Blake's poetry as fantasies of female power, phallic mothers, and impregnably mysterious parental authorities. She has perceptively noted that the hermaphrodite tropes the "child's own feelings of aggression toward the parents transformed into the hybrid monster and directed

that sexual separation can take, as if he were parodying Aristophanes' account of the three original beings in the *Symposium,* and then he states that the only escape from history as a panorama of sexual conflict and religious perversion lies in transforming the sexual altogether.

In addition to informing Blake's vision of history, the hermaphrodite in his poetry serves a crucial function at the conclusion of each of the epics. Before salvation can occur, the central figures consistently confront the horrible figure of the hermaphrodite. In *The Four Zoas* VIII, the hermaphroditic form appears as haunting and demonic every time the characters move toward redemption. First it is Urizen who beholds the emblem of his life as a fallen, separate self: "a Shadowy hermaphrodite black & opake / . . . unformd & vast / . . . hiding the Male / Within as in a Tabernacle Abominable Deadly" (E, 374; K, 343). The voices from Eternity repeat the message of salvation, that humanity must "put off the dark Satanic body" in order to regain the spiritual and imaginative (E, 376; K, 346). But the wars of redemption are not easily won, for the forces of the fallen world assume "a Vast Hermaphroditic form" that attacks Jerusalem's Gates. This horrible hermaphroditic form bursts to reveal its internal force, Satan, "dishumaniz'd monstrous / A male without a female counterpart . . . Yet hiding the shadowy female Vala as in an ark & Curtains" (E, 377; K, 347).

Satan's identity as a hermaphrodite is important for an understanding of *Milton,* for Milton's spectre appears as hermaphroditic. *Milton* 14 presents Milton's realization that his masculine portion, his spectre, is a satanic selfhood that must be purged before he can reunite with Ololon, his true counterpart. But just as in *The Four Zoas* Urizen had to face the ultimate fallen form before his movement to regeneration could begin, so Milton confronts his own "Shadow; / A mournful form double; hermaphroditic: male & female / In one wonderful body" (E, 108; K, 496). For Blake, then, the hermaphrodite is a sterile monstrosity not because it is asexual, but because it is multisexual; it yokes together by force the two sexes in their fallen forms.

As it does in *The Four Zoas,* the hermaphrodite appears near the conclusion of *Jerusalem* as the embodiment of the final and most fallen of earthly forms. As Los and Enitharmon rage during their struggle for dominance over each other, "A terrible indefinite Hermaphroditic form" appears with "A Wine-press of Love & Wrath double Hermaphroditic" (*J* 89: E, 248; K, 734). The figure appears at this moment as an accusation and a reminder of what divided sexuality has

---

against the threat that the monster poses to the social order." See her "Blake and Women," *Narcissism and the Text,* ed. Layton and Schapiro, 106.

produced throughout history. These hermaphroditic figures are the return of the Satan-Tirzah figure and the Satan-Rahab figure, the curses of history—war, Nature, and institutionalized religion. They appear at this moment to emphasize humanity's historic enslavement to their power. They are "Religion hid in War, a Dragon red & hidden Harlot / Each within other, but without a War-like Mighty-one / Of dreadful power" (E, 249; K, 735).

Jerusalem 90, however, presents Blake's most explicit statement on the nature of the sexes and the necessity for androgynous reintegration. As Los explains,

> When the Individual appropriates Universality
> He divides into Male & Female: & when the Male & Female,
> Appropriate Individuality, they become an Eternal Death.
> (E, 250; K, 737)

When Los finally defeats his Spectre and awaits his reunion with Enitharmon, he assures her that neither of them is being annihilated in their eternal, psychic forms, only in their fallen manifestations: "'Sexes must vanish & cease / To be, when Albion arises from his dread repose'" (*J* 92: E, 252; K, 739). That is, the perverted forms that sexual bodies take in the fallen world must be transformed to androgynous "bodies" based on asexual consciousness. The hermaphrodite, then, symbolizes the attempts made by the anti-Christ figures of Satan, Rahab, and Tirzah to form a substitute androgyne. This parody of the spiritual ideal glories in the duality of the sexes and as such exemplifies the horrors of cruelty and jealousy indigenous to the separate and exclusively male and female psyches.

In opposition to the hermaphroditic Satan, Blake endorses the ancient belief in the androgynous ideal, represented in his poetry by Jesus, the second Adam who has the power to reinstitute the androgynous harmony of the original creation. In *Love's Body* Norman O. Brown observes that

> [t]he fall of man is the fall into the division of the human race, the dismemberment of the first man, Adam; and the resurrection or rebirth through the second man, Christ, is to reconstitute the lost unity. . . . The unification of mankind into one is also the unification of humanity and divinity; "Christ, by

> whome all mankind was united into divinity." Unification is deification.[8]

The androgynous ideal in Blake's poetry, then, stands as a fictional and apocalyptic union within the self that simultaneously redeems the internal and external worlds. The model for Blake was Jesus, who was aware as no other human being has been of his own divinity and inner integration. Blake's art aims ultimately to depict and valorize New Testament ideology by embodying the fantasy that the recovery of Paradise must take place within, creating a state in which humanity is perfectly integrated with God, that is, integrated within itself.

The androgynous reunion of Albion and Jerusalem forms the focus of Blake's final epic, *Jerusalem*. Because of its subject matter, then, *Jerusalem* is a psychomachia, for the warfare between Albion and Jerusalem is internal. They are not searching for anything outside the self; rather, they seek their own integration. As Blake believed that all reality is ultimately mental, so are the landscapes in his poems eerily dreamlike because they are internal. All activity in the poems, in fact, takes place as warfare within the fallen Albion, Blake's depiction of archetypal "man" who in "his" unfallen condition integrates the four Eternal principles.

Bloom admits that Albion does "faintly resemble the *Adam Kadmon* or Divine Man of Jewish Cabbalist tradition," but he denies Blake's debt to the tradition of androgynist theorizing, stating that "Albion is not a speculative product of the Platonizing imagination." It seems unlikely, however, that Blake's Albion stands radically apart from two thousand years of thought about a primal being who contains all reality within itself. Even Bloom echoes the many descriptions of the androgyne when he describes Albion as "a great Adam, a man who contains all of reality himself, and who is therefore human *and* divine, male *and* female, and a fourfold balance of the faculties of intellect, imagination, emotion and instinct."[9]

8. Norman O. Brown, *Love's Body* (New York: Random House, 1966), 83. The most helpful discussion of "The Audience of Jesus" in *Jerusalem* is Morris Eaves's "Romantic Expressive Theory and Blake's Idea of the Audience," *PMLA* 95 (1980), 784–801; *William Blake's Theory of Art*, rpt. and rev. (Princeton: Princeton University Press, 1982).

9. Harold Bloom, *Blake's Apocalypse*, 189–90. On the same point, see Leonard Trawick, "Blake's Empirical Occult," *WC* 8 (1977), 161–71; Abrams, *Naturalism Supernaturalism*, 146–54 and Howard O. Brogan, "Blake and the Occult: 'The Real Man the Imagination which Liveth for Ever,'" *WC* 8 (1977),

Significantly, Albion first appears in Blake's writings as a female. In the early fragment, "Prologue to King John," Albion is the spirit of England, an abused harlot, whose "sins are crimson dy'd." In battle Tyranny stains "fair Albion's breast with her own children's gore," but in a final scene each is restored and the poet hopes, "O yet may Albion smile again, and stretch her peaceful arms, and raise her golden head, exultingly" (E, 439; K, 34). Blake's Albion differs from the *Adam Kadmon* of the Kabbalists precisely because of this feminine aspect. Blake's illustration of the Cosmic Man in *Jerusalem* 25 (see Figure 1), in addition to being derived from Poussin's "Martyrdom of St. Erasmus," bears a striking resemblance to the cosmic androgynes depicted in theosophical manuscripts of the late eighteenth and early nineteenth centuries (see Figures 2 and 3).[10] But Blake presents his Cosmic Man as the victim of the females who torture him by pulling out his entrails. Immediately following this plate Blake addresses the Jews in a mocking, even chiding tone about their tradition of a Cosmic Male. Blake attempts to correct this male-dominated version of the image by emphasizing the equality of Jerusalem as the counterpart of Albion. He writes, "You have a tradition, that Man anciently containd in his mighty limbs all things in Heaven & Earth." But he continues this description by pointing out that Jerusalem is "the Emanation of the Great Albion! Can it be? Is it a Truth that the Learned have explored? . . . It is True, and cannot be controverted" (*J* 27: E, 171; K, 649).

47–60. Sheila Spector's "Kabbalistic Sources—Blake and His Critics," *B:IQ* 17:3 (1983–84), 84–101, provides the best survey of Blake's knowledge of the Kabbalah, while Morton D. Paley's work explores Blake's "complex and shifting attitude" toward Swedenborg and other mystical precursors (see his *Energy and the Imagination: A Study of the Development of Blake's Thought,* and " 'A New Heaven is Begun': William Blake and Swedenborgianism," *B:IQ* 13:2 [1979], 64–90).

10. The source for these illustrations is Albert Béguin, "L'Androgyne," *Minotaure* 11 (October 1938), 11, 13. He identifies them only as "from a Russian Theosophical manuscript." Theosophy and Freemasonry reached Russia after 1750 and both were politically suppressed during the 1820s. The illustrations, then, can be placed during that seventy-year period, also roughly the period during which Blake was writing. Fred Gettings's chapter "Sex Sacred and Profane: Heretical and Occult Symbols Connected with the Fall of Man and Gods" in *The Occult in Art* (New York: Rizzoli, 1978), discusses several visual illustrations of what he calls the "complex secret geometry as symbolic substructure, hidden commentary" in works of occult art that Blake would have seen in Ebenezer Sibly's *New and Complete Illustration of the Occult Sciences* (1790).

Blake's depiction of Albion-Jerusalem as the androgynous cosmic being is an attempt to correct the "learned" Kabbalistic traditions that present the original being as a supreme male with no female counterpart. For Blake this cosmic male can only be a giant spectre who will be perpetually tortured by the female because he has rejected her and made her alien to himself.

Jerusalem as muse is, then, the focus and redemptive power in this final version of the fall and salvation. In *The Four Zoas* Tharmas's opening lament implies that Jerusalem is the universal feminine and that all female characters are ultimately derived from her. Tharmas asks Enion why she has taken "sweet Jerusalem from my inmost Soul" (*The Four Zoas* IV: E, 301; K, 265). Jerusalem tropes the fantasy that there is an unfallen feminine component within every being who must be reconciled with each of the Zoas before she can reunite with Albion. Jerusalem, then, is not an appendage of Albion; she is the exact feminine equivalent who is fallen and incomplete when separated from Albion. She also needs to experience the return to her original androgynous union with Albion in order to redeem all her fallen manifestations. Humanity is reintegrated by Jerusalem, the "Emanative portion: / Who is Jerusalem in every individual" (*J* 39 [44]: E, 187; K, 675). David Wyatt characterizes Jerusalem as an oxymoronic principle; "she is a saving imperfection. Her completed image in text and illustration creates a woman who is at once her own contrary, both a natural and visionary form. Without such a woman, there is no progression." [11] But such a reading uncritically accepts the ideology of Woman as Other and merely accepts one side of Blake's depiction of the split female muse at face value, without recognizing that Jerusalem's split identity as Vala is a crucial component in Blake's vision of the female muse as doubled.

Within the fiction of the poem, then, Albion learns the lessons of salvation through an understanding of Jerusalem's composite identity. As the poem opens, Albion reveals his mistaken beliefs: "'We are not One: we are Many,'" while he also believes that "'Jerusalem is not! her daughters are indefinite: / By demonstration, man alone can live, and not by faith'" (*J* 4: E, 147; K, 622). Albion is fallen because he no longer

11. See his "The Woman Jerusalem: Pictura versus Poesis," *BS* 7 (1975), 105–24. Webster (in *Blake's Prophetic Psychology*, 286) perceptively notes that Blake idealized "feminine" traits such as tenderness and maternal care because they allow Jerusalem as the idealized woman "to care for the Male Genius; on the other hand, the poet can incorporate and use them in creation and in drawing close to other men." In either mode, the feminine exists as a projected principle to be consumed by the male poet-hero.

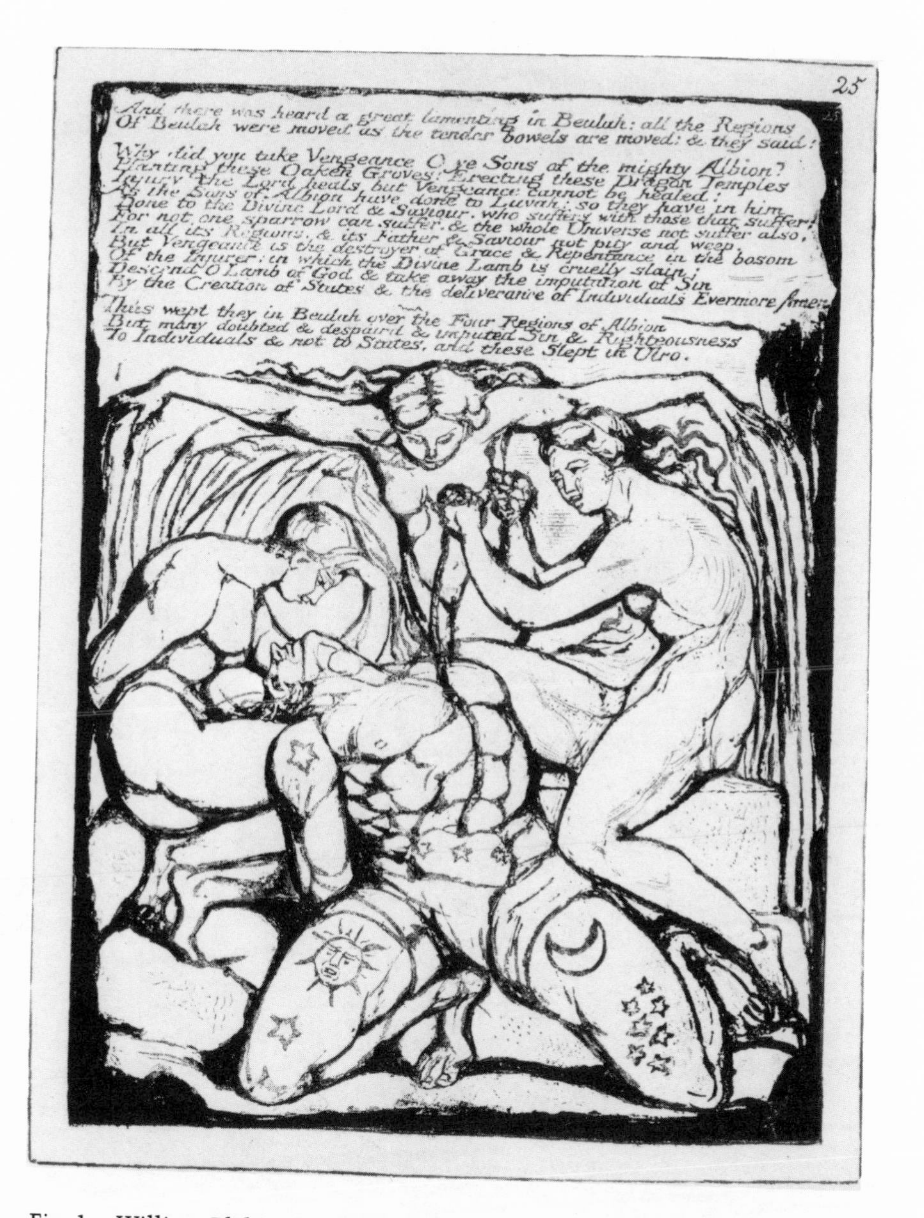

Fig. 1. William Blake, *Jerusalem* 25. Courtesy of the Houghton Library, Harvard University.

Fig. 2. *Adam before the Fall.* Courtesy of the University of Illinois Library.

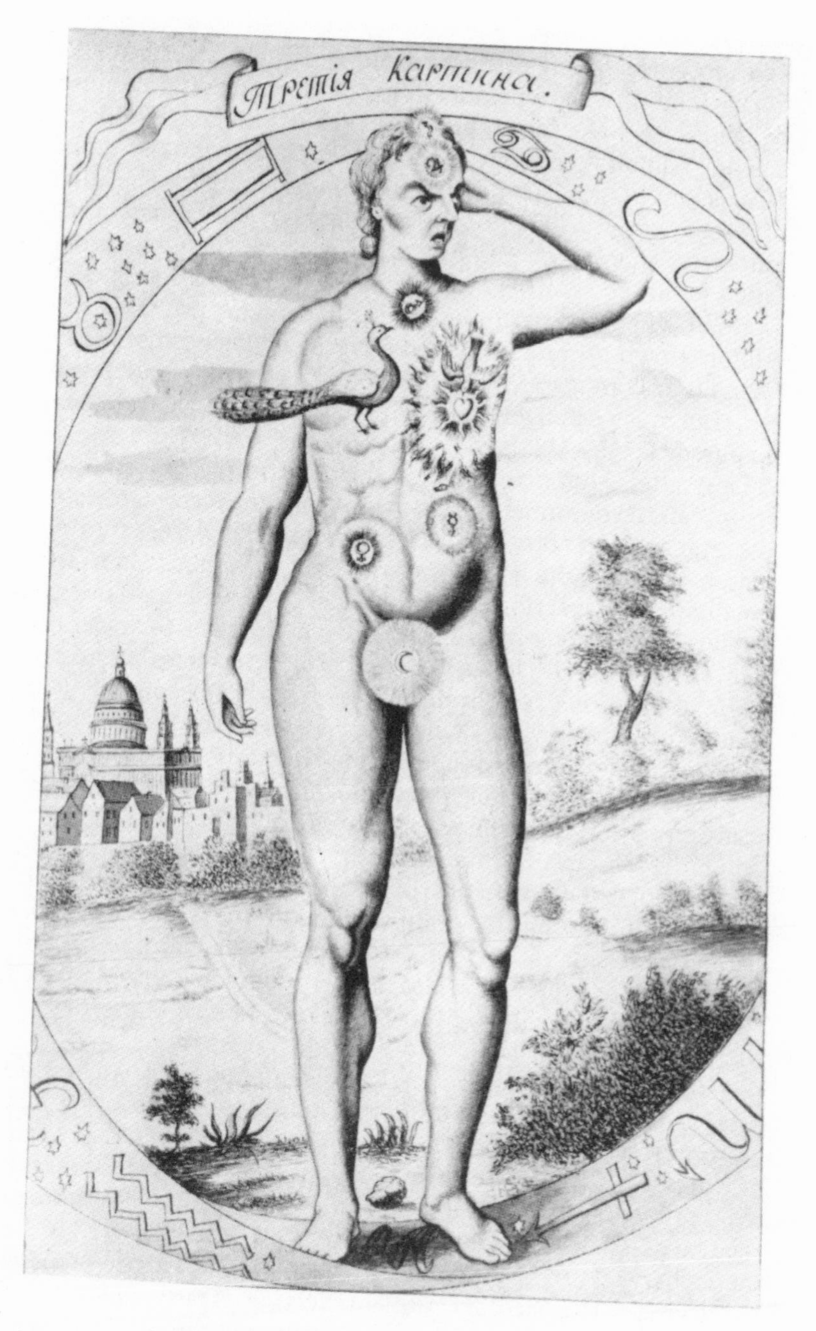

Fig. 3. *Adam after Reintegration.* Courtesy of the University of Illinois Library.

can recognize his own divinity; he worships instead a "God in the dreary Void... wide separated from the Human Soul." Because of these delusions he sinks into "this dark Ulro & voidness" (*J* 23: E, 168–69; K, 646). Albion's errors are those of fallen man who has embraced the false beliefs of rational and masculine individualism. The fallen faculty of reason, with its belief in the individual as self-sufficient, denies the fantasy of androgyny. Vala functions, then, as the embodiment of the fallen feminine faculties, who tempts Albion to a living death in the world of generation. Jerusalem is the true saving principle who honors Albion's "own Minute Particulars" because "They are of Faith & not of Demonstration" (*J* 45 [31]: E, 195; K, 657). But in the fallen world Vala's power is much stronger, for it is based on the "Sexual Reasoning Hermaphroditic" (*J* 29 [33]: E, 175; K, 659).

Only after Albion "dies," which occurs in the exact middle of the poem, can the movement toward salvation take place. Only after he has given up his own efforts can reunification take place. From the earth's center, "Beneath the bottoms of the Graves" where "Contrarieties are equally true," the action of salvation begins—Maternal Love awakes Jerusalem, who bursts from her tomb and struggles to "put off the Human form" (*J* 48: E, 196–97; K, 677–78). Jerusalem has to reject the "Human form" because, in Erin's words, it has become a "Polypus of Death" ruled over by the "One Great Satan... the most powerful Selfhood," who has murdered the "Divine Humanity" (*J* 49: E, 198; K, 679). Erin claims that salvation is possible only when humanity "shall arise from Self / By Self Annihilation into Jerusalem's Courts & into Shiloh / Shiloh the Masculine Emanation among the Flowers of Beulah" (*J* 49: E, 199; K, 680). Salvation is possible only when the masculine rejoins Jerusalem and the feminine rejoins Shiloh. In the world of Beulah sexual distinctions remain, but the sexes function in harmony, forgiveness, and love. Blake depicts this ideal as "Jerusalem in every Man / A Tent & Tabernacle of Mutual Forgiveness Male & Female Clothings" (*J* 54: E, 203; K, 684).

Although Jerusalem ultimately redeems Albion, it is Los who functions as instructor. When Albion mistakenly prays to a deity external to himself, Los condemns "Calling on God for help; and not ourselves in whom God dwells." Los also repudiates the "bloated General Forms" that reason creates because they insult "the Divine- / Humanity, who is the Only General and Universal Form" (*J* 38 [43]: E, 185; K, 672). Los is the archetypal artist, representative of the male artistic process itself. He valorizes the ideologies of intellectual creative activity and the power of the human imagination to transcend the limitations of space and time. When Los and Enitharmon reunite to form Urthona, they present a model for salvation to Albion and Jerusalem. Since Los symbolizes Albion's imagination, his fall and redemption parallel Albion's. In this final poem, Los's fall is presented in abbreviated form. During a war between "Abstract Philosophy" and "Imagination . . . the Divine Body of the Lord Jesus," Urthona's "Emanation divided, his Spectre also divided" leaving Los a "frightened wolf" (*J* 5–7: E, 148–49; K, 624–25). Los scorns his Spectre's taunts and yearns for the day when Albion will be reunited with Jerusalem and the united Zoas will compose the complete androgynous being: "tenfold bright, rising from his tomb in immortality." Los already knows that it is through love and "mutual forgiveness between Enemies" that the fallen world of Generation will be transformed into the unfallen realm of "regeneration" (*J* 7: E, 150; K, 626).

Los also knows that Albion is fallen because Los's "Emanation is divided from him" and continues to divide. Los mourns, "What shall I do! or how exist, divided from Enitharmon?" (*J* 12: E, 155; K, 631). This state of divisive warfare between the sexes is at the root of the fallen state in Blake's poetic world. After Los reunites with Enitharmon, he can understand the divisions that precipitated the fallen state of hermaphroditic/fallen sexuality:

> The Feminine separates from the Masculine & both from Man,
> Ceasing to be His Emanations, Life to Themselves assuming!
> . . . that no more the Masculine mingles
> With the Feminine. but the Sublime is shut out from the Pathos
> In howling torment.
>
> (*J* 90: E, 249; K, 736)

When Los reunites with Enitharmon and his Spectre, "the Divine Vision" appears with him, and he prays to Jesus in a passage that repeats Blake's belief in the androgynous ideal:

> Humanity knows not of Sex: wherefore are Sexes in Beulah?
> In Beulah the Female lets down her beautiful Tabernacle;
> Which the Male enters magnificent between her Cherubim:
> And becomes One with her mingling condensing in Self-love
> The Rocky Law of Condemnation & double Generation, & Death.
> (*J* 44 [30]: E, 193; K, 656)

Jerusalem echoes this statement when she accuses Vala of bringing only death to the world through her separate sexual identity. The hermaphroditic Vala endorses a divided male and female, "hardening against the heavens / To devour the Human." Jerusalem retorts,

'O Vala! Humanity is far above
Sexual organization; & the Visions of the Night of Beulah
Where Sexes wander in dreams of bliss among the Emanations
Where the Masculine & Feminine are nurs'd into Youth & Maiden.'
(*J* 79; E, 236; K, 721)

Los repeats this belief when he proclaims, "Sexes must vanish & cease / To be, when Albion arises from his dread repose" (*J* 92: E, 252; K, 739). But Albion cannot awaken until Enitharmon and Brittania, voices of the Female Will, renounce their dominion. Enitharmon is terrified of losing her separate existence, for she has forgotten her original identity as Urthona. All of the Zoas must learn the lesson presented by Jesus, the divine/human androgyne who appears in "the likeness & similitude of Los" to instruct Albion in love and forgiveness: "And if God dieth not for Man & giveth not himself / Eternally for Man Man could not exist. for Man is Love: / As God is Love" (*J* 96: E, 256; K, 743).

Only when Albion throws himself into the furnaces of affliction to save his brother can the Zoas reunite in harmony and again reside in his being. Ultimately, however, it is Jerusalem who must awaken and assume her proper station if the composite androgynous being is to participate in the continual flux between Eden and Beulah. By accepting and redeeming Beulah, the world of generation, Blake's fantasy of an erotic apocalypse leads to the assumption of a new "body"—a spiritual, androgynous psyche in imitation of the resurrected Jesus. The androgynous ideology in Blake's poetry corresponds to the Christian belief that if the Kingdom of God can be found on earth, it must be found within, that is, as a self-created and self-sustained fiction.

In this final epic and throughout his life, Blake believed, as he declared in "All Religions are One," that the "Poetic Genius is the true Man. and that the body or outward form of Man is derived from the Poetic Genius." The Poetic Genius, supposedly humanity's divine imaginative power, is "the source" of the "true Man" (E, 1–2; K, 98). These statements support the view that the androgynous ideology in Blake's poetry is an imaginative construct that sought to act as a substitute religion based on the fantasy that the human mind can reintegrate its splintered components, troped conventionally as the "masculine" and the "feminine." Blake chose the androgyne because the image was based on distinct sexual identities and polarities, yet repudiated both and became the most paradoxical state the human mind could imagine. The concept of the androgynous is based on the oxymoron, an artifice that combines contradictions and attempts to grasp the ideal as imaginative reality. For, as Blake pointed out in his Annotations to Berkeley's *Siris*, every object's "Reality is its Imaginative Form" (E, 664;

K, 213). "Reality" is not what the fallen senses perceive, but what can be imagined. If humanity can imagine itself as androgynous and harmoniously unified, then Blake posits that imaginative vision as humanity's ultimate form—but all of this is a case of special pleading, the fantasy of an escape from the real into the ideal.

And if Blake's vision is but one variation of what Abrams and Bloom see as the "internalization" of the quest-romance during the period, then we can see that Jerusalem/Vala's role and identity as split-muse is crucial to the centripetal movement of his characters toward salvation. By reshaping and absorbing the external world, Nature as the feminine, Blake allows his hero Albion (and, by extension, his audience) the illusion that there can be an escape from the ravages of the fall, identity, and self-consciousness, not to mention capitalism. In swallowing, introjecting, and cannibalizing the internal feminine, Albion redeems not only himself but all of those who have participated as readers in his creator's fiction. The wedding of internal and external, male and female, thought and action constitutes the fictional moment that Blake and his readers fulfill the promise and meaning of Jesus—redeem themselves through belief in their most arrogant self-created fantasies. Blake's creation of Jerusalem as the muselike feminine within (along with his silencing of Vala) stands in his imaginative cosmos as the moment of epiphany. By paradoxically defining and redefining the woman as Nature goddess, in transforming her into a desexed muse, he creates his final saving remnant, Jerusalem, the rightful ancestress to Isis, Sophia, the Shekhinah, Mary, and all those other women who have functioned throughout the patriarchy as internal fetishized objects. Blake's poetic vision, then, is based on merging the ideology of the male creative artist (Los) with the ideology of the woman within (Jerusalem). Because Blake presents a corpus that stands as a whole, his readers participate in his texts as a sustained and evocative panegyric that conceals its essentially conservative nostalgia for an earlier and fantasied world of the potent male mind/body as self-sufficient cosmos. In Blake's universe, then, the fantasy of male escapism takes its most extreme form; this is a world where women joyfully extinguish themselves.

II Wordsworth: "Characters of the great Apocalypse"

In a passage intended as the first section of his never-completed masterpiece, *The Excursion,* a poem that would have included *The Prelude* as only an introduction, Wordsworth announces his theme:

—I, long before the blissful hour arrives,
Would chant, in lonely peace, the spousal verse
Of this great consummation:—
Preface to *The Excursion,* 56–58

The consummation of which he sings is the union of the mind of man to the "goodly universe," a union that can be understood as a displaced androgynous quest to merge the internal world—the masculine mind—to the exterior world—the feminine natural realm. The ideal union of masculine and feminine in Wordsworth's poetry is not imaged as a merger between an adult male and female, but most often as an infant embraced and nurtured by a great mother/muse. This pair represents an image of humanity totally at peace with the larger universe:

Immense
Is the Recess, the circumambient World
Magnificent, by which they are embraced.
They move about upon the soft green field:
How little They, they and their doings seem, . . .
Through utter weakness pitiably dear,
As tender infants are: and yet how great!
Prelude, VIII, 46–54

An infantilizing of the male occurs here and throughout Wordsworth's work that bespeaks his anxiety in the face of the all-powerful feminine force. It would almost seem that the male presents himself as nonthreatening to the great mother/muse Nature so that he can live in peace, in harmony with her. But there are a number of differing opinions as to why Wordsworth overdetermines the image of Nature as a (M)Other in his works. In his psychoanalytical study of the poet, Richard Onorato claims that the death of Wordsworth's mother, which occurred when Wordsworth was eight years old, caused the poet to seek out substitutes for her in his highly fictionalized relationship with Nature: "The journey metaphor begins with the death of the mother and her disappearance from the original vale." Nature, then, "stands for the protective and feeding mother recollected and desiderated." [12] Without privileging any of the various biographical explanations,

12. Richard Onorato, *The Character of the Poet: Wordsworth in The Prelude* (Princeton: Princeton University Press, 1971), 72; Schapiro, *The Romantic Mother,* 94. On the same subject, see also James Heffernan's "The Presence of the Absent Mother in Wordsworth's *Prelude,*" *SIR* 27 (1988): 253–72.

it is certain that Nature does assume maternal characteristics—both positively and negatively—but that "her" dominant role is as an instructor, a muselike force who teaches the poet both gently and sternly about the comforting and harsh realities of life.

As E. D. Hirsch has demonstrated, Wordsworth's concept of Nature bears uncanny resemblances to Schelling's as developed in his *Naturphilosophie.* For Schelling, Nature is dual-visaged: Either an appearance (*natura naturata*) or Nature in herself, as merged with the Absolute, the infinite Being-affirmed of God (*natura naturans*). Coleridge, following George Berkeley's *Siris,* believed these two forces took on masculine and feminine qualities, with *natura naturata* or the bodily world represented by the female, while *natura naturans,* identified with God, was clearly male. The philosophical issue at stake here is the relationship between the mind and the external world. That is, does man seek value through himself, his own imagination, his own self-created projections, or does he find value imposed on him through his perception of Nature as a symbol of some external divine order? This is the crux of the problem of women in Romantic poetry. If women exist primarily as metaphors, as male-created symbols of value, then they can have no ontological reality. But if they are an essential element of a supposedly dual reality, the androgynous imagination, then they must exist as one side of an essentially dialectic reality. In either case, however, women do not exist as "real," but only as metaphors for process or product.

Herbert Lindenberger has claimed that Wordsworth, under the influence of Boehme and more directly Coleridge, developed the image of Nature as having nourishing female breasts in order to represent the sexual aspects of the interaction between the mind and Nature. He reads the passage: "The perfect image of a mighty Mind, / Of one that feeds upon infinity" (*Prelude,* XIII, 70–71), as developing the complex and ambivalent relationship that occurs between an object of Nature visible to man (the masculine "mighty Mind") and the higher realm from which it and man draw their nourishment (the feminine "infinity"). The image of the nourishing female breast appears at least a dozen times throughout *The Prelude,* most strikingly in the scenes in which the child is compared to an infant suckling at the maternal breast (one is reminded here of Keats's "Intellect nourished at the teat of emotion"). This oral greediness tropes the mouth that ingests first the maternal and all of her later manifestations—it lends a very real literalness to the image of the "women within."

In *The Prelude,* I, after settling on the theme of his epic and describing his first childhood memories, Wordsworth comments on his larger concern—the mind's relation to the feminine world of Nature:

> The mind of Man is fram'd even like the breath
> And harmony of music. There is a dark
> Invisible workmanship that reconciles
> Discordant elements, and makes them move
> In one society.
>
> (351–55)

In fact, Wordsworth states that Nature can teach the mind either through "gentlest visitation" or through "Severer interventions, ministry / More palpable, and so she dealt with me" (367, 370–71). The double visage of Nature has been traced by Abrams to the theological tradition enunciated by Thomas Burnet's *Sacred Theory of the Earth* (1681–89), in which Nature is seen as the external emblem of both the beneficent and the terrifying attributes of God, while Spivak sees it as troping the split between Nature and Culture, Lucy's kinship contrasted to Annette's "illegitimacy." Another possible source, however, can be found in Wordsworth's readings in both Jewish and Christian mystical writers. In the Kabbalistic tradition, for instance, the Lord's feminine aspect is called the Shekhinah, who embodies eternal, mystical Silence, the Grace of the Holy Spirit, and the powers of Wisdom (here the Greek is "Sophia" for the Hebrew "Hokhmah"). In a revealing appropriation of the mother's identity, an early Gnostic text written by Clement of Alexandria (ca. A.D. 180) describes the child feeding from his father's breast:

> The Word is everything to the child, both father and mother, teacher and nurse. The nutriment is the milk of the Father and the Word alone supplies us children with the milk of love, and only those who suck at this breast are truly happy. For this reason, seeing is called sucking; to those infants who seek the Word, the Father's loving breasts supply milk.[13]

13. Herbert Lindenberger, *On Wordsworth's Prelude* (Princeton: Princeton University Press, 1963), 308–9; E. D. Hirsch, *Wordsworth and Schelling* (New Haven: Yale University Press, 1960), 30; Abrams, *Natural Supernaturalism*, 99–105. Gayatri Chakravorty Spivak, "Sex and History in *The Prelude*," *TSLL* 23 (1981), 333. Clement of Alexandria quoted in Pagels, 81; for the fullest discussion of androgynous imagery in Gnostic texts, see "God the Father/God the Mother," in Elaine Pagels, *The Gnostic Gospels* (New York: Vintage, 1979). On the "Judaic quality" of Wordsworth's thought, see Lionel Trilling, "Wordsworth and the Rabbis," in *The Opposing Self* (New York: Viking, 1955). According to Gershom Scholem, "in Talmudic literature and non-Kabbalistic Rabbinical Ju-

But the more contemporary Christian mystic, Jacob Boehme, was decidedly more influential in shaping Wordsworth's vision of a sexualized deity. Even Byron recognized Boehme's influence on Wordsworth's work and attacked it by depicting Wordsworth as

> this new Jacob Behmen, this ***** whose pride might have kept him true, even had his principles turned as perverted as his *soi-disant* poetry.

Two volumes of Boehme's works were found in Wordsworth's library, as was Edward Taylor's *Jacob Behmen's Theosophic Philosophy Unfolded* (1691) after his death, and Stallknecht has asserted that the William Law translations of Boehme that Wordsworth owned present a philosophy that stood as a transition between the biblical idea of divine creation and the Romantic notion of artistic/aesthetic creation, thus lending a religious significance to the latter. For the Christian mystics, God's act of creation is continuous, not limited to one exclusive "making," while a feminine Nature is constantly creating and manifesting God in those creative *fiats*.[14] And although Wordsworth occasionally uses masculine attributes to describe Nature (much like the Gnostic "Father's breast"), Nature is most typically portrayed throughout *The Prelude* as a primarily feminine power in the tradition of the Shekhinah-Sophia. She embodies the love of the mother, but she is also the stern judge and harsh instructor of Hebrew tradition, and it is here

---

daism the Shekhinah means the in-dwelling of God in this world, God's face, and is not separated from God: but in Kabbalah the Shekhinah is an aspect of God, a quasi-independent feminine element within God" (see his *On the Kabbalah and Its Symbolism*, trans. Ralph Manheim [London: Routledge and Kegan Paul, 1965], 105). Coleridge was so deeply read in Kabbalistic sources that he routinely referred to the "Shechinah of the Conscience," and the "Shechinah in the heart" (see Beer, *Coleridge the Visionary*, 59).

14. Byron's comment can be found in a letter to Thomas Moore, 1 June 1818. Boehme's influence on Wordsworth (largely via Coleridge) has been analyzed by Newton P. Stallknecht in *Strange Seas of Thought: Studies in William Wordsworth's Philosophy of Man and Nature* (Durham: Duke University Press, 1945), 43. Lionel Trilling sees Wordsworth's quietude, carried to an extreme, as a "denial of sexuality" (see his "Wordsworth and the Iron Time," in *Wordsworth: A Collection of Critical Essays*, ed. Abrams [Englewood Cliffs: Prentice-Hall, 1972], 56). Similarly, G. Wilson Knight claims that Wordsworth's preference for a stern Nature stems from his lack of sexual drive (see his "Wordsworthian Profundity," in *The Starlit Dome* [1941; rpt. London: Oxford University Press, 1971]).

that we can see the dual/split qualities of Wordsworth's muse most clearly.

In Book II we see Wordsworth as an "infant Babe" "Nurs'd in his Mother's arms, the Babe who sleeps / Upon his Mother's breast" (237; 240–41), but we also see a Nature who teaches not only through "beauty" but also through "fear" (I, 306). Nature is, like mother's milk, the "nourishment" that the poet has "fed" on so that he has come to know a "never failing principle of joy, / And purest passion" (II, 462–66). But Nature also has the power to unify thoughts with emotions, or, as Wordsworth says, "From Nature and her overflowing soul / I had receiv'd so much that all my thoughts / Were steep'd in feeling" (II, 416–18). The interaction between Wordsworth's mind and the presence of Nature had already been established as a "spirit of religious love" by the time he was seventeen (II, 376). But Nature is not his God in any simplistic formula; rather, his mind and its interactions with the feminine within—troped as a semiotic/Imaginary Nature—form a power that allows him to imaginatively transform both his external and internal worlds: "An auxiliar light / Came from my mind which on the setting sun / Bestow'd new splendor" (II, 387–89). As Weiskel has shrewdly noted, Wordsworth's "regressive attachment to Nature" had to be concealed if not denied. Throughout *The Prelude* he speaks of Nature leading him on—"(surely I was led by her)"—like a woman leading on a man toward whom her intentions are not wholly honorable: "Nature is thus responsible for both the sense of loss or deprivation, felt as betrayal, and for the fear itself. . . . But beyond the formulas of betrayal there is the possibility that Nature herself enters into the object of fear in a constitutive fashion. She does not merely employ fear and pain to strengthen the young mind; she is herself a source of pain and terror" (102). Wordsworth is redeemed by the exquisite harmony of mind and Nature, masculine and feminine, an idea that ironically almost caused Blake a fit of apoplexy.

The Preface to Wordsworth's *Excursion,* for instance, praises the exquisitely fitted individual Mind functioning in perfect harmony with the feminine world of Nature:

> How exquisitely the individual Mind
> (And the progressive powers perhaps no less
> Of the whole species) to the external World
> Is fitted:—and how exquisitely, too—
> Theme this but little heard of among men—
> The external World is fitted to the Mind;
> And the creation (by no lower name

Can it be called) which they with blended might
Accomplish:—this is our high argument.
(63–71)

After reading these lines, Blake responded violently: "You shall not bring me down to believe such fitting & fitted I know better & Please your Lordship" (E, 667; K, 784). The irony here, of course, is that Blake's own theories were so similar to Wordsworth's vision. Wordsworth, in fact, once told Crabb Robinson that he had no need for a redeemer, for that sentiment, the belief in the divine power of the poet's reintegrated imagination, is identical to Blake's own fantasy of himself as a grandiose self, the androgynous/apotheotic artist.

The Prelude III depicts Wordsworth retreating to the "caverns" within his mind (246) and living within his own self-created universe (142–43) rather than the freakish world of the city or the sterility of Cambridge. But no one can exist for long in that sort of escapism; Wordsworth himself admits that his life at Cambridge was "rotted" and like a "floating island, an amphibious thing, / Unsound, of spungy texture" (339–41). And so to renew himself spiritually Wordsworth returns to his home during a summer vacation and there undergoes a mystical, quasi-sexual experience in the presence of Nature:

Gently did my soul
Put off her veil, and, self-transmuted, stood
Naked as in the presence of her God.
(IV, 140–42)

And later Wordsworth contents himself with the realization that once more in the presence of Nature he has "glimmering views" of

How Life pervades the undecaying mind,
How the immortal Soul with God-like power
Informs, creates, and thaws the deepest sleep
That time can lay upon her.
(IV, 154–58)

The soul of the male poet is clearly feminine here, but so is the world of nature; that is, the male perceives both the internal and his external worlds as "other" to him. His "true" self, in other words, is his totally male mind—his reason—divorced from contamination from alien forces assaulting it both from within and without.

It has long been noted that Wordsworth actually bases many of his poetic structures on the notion of contraries, dualities, and oppositions that he then attempts to resolve. For instance, Langbaum has observed that what he calls the "evolution of soul" in Wordsworth's poetry often evidences itself in the "composite experience of river and towers" that is also an "experience of female and male principles." The river, water imagery, the running stream we see throughout *The Prelude* and other poems represents the feminine-semiotic force, while the tower and stone consistently image the Symbolic/phallic.[15] We can see the struggle between these emblems most clearly in *The Prelude,* V, 72–89. Here the Arab appears to the poet in a dream as a "guide" who would lead him through the "desert." The Arab carries "underneath one arm" a stone, while "in the opposite hand a shell." The stone represents "Euclid's Elements," that is, rational thought and the phallic/Symbolic, while the shell is "something of more worth," poetry, the semiotic/Imaginary, the feminine. The poet as dreamer has to incorporate both forces within himself before he can continue on his journey to self-knowledge. Throughout Wordsworth's poems we see these dichotomies, and recognize the concealed sexual nature of the compulsion to posit irreconcilable oppositions. Charles Smith has noted that "Wordsworth had a very strong habit of thinking in terms of paired opposites or contrarieties. Everywhere, in nature, in individual man and in society, he saw a constant interplay of opposing forces."[16] The androgynous quality of this tendency has been implicitly recognized by critics who speak of the mind's relationship with Nature as a poetry of "union," "fusion," and "fulfillment." Thus Wordsworth's declaration of a "spousal verse" and a "great Consummation" requires that his poetry be written on the premise that man and Nature, like man and wife, live by the bourgeois ideology of mutuality and reciprocity.

Book VI's famous description of the poet's journey through the Simplon Pass stands at the exact center of *The Prelude,* and, as such, represents the contradictory nature of Wordsworth's vision of feminine Nature as transformed by the mind. When Wordsworth realizes that he and his friends have already crossed the Alps without realizing it, there is an ironic anticlimactic tone. Wordsworth stands back from the remembrance of the experience and muses that it is the mind, the

15. Robert Langbaum, "The Evolution of Soul in Wordsworth's Poetry," *PMLA* 82 (1967), 266; also see Florence Marsh, *Wordsworth's Imagery: A Study in Poetic Vision* (New Haven: Yale University Press, 1952), 96.

16. Charles Smith, "The Contrarieties: Wordsworth's Dualistic Imagery," *PMLA* 69 (1954), 1181.

"Imagination" (525), that leads us to "Our destiny, our nature, and our home," which is ultimately not the natural world (proven to be disappointing), but is instead "infinitude" (538–39). After making this observation, Wordsworth retraces his steps and comes once again on the sight he had wanted to experience—not simply see, but recreate in his own mind:

> The unfetter'd clouds, and region of the heavens,
> Tumult and peace, the darkness and the light
> Were all like workings of one mind, the features
> Of the same face, blossoms upon one tree,
> Characters of the great Apocalypse,
> The types and symbols of Eternity,
> Of first and last, and midst, and without end.
> (566–72)

In this oft-quoted passage we can discern a displaced version of Wordsworth's androgynous ideal. The contraries of male and female are displaced and replaced by the contraries of tumult and peace, darkness and light. But we are confronted with a sort of mystical perception of the "one mind," the unified face, the fantasy of the primordial being who was the only reality at the beginning of creation and will be the only reality at the end. The sexual implications of this passage need to be noted, however, if we are to appreciate Wordsworth's appropriation of the feminine muse into that "one mind" that creates all of reality both within and without the self. Marlon Ross has perceptively noted that Wordsworth's depiction of the Imagination as "unfather'd" (VI, 527) suggests that for Wordsworth, Fathering is prior and superior to Mothering: "In Wordsworth's scheme, mothering does not justify and order existence, it merely enacts and nourishes what has already been ordained by motherless fathering. By making imagination father itself, and by unmothering the originating act of fathering, Wordsworth, following Judeo-Christian tradition, manages . . . to defeminize the conquest that has been made possible through the good auspices of feminine nature."[17] In other words, Wordsworth needs to redefine Nature much as Blake redefined Vala into Jerusalem. His split muse—Nature as harsh and Nature as beneficent—was finally so fearful a power that it required him to escape a female Nature altogether, thus

17. See Ross, "Romantic Quest and Conquest," in *Romanticism and Feminism*, ed. Mellor, 47–48.

the invention of a masculine "Father Nature," surely one of the patriarchy's most convoluted acts of self-deception.

The companion passage to the image of the "one mind" can be found in Book XIII's meditation on the "perfect image of a mighty Mind." In this passage we have another of Wordsworth's cosmic visions of unity between mind, Nature, God, nourishment, and imagination. Wordsworth in his conclusion to the poem is moved by the sight of Snowdon, a "lonely Mountain" and a revised version of the Mount Blanc of Book VI, so that in perceiving it he no longer sees the actual mountain, but instead

> The perfect image of a mighty Mind,
> Of one that feeds upon infinity,
> That is exalted by an underpresence,
> The sense of God, or whatsoe'er is dim
> Or vast in its own being.
> (XIII, 69–73)

Wordsworth spent a good deal of time and trouble endlessly revising this passage, suggesting that it was of major importance to his purpose in concluding the poem, and Stephen Gill has pointed out that it is intended to support Wordsworth's notion that we all possess an interior life "In which all beings live with God, themselves / Are God, existing in the mighty whole." The apocalyptic impulse in Wordsworth's poetry requires that the mind and Nature exist as equal powers in his essentially fictitious presentation of an androgynous balance of imagination and reality, but this is not possible in a poet so anxious about the encroaching power of the feminine. The passage, like the Mount Blanc section, presents the belief that the mind transforms the external world in such a way that the actual Snowdon becomes both an image or analogue for the mighty mind of man and an imaginative projection or creation of the mind itself. In both scenes Wordsworth states his belief in the mind's ultimate supremacy over the natural world, another manifestation of his belief that the Symbolic/masculine was to be valued over the semiotic/feminine, a theme he had developed earlier in "Nutting."

Wordsworth further claims in this final poetic summation that love has been one of his major thematic concerns since it is the power of love that makes the soul divine (XIII, 158). But he is speaking here of a particular kind of love:

> This love more intellectual cannot be
> Without Imagination, which, in truth,
> Is but another name for absolute strength
> And clearest insight, amplitude of mind,
> And reason in her most exalted mood.
>
> (159–63)

In fact, the love Wordsworth endorses is a form of the imagination, "intellectual love, / For they are each in each, and cannot stand / Dividually" (179–81). As Spivak points out, this passage endorses both an "intimation of androgynous plentitude through the thematics of self-separation and autoeroticism" and "a picture of indeterminate coexistence with a strong aura of identity."[18] In a passage that is often seen as Wordsworth's declaration of imaginative independence, he states that man must find this imaginative power and love totally within himself. He claims:

> Here must thou be, O Man!
> Strength to thyself; no Helper hast thou here;
> Here keepest thou thy individual state:
> No other can divide with thee this work,
> No secondary hand can intervene
> To fashion this ability.
>
> (181–86)

But this passage reads more as a wish than a statement reflecting the facts of Wordsworth's experience. It is, as Keats recognized so clearly about Wordsworth, a manifestation of his "egotistical sublime." Wordsworth's poetic history is finally a veiled and obscured record of his debt to the feminine within—whether that feminine is troped as Nature's breasts or his sister's ministering direction. As William has stated over and over again throughout *The Prelude* as well as earlier poems, his sister Dorothy and his friend Coleridge have assisted him at all crucial points in his imaginative development, and they have completed his being by representing to him throughout his life the masculine and feminine ways of being and seeing. William would like to stand as a sort of imaginative titan,the embodiment of the purely masculine egotistical sublime, alone with the universe. But the poem ex-

18. See Wordsworth, *The Prelude,* ed. Stephen Gill (London: Oxford University Press, 1970), 317. All quotations from *The Prelude* are from this edition. Also see Spivak, "Sex and History," *TSLL* 23 (1981), 335.

presses instead William's ambivalent reliance on Dorothy as muse, "Sister of my Soul!" whose "sweet influence" and love have softened William's self-confessed tendency to "over-sternness" (204, 209, 220). Dorothy has taught William the value of the feminine so that he has given up his "countenance severe" and has returned to an appreciation of Nature when it "in my affection, had fallen back / Into a second place." Dorothy as anima, muse, second self is praised first of all creatures; she is "a kind of gentler spring / That went before my steps" (223, 231–32, 238–39).

If Dorothy functions throughout the poem as both herself and William's feminine element, Coleridge plays both an actual and a symbolic role as well. William addresses him as a "most loving Soul," a "gentle Spirit to my heart of hearts," whose function has been to "shed the light of love" (241, 245, 243). William praises Coleridge, however, in somewhat ambiguous terms. For instance, Coleridge is a "human Creature, be he who he may" a "Poet, or destined for a humbler name" (252–53). The implication here is that Coleridge is a flawed man; although still worthy of some modicum of respect, he will never be the poet William is, though he may prove someday to be a philosopher (a humbler vocation). This ambivalence toward Coleridge's identity parallels his equally deep ambivalence toward Dorothy, expressed most clearly in "Tintern Abbey." William was all too aware of how deeply dependent he was on both of these people, and his poetry reflects that he found this dependence both threatening and embarrassing, something that he attempts to elide at every opportunity.

Dorothy and Coleridge function in *The Prelude* as symbolic aspects of William's fragmented psyche, and in Book XIII he came close to openly admitting as much. Immediately after declaring his independence from all human and natural mediation, he contradicts himself:

> For all that friendship, all that love can do,
> All that a darling countenance can look
> Or dear voice utter to complete the man,
> Perfect him, made imperfect in himself,
> All shall be his: and he whose soul hath risen
> Up to the height of feeling intellect
> Shall want no humbler tenderness, his heart
> Be tender as a nursing Mother's heart;
> Of female softness shall his life be full,
> Of little loves and delicate desires,
> Mild interests and gentlest sympathies.
> (193–203)

This passage, in several revealing ways, announces William's awareness that his theme has been his own completion as a whole human being, for he admits that as a singular self he has been "imperfect." Here William acknowledges that he, Dorothy, and Coleridge form a sort of trinity, a humanized and composite divine self. Whereas he began his poem by tracing the growth and development of his individual mind, he concludes by admitting that he cannot exist in isolation or apart from his complements: Coleridge as the son-figure, the *logos,* and Dorothy as the creative spirit, *sophia.* In this sense *The Prelude* is a very Christian poem, or at least a poem that admits traditional Christian ideologies in its valorization of human wholeness.

Further, the passage also uses breast imagery and dwells on the feminine aspects of William's fantasy of psychic completion. In fact, his use of the words "feeling intellect" expresses the displaced nature of the androgynous impulse throughout his work. William wants not simply to think in a Symbolic/masculine manner, but to have his intellect tempered by the emotions traditionally associated with the semiotic/feminine and embodied in his sister Dorothy. The androgynous quest in William's poetry is displaced and muted, but he concludes his major work with the image of his sister's intervention, as well as Coleridge's model of the masculine thought processes. Unified, the three form a composite deity, "Prophets of Nature," singing the beauties of the "mind of man": "In beauty exalted, as it is itself / Of substance and of fabric more divine" (435–45). That "fabric," the fantasied body of the androgynous imagination, stands as Wordsworth's final attempt to absorb/consume the feminine principle, sometimes imaged as the (M)Other, sometimes as the female world of Nature, and sometimes as Dorothy, the infantilized sister/second self. But throughout the various contortions that the feminine takes in Wordsworth's poetry, we can discern a distinct pattern of negation, a tracing out of existence. The woman in Wordsworth's poetry ultimately disappears, erases herself at the moment that Wordsworth as cosmic masculine mind achieves his own apotheosis.

III Keats: "A power within me of enormous ken, / To see as a God sees"

Keats presents both faces of the feminine muse as fetish—loving and fearful—but he splits this presentation between two female figures:

Psyche and Moneta. Both "women" are primarily troped as the feminine aspect within the poet/hero, and both are seen as vital to the poet/quester's mission of self-knowledge. But whereas Psyche can finally be assimilated in a fictionally harmonious fashion by the male, Moneta cannot. The poet ends his quest in failure with her visage—impenetrable and unyielding—before him. Both Psyche and Moneta, however, also engage in a sort of ritualized dance with the protagonist-poet Keats, who experiences himself as increasingly feminized throughout his poetry. His poems, that is, reflect his own sense of castration at the hands of a feminine marketplace, increasingly dominated by women as both readers and writers of literary texts. Psyche or Moneta as muses function, then, not simply as internal aspects of Keats the poet; they also reenact the historical conditions of a literary marketplace in which the male writer felt more than ever like a prostitute, selling himself and his works to the highest bidder in order to survive.

Keats read Thomas Taylor's translation of Apuleius's version of the Psyche story, published in England in 1795, and Taylor's commentaries on the work are illuminating for shedding light on Keats's adaptation of the myth. For Taylor, Psyche's marriage to the invisible Eros represents the soul's union with Love, the power of Desire itself, which can never be contained in any external form. Her interfering sisters, the ones who demand that Psyche must view the body of her husband, symbolize for Taylor the Imagination and Nature—two traditionally idealized and feminine powers within Romantic ideology. Their interference, their need to give internal vision external form and reality, cause the fall of Psyche and her descent into Hades before she is rescued by her husband and taken to her earned immortality. The significance of the tale, then, lies in the fact that Psyche was not born a goddess, just as Keats was not born into the class that traditionally supplied England with its poets. Psyche won her status through suffering and learning about the false lure of both the Imagination and the external world—a lesson that Keats as a poet personalizes in his own meditation on the psychological and economic meanings of the mythoso.[19]

19. For the most pertinent discussions of the feminization of the literary marketplace during the early nineteenth century, see Marlon B. Ross, "Scott's Chivalric Pose: The Function of Metrical Romance in the Romantic Period," *Genre* 18 (1986), 267–97, and Sonia Hofkosh, "The Writer's Ravishment: Women and the Romantic Author—The Example of Byron," in *Romanticism and Feminism*, ed. Mellor, 93–114. Also see Marilyn Butler, *Romantics, Rebels, and Reactionaries*, 132–37, for historically contemporary treatments of Psyche.

We enter Keats's "Ode to Psyche" and are supposed to be immediately overwhelmed by the fictional power of the female to create and inspire imaginative visions: "O Goddess! hear these tuneless numbers, wrung / By sweet enforcement and remembrance dear" (1–2). The "remembrance dear" recalls the stories of our primal origins, lovingly preserved in the world of myth and metaphor, which Psyche herself embodies. But Keats is a poet, a creator as well as a re-creator of myth himself. He places his poem in the past not simply as a nostalgic gesture, but to conceal his very real present concerns. The poem disguises its meanings, then, by its invocation of the past, a historical moment that it presents as universal in significance and therefore "transcendent." But Keats's concerns with his own middle-class status and his increased sense of emasculation at the hands of his culture are perhaps nowhere more in evidence than in this poem. When Keats begs Psyche to "pardon that thy secrets should be sung / Even into thine own soft-conched ear" (3–4), we know that this is simply another way of admitting that his poems are attempts to sing into his own ear, his own psyche. We realize most clearly here that Psyche has been (re)invented by Keats as an avatar not only of his own poetic belatedness, but also of his own increasingly obvious femininity as a writer of "Romance" and "women's" literature as well as his embarrassing middle-class status. She is his imaginative creation and projection, his muse, his feminine self, his self-created "Other," but she also tropes his sense of inferiority in a marketplace that has failed to accept him, failed to accord him the right to a living as a writer. Psyche's courtship by Eros images Keats's own courtship of the literary marketplace, a marketplace that has rewarded instead the writings of that flagrant self-promoter Byron or the even more unworthy productions of a Felicia Hemans or Letitia Landon.

To court the feminine and feminized literary marketplace, then, Keats invents Psyche, a projection of himself as both poet and product, artistic production and object of consumption. He commodifies himself, so to speak, as a woman, in thrall to and under the domination of forces out of "her" control. But if the poet's role is to create and celebrate his feminine aspect, he must also be able to sustain the fiction, at least as long as the duration of the poem. This act of artifice, which is, after all, the poem's *raison d'être,* is immediately undercut by the poet's question, "Surely I dreamt to-day, or did I see / The winged Psyche with awaken'd eyes?" (5–6). Can Psyche be seen except in an internal vision? Here Keats asks if the mythic power of the feminine and adherence to the economic demands of the marketplace have the ability to make our self-created ideals a reality. The answer would seem to be affirmative, at least as far as the wish-fulfillment structure of the poem is concerned. After supposedly wandering through the forest "thoughtlessly" (7), perhaps only the Apollonian powers of thought suspended, the poet stumbles onto the loving pair, Psyche and Eros, "couched side by side / In deepest grass," beneath a roof of blossoms and next to a running stream (9–11). The lovers, amid their sensually delightful Eden, are "calm-breathing," but

> Their arms embraced, and their pinions too;
> Their lips touch'd not, but had not bade adieu,
> As if disjoined by soft-handed slumber.
> (15–18)

Much has been made of the similarities of this scene to the depiction of Adam and Eve in *Paradise Lost,* and that myth surely informs Keats's portrayal.[20] It is precisely because Milton's Adam and Eve are self-consciously fictional, metaphorical, the creations of a poet's attempt to reanimate Christian myth that they are invoked here in Keats's attempt to reanimate pagan myths through what Lacan has called the *gaze.* For there is a sense in which Milton, like his serpent, was the voyeur in that Eden, the uninvited yet crucial guest in what was, after all, a primal scene. But the primal scene exists only if it is viewed by someone, someone without sexual power, someone who stands, that is, in a castrated posture to the principal actors. It would seem that Keats is trying here to convey that voyeuristic sense as he purposefully blunders into witnessing this embrace between the male and female, the father and mother, but transformed by the child's mythic memory of what parents seem to represent—power, beauty, love. It is important here that the poet clearly recognizes and identifies the male figure as Eros, but that he is uncertain about the female. He lapses into wish-fulfillment and finally realizes that she is Psyche, actually a projection of his own poetic consciousness and assumed cultural identity. In a sense, then, he is witnessing himself as "Other" in the arms of poetic desire. We can even go so far as to see the text making love to itself here, in an epiphany of self-reflexive desire. But we are also witnessing a scene of commodity exchange masquerading as "love," for Psyche, like Keats the poet, has sold herself to gain the power and prestige of Eros. In embracing Eros, Psyche gains fame and the im-

20. On the Miltonic and Wordsworthian echoes in the poem, see Harold Bloom, *The Visionary Company* (New York: Doubleday, 1961), 421, and *A Map of Misreading* (New York: Oxford University Press, 1975), 152–56.

mortality that she could not possess in her own right. In creating and becoming Psyche, Keats, by extension, attempts to grasp the elusive "woman" fame for himself; he attempts to deny his masculine identity and the qualities of self-mastery and aggression that have failed to prosper in the new female-dominated marketplace.

The poem's third stanza recapitulates Psyche's mythic history and associates her even more clearly with Keats's own identity as a poet. She is the "latest born and loveliest vision far / Of all Olympus' faded hierarchy!" (24–25). Fairer than Phoebe or Vesper or any of the other established deities, Psyche is the loveliest because she is worshipped only secretly, internally, through the mind. She has no "altar heap'd with flowers," no "virgin-choir to make delicious moan / Upon the midnight hours; / No voice, no lute, no pipe, no incense sweet" (29–32). The poem here is a virtual catalogue of negatives. Psyche has nothing; Psyche *is* nothing? According to Paul Fry, Psyche as soul "finally cannot be signified—it *is* the empty space—because it is unsignifying; Psyche is the simple quiddity of things known for what they are. She has no wings, no figure at all, and to interrupt the erotic embrace that represents her inseparability from things as they are, to 'transport' or transcendentalize her, is to annihilate her nature." We are again, then, in the realm of the absent woman in the poem, buried under so much hyperbole that she is negated at the moment of her ostensible triumph. But we are also at the moment that Fredric Jameson (following Bakhtin and Kristeva) labels an *ideologeme,* a ideostructural maneuver that allows Keats to conceal the cultural and economic conflicts that concern him while simultaneously positioning his audience ideologically in relation to the conflicts.[21] The absent altar and choir trope the displacement of the male poet by the female writer and audience, at the same time that they paradoxically celebrate the domestic ideology as a middle-class fantasy. Psyche can be read on some level as the triumph of the middle-class woman author, while she is also Keats's appropriation of that role for himself as male and middle-class poet.

21. Paul Fry, *The Poet's Calling in the English Ode* (New Haven: Yale University Press, 1980), 231. Jameson's use of the concept "ideologeme" (in *The Political Unconscious: Narrative as a Socially Symbolic Act* [Ithaca: Cornell University Press, 1981], 73, 87–89) can be traced to P. N. Medvedev and M. Bakhtin, *The Formal Method in Literary Scholarship: A Critical Introduction to Sociological Poetics,* trans. Albert J. Wehrle (Baltimore: Johns Hopkins University Press, 1978), 3, and Julia Kristeva's "The Bounded Text," originally published in France in 1969, available in *Desire in Language,* 36.

Without making too much of Bloom's theory of poetic belatedness, it is surely striking that the belatedness of Psyche, as well as her déclassé vulnerability, endear her to the poet. Psyche is "too late for antique vows, / Too, too late for the fond believing lyre" (36–37). She was not created when Greek myth was at its height, when air, woods, water, and fire were seen as sacred (38–39). And so Keats admits his role as self-creator of both the dream and the dreamer: "I see, and sing, by my own eyes inspired" (43). Where there were once negatives, emptiness, false and artificial myths, the poet as self-invented mythic hero steps in and begs to become Psyche's "choir," "lute," "pipe," and "incense sweet" (44–46). Psyche, like Keats the belated poet, is a fiction of herself; her fame is her own fantasy. As Fry has pointed out, in this insight Keats is implying, like Blake before him, that religious "worship from now on will simply consist in cultivating one's awareness of selfhood." But social responsibility as well as reality demand that "the poet cannot rest satisfied with the worship of his sole self, [he] needs the image of a sentient double, of the self as other, even if bowing to that need entails repeating all the old postures of worship."[22] Keats needs to worship Psyche because she holds the power not only to spiritually redeem him, but to economically ensure his own existence as a poet. Courting the muse within becomes an act of faith in his own fame as a writer in a marketplace that demands that the male poet become as much like a woman as possible.

In the final stanza the poet blatantly assumes his role as mythmaker and literary raconteur. Psyche as self is his own creation, and through assuming the position of her "priest," he worships himself as feminine. He will "build a fane / In some untrodden region of [his] mind" (50–51). In worshipping Psyche/Eros within that "untrodden" sacred region of his own mind, Keats has also assumed powers that the traditional alchemists associated with the philosopher's stone, the *rebis;* he can reconcile opposites and transform dull matter into its spiritualized essence. Thus the poet can inhabit an area of his mind "new grown with pleasant pain" where "pines" will be transformed into "branched thoughts" (52–53). Clearly, this is the fiction of a totally humanized

22. Fry, 229. For another interpretation of the narcissistic involution leading to unisexual figures in the "Ode," see Jean Hagstrum, "Eros and Psyche: Some Versions of Romantic Love and Delicacy," *CI* 3 (1977), 521–42. And for a suggestive treatment of the poem's "androgynous consciousness attained through self-reflexivity," the "self-enchantment" that the Romantic fantasist uses to enchant others, see Karl Kroeber's *Romantic Fantasy and Science Fiction* (New Haven: Yale University Press, 1988), 105.

universe, the logical result of making the external internal. This image, however, also contains the middle-class and masculinist notion that the material world exists only to be transformed into goods of production and consumption, an ideology that tropes Keats's appropriation of the feminine as an object of exchange. In the midst of this fantasied idyllic human landscape, the poet will build a "rosy sanctuary . . . With the wreath'd trellis of a working brain" (59–60). The brain is feminized here, troped as a trellis, supporting flowery thoughts. This curiously artificial image actually is appropriate to the hysterical promises that are being made here to Psyche and self. In fact, the poem is consistently written in the future tense. The tone, however, becomes increasingly shrill, even desperate, as if the poet recognizes all too well the artificiality of his defenses against the woman and her sexual and economic power.

The literary work of building a shrine for Psyche must be carried on by the "gardener Fancy" who must use a good deal of "feign" in his productions (62). Keats by this time is failing to sustain the artificiality of his own poetic recreation. He hopes for flowers, no two of which are the same (63), while fantasizing that Psyche is reposing on a bed of "soft delight / That shadowy thought can win" (64–65), with a "bright torch, and a casement ope at night, / To let the warm Love in!" (66–67). The unification of Psyche and Eros obviously cannot be sustained continually or indefinitely in the poet's mind. All he can hope for is the power to occasionally "let the warm Love in" through the use of the "torch"—the poetic insight and inspiration of the casement, the portal to the fictionalized feminine within the self and culture. Psyche stands, then, as another erased and absent woman within. Her absorption into the body of Love represents her role and identity as a self-created and self-consumed image, much like the increasingly feminized poet Keats. In picturing his female muse as a displaced and harassed woman, struggling to gain acceptance ("love" and economic status), Keats conceals his distaste for the feminized literary marketplace and his own castration at its hands while supposedly celebrating the power of the feminine to redeem the masculine realm of the mind, Eros. The dichotomy between these two forces, continually at war with one another, finally produces a poem notable for its depiction of "love" as barely concealed sexual politics/economics.

Keats's final major and incomplete works, the *Hyperion* poems, present the feminine muse as both the woman within and the increasingly feminized marketplace. The two versions we have of Keats's final attempts to compose an epic reveal that the ostensible topic of the epic, the overthrow of Saturn and the Titans by the Olympian Apollo, is also a displaced version of Keats's own struggle to define his identity as a strongly male poet within the larger pantheon of British literature. But—as was evidenced in "Psyche"—Keats can assert himself as a strong son against a feared and respected father-figure only by making himself feminine, or, at the very least, androgynous. Saturn, the imposing male figure who dominates the first *Hyperion* poem, *Hyperion: A Fragment,* represents both his feared rivals (Milton and more covertly Wordsworth) at the same time he embodies Keats's idealized vision of himself as a strong male writer, untainted by the sensibility, affectation, and weakness that characterized "romance" or women's writing during Keats's era. But equally fearful and finally overwhelming in both poems is the female presence—Mnemosyne/Moneta—Keats's muse, his projected feminine side, his dreaming tendencies, and the feminine cultural values that he realizes are at war with the masculine and patriarchal realm to which he ideally aspires.

Most revealing as evidence of Keats's extreme ambivalence toward the masculine powers of reason—the Milton within him—is his abandonment of *The Fall of Hyperion* after writing the first sixty-one lines of the second canto. In a letter to Reynolds (21–22 September 1819), he explained:

> I have given up Hyperion. . . . Miltonic verse cannot be written but in an artful or rather artist's humour. I wish to give myself up to other sensations. English ought to be kept up. It may be interesting to you to pick out some lines from Hyperion and put a mark X to the false beauty preceeding from art, and one // to the true voice of feeling. (*Letters,* II, 167)

In his final poem, Keats confronted his creative impulses as simply the power of imitation, more specifically as Milton's "artful" influence. But this denunciation of Milton is most patently a nostalgic gesture, a reference to that more pristine time in England's literary history, the era before women in large numbers not only made their way into print, but finally dominated the marketplace. The fact that Keats cannot distinguish between "false beauty" and "the true voice of feeling" suggests his confusion about his culture's demand to write poetry that appeals to women and lower-class readers in opposition to the stronger, masculine voice of Milton. Overwhelmed by the confusion to court a composite muse who demanded loyalty to conflicting literary traditions, Keats gave up the poem in impotent frustration.

Bloom has conjectured that *The Fall of Hyperion: A Dream* begins with a bitter polemic against the two imaginations that had most intimidated Keats. He speaks of the "Fanatics" with their "dreams, wherewith they weave / A paradise for a sect" (1–2), which he reads as a reference to Milton's radically Protestant vision and *Paradise Lost's* dominating poetic creation of Eden. The other imagination represented here is the "savage" who "Guesses at Heaven" (2–4), most likely Keats's portrait of Wordsworth and the "Prospectus," ironically Wordsworth's own aborted attempt to transcend Milton. But one can also see these references as echoes of Keats's own earlier work in *Hyperion: A Fragment*, thus making the poem an exercise in self-confrontation and narcissistic anxiety.[23] One has to be struck, however, by the sexual displacement of the feminine in Keats's vision of artistic creation. According to the vision Keats proffers, he is heir to a radically male line of poetic precursors, a literary patriarchy that has assumed quasi-religious status for both him and his society. The muses who appear in the two *Hyperions* can be read, then, as the resurgence of the repressed feminine principle, both within the mind of Keats and in literary and economic history.

In lines 19ff. the poet again finds himself in the paradise of Milton (*Paradise Lost,* V, 321ff.), where he eats the fruit left from the last meal of Adam and Eve before their expulsion from the garden. After eating, the poet drinks to the presence of all the dead and of course male poets whom he claims he will confront on his mission of self-justification (44–46). After recovering his senses, the poet makes his way westward to receive Moneta's hyperbolic challenge to "ascend / These steps" or die at the base (107–8). The extremity of the challenge expresses Keats's own bitter struggle to accept his poetic efforts in the face of his growing awareness of not only the death that would claim him before he reached those "immortal steps" (117), but also of his own increasing feminization, experienced as an artistic castration. Moneta's challenge might very well have been voiced by Keats's conception of Milton as the castrating father with his "tyranny," "fierce threat," and "hard task proposed" (119–20). He remarks, after all, that he looks and hears "two senses both at once" (118). The blending here of the visual and the auditory suggests a fictionalized merging of the masculine and feminine, but the balance appears to be more wish than actuality. The poet cannot reconcile his desire for literary fame with the compromises and

23. See Marjorie Levinson, *Romantic Fragment Poem*, 177, 256. In another attempt to read the later "Fall of Hyperion" as informed by the earlier "Hyperion," Anne K. Mellor interprets the face of Moneta as Keats's "total image" for suffering and beauty (see her "Keats's Face of Moneta: Source and Meaning," *KSJ* 25 [1976], 8, and her *English Romantic Irony,* 99–106).

concessions he has to make to the realities of the marketplace. He is left with the sense of the "Prodigious" (121) task made more impossible by the increasing symptoms of his own physical decline through tuberculosis: "palsied chill," "cold grasp" (122–24). The poet, however, struggles to gain even the lowest step and is ironically and cruelly rewarded by being told that he is of a lesser poetic brethren, not of the company of Milton and Wordsworth.

The dominant question Moneta raises in regard to Keats's poetic efforts is "'What benefit canst thou do, or all thy tribe, / To the great world?'" (167–68). The conflict between contemplation and action is surely a question that concerned Keats, but it seems more likely that Moneta's query, "'Art thou not of the dreamer tribe?'" and her subsequent reply, "'The poet and the dreamer are distinct, / . . . The one pours out a balm upon the world, / The other vexes it'" (198–202), are the central passages in which Keats comes to terms with both the demanding muse within himself and the realities of surviving as a poet in a marketplace that would shun a Milton for a Hannah More. Although Keats would like to identify himself as a member of the company of Milton and Wordsworth, he fears that his poetry has more clearly placed him in the company of the dainty women poets who were popular during the early nineteenth century. Moneta's challenge specifically demands that Keats distinguish himself as either a strongly "male" poet, a writer of histories and war epics, or a feminized poet, a writer of romances and love poetry. But the challenge is unresolved and the poem's power and "true voice of feeling" diminish after this climactic moment. Keats had become all too aware that his poetry was not only obsessed with "Miltonic verse," but with the presence of masculinity, the power of the strong male voice, uncompromised by the economy. Keats abandoned the poem and his own efforts to attain an equal footing with Milton, and in these confessed failures we can see the tragic outcome of a poet unable to come to terms with his anxiety toward both the feminine and the marketplace.

The poet-narrator of the second *Hyperion* poem sees his mission as one of combining Apollo's "knowledge enormous" with Moneta's memory so that he can see and create androgynously, as both fully masculine and feminine:

> there grew
> A power within me of enormous ken,
> To see as a God sees, and take the depth
> Of things as nimbly as the outward eye
> Can size and shape pervade.
>
> (I, 302–6)

But such a goal is a purely nostalgic, idealistic, and fantasied wish, for the poet knows that the masculine values he valorizes have been supplanted long ago by a feminine marketplace that demands their eradication. Whereas Keats would like to think that the masculine realm is not under siege, he knows from his own ambivalent courtship of fame that such nostalgia is simply not the case. We can see the shift in his consciousness by contrasting this poem to the earlier version, which uses phrases to describe Saturn, the father-figure, as the "real self" and the "strong identity" (I,114), to the second version, which presents an almost self-effacing poet-narrator who seeks his identity in the enigmatic face of the goddess Moneta: "a wan face, / Not pin'd by human sorrows, but bright-blanch'd / By an immortal sickness which kills not" (I,256–58). The face of the immortal feminine, the idealized muse, haunts Keats here because he knows that he has tried to forsake her, has denied her in his own attempt to become a fully masculine poet, a worthy heir to Milton and Wordsworth. Moneta as muse is the last of the Titans, the one who is preserving their memory even as Keats is trying to destroy it. His reaction to her is one of ambivalence and guilt; he has been drawn to her as he has been lured to fame, that "immortal sickness which kills not." He has courted this woman, this "prostituted muse" (Byron's expression) because she tropes both his best hopes for fame and his worst fears about the price he has paid for it. But he does not, indeed he cannot, forsake Moneta. Her power as preserver of the shrine to the Titans also represents her role as perpetuator of Keats's own eventual fame (he hopes) as a poet in the masculine pantheon that exists as a myth about male privilege and power (now masquerading as the "canon"). Just as Saturn is never totally eradicated, neither, he hopes, will be his memory. But there is ambivalence here, an ambivalence reflected in the nature and identity of Moneta herself. She is both an emblem of the idealized Romantic Imagination and a critique of that ideology. As McGann has observed, "The Romantic Imagination does not save, it offers, like Keats's Moneta, a tragic understanding. And for the Romantic poet, the best and worst knowledge it brings is the critique of the ideology upon which Romantic poetry is itself founded."[24] But the ideology that is criticized here is the ideology of the feminine as fetish; the veiled woman as an ambivalent figure who cannot be embraced or even understood by the Romantic poet because she exists as both his objectified fear of the female and his

24. McGann, *Romantic Ideology,* 132. Other critics have pointed out the association of Moneta with monetary matters: K. K. Ruthven, "Keats and *Dea Moneta,*" *SIR* 15 (1975), 445–59, and Beth Lau, "Keats's Mature Goddesses," *PQ* 63 (1984), 323–41.

horror at the power of the feminizing and castrating literary marketplace.

We can, then, perhaps best understand the two poems by examining the two female figures who function in both versions. Thea, original embodiment of the feminine muse, lays one hand on her own heart and another on Saturn's neck in both versions (*Hyperion*, 42–51; *The Fall*, I, 344–53). This repeated gesture indicates in a powerfully semiotic manner the role of Thea as godlike mediatrix between the feminine emotions and the masculine powers of reason and thought. In this capacity, Thea attempts to communicate, as Keats the poet also hopes to, between the polarized extremes that bourgeois sexual ideology has created and valorized. In another revealing episode, Mnemosyne appears toward the conclusion of *Hyperion* III and actually presides like a midwife at Apollo's painful birth-transformation as a god. As he "Die[s] into life," she holds up his arms, the same "limbs" that have become "Celestial" at the breaking-off point of the poem (130–36). What is important here is that Apollo, embodiment of the strongly male voice, needs the feminine to assist at his transformation. As a solitary male he needs her answers to his continual questions, just as he needs her role as the Great Mother/muse to bring him both physical and imaginative life. Keats implies through both images that he and his culture aspire to some sort of a fictitious harmony between the masculine and the feminine, exactly that sort of androgynous balance that the ideology posits as an escape from sexual warfare. But the images, like the poem, are inconclusive. The dichotomies cannot be transformed into some fictional and mythic balance as in "Psyche," or some nostalgic escape from historical and economic reality as in "The Eve of St. Agnes."

And so in the final climactic scene of *The Fall*, the poet-narrator finds himself facing three silent "fixed shapes" (391)—Thea, Moneta, and Apollo—the embodiments of the old order who are frozen until the poet brings them back to life, so to speak, within the dream-memory that is the vision of the poem. Their artificiality accentuates the entire artifice of the poem, suggesting the transience of the poet's vision as well as his eventual fame. It is no coincidence, then, that Keats could not finish the *Hyperion* poems, and that he stumbled particularly when he confronted his own poetically and sexually split identity. Could he recapitulate the masculine vision embodied in Milton or would he accept his own castration at the hands of the feminine powers represented by Moneta? He was not able to reconcile the two forces within himself, and his career as a poet abruptly ended on this unresolved dilemma. The androgynous ideology in Keats's poetry reveals, then, that a successfully sustained and fictional reconciliation of masculine and feminine within requires an acceptance and endorsement of the feminine as a complex but not destructive power. Keats was finally unable to envision the feminine as a positive force, not only because of his own personal history, but because of the unassailable power of the feminizing marketplace in which he had struggled to survive.

IV Shelley: "The breath whose might I have invoked in song"

Shelley's creations of the feminine muse within conform in striking ways to the issues of sexuality, creativity, and self-irony that we have seen in Keats's works. In his poetic idealization of the Witch of Atlas and her ironic creation, the hermaphrodite, we see the essentially positive face of the feminine muse, while in Urania of "Adonais" we see a figure who uncannily resembles Keats's Moneta—a desexed and castrating mother/muse. Finally, in his last uncompleted poem, "The Triumph of Life," Shelley concludes his poetic career staring into the inscrutable face of the "Shape," the feminine muse as castrator and usurper of male literary privilege.

Shelley's treatment of the conflict between love and self-love is a persistent theme throughout his poetry, most noticeably present in *The Witch of Atlas*, a poem that uses a feminine muse to represent the inherent contradictions found in poetic creativity—by externalizing our ideal conceptions we are doomed to disappointment. In addition to the love/self-love theme, Shelley returns in this poem to themes that were prominent in his earlier poetry, namely, the poetic and human need to transcend the limits of poetry by creating and pursuing inherently flawed ideals. In earlier poems this ideal was embodied in a woman, but these "women," for instance, the visionary maiden in *Alastor* or Pandemos in *Prince Athanase*, prove false because they have no ontological reality; they are ultimately projections of the hero's mind.

The Shelleyan hero has been criticized, therefore, for loving idealized projections of himself rather than "real" women. And Shelley himself gave credence to this interpretation of both his poetry and his person in a later letter on the subject of Emilia Viviani: "I think one is always in love with something or other. The error, and I confess it is not easy for spirits cased in flesh and blood to avoid it, consists in seeking in a mortal image the likeness of what is perhaps eternal."[25]

25. Letter #715 to John Gisborne, 18 June 1822, in *Letters*, II, 434.

The Witch of Atlas is, then, an interesting variant on Shelley's prototypically fictional quest for union with the ideal; the Shelleyan hero has been replaced, however, by a woman, a Witch, and her ideal creation takes the form of a sleeping hermaphrodite. Shelley seems in this poem to be gently poking fun at himself, his literary obsessions, his idealizing tendencies, and his poetic failures to achieve erotic apotheosis. Or perhaps he is suggesting that any attempt to make external what must of necessity be internal is doomed to fail, his own ideals notwithstanding. He sought a selfless self on the one hand; on the other hand, he idealized the notion of merger with a feminine Other who would complete his identity. He knew on a deep and intuitive level that his personal and poetic quests were bound up with the permutations and limitations of sexual identity, that neither sex can ever escape its gendered consciousness long enough to accept the Other as a complement rather than a threat to the self. Ultimately, Shelley, like the other English Romantic poets, found himself fleeing the feminine in all of her guises, rejecting all of the women within himself.

Understanding the identity of the Witch and the hermaphrodite in the context of this poem, however, has been consistently confused by a basic misunderstanding of the differences between the androgyne and the hermaphrodite. A profound student of mythology, Shelley deliberately utilized a hermaphrodite, but his critics have mistakenly interpreted the meaning of the figure and, in the process, obscured the poem's intent.[26] The androgynous reunion of masculine and feminine principles in the psyche has long been confused with the literal and sexual union of male and female. The latter union produces a sort of physical monstrosity that merely accentuates the differences between the sexes. The androgynous, on the other hand, is a merger of psychic

26. In *Mythology and the Romantic Tradition,* 142, Douglas Bush sees the hermaphrodite as "a companion of ideal perfection" for the Witch, while G. Wilson Knight (in *The Starlit Dome,* 228) sees the hermaphrodite as the "symbol of the purified, yet inclusive, poetic consciousness." In *The Meaning of "The Witch of Atlas,"* (Chapel Hill: University of North Carolina Press, 1935), 22, Carl Grabo also sees the hermaphrodite as an androgyne: a "symbol of unity and perfection, of the harmonizing of the male and female principles in nature," as does Carlos Baker in *Shelley's Major Poetry* (Princeton: Princeton University Press, 1948), 221: "love is capable of blending opposite sexes." In *Light from Heaven,* 170, Beaty sees the hermaphrodite and Witch as "Lovers so perfectly whole that in their androgynous union they become not only double-sexed but spiritually unsexed." More recently, Nathaniel Brown discusses the "unequivocally androgynous Hermaphroditus" in his *Sexuality and Feminism in Shelley*, 23.

characteristics within the imagination. The image of the androgynous expresses, then, the restoration of the psyche to its original, asexual wholeness. This view of the androgynous, as we have seen, enjoyed wide currency in the early nineteenth century. If the androgynous embodies the fiction of a redeemed asexual psyche, then the hermaphrodite represents an earthly and physical parody of that state.

Because critics have failed to understand the distinction between the androgyne and the hermaphrodite, criticism of the poem is divided between those who see Shelley's portrait of the hermaphrodite as an ideal spirit and those who see it as an attack on that ideal. An examination of Shelley's sources as well as his other works leads to the conclusion that this hermaphrodite is a parody of the androgynous ideal and a satirization of the self-love his poetic personae have been forced to embrace. As such, *The Witch of Atlas* assumes a critical importance that has been denied it in the past, for the poem functions to a large extent as Shelley's own veiled commentary on his earlier works. In his technique of juxtaposing pagan, Platonic, and literary myths, Shelley wrote a poem that self-consciously deflated the creative process as he himself had experienced it. In particular, he satirizes his own presentation of feminine figures by presenting them as flawed even in their supposedly highest function as godlike muses.

The Witch as muse, like Shelley the poet, has the power to create her perfect love object. In creating the hermaphrodite she makes an ironic comment on her abilities and values, for the hermaphrodite hardly proves an appropriate love object for this world. If the androgyne is the true reconciliation of masculine and feminine, spirit and psyche, then the hermaphrodite is all flesh, a mockery of the possibility of spiritual transcendence. The visual source for the Witch's creation was the statue of the sleeping hermaphrodite that Shelley saw in the Borghese palace in Rome, where he spent a good deal of time writing short pieces on several classical subjects. His reaction to the hermaphrodite is recorded in some rejected fragments of *Epipsychidion* when he compares Emily to a hermaphrodite:

> Like that sweet marble monster of both sexes,
> Which looks so sweet and gentle that it vexes,
> The very soul

Here the implication is clear: the hermaphrodite's beauty is of a perverse nature, "sweet" as well as monstrous. Similarly, Shelley's most serious charge against Elizabeth Hitchener was that she was a "hermaphroditical beast of a woman." [27] In spite of these negative characterizations of the hermaphrodite, several critics persist in interpreting the hermaphrodite in *The Witch of Atlas* as if it were an androgynous ideal.

Shelley's use of the hermaphrodite has been misread because he employed a distinct pagan image with a definite meaning, while his critics were inclined to interpret the image as its opposite, a Platonic ideal.[28] The mythic allusions become thicker in the poem, and the same confusion prevails in Shelley's depiction of his female alter- ego, the Witch. In characterizing her, Shelley combines Spenserian allusions with his own previous poetic creations in order to make the Witch an androgynous foil to the hermaphrodite. The Witch represents Shelley's True Florimell, the true love object who is androgynous and immortal, while the hermaphrodite is the false copy, a purely physical love who lures the poet into the realms of self. Shelley's comparison of Emily and Elizabeth to the hermaphrodite reveals that for Shelley the hermaphrodite was associated with feminine figures. Shelley's disillusionment with these women is contrasted to his belief that somewhere his immortal complement, the Witch, exists. Graham Hough's comment on the Florimell figure highlights Shelley's theme of the conflict between affection and sensuality, spirit and flesh as embodied in women: "Florimell stands for woman as the object of desire, . . . who splits into two; the true Florimell, the right object of love; and the false Florimell, its factitious and deceiving semblance." [29]

The Witch of Atlas, then, contrasts the two forms that love and women have assumed throughout Shelley's poetry. The Witch is in the tradition of Asia and Cythna, idealized beloveds who inspire the heroes with the power to attempt androgynous reintegration. Also like Cythna and Asia, the Witch lives for a time "Within a cavern, by a secret fountain" (56) in order to gain the wisdom necessary for her re-

27. Canceled passages from *Epipsychidion* in *JW,* VI, 378; Letter #211 to Thomas J. Hogg, 3 December 1812 in *Letters,* I, 336.

28. In *Shelley* (London: Weidenfeld, 1974), 605, Richard Holmes sees the poem as an expression of Shelley's attraction to homosexuality, while Bloom, in *Shelley's Mythmaking,* 200, sees the hermaphrodite as a "toy" and "distraction" for the Witch. Similarly, Sperry sees the hermaphrodite as "harmless," a metaphysical "idiot" (see his *Shelley's Major Verse,* 153–54), while Andelys Wood sees the Witch's creation of the Hermaphrodite as an anachronism (see her "Shelley's Ironic Vision: *The Witch of Atlas,*" *KSJ* 29 [1980], 67–82).

29. Graham Hough, *A Preface to The Faerie Queene* (New York: Norton, 1963), 135.

demptive activities. The Witch is so brilliantly beautiful that she "made / The bright world dim, and every thing beside / Seemed like the fleeting image of a shade" (137–39). Like Asia, she also must be veiled, and she weaves a "shadow for the splendour of her love" (151). In one tradition, androgyny in literature is imaged by the combination in one person of the "best" psychic and emotional traits of each sex. Fittingly, the Witch is described as the embodiment of "gentleness and power" (96), possessing the power to institute an apocalyptic harmony: within the "magic circle of her voice and eyes / All savage natures did imparadise" (103–4). Like Spenser's Una, the Witch has the power to tame the savage, although the source of her power is intellectual rather than spiritual (89–91). And like the poet of *Alastor,* the Witch has a cave "stored with scrolls of strange device. / The works of some Saturnian Archimage" (185–86). It was, of course, Spenser's Archimago who created Duessa, the false image of Una, to deceive the Red Cross Knight. As the motif of doubled women runs throughout Spenser's epic, so does it recur in Shelley's vision of the muse. As Marilyn Butler has recently observed, the Witch "is both myth herself, and the sophisticated modern poet's meditation upon myth, and, perhaps beyond that again, a projected *alter ego* to convey his anxieties about his own creativity."[30]

The Witch is that ideal "soul within the soul," immortal, the possessor of the "inmost lore of Love," as well as the knowledge that can be obtained only through the "scrolls of dread antiquity" (199, 250). She is similar to the poet as described in the Preface to *Alastor* who has unified the wonderful, wise, and beautiful, the functions of the imagination, the mind, and the heart. But like the hero of *Alastor,* the Witch is not content with her own self-integration; she must have a double who will reflect her own integration as in a mirror. The Witch begins her search by choosing a boat that Love has created and lit by infusing a "living spirit within all its frame" (314). In a parody of the *Alastor* hero's quest, the Witch begins to create the hermaphrodite:

> Then by strange art she kneaded fire and snow
> Together, tempering the repugnant mass
> With liquid love—all things together grow
> Through which the harmony of love can pass;
> And a fair Shape out of her hands did flow—
> A living Image, which did far surpass
> In beauty that bright shape of vital stone
> Which drew the heart out of Pygmalion.

30. Marilyn Butler, *Romantics, Rebels, and Reactionaries,* 132.

> A sexless thing it was, and in its growth
> It seemed to have developed no defect
> Of either sex, yet all the grace of both—
> In gentleness and strength its limbs were decked;
> The bosom swelled lightly with its full youth—
> The countenance was such as might select
> Some artist that his skill should never die,
> Imaging forth such perfect purity.
>
> (321–36)

This superficially idealized portrait of the hermaphrodite, however, is countered by the hermaphrodite in a perpetual state of lethargy. That is, the hermaphrodite spends most of its time in the poem reclining in the Witch's boat "with folded wings and unawakened eyes" (362). The tone of the description, moreover, implies that the hermaphrodite is a sterile "Image" and "shape," a physical anomaly, a "sexless thing." As the Witch was earlier described as the embodiment of "gentleness and power," so is the hermaphrodite (332). The immediate allusion is to the creation of the False Florimell, for the creation of the hermaphrodite is a mockery of the Witch's androgynous perfection. There are also allusions to Ovid's version of the tale of Hermaphroditus, Plato's *Symposium,* and perhaps Mary's *Frankenstein*—the sheer weight of literariness increases the artificiality of not only the Witch, but most definitely the hermaphrodite. Further, the hermaphrodite's qualities are phrased in tentative terms, that is, "It seemed to have developed no defect," but the poet implies that there is some uncertainty; these graces *seemed* to be there or at least there *seemed* to be no defect.

The hermaphrodite's only function in the poem is to unfurl its wings, which causes the boat to journey upstream against the current (393–408). This act seems to suggest that the hermaphrodite does possess some sort of transcendent power over the world of Nature. David Rubin claims that when the hermaphrodite unfurls its wings it is "one of Shelley's most complete symbolic embodiments of the mediating position and function of poetry." But Rubin admits that there "is a disturbing quality in the sexlessness of the hermaphrodite," because it renders the hermaphrodite "a mere artifact which mocks its maker and the reader alike, expressing the severe limitations of all artistic creation."[31] The hermaphrodite, however, does not symbolize poetry as

31. David Rubin, "A Study of Antinomies in Shelley's *The Witch of Atlas,*" *SIR* 8 (1969), 223. Also see Jerrold Hogle's "Metaphor and Metamorphosis in Shelley's *Witch of Atlas,*" *SIR* 19 (1980), 327–53, for a discussion of the poem as

much as it embodies the subject matter which Shelley had most frequently developed—the disillusionment that derives from solipsism.

The hermaphrodite in Shelley's poem represents the false love of self, the solipsistic love that sees all others as reflections in a pool. The hermaphrodite parodies the androgynous feminine muse, the Witch, the goal of ideal love. Although Shelley's poetry has been accused of expressing egoism, Shelley himself waged a personal campaign against the dominion of the self. His letters particularly reveal the struggle that his impulses toward charity and altruism waged against the self-centered ego. In an early letter to Hogg, he refers to "that hateful principle," the self, while he declared, "I am sick to Death at the name of *self.*" As late as 1819, a few months before writing *The Witch,* Shelley complained to Hunt, "*self,* that burr that will stick to one. I can't get it off yet."[32]

Only with the hermaphrodite's absence from the poem, and its exit is marked with considerably less ceremony than its entrance, does the Witch begin to use her powers seriously. She uses her eyes, like a poet, to see the "naked beauty of the soul . . . / And often through a rude and worn disguise / She saw the inner form most bright and fair." She is then able through a "charm of strange device" to "make that Spirit mingle with her own" (571–76). This achievement is similar to the ideal goal of the alchemist, who seeks the essential form in an attempt to rejoin it and thereby redeem himself and his world. The Witch's power ultimately has poetic and spiritual implications, for she attempts to rejuvenate a dead man by transforming his lifeless, mortal body into a body that is "Mute, breathing, beating, warm, and undecaying, . . . And living in its dreams beyond the rage / Of death or life" (610–14). Of course, the Witch cannot return the man to life, but she can instill the dreams of imagination that have (supposedly) their own immortality. The poet can hope for no more from his art. *The Witch of Atlas* concludes, then, by juxtaposing pagan, platonic, and literary myths in order to present Shelley's own personal view of poetic creation as frustrated and frustrating. As such, *The Witch* is a poem, not only about the use of mythology as a subject for poetry, but about how the androgynous imagination transforms sexual mythologies to express a cosmic vision of potentiality. The image of woman functions within

---

evoking what it is to live with never-ending transformations, as well as his more recent reading, "Free Mythography in Action: *The Witch of Atlas,*" in *Shelley's Process,* 211–19.

32. Letter #34 to Thomas J. Hogg, 1 January 1811, in *Letters,* 1, 34; Letter #508 to Leigh Hunt, 15 August 1819, in *Letters,* II, 109.

that mythology to either impede or compel the vision, but her celebration, Shelley implies, is hopelessly complicated by the fact that she is always a self-created fiction of the male mind, a phantasm and projection of his best and worst imaginings.

Perhaps as a rejection of the image of woman as a poetic and sexual ideal, Shelley chose to celebrate Keats as a sort of masculinized muse figure in *Adonais.* In eulogizing the dead Keats, Shelley has totally removed his quest for union with another from the realm of the feminine. Keats is presented as nearly identical to Shelley; most significantly, they are of the same sex. By celebrating Keats as an image of the self, Shelley perceives his ideal prototype within himself as a fantasy of the suffering and martyred male artist. Keats as Adonais, however, undergoes a quasi-androgynous union with Urania, the dominant and doubly ambivalent feminine muse in the poem. Urania is the embodiment of Nature and organic growth and decay, the "mighty Mother" (10), as well as the psychic mate of Milton. In her role as Venus Genetrix, she must, then, function in an incestuous manner toward her son Adonais. As such, she is a dark and demonic figure binding the poet to the false and deceiving life of Nature. But Urania is also the muse of astronomy, the muse Milton had invoked and unified with in order to find divine aid during the composition of *Paradise Lost.* Her dual visage recalls the doubleness of all of the muse figures who function throughout Romantic poetry to both proclaim and conceal the fiction of castration.

When Urania begs Adonais to kiss her (227), it is as if she were trying to lure him into her cave of death to feed off his youth. Like a female vampire, she seeks to consume his vitality in a futile effort to perpetuate her own existence. She is, as she is forced to admit to Adonais, "chained to Time, and cannot thence depart!" (234). And so to embrace Urania as mother/lover/muse is to embrace the death that is an integral feature of Nature. As Shelley realizes, Urania can only bestow "vain caress[es]" on her beloved Adonais because her ultimate gift can only be death (225). As the *Alastor* poet learned that the object of his love did not exist in the world of Nature but in his own mind, so does Adonais (and Shelley his creator) realize the same truth. But to simply escape Nature/Urania is not the solution. In the final third of the poem, the poet traces how Adonais, the son, actually redeems Nature through union with her. In this androgynous union of masculine and feminine, Adonais represents the power of the mind, creativity, consciousness, and poetry, while Urania embodies the world of the senses that both "Attracts" and "repels" the poet (474).

Only by merging with Urania can Adonais redeem not only her, but himself; he is made one with her and becomes "a portion of the loveliness / Which once he made more lovely" (379–80). She disappears in this last section of the poem because she has been absorbed by Adonais and Shelley the poet. They cannot flee from Nature nor can they worship her, marrying her with their minds as Wordsworth would have them do (and as delineated as the theme of his *Excursion*). It is as if Shelley's Urania was both Vala and Jerusalem; Shelley's apocalypse, like Blake's, is predicated on a redemption of and fusion with the feminine as both Nature and spirit, body and mind. Urania as the feminine principle is fallen in the first part of the poem because her faculties are divided and her perceptions flawed. She is seen sitting "With veiled eyes" in a false escape where she hears only "fading melodies," weak poetry that fails to prepare her for the "coming bulk of death" (13–18). She must be awakened from this state, as well as from the time-bound cyclical world she inhabits in the second section of the poem. She cannot achieve this transformation apart from the imagination of the poet who, in embracing her, accepts her limitations and absorbs her strengths. (Urania was, after all, Milton's "heavenly muse.")[33]

Adonais is "made one with Nature," and he and the redeemed Urania compel all phenomena to change their "forms" and "likeness" until they, too, are "bursting in its beauty and its might / From trees and beasts and men into the Heaven's light" (370; 383–88). "Light," "Beauty," "Benediction," and "Love" descend on the poet of *Adonais* and sustain his faith in his creative powers (477–81). He knows that all things—even Rome—are mortal and will suffer the mutability we call death, but the "breath whose might I have invoked in song," the image of Keats united with Urania, his redeemed muse, will continue to inspire Shelley by convincing him that there is some comfort in the fantasy of the transforming androgynous imagination, presenting as it does a fictionalized escape from "cold mortality" (487, 486).

33. Wasserman was the first critic to recognize that Urania's identity as mother caused her to be an ambivalent force in the poem (see his *Subtler Language* [Baltimore: Johns Hopkins University Press, 1964], 352.) More recently, the fullest and most helpful discussions of Urania's ambivalent role and identity can be found in Ross Woodman, "Milton's Urania and Her Romantic Descendents," *UTQ* 48 (1979), 189–208, and his "Shelley's Urania," *SIR* 17 (1978), 61–75. Also see Hogle's "*Adonais* as the Confluence of Two 'Eternal Flights,'" in *Shelley's Process*, 307–19.

Shelley returns to the theme of the deceiving lure of women in his final and incomplete poem, "The Triumph of Life." The guide through this phantasmal horror show is Rousseau, an "old root" with "holes" for eyes (183; 187–88).[34] After the transparently evil politicians and clergymen are introduced and deflated, Rousseau leads the poet to the most deceptively evil force of all, the doubled feminine presence in the poem, a "shape all light" who appears in a dream to Rousseau: "And the fair shape waned in the coming light / As veil by veil the silent splendour drops / From Lucifer" (412–14). Although this "fair shape" eventually fades to only a glimmer, "forever sought, forever lost" (431), she is complemented by a very different "Shape" who appears in the triumphal car of life. This woman is deformed, crouching, associated with death and decay (88–93). Although ostensibly the first woman is the embodiment of life, hope, and optimistic renewal and the second woman tropes the opposite qualities, we are once more clearly in the psychological territory of the virgin/whore syndrome. Both women, that is, are reflections of Rousseau's alternating states of mind, both toward himself and toward what life has to offer. The compulsion to idealize, reflected in the "shape all light," is as false and fictitious, as self-deluded and naive, as the tendency to despair. The psychological pattern of this final work repeats the images developed in *Alastor* and *Epipsychidion*. The split female figures trope the poet's own ambivalence and uncertainty toward his masculinity and his imaginative capacities as they come into conflict with the feminine and material realm. That is, in her idealized manifestation the female represents the poet's belief that his imagination can restore and redeem the fallen world of the senses (hence the celebration of Asia). But in her dark guise the female stands as an indictment of such optimistic and naive fantasies. As the embodiment of disappointment and death, she expresses Shelley's growing certainty that the world of the flesh could never be redeemed.

The "shape all light" is accompanied by another female-identified power, Iris the rainbow, much as Jerusalem was ironically and necessarily complemented by Vala. Iris, with her "many-coloured scarf' and "chrystal glass," is presented as a mockery of the "white radiance of Eternity" (357–58). But the emphasis here is on the Shape all light, now simply called the "Shape," supposedly the final embodiment of the re-

34. Edward Duffy characterizes Rousseau as the embodiment of masculine faults: "egotism and pride of intellect" in his confrontation with the female "Shape" (see his *Rousseau in England: The Context for Shelley's Critique of the Enlightenment* [Berkeley: University of California Press, 1979], 133).

deeming female in Shelley's corpus. Sperry, Brisman, and Paul de Man identify her as the incarnation of Shelley's ideal muse,[35] but surely there is more than a little ambivalence in her portrait. In the description of the Shape we see again the dehumanizing impulse behind so many depictions of symbolic women. Women in Romantic poetry are more than likely to be troped as things of either a purely physical or mental nature. They find themselves imaged, then, as objects or ideas. In her promise to renew Nature with "Dew" and "invisible rain" (353–54), the Shape is strikingly similar to Blake's Vala, a false redeemer who entraps humanity in the world of fallen Nature. Rather than inspiring humanity at least with fantasies of the ideal, the Shape only serves "to blot / The thoughts of him who gazed" on her so that "the gazer's mind was strewn beneath / Her feet like embers"; and she, "thought by thought, / Trampled its sparks into the dust of death" (383–88). The Shape is the ultimate negative muse; she leads not to the sublime but to the void. She "blots," but that verb can also be read as a noun, expressing her own absence in the poem and in Rousseau's vision of her, for he is, after all, her creator. She deceives both Rousseau and his creator, Shelley the poet, with her false claims about her Natural power. Like Urania and the other manifestations of the fearsome muse, she can only deliver on the promise of death because that is her function within the male-created ideology of the Eternal Feminine. She is a "blot" because she is a void, a hole, with all of its sexual and ontological meanings.

35. See, for instance, Stuart Sperry's idealization of the Shape as "the archetype of Shelley's dream women. . . . the inspiration of the poet's verse, his muse" (in *Shelley's Major Verse,* 191); Leslie Brisman's celebration of the Shape as the type of "all the psychidions of his poems and others" (in his *Romantic Origins* [Ithaca: Cornell University Press, 1978], 178); or Paul de Man's identification of the Shape with the metrical power of poetry (in "Shelley Disfigured," *Deconstruction and Criticism,* ed. Harold Bloom [New York: Seabury, 1979], 504). An overview of the critical interpretations of the Shape can be found in Linda E. Marshall, "The 'Shape All Light' in Shelley's *The Triumph of Life,*" *ECS* 5 (1979), 49–56. Other recent interpretations can be found in David Quint, "Representation and Ideology in *The Triumph of Life,*" *SEL* 18 (1978); Merle R. Rubin, "Shelley's Skepticism: A Detachment Beyond Despair," *PQ* 59 (1980); Tilottama Rajan, *Dark Interpreter* (Ithaca: Cornell University Press, 1980), 62–73; Richard Cronin, *Shelley's Poetic Thoughts* (London: Macmillan, 1981); Angela Leighton, *Shelley and the Sublime* (Cambridge: Cambridge University Press, 1984); Jerrold Hogle, "The One as Its Different Forms in Tandem and as a Poser of Questions: *The Triumph of Life,*" in *Shelley's Process,* 319–42.

In another similarity to Blake's Vala, the Shape also symbolizes the power of reason, that "Treads out the lamps of night" and "like day" makes the "night a dream" (390–93). She destroys the imagination and creative powers by giving Rousseau the draught that he has requested to know "whence I came, and where I am, and why" (398). The potion she provides, instead of enabling him to gain such knowledge, turns his brain to "sand" (405) and causes the entire vision to vanish. The Shape vanishes from Rousseau's mind to be succeeded by the spectre of Love. Shelley (as well as Rousseau) had earlier in his work idealized this figure, powerful and divine Love. But now we see the figure of transitory Love boasting, "In words of hate and awe, the wondrous story / How all things are transfigured, except Love," but life's inhabitants cannot hear this reassurance. Love's promise is called a "rhyme," a fable, a fiction, while love's permanence is a lie (475–79) that lures the naive into participation with its fantasies. In the poem's concluding apocalyptic vision, "Mask after mask fell from the countenance / And form of all" in the "ghastly dance" of death/life (536–37; 540). The poet cannot bring himself to accept this vision of reality; therefore, the poem concludes with the shrill and desperate question, "'Then, what is Life?'" (544). The only answer we are given lies in the cripple's hopeless gaze. Shelley's apocalypse has led to this desperate rejection of the Natural world and the feminine. His concept of Eros simply could not redeem either humanity or the physical world. Eros cannot become *agape;* the lower Venus cannot become the higher Venus; humanity cannot become God, only a "horrible root," an image that expresses both the Romantic male fear of the isolated phallic principle and at the same time its ironic valorization.

Afterword

In 1808 Hannah More published her most popular novel, *Coelebs in Search of a Wife*, a work that reveals how completely and quickly the domestic ideology of woman had been accepted by middle-class women themselves. In this novel a young man considers a variety of women for marriage, but each one disqualifies herself because she possesses one of several possible female faults. The hero finally meets one Lucilla Stanley, a passive, polite, and pious paragon. But do not think that Lucilla is unintelligent; she studiously performs good works in the local village and spends her leisure hours studying botany, her hobby. More's explicit dictum to her female readers was that no woman completely "of the world" could find happiness there, for society was ultimately a male domain, while the home and extensions of it—like the Church—were the natural spheres for women. As Anna Letitia Barbauld (a friend of Coleridge) succinctly expressed it, men could have many duties, but "women have but one, and all women have the same."[1] The new

1. For a discussion of Hannah More and Anna Barbauld, see Priscilla Robertson, *An Experience of Women: Pattern and Change in Nineteenth-Century Europe* (Philadelphia: Temple University Press, 1982), 18. Robertson's massively documented study of women includes several chapters on "The New Domesticity" as it affected women in France, England, Germany, and Italy at various specific points in their lives. Almost equally rich as a source for primary documents from the period is Barbara Taylor's *Eve and the New Jerusalem*. Consider her perceptive observation: "An ideal of femininity which

middle-class woman of the early nineteenth century, enshrined as a goddess at the hearth of her home, stood as the fictional creation and triumph of the emerging modern bourgeois intelligence. As John Lukacs has noted, the role of the domesticated woman was crucial in the development of what he calls the "interiors" created by the new bourgeoisie—both private homes and private psychic spaces—as well as the growing sense of the power and importance of the unconscious mind during the age.[2] One manifestation of that impulse to increased privatization in all areas was, as I have argued, the invention and celebration of the internal woman in English Romantic texts written by the six canonical male poets.

In the introduction to this volume, I observed that the symbolic women who appear throughout English Romantic poetry can be read as various manifestations of the same woman—eerily transformed only by the current psychic needs of her male creator. The same observation, to a certain extent, has been made about the historical portraits we have of "real" middle- and upper-class women during the late eighteenth and early nineteenth centuries. These women largely accepted their society's vision of their nature, role, and destiny. In fact, they embraced the fact, as Barbauld expressed it, that they were united in their identical duties as wives, mothers, sisters, and cultural guardians. Because they shared this (largely hystericized) identity, at least in the eyes of their culture, we can conclude that to some extent they had little if any reality outside of their own homes, either in their own eyes or society's. "Real" women in the historical *milieu* actually did take their identities from their roles as mothers, sisters, wives, and mistresses to men. What is one to make of Maria Edgeworth's statement in *Letters for Literary Ladies* (1795) that "women must always see things through a veil, or cease to be women"? Or consider the outrageous observation made by one Laetitia-Matilda Hawkins in her *Letters on the Female Mind* (1793): "Our Maker never designed us for anything but what he created us, a subordinate class of beings; a sort of noun adjective of the

---

combined holy love with social subordination not only served to suppress women, it also tamed and contained the anti-capitalist implications of Christian love itself. Domesticated Christianity, like domesticated womanhood, was the most comfortable kind for a bourgeois man to live with" (126–27). And see Mitzi Myers ("Reform or Ruin: 'A Revolution in Female Manners,'" *SECC* 11 [1982], 199–216) for a revisionary reading of More and her contemporaries as forerunners of a militant Evangelicalism that sought to "revitalize the world to conform to the values of home, not the materialistic marketplace" (204).

2. John Lukacs, "The Bourgeois Interior," *AS* 39 (1970), 623.

human species, tending greatly to the perfection of that to which it is joined, but incapable of sole-subsistence."[3] By the 1840s, Sarah Stickney Ellis could publish a series of etiquette manuals that provided all the essential information needed for middle-class women at every stage of their lives: *The Mothers of England* (1843), *The Daughters of England* (1845), and *The Wives of England* (1846). Even though it may be uncomfortable to admit as much, the poetry of the Romantic period does, indeed, complement the reality of women's historical and familial situations.

As we have seen, then, the confluence of the ideological and the psychological is evident both in concealed form in the poetry and in a rather more overt manner in representative philosophical texts of the period. For instance, as Hegel observed in his *Phenomenology of Mind*:

> Since the community gets itself subsistence only by breaking in upon family happiness and dissolving self-consciousness into the universal, *it creates itself in what it represses* and what is at the same time essential to it—womankind in general, its inner enemy. Womankind—the eternal irony of the community—alters by intrigue the universal purpose of government into a private end. (trans. Baillie [1931], 496)

Society, it would seem, can only be (re)formed if woman can be properly defined and willingly confined to her proper sphere. One is reminded (unfortunately) of the statements by the notorious German "scientist" Otto Weininger: "Women have no existence and no essence; they are not, they are nothing. Mankind occurs as male or female, as something or nothing. Woman has no share in ontological reality, no relation to the thing-in-itself, which, in the deepest interpretation, is the absolute, is God." Man, identified with the ultimate patriarch, signifies; woman can only stand, then, as the negation of meaning, a man-

3. Not all women, of course, unquestioningly accepted the imposition of the new domesticity. Frances Wright (1795–1852), a pioneering feminist, saw all too clearly the regression that it would lead to for women. See the discussion of Wright in Arnita Jones, "From Utopia to Reform," *HT* 26 (1976), 393–401. Edgeworth and Hawkins are discussed in Alice Browne, *The Eighteenth-Century Feminist Mind* (Detroit: Wayne State University Press, 1987), 29, 160. Edgeworth's adherence to "new-style patriarchy" through "compelling inner needs"—"guilt and obligation"—has also been discussed by Beth Kowaleski-Wallace, "Home Economics: Domestic Ideology in Maria Edgeworth's *Belinda*," *EC* 29 (1988), 242–62.

ifestation of the void. We amuse ourselves when we dismiss the ravings of Weininger as inconsequential historical marginalia. His observations come perilously close, after all, to Lacan's position on the woman as a self-negating signifier for male consciousness.[4]

Simone de Beauvoir has remarked that humanity has always defined itself as male and seen woman "not in herself but as relative to him; she is not regarded as an autonomous being. . . . [S]he is simply what man decrees; thus she is called 'the sex,' by which is meant that she appears essentially to the male as a sexual being. For him she is sex—absolute sex, no less. She is defined and differentiated with reference to man and not he with reference to her; she is the incidental, the inessential as opposed to the essential. He is the Subject, he is the Absolute—she is the Other."[5] As de Beauvoir demonstrates, woman has acquiesced and accepted her status as "other" in relation to man for a variety of ideological reasons—all of them socially/economically/religiously imposed and legislated. But the historical situation for women was actually much more complex than the brief summary here (or de Beauvoir's) can suggest. Under capitalism women have functioned as repositories of male fantasies; they have been deemed closer to the emotions, closer to Nature, closer to the spiritual forces that man has had to both disown and appropriate in order to remake himself into a Culture Hero. Consider William Duff's pronouncements in his *Letters on the Intellectual and Moral Character of Women* (1807): Women are superior to men in "patience and resignation in particular," as well as in piety and fortitude. Or note the lecture given by Henry Thomas Buckle at the Royal Institution in 1858, revealing that by that date the domestic ideology had assumed mythic/religious status. He declared that it was solely woman's influence that kept men from sinking into cruelty, selfishness, and wanton violence. And the next year James Thomson published "The Deliverer," a poem that celebrates the bourgeois wife as

4. Otto Weininger, *Sex and Character* (London: Heinemann, 1906), 286. For a typical contemporary discussion of Weininger, see *Masculine/Feminine: Readings in Sexual Mythology and the Liberation of Women*, ed. Theodore Roszak and Betty Roszak (New York: Harper and Row, 1969), 89. One cannot fail to note that Weininger's vicious Kantian Platonizing: "Man is form, woman is matter. . . . Matter needs to be formed: and thus woman demands that man should clear her confusion of thought, give meaning to her henid ideas" (293) bears an uncanny resemblance to Lacan's position: "For the soul to come into being, she, the woman, is differentiated from it . . . called woman and defamed"; "A woman is a symptom. . . . A manifest instance of the hole" (*Encore*, in *Feminine Sexuality*, ed. Mitchell and Rose, 156, 168).

5. Simone de Beauvoir, *The Second Sex*, xvi.

a veritable angel, the cause of man's salvation and escape from the ravages of capitalism:

> So thou, the man, the circle incomplete,
> Shalt find thy other segment and be whole;
> Thy manhood with her womanhood shall meet
> And form one perfect self-involving soul.

But this supposedly superior status was available to women, of course, only if they willingly complied in their culture's suppression and/or fantasied notions of their (absent) sexuality.[6]

During the initial impetus of the Industrial Revolution, the urge to celebrate the Eternal Feminine regained currency, and women became the last bastions of sexual nostalgia, the literal embodiments of sensibility and feeling; they stood as reminders of the preindustrial world that was quickly disappearing. No matter that lower-class women and children were the raw material on which the engine of Britain propelled itself into the technological promised land, selected women (and children) were idealized as being above the mundane, above the degradation that was infecting the real/male world. They had to be celebrated in their nurturing capacities in order to keep alive the vestiges of belief in an earlier, idealized way of life. The fact that this earlier life was itself a fantasy was of no real import to the poets or to the culture. The illusion had to be maintained, and properly positioning middle-

6. See William Duff, *Letters on the Intellectual and Moral Character of Women* (Aberdeen: 1807); rpt. and ed. Gina Luria (New York: Garland, 1974). For the lecture by Buckle, see Robertson, *An Experience of Woman*, 31, and for a discussion of Thomson's poem, see Eric Trudgill, *Madonnas and Magdalens: The Origins and Development of Victorian Sexual Attitudes* (New York: Holmes and Meier, 1976), 77. On the same point, consider the observation of Jeffrey Weeks that "it was not until the nineteenth century that sexual ideology attempted to deny female sexuality altogether" (see his *Coming Out* [London: Quartet, 1977], 5; as well as the chapter "'That Damned Morality': Sex in Victorian Ideology," in his *Sex, Politics, and Society: The Regulation of Sexuality since 1800* [London: Longmans, 1981], 19–37). By the Victorian period the Eternal Feminine was celebrated as the "Angel in the House," a cultural icon that has persisted (with brief respites) throughout the twentieth century. For a discussion of one of those brief respites, see Carroll Smith-Rosenberg, "The New Woman as Androgyne: Social Disorder and Gender Crisis, 1870–1936," in *Disorderly Conduct: Visions of Gender in Victorian America* (New York: Knopf, 1985).

and upper-class women became a crucial component in preserving the cultural deception.

In addition to the industrial transformations that were reshaping society, the political turmoil inaugurated by the French Revolution and a period of virtual class warfare caused women to be seen not as equal participants in the increasingly serious struggle for political and social equality, but as embodiments of the home, goddesses of the hearth. The male Romantic poets envisioned an ideal political realm, but the role and function of women in this utopia were never clearly defined. Shelley and even Blake to some extent may have fancied themselves supporters of women's political rights, but the evidence of their texts (not to mention their lives) indicates something a bit less idealistic.[7] Woman was not viewed as an equal partner in "real" social, economic, and political reform; her identity as a spiritual essence and an "ideal" internal component of the male psyche was too strong and persistent to allow the "real" to interfere with the poetic "ideal," manifested in the poetic language we recognize as ideology.

The historical situation was simply so volatile, so dislocated, and so threatening that the culture had to turn to some fable, some fiction, some discourse to preserve its sense of stability, harmony, and unification. In desperation, then, the poets and their culture found themselves attracted to the mythos of the androgynous union of masculine and feminine. The myth was recognized as hopelessly fictitious even as it was celebrated, just as women in the poetry were acknowledged on some level to be "real" at the same time they were internalized and idealized. Through the confluence of these factors and fables, then, the male Romantic poets created a new Culture Heroine—the Woman Within. This woman assured male dominance and cultural hegemony through her very fictitiousness. She met the male's every spoken and unspoken need; she ministered to his very real fears; she shored up his shaken beliefs in his own importance. She could appear and disappear in ways that bespoke her compliance with the culture's dominant fantasies. She was emotion incarnate; she was pure spirit or pure flesh, whatever the situation demanded. In creating her, the male Romantics projected their very real fears and fantasies about both personal and his-

7. The strongest case made for Shelley as a "feminist" appears in Nathaniel Brown's *Sexuality and Feminism in Shelley*, particularly his chapter "In Defense of Women," 164–96. But despite his best efforts to paint Shelley as a veritable "androgyne" himself, Brown has to admit that Shelley opposed suffrage for women, as well as access to birth control (197–211). To date, no one has managed to make a convincing case for Blake as a feminist.

torical abandonment. In their vision of the woman within, however, they finally created an emblem of their own desire to appropriate the external world, troped as the feminine, at the same time they declared the supremacy of the internal realm—the masculine mind. Both gestures were, of course, escapist and middle-class fantasies.[8] The woman within was as much a product of the egotistical sublime as she was the last gasp of high Romantic bourgeois culture. Replacing "real" women with the principle of the Eternal Feminine became both an ambivalent deconstructive/reconstructive movement, a self-conscious and increasingly futile attempt to recapture a lost world where complete male dominance was unquestioned and assured because women were, after all, within.

8. On the nature of Romantic escapist fictions, consider this statement by McGann from *Romantic Ideology*:

> Ideas and Ideology therefore lie at the heart of all Romantic poetry. Its entire emotional structure depends upon the credit and fidelity it gives to its own fundamental illusions. And its greatest moments usually occur when it pursues its last and final illusion: that it can expose or even that it has uncovered its illusions and false consciousness, that it has finally arrived at the Truth. The need to believe in such an achievement, either immediate or eventual, is deeply Romantic (and therefore illusive) because it locates the goal of human pursuits, needs, and desires in Ideal space (134).

Index

DATE DUE

DEC 0 7 1999